Inside Urban Politics

Inside Urban Politics

Voices from America's Cities and Suburbs

DICK SIMPSON

University of Illinois at Chicago

PEARSON
Longman

New York   San Francisco   Boston
London   Toronto   Sydney   Tokyo   Singapore   Madrid
Mexico City   Munich   Paris   Cape Town   Hong Kong   Montreal

Vice President and Publisher: Priscilla McGeehon
Executive Editor: Eric Stano
Senior Marketing Manager: Megan Galvin Fak
Production Manager: Joseph Vella
Project Coordination, Text Design, Photo Research, and Electronic Page Makeup: Shepherd, Inc.
Senior Design Manager/Cover Designer: Nancy Danahy
Cover Photos: The photographs on the front cover from left to right are: The New York City
    Council Chamber and Dallas Mayor Laura Miller conducting a meeting at City Hall.
    Pictured in the bottom photo (left to right) are Beverly O'Neill, Mayor of Long Beach,
    California; Alex Padilla, President of the Los Angeles City Council; and Jim Hahn, Mayor
    of Los Angeles.
Manufacturing Buyer: Roy L. Pickering, Jr.
Printer and Binder: Courier Corp., Stoughton
Cover Printer: Phoenix Color Corp.

For permission to use copyrighted material, grateful acknowledgment is made to the copyright
holders on pp. 315–317, which are hereby made part of this copyright page.

Library of Congress Cataloging-in-Publication Data

Simpson, Dick W.
    Inside urban politics : voices from America's cities and suburbs. Dick Simpson.
        p. cm.
    Includes bibliographical references and index.
    ISBN 0-321-09567-7
    1. Municipal government—United States. 2. Community development, Urban—United
States. 3. United States—Economic conditions—1981–2001. 4. United States—Economic
conditions—2001– 5. United States—Social conditions—1980– I. Title.
JS331.S495 2004
320.8'5'0973—dc22

                                                                        2003066392

Please visit our website at http://www.ablongman.com

ISBN 0-321-09567-7

1 2 3 4 5 6 7 8 9 10—CRS—06 05 04 03

For my wife Sarajane

Who put up with the turmoil of writing this book;

For the students

Who helped to teach me about real urban politics;

And for the activists

Who would make our cities and suburbs better.

Contents

Part Three Race, Class, and Poverty

Part Four Political Power in American Cities

Inside Urban Politics focuses broadly on the economic and social renaissance in U.S. cities and suburbs in the 1990s, and on the decline during the recession following the terrorist attacks of September 11, 2001. It paints the broad mosaic of urban politics in terms of the changing social, economic, political, and governmental conditions of our metropolitan regions.

The collection of readings found in the text is unique amongst those found currently in the urban politics course. The selections detail the struggle for power and bring into the foreground the people engaged in that struggle in urban America. Participants speak for themselves in these pages while journalists and social scientists describe urban life. What emerges is a complex picture of the real urban world today.

This reader is intended to supplement urban politics textbooks, provide gripping stories, and add depth to newspaper and mass media accounts. It provides a framework for the latest social science theories, and explains the context within which individuals act. Among the topics covered in these pages are:

- The Renaissance of U.S. Cities
- The Social and Economic Conditions
- Immigration and the Global Economy
- Race, Class, and Poverty
- Political Power in American Cities
- Government Structures and Processes
- Citizen Participation and Evaluation of Local Government
- Metropolitan Politics
- Urban Politics Since September 11, 2001

It is my hope that the articles in *Inside Urban Politics* will make readers think about the fate of their own cities and suburbs. To help accomplish this, it raises the following questions and provide new ways of answering them:

- How did U.S. cities make such a come back in the 1990s?
- Why did the recession following the terrorist attack hit urban areas so hard?
- How is the cycle of immigration, urban renewal, and neighborhood destruction changing in the 21st century?
- What are the effects of the global economy?
- What are the links between race, class, and poverty? Have racial discrimination and urban poverty changed since the Civil Rights era of the 1960s?

- How are racial, cultural, and gender politics changing in urban areas today?
- Who are the leaders in cities? Should others have power instead?
- How do governmental structures, as created by city charters and laws, affect urban politics? Should they be reformed or changed in any fundamental ways?
- How do citizens evaluate and participate in local government?
- Why are metropolitan politics fundamentally different from other forms of local politics?
- How are our cities changing after September 11, 2001 and how can we make them better?

Inside Urban Politics differs from most other readers or anthologies on urban politics in bringing first-hand accounts of city life, struggles for power, and city governance. Many of the points of view of the authors are in conflict and their conflicts illuminate the political battles over our cities and suburbs in the way that the more standard collections of social science journal articles on urban politics do not. These real-world materials bring the passion, insights, and conflicts to you the reader. They should facilitate debates over our urban future in the classroom and in city hall. While *Inside Urban Politics* provides some of the top scholarship in the field to help provide a context within which to analyze and understand what is happening, it is focused on the real politics and the real governmental problems of today's urban areas.

Through exercises, as well as the articles, *Inside Urban Politics* provides readers with the tools to analyze their own city, suburb, and metropolitan area to determine its social, economic, political, and governmental conditions for themselves. It is my hope that listening to the voices from one's own city and suburb provides a deeper and richer understanding of where we each live.

ACKNOWLEDGMENTS

This book would not have been possible without help from my graduate students in the urban politics class that I teach. Over several years they researched, as part of the course, first-hand accounts of urban politics in cities around the country. While I have not been able to include all the speeches, newspaper accounts, historical documents, and memoirs that they found in the final version of this book due to space limitations, they helped to uncover an unremembered story of life and politics in American cities. Hopefully, this will inspire other scholars and students to collect these documents more carefully and to decode their meaning for the past, present, and future of metropolitan America.

I am grateful to my agents Michael and Barbara Rosenberg for getting this book accepted and for Eric Stano, Senior Political Science Acquisitions Editor at Longman, who agreed to publish it and supervised the laborious publishing process which has produced a much better book.

Inside Urban Politics has been reviewed and improved by a number of political science colleagues. I wish to thank especially the following urban scholars for guiding the many revisions of the manuscript: A. Hunter Bacot (University of North Carolina-Charlotte), Janet K. Boles (Marquette), Stefanie Chambers (Trinity College), Timothy B. Krebs (University of New Mexico), Neil Kraus (Hamline), Robert LaPorte, Jr., (Pennsylvania State), Suzanne Leland (Kansas State), Richard T. Middleton, IV (Jackson State), Jeffrey Sadow (Louisiana State University in Shreveport), Linda K. Shafer (Allegany), Joseph Stefko (University of Buffalo, SUNY), Elizabeth Strom (Rutgers), and Robyne S. Turner (Florida Atlantic).

While I did not consult him personally, I found Professor Peter Dreier's syllabus for his urban policy courses to be very helpful in finding many current publications from cities around the country. Some of those are included in this anthology. His course Website is http://comm-org.utoledo.edu/syllabi/dreierurbpol.htm. It is my hope that other urban faculty will post similar listings of up-to-date first-hand sources for all of us to use. As the Urban Politics Section of the American Political Science Association continues to expand at the APSA Website, http://www.apsanet.org/~urban/, it should include stories of importance from different cities such as some of the ones in this text. Already the urban politics section Website has a list of data sources which is most useful.

Finally, I wish to thank Celeste Parker Bates for helping me gain the permissions to publish the articles, and Ken Harrell and Shepherd Incorporated for coordinating the production of *Inside Urban Politics*.

DICK SIMPSON

Inside Urban Politics

Introduction

An Insider's View

Most anthologies on urban politics are composed of professional journal articles or book chapters by social scientists writing about the city in a detached analytical way with a lot of jargon and statistics. This book differs from those in its emphasis on the first-hand accounts—speeches by politicians, newspaper stories, editorials by journalists, interviews with political activists, memoirs and biographies of famous people, and research reports advocating change. Some writings by social scientists are included because of the perspective they bring to understanding the city and its problems —and sometimes, social scientists are advocates. In general, I bring you voices of passion, insight, and conflict.

I served as Chicago alderman for eight years and have taught courses on urban politics with guest speakers in a debate format for nearly thirty years. From these experiences I have learned how important real debates about urban politics can be. I have tried to achieve that here. There are no easy answers, no single truths about urban politics, but these case studies, speeches, and editorials help us better understand our cities and suburbs and challenge us to take up sides in the battles to reshape our metropolitan regions. The goal of this book is to engage you in improving our cities and suburbs.

The book is divided into sections on social, economic, political, and governmental conditions. There are, of course, other ways of organizing the study of urban politics. Among the most significant subfields that have emerged are: (1) the study of power structures and regimes, (2) government structures and processes, (3) race and poverty, (4) political economy and private and public decision making, (5) metropolitan politics and government, and (6) the emerging global society and economy. In the introductions to various sections, I provide a summary of some of the seminal ideas in each of these subfields which provide a context for the readings here.

These articles provide information and arguments that make us think about our cities and what they are becoming. Of course, every city is different and you are probably most interested in your own city or metropolitan region. Exercises at the end of each section show you how to find out what is happening in your city and even, perhaps, what you can do about it.

To explicitly link these articles to the most frequently used textbooks, references are provided at the end of introductory essays to Dennis Judd and Todd Swanstrom's *City Politics* (Longman) and Bernard Ross and Myron Levine's *Urban*

1

Politics (Peacock). Similar linkages can be supplied by instructors to other urban politics texts.

This collection of first-hand accounts is meant to provide an insider's view of how our cities have evolved in the last century and a half, who the movers and shakers that make decisions are, and how local governments work and fail to work. The challenges facing our metropolitan regions are set forth. What we will do about them is up to each of us.

Urban politics have changed since the terrorist attacks on New York City and Washington, D.C. on September 11, 2001 and the recession that followed. Restrictions on government budgets and services during the current economic recession have been inevitable. These economic pressures have increased with the need to pay for the war in Iraq. We don't yet know all the profound and long-term effects that will follow from these events. This is something that citizens, governmental officials, and scholars are still discovering.

Since this is the first edition of this book, I hope as it is used in college classes and by public officials and citizens trying to improve their cities and metropolitan regions, that readers will recommend new articles so that this anthology can be kept up-to-date and relevant. This book emphasizes the importance of what insiders—journalists, politicians, bureaucrats, and citizen activists—as well as urban scholars have to teach us about the cities and suburbs in which most Americans now live. As the debate over the future of metropolitan regions continues, this anthology will evolve and change.

Cities at the Millennium

After the trials and tribulations of World War II, the 1950s were a time of growth and prosperity. Suburbs blossomed and cities began to take the shape of the metropolitan regions that are the standard today.

The 1960s were swept up in the civil rights movement. Programs of urban renewal, "Model Cities," and the "War on Poverty" began to provide cities with money to attack poverty and physical ghettos. Then the 1970s and 1980s were marked by inflation, stagnation, and a steady retreat by the federal government from funding social service programs. At the same time, a switch from the manufacturing economy brought closed factories and lost jobs. Downtowns stagnated, the middle class fled, and factories moved from central cities to the suburbs, southwestern United States, and abroad.

These trends mostly continued through the economic recession at the beginning of the 1990s. However, after 1992, American cities rebounded. Downtowns were redeveloped, tourism and convention business increased, and many middle- and upper-class families rediscovered the advantages of living in cities. In the 1990s and at the turn of the twenty-first century the outlook was much more positive. U.S. cities experienced a renaissance until September 11, 2001. Since then cities have faced a continuing recession and are trying different ways to cope with it.

Paul Peterson in his now classic book, *City Limits*, proposed that city governments basically do three different kinds of things. They provide: (1) allocative services for all citizens like garbage collection, street sweeping, and police protection; (2) redistribution of resources like public housing, free shelter for the homeless, and welfare payments; and (3) economic development.[1]

From the 1990s until the economic recession following the terrorist attacks, cities made progress on two fronts—allocative services and economic development. The early 1990s saw the ascension of "manager mayors," pragmatic public officials, whether Republicans or Democrats, who cut wasteful spending, brought urban government bureaucracies under control, and saw that city services were delivered more effectively, economically, and fairly. They were frugal and often even cut taxes on businesses and property owners.

The end of the twentieth century and the beginning of the twenty-first were a time of affluence, growth, economic development, and redevelopment. Gone were the dirty smokestacks of the earlier industrial era. New office skyscrapers housed the new service industry in the global economy. Museums, malls, waterfront playgrounds, convention centers, and fancy new restaurants attracted tourists from around the state, nation, and world. Dilapidated downtowns and public housing were bulldozed and replaced with bright new buildings, parks, and shopping meccas.

Cities throughout the country had a spurt of economic development not seen for decades while the suburbs with their new homes, clean new factories, and sparkling shopping malls continued to spread outward from the central cities like dandelions popping up in endless suburban fields.

One indication of the successful development of cities at the end of the twentieth century were the positive, upbeat speeches of their mayors. Most mayors from towns and cities across the country could claim at the turn of millennium that they had led their cities through major renewals that represented a renaissance. For instance, in the spring and summer of 2001, then-Mayor Rudy Giuliani of New York City bragged that in his term in office he had reduced or eliminated 23 city taxes, saving taxpayers $3 billion in 2001 alone. He argued that the previous high rate of taxes had cost New Yorkers 330,000 jobs in the first three years of the 1990s but that his tax cuts had brought a resurgence of 480,000 jobs back to the city by the end of his term in office. Along with reduced crime, the mayor credited his tax policies with bringing about the renewal of the largest city in America.

Mayor Wellington E. Webb of Denver was similarly upbeat. He claimed four cornerstone principles as the basis of Denver's revival: (1) increased public safety, (2) increased parks and open space, (3) elimination of budget deficits by cutting waste in city services, and (4) improved schools. Beyond these cornerstones, Denver embarked upon the redevelopment of its downtown including retail and office space, housing developments and sports arenas. It redeveloped vacant buildings, warehouses, and department stores and built extensive new housing. Renewal of the downtown was central to Denver's renewal from the 1990s to the turn of the twenty-first century.

By the end of the 1990s, successful economic development like New York's and Denver's had become more important than merely providing "allocative services" like good garbage collection. Redistribution of resources, other than the now limited programs of the federal government, remained beyond the capacity of cities to provide.

At his inauguration in 1999, Mayor "Buddy" Cianci of Providence, Rhode Island recounted the history of that city from his first inauguration back in 1975 when the downtown, the neighborhoods, and the waterfront were all in economic distress. He proclaimed that Providence was now "a shining example of a city reborn." He spoke of new shopping malls, hotels, performing arts centers, and a skating center as some of the new beginnings in Providence. Since 1990, the city had invested more than $300 million of public money in the neighborhoods. Forty-two parks and playgrounds were refurbished, 225 classrooms built, and the police department had more officers in uniform than in the last 20 years. The crime rate had fallen more than 40 percent, a statistic true of many American cities. The city was also the site of a very successful national TV series named after it. Finally, Mayor Cianci looked forward to developing three industrial sites as high quality, commercial, institutional, and residential uses on such a grand scale that he called each a "New City." He argued that "in the twenty-first century, the rivers of Providence will be the centerpiece of a revitalized and vigorous city . . . a great city on the hills and the plains overlooking the rivers and the bay . . . a New Providence." Despite Mayor Cianci's vision and accomplishments, however, he was convicted of corruption and sent to jail, after Providence had its renaissance.

In 1998 when Paul Schell became mayor of Seattle, before the demonstrations at the 1999 World Trade Organization meeting went uncontrolled and doomed his reelection, he wrote an open letter to the citizens about building "a City of Choices." As mayor, he saw his job as providing citizens with "as many good choices as possible to allow each citizen to lead the richest and most complete life possible." To do that, the city had not just to grow but to "grow with grace." He advocated "smart growth," which protected the surrounding environment by growing within existing urban boundaries in ways that were sustainable. To give citizens their money's worth the mayor exhorted city employees to do the public's business in "a businesslike manner." He ended by proclaiming that "In a time of economic health such as this we have the chance—the moral obligation—to invest in more than just basic maintenance. . . . We have the chance to show that a city can grow while at the same nurture its local culture . . . [create] a healthy environment, [and have] compassion for those in need." While Seattle Mayor Schell was tossed out by the voters in the mayoral primary election on September 18, 2001, his vision of a city of choices had become more widespread among U.S. cities in that period of affluence. While economic development is an important goal for every city, "smart growth" is an alternative to just growth for growth's sake. As a result, Seattle continues to be one of the most livable cities in America.[2]

Midwestern cities like Chicago also experienced significant growth during the 1990s. Mayor Richard M. Daley in his State of the City address on January 19, 2000, reflected the optimistic outlook of the time. He believed that the city would continue "to build a better and brighter future" and referred with pride to the $5 billion which had been invested in Chicago neighborhoods during the past decade. He announced the Neighborhoods Alive 21 Program, an $800 million dollar investment projected over the next four years to build or fully rehab 25 police stations, 20 new state-of-the art firehouses, new and improved branch libraries, and 100 school campus parks. Between 1998 and 2000 the city had attracted or retained over 32,000 jobs in neighborhoods in addition to the rapid job growth downtown.[3] He was successfully reelected to a fifth term in 2003.

Not only larger cities, but middle-sized cities like Duluth, Minnesota made advances during the 1990s. In his 2001 State of the City address, Mayor Gary Doty stressed what had been achieved along with the plans for the first decade of the twenty-first century. In 2001, two "world class" projects opened, the Duluth Technology Village and the Great Lakes Aquarium. The city's Convention Center was in the midst of a $20 million expansion along with a 600-car parking garage and upgraded hockey facilities. Duluth's Bayfront Festival Park was expanded, a 33-acre nature preserve added, and a number of businesses grew. Mayor Doty explained that each new building and each expansion "requires more people to work inside them. This means new opportunities for Duluthians. And hopefully more income to support their families." During eight years at the end of the 1990s, more than 10,000 jobs were added to the Duluth economy. Mayor Doty ended his speech with a claim that would probably be embraced by all mayors of U.S. cities of all sizes. "Sure this isn't a perfect community. But we're getting closer all the time."

Cities which had been less successful in modernization and development were anxious to catch up. During the summer of 2002, Mayor Bill LaFortune of Tulsa, Oklahoma held a series of Mayor's Vision Summits on urban revitalization for the Tulsa Metropolitan Region. As Mayor LaFortune argued, "This [developing the city] is not just about attracting conventions and tourism; it is also about retaining the best and brightest people in our city." The mayor maintained that Tulsa had to offer "recreational and quality-of-life opportunities that other cities its size have, or we're not going to retain or attract [the best and brightest people]."[4]

Since September 11, 2001, the affluence, economic development, and job growth of the previous decade has been reversed. According to reports from the New York City Partnership, the Chamber of Commerce, and the City Comptroller, the attack on the Word Trade Center caused $83–$95 billion in economic losses in addition to the loss of 2,819 lives and 146,000 jobs to New York City alone. In 2002, New York City lost another 46,000 jobs. There were projections of a net loss to the city's economy of at least $16 billion even after insurance payments and federal funds defrayed most of the costs.[5] The economic downturn in the nation produced job freezes, job cuts, reduced revenues, and cuts in services in other cities as well. Before these events, American cities were on a crest of renewal. Now their immediate future is less certain.

Reference

Some of these themes discussed by mayors are further elaborated in Judd and Swanstrom's *City Politics: Private Power and Public Policy,* (2003 edition) Chapter 13: "Reviving the Central Cities" and Ross and Levine's *Urban Politics: Power in Metropolitan America,* (2001 edition) Chapters 1 and 2: "The Urban Situation" and "The Evolution of Cities and States."

Notes

1. Paul Peterson, *City Limits,* Chicago: University of Chicago Press, 1981.
2. The excerpts are from Mayor Paul Schell, "An Open Letter to the People of Seattle," January 6, 1998 and was available previously on the Seattle Website. (http://www.cityofseattle.com)
3. Mayor Richard M. Daley, "State of the City Address," January 19, 2000. Available on the City of Chicago Website, (http://www.ci.chi.il.us).
4. P. J. Lassek, " 'Vision Summit' to Begin," *Tulsa World,* July 7, 2002, pp. A-1 and A-8.
5. The estimates of total losses continue to change. The City of New York in the end of 2001 estimated the total costs to be in the $90–$105 billion range and asked the federal government for more than $50 billion in relief grants, not all of which were granted. Office of the Comptroller, "The Impact of the September 11 WTC Attack on NYC's Economy and City Revenues," New York City Office of the Comptroller, New York (2001), quoted in David Wildasin, "Local Public Finance in the Aftermath of September 11," *Journal of Urban Economics,* Vol. 51, No. 2 (March 2002), p.230. The study as of September 2002 by the City Comptroller was reported by Lisa Anderson, "NYC's 9/11 Bill Put at $83 Billion and Rising," *Chicago Tribune,* September 5, 2001, p. 10.

1. Renaissance Budgeting and the Resurgence of New York City

Mayor Rudy Giuliani

These budget messages were written before the terrorist attacks on the World Trade Center on September 11, 2001. They give a description of the recovery of many U.S. cities at the beginning of the twenty-first century from the earlier recession of the 1980s and 1990s. Mayor Giuliani attributes New York's recovery to certain urban policies, but other cities followed different strategies and also experienced renovation during this period of economic growth and affluence.

Late last week the City Council and I agreed on a final budget that solidifies the gains we've made over the past eight years. Our historic crime-reduction efforts and the reforms that are bringing record numbers of New Yorkers from welfare to work will continue. Spending for senior citizen services has increased by over 90 percent since 1994, while funding for public education is at the highest level it has ever been in our City's history. But one of the most significant aspects of this budget is the almost $500 million in new tax cuts that have been achieved while government spending has been kept under control.

What we have achieved together is a fundamental change in the way New York City government approaches taxation. In the past, chronic fiscal irresponsibility coupled with a tax-and-spend philosophy led to frequent tax hikes. The efforts of businesses and hard working men and women were taken for granted. That high rate of taxation contributed to the exodus of businesses from our City during the early 1990s, when New York lost nearly 330,000 jobs in just three years.

New York's resistance to tax cuts began to change in my first budget— when we proposed reducing the hotel occupancy tax, which resulted in higher revenue from the lowered tax. The political landscape has shifted dramatically over the last eight years, to the point that the Council and I frequently debate which taxes to cut and by how much, as opposed to which taxes to raise and by how much. In fact, since 1994 we've reduced or eliminated 23 different city taxes, saving taxpayers more than $3 billion in fiscal year 2001 alone. These tax reductions include:

- Elimination of sales tax on clothing and footwear purchases of less than $110.
- Reduction of the commercial rent tax; eliminating it in every borough but Manhattan south of 96th Street.

SOURCE: Mayor Rudy Giuliani, "Renaissance Budgeting," *Mayor's Weekly Column* on New York City's government Website, June 11, 2001 and "Mayor Giuliani Unveils $39.5 Billion Executive Budget," press release, April 25, 2001. http://www.nyc.gov/html/om/html/2001a/weekly/wkly0611.html and http://www.nyc.gov/html/om/html/2001a/pr125-01.html. Reprinted by permission.

- Reduction of the personal income tax surcharge.
- Reduction of the co-op and condo property tax.

In all, the tax burden on New York City residents and business has been reduced 17 percent—to its lowest level in more than three decades. These tax cuts have spurred the private sector to create a record 480,000 new jobs, outpacing both the state and national job growth. And job growth is thriving in all five boroughs, while property values have increased by 32 percent citywide since 1998. In fact, Queens and Staten Island are leading all boroughs in job growth. Queens has experienced 12.5 percent private sector job growth since 1993. Staten Island has experienced 24.5 percent job growth since 1993. Brooklyn and the Bronx are at 9.4 percent and 7.7 percent respectively. And Manhattan has experienced private sector job growth of 17.3 percent.

New York City's renaissance has been built upon fiscally responsible budgets as much as reduced crime and the improved quality of life. Together, we have turned chronic budget deficits—that reached $2.3 billion when my predecessor left office—to multi-billion dollar surpluses. We've kept the rate of spending at or below the rate of inflation. And we've created a budget stabilization account that will insulate New Yorkers from any future downturns in the economy and reduce the temptation to turn back the clock to the failed tax-and-spend politics of the past. In this final budget we have once again demonstrated that a City in control of its destiny is committed to fiscal responsibility and tax policies that reward the entrepreneurial spirit that has always made New York City the Capital of the World. . . .

The Budget [for 2002] reflects one of the Giuliani Administration's fiscal priorities of reducing spending year-to-year, with a decrease of 2.8 percent. The Plan further reflects the Administration's success in reducing taxes by $3.2 billion since 1994, and funds an additional $494 million in tax cuts, which increase to $1.3 billion by 2005. The Plan projects a surplus of $2.76 billion in FY2001 and contains a Budget Stabilization Account for FY2002, to assist in the event that the City is faced with an economic slowdown.

"This budget is the capstone of nearly eight years of sound fiscal management by this Administration," the Mayor said. "Today, the City is much stronger, leaner and safer.

"We have worked hard to ensure that New York City is an ideal place to raise a family, start a business, or take a wonderful vacation. And there are indications everywhere that our efforts to turn New York around have paid off: Since 1993 City population rose 9.3 percent, personal income shot up 49.1 percent, new construction permits increased 49.2 percent, and private employment is up 16.6 percent. All this while crime plummeted to near-historic levels.

"This budget was designed to build on our past successes," the Mayor said. "But we need to be mindful that with the national economy slowing, the City must remain dedicated to exercising fiscal restraint.

"In this last year of my Administration, I feel confident that with the budget I'm presenting today—along with the many creative programs that we've implemented over the last seven and a half years—the City is on a fixed course of continued fiscal stability," the Mayor concluded. . . .

TAX CUTS

Since 1994, the Mayor has reduced taxes by $3.2 billion. This Executive Budget proposes an additional $494 million in tax cuts, which increases to $1.3 billion by 2005. This Plan is designed to help reinvigorate the economy, stimulate job development and keep government spending in check.

Tax cuts that are proposed in the Executive Budget are:

- Reduction of the Personal Income Tax Surcharge by an additional 25 percent (effective July 2001);
- Elimination of the Commercial Rent Tax;
- Extension of Co-op/Condo Property Tax Relief;
- Creation of a PIT Credit for "S" Corporations;
- Introduction of a City Earned-Income Tax Credit;
- Repeal of the $2 flat fee tax on hotel rooms, with a reduction for Bed and Breakfast establishments;
- Elimination of the Sales Tax on clothing and footwear;
- Business tax reform;
- Extension of the Lower Manhattan Revitalization Program. . . .

COMPARATIVE ANALYSIS

To properly gauge the resurgence of the City in economic and quality of life terms from 1993 to the present, the following comparative statistics are offered:

TABLE 1.1   Then and Now

	1993	2001	1993–2001
Population	7,329,079	8,008,278*	9.3%
Personal Income (billions)	$202.9	$302.5*	49.1%
Total Construction Permits	46,048	70,442*	53.0%
Private Employment (thousands)	2,703.6	3,152.6*	16.6%
Hotel Occupancy Rate	69.5%	84.6%*	21.7%
Public Assistance Recipients	1,112,490	518,823**	(53.4%)
Unemployment Rate	10.4%	5.1%**	(51.0%)
Tax Burden	8.8%	7.3%	(17.0%)
Fresh Kills Landfill Avg. Daily Tons	14,911	0	(100%)
Full-Time City-Funded Employees	222,836	215,891	(3.1%)
Police Uniformed	36,340	40,710	12.0%
Board of Ed.-Pedagogues	69,002	77,843	12.8%
All Others	117,494	97,338	(17.2%)
Murders	1,946	673*	(65.4%)
Overall Crimes	600,346	288,368*	(52.0%)
Vehicle Thefts	112,464	35,847*	(68.1%)

*Data is through December 2000
**as of March 2001

2. Reviving Downtown

Mayor Wellington E. Webb

Denver, located in the western United States, differs from New York in many ways. Mayor Webb's policies are more traditional economic development policies in contrast to Mayor Giuliani's policies of tough policing and tax cuts. He describes a four-fold policy of public safety, open space, fiscal reforms, and education improvements as a strategy for improving Denver, but especially focuses on downtown redevelopment as the key to a more positive future. Like New York, Denver in the late 1990s had considerable success. But Mayor Webb also looks to a new partnership between the cities and the federal government which has yet to emerge in order to create "The Great American City."

O ur topic of discussion is the Future of the American Downtown. But we can abbreviate this title. We are really speaking about the Future of America.

Statistics suggest that our nation's cities are shrinking in population and that our suburbs are the new growth centers for political and social and economic influence.

But, in fact, we know that the opposite is true.

As Americans become more transient and disconnected, as three-generation households and one-job careers become increasingly rare, our cities become even more important to our sense of community and identify.

As the older suburbs face the same challenges as their urban neighbors—on issues such as public safety, housing stock, and outmigration of wealth—it is clear that the agenda of the cities has become even more critical.

As urban sprawl imposes an increasing burden on our citizens, whether they live in century-old neighborhoods or brand new exurban subdivisions, we realize the value of the city's compact development and efficient use of existing infrastructure.

As study after study establishes the interdependence between the vitality of the central city and the economic success of entire regions, it is clear that the agenda of the cities is an essential part of our nation's agenda.

Essential for sustainable growth;

Essential for our economic development;

Essential for our sense of place and belonging;

And essential for the values that define and enrich us.

And at the heart of each of our cities is a downtown. It is the hub from which a city's success or failure will be determined.

SOURCE: Mayor Wellington E. Webb, "Reviving the Roost: The Return of the Great American City," Speech to the James W. Rouse Forum on the American City, September 28, 1998, Washington, D.C. Available at the Denver, Colorado Website. http://infodenver.denver.co.us/~mayorden/speeches/rouse.htm. Reprinted by permission of Denvergov.org.

And so the following question is one of national importance:

How do we revitalize our nation's blighted downtown areas, and how do we sustain the successes that we have achieved?

Let me talk, first about the success. As Bruce Katz has emphasized on many occasions, the cities are the beneficiary of two very promising national trends: a strong market, and demographics.

The population is getting older. People are having kids later. This offers our cities an enormous opportunity. It's an opportunity to bring the empty nesters back to the central city.

But it's an opportunity for success. It's not a guarantee.

Fulfilling that opportunity requires a focused civic and government leadership.

In Denver, our city-wide strategy encompasses four priorities, what I refer to as the cornerstones of a great American city.

First, we restored a sense of public safety. We know that people will not return to the city, despite all of its appeal, if they don't feel safe. And we know that many people have exaggerated impressions of urban crime. In Denver, we've reduced our crime rate by 25 percent over the past five years alone.

Second, we reclaimed our open space. Since 1991, we have increased the parks and open space program by 50 percent, from 4,000 acres within the City's boundaries to 6,000.

Third, we put our fiscal house in order. We transformed a $33 million cash deficit at Denver General Hospital into a positive annual surplus, we obtained an enhanced evaluation of the city's overall credit rating, and, in a steady fashion, we tripled the general fund balance, from $29 million to over $99 million. We made the delivery of services to our residents and businesses more cost-efficient and customer friendly, and we have consolidated city agencies and functions to cut waste and improve ease of access for our citizens.

And fourth, we have made kids and schools a priority. The success of any great American city depends, in large measure, on the quality of the education its children receive. In Denver, the school district is independent of city government. However, our futures are clearly interconnected. Over the last five years, we have provided more than $20 million to fund police officers in schools, early childhood education programs, summer youth employment, after school career clubs, and a strict and nationally recognized curfew program. We also took over and re-energized a struggling Head Start Program.

Beyond these four cornerstones, we developed a very specific strategy for our distressed downtown area.

One of the first things I did when I became Mayor in 1991 was convene a Downtown Summit. And I made it clear that our top priority would be housing. Up to that point, the emphasis downtown had not been on housing, it had been on retail. But, as many of you know, if you establish a residential population, the retail will follow. Out of the Summit, came several initiatives:

- We created a downtown housing office to proactively market downtown's inventory of vacant buildings to housing developers and to provide developers and investors with accurate information on properties and market conditions.

- We made sweeping changes in downtown zoning to encourage housing and transit oriented development and to protect historic buildings. The land use regulations in place at the time actually inhibited housing. We used higher density as an incentive for housing projects, and created design standards and review. As a result of these changes, we were able to save a critical mass of our older buildings downtown. They may not have been functional for office space, but they were functional for housing.
- We also eliminated parking as a "use by right," which further strengthened our effort to preserve historic buildings and stimulate residential development. We know that once a downtown is more than one-third parking lots, it loses its character and sense of place
- We provided housing financing on unconventional projects. As these projects achieved success, they were supported by conventional lenders.
- We directed all of our private activity bond allocations toward downtown housing projects for at least three years.
- We created a 1 million-dollar revolving loan fund for housing, thanks to the outstanding work of Ann Wheelock when she was Director of our Community Development Agency.

In 1995, I convened another Summit to take our success one step further. Our lower downtown was booming, and our midtown was under renovation. The time had come to expand our focus to the inner ring neighborhoods right around downtown. These areas were not benefiting from the economic resurgence. But they offered lower property and building costs, and a strong downtown as an anchor.

We also continued several other important elements of Denver's long-term strategy, which includes:

- Placing our sports arenas downtown;
- Emphasizing and supporting the Denver Performing Arts Complex;
- Providing free shuttle bus service on our downtown mall, which offers easy access for employees, residents and visitors; and
- Maintaining downtown as the hub of the regional transporation system, including the first phase of the light rail system.

In Denver, our focus is on development of a transit system not only to enhance the mobility of our residents but also to shape land use and support economic development. To that end, we have initiated a station development program which has brought together city agencies, the Regional Transportation District, the Colorado Department of Transportation, and the private sector. The goals are to revitalize those areas of the central city served by rail and to enhance ridership of the system. In this way, we can address transportation, housing, jobs, and containment of urban sprawl.

What are the results of these efforts?

Since 1991, 51 vacant buildings have been redeveloped in downtown Denver, including more than 2,000 residential units, 1200 hotel rooms, and over 400,000 square feet of commercial space.

Warehouses, office buildings, and banks have been transformed into residential developments. Light industrial buildings have been converted into mixed-use developments. Department stores have been successfully re-used, as hotels, retail space, offices, and lofts. Too often, the empty spaces left by department stores symbolize the flight of prosperity from the cities to the newer suburbs. We were determined to avoid that fate.

In addition, 2,600 residential units in downtown Denver are currently under construction or proposed for construction. Included among these are two very large multi-family rental developments. West Commons Park is being developed in the Platte Valley across the river from a new urban park. The other large project consists of 500 units on the site of a former hospital.

And in our upper downtown, we have just completed a two-block, 350,000-square-foot entertainment and shopping project.

Essential to this success has been a constructive partnership between the public and private sector. Just yesterday, the International Downtown Association awarded Denver its Outstanding Achievement Award for 1998, and said that "the collaboration of the City and County of Denver, the Denver Urban Renewal Authority, and the Downtown Denver Partnership provide a model for cities all over the world."

What are the lessons learned from the Denver experience and from the revival of other downtown areas?

First, we know that the revival of our nation's downtown areas is a serious and very positive trend for our cities. And we need to do all that we can do to leverage this to the maximum extent possible.

Second, the downtown experience reflects how we should think about urban policy generally. It offers a strategy for building a competitive urban agenda that takes full advantage of the real market and demographic trends that are shaping the country.

As CEOs of municipal corporations, Mayors have to try to understand our cities' functions, and to exploit our assets.

It means that we should not try to involve ourselves in sectors of the economy that started to diminish 50 years ago. And it means that we should think about key sectors of the economy, such as retail, publishing, financial services, and other higher-end services in the new, knowledge-based economy. These are services that belong in our cities because of our infrastructure and our compactness. These are the economic advantages of density.

Related to this is the message of Michael Porter at Harvard and of William Goodyear, Chairman of the Bank of America of Illinois. We have untapped retail markets in our inner cities. And, for too long, we have understated or ignored their enormous potential for profit.

There are other assets as well. Every person living downtown is a person who is not stuck in a 45-minute commute.

In short: The 24-hour downtown represents a more sustainable form of development, both fiscally and environmentally.

What lessons do we have to offer the federal government?

Cities remain a power in the new economy. They are places to invest in, and they are not places to disinvest.

Many of our cities are in good shape. Crime is down. Unemployment down. We have balanced budgets. We are run by pragmatic administrators.

We are not overly political and we are not ideological. There is a new urban environment and it warrants a new and enhanced partnership with the federal government.

That means investments that are sound. And that means "do no harm."

In many ways, the federal government has been enormously helpful and inventive. Examples include the Empowerment Zone and Hope VI grants and the cleaning up to Brownfield sites. ISTEA, and now TEA-21, provide needed flexibility in developing transportation systems that best serve local needs.

And we are fortunate to have an Administration that has reinvigorated the dialogue about our nation's urban agenda. Vice President Gore's remarks at the Brookings Institution earlier this month reflected a deep and impressive appreciation for the importance of the cities in the formulation of federal policies.

I commend him for his leadership.

Among the new initiatives the Vice President announced was FANNIE MAE's program to promote location-efficient mortgages. This is a good example of how the market place can recognize and reward the cost savings enjoyed by families that live in centrally located areas, near existing transportation and other infrastructure.

The Vice President also defined an important element of a new and more vigorous urban agenda when he challenged us to reexamine federal policies that have the unintended but very real consequence of subsidizing urban sprawl, the kind of growth that is unsustainable and harmful to our cities.

I embrace this challenge.

The first step, which we are doing today, is to recognize and underscore the central role of the cities and inner ring suburbs to the nation's prosperity.

Once we do that—once we appreciate that cities are essential to our country's well being—then we can go forth with an agenda that unites our great urban centers in a new and expanded alliance.

An alliance that includes older suburbs, financial institutions, major corporations, and faith-based organizations.

With this expanded alliance, we can forge a new partnership between the cities and the federal government. We can look closely and seriously at the way in which federal tax policies and transportation dollars impede and even reverse the hard-fought progress we have achieved in our nation's cities. And we can establish the public and private sector coalitions necessary to implement a real urban agenda that encompasses the full scope and potential of the great American City.

A place where commerce, smart growth, opportunity, and culture intersect with tradition and faith and family and hope.

A place that is textured and reassuring, that is rich with history and a sense of continuity and belonging.

A place where I know and respect my neighbors and where I can walk to restaurants and shops, sometimes to spend money and sometimes just to exchange stories with old friends.

A place that millions of Americans call home.

And a place that millions more would like to call home.

3. Revitalization in Providence

Mayor Vincent Cianci

Mayor "Buddy" Cianci was the longest-serving mayor in the history of Providence and served longer than any big-city mayor in recent years. He dominated local politics. He was first elected mayor in 1975 and was last reelected in 1998 with 97 percent of the votes cast. He was convicted of assaulting his wife's boyfriend in 1984, received probation, and was forced to resign. But he came back to win reelection just a few years later.

The federal corruption investigation in Providence caused 30 members of the mayor's administration to be convicted. Mayor Cianci was convicted of racketeering conspiracy and corruption in federal court and received a five year sentence. At one of the trials, Judge Ronald R. Lagueux said from the bench. "In this mayor's two administrations, there has been more corruption in the City of Providence than in the history of this state." (*New York Times Magazine,* December 31, 2000, p.24.) Despite his personal troubles, Mayor Cianci led Providence in its physical renovation over several decades. In his 1999 Inaugural Address he spelled out with pride his vision of the "New Providence," which parallels the vision of economic development that many mayors had for their cities at the turn of the millennium.

On this very spot, almost a quarter-century ago, I delivered my first Inaugural Address to the people of Providence.

I surveyed the city before me in 1975, and saw a downtown in economic distress, neighborhoods in desperate need of new investment, and a waterfront that contributed almost nothing to the well-being of our people.

I argued that Providence had many assets upon which to rebuild: strong neighborhoods, great colleges and hospitals, beautiful buildings, an impressive setting at the head of Narragansett Bay. I called for a "new beginning," a new "spirit of adventure and excitement"—a new commitment to progress in the center city, the neighborhoods, and the waterfront.

How far we have come in the 24 years since that day. At the dawn of a new century and a new era, Providence is in the forefront of American cities—a shining example of a city reborn. Everywhere there is evidence of urban energy and vitality.

To my left, a magnificent new shopping mall rises majestically in Capital Center—once the site of bleak railroad yards and ugly buildings. Now sleek new hotels sprout up around the Rhode Island Convention Center. During the Christmas season, Providence College hosted Notre Dame at the Civic Center,

SOURCE: Mayor Vincent A. Cianci, Jr., "Inaugural Address," January 4, 1999. Available at the Providence, Rhode Island Website. http://www.ProvidenceRI.com/InauguralAddress1999.html. Reprinted by permission of the Mayor's office.

Showboat played to a full house at the grandly restored Providence Performing Arts Center, and *A Christmas Carol* held the stage at the Tony Award-winning Trinity Repertory Company. On gentle summer evenings, thousands assembled along our riverwalks as *Waterfire* weaved its mystical spell. Waterplace Park is a magical transformation of old industrial rivers into a grand focal point of urban inspiration. And the new Fleet Skating Center captivates young and old alike on crisp winter evenings.

There is a new spirit of hope and confidence in the neighborhoods as well. Here are some reasons why:

- Since 1990, we have invested more than $300 million of public money in the neighborhoods of the city—far more than we have invested in the downtown.
- In this time, 73 miles of city streets have been resurfaced.
- 42 parks and playgrounds have been refurbished.
- 1,700 houses have been painted or refurbished.
- Thousands of sidewalks have been resurfaced.
- 225 new classrooms have been built.
- Some of the newest and best-equipped public schools in Rhode Island have been built on the South and West sides of the city.
- Property values are rising in most parts of the city.
- New, much-brighter streetlights have been installed in 80 percent of the city.
- The police department has new cruisers, new technology, and a state-of-the-art fingerprint identification system.
- The police department has more officers in uniform than in any other time in the last 20 years.
- The Gun Court that we created has put more than 350 gun criminals in prison.
- The crime rate in the city has fallen by more than 40 percent since 1990. In fact, crime in 1998 was at its lowest level since the 1960s.
- And our arguments on behalf of property tax relief have been heard in the State House. Starting this July, we will finally begin to phase out the automobile tax and the inventory tax.

Repaved streets, refurbished playgrounds, restored housing, rising property values, computer-centered classrooms, first-rate equipment for the public safety forces, brighter and safer streets, repealed taxes on automobiles and inventory: These are the dreams of 1975 that become the reality of 1999!

In that first election, in 1974, I was elected by the slimmest of margins—only 709 votes. Five elections later, in November of 1998, I received 97 percent of the vote—and I will be forever grateful. The meaning of the November election is clear: There is almost universal support for the progress we have made in the center city and the neighborhoods. I interpret the election as a mandate—a mandate to press on with even greater determination in the renewal enterprise—always reaching for that lofty standard that makes a city great in the eyes of its people, and in the pages of history.

In the next four years, these will be my priorities, and not in any particular order: One, accelerate the pace of redevelopment and economic renewal in our downtown and our neighborhoods; two, bring about reductions in the tax burden on business; three, accelerate school reform, so that the public schools become an important reason why people choose to live in this city; four, implement a tax revaluation that strengthens our neighborhoods; and, five, build a new public safety headquarters that fully meets the needs of the city well into the twenty-first century.

I believe we can build on our successes to date and really achieve something extraordinary in this city. Our reputation has never been higher; the Providence Renaissance is a model for other American cities, now is the time to attract quality employers and talented individuals to our city. . . .

A generation ago, Providence was a town of crumbling mills and empty storefronts. Today we are a great city, celebrated for our theater, our restaurants, the preservation of our historic architecture, our institutions of higher learning, and the grand reconstruction of our public spaces. In a burst of creativity, we have produced Waterplace, *Waterfire*, and the Fleet Skating Center in rapid succession. On Friday, a new TV series set in the City of Providence will have its national premiere. And the new association with our Partnership City of Florence will bring paintings and art works, along with visiting artisans, craftsmen, and gourmet chefs from Florence to our city.

We cannot rest on our laurels. The time has come to set our sights even higher. With the foundation that we have laid in the last 25 years, Providence is ready to take another great leap forward. In a few weeks, I will announce plans to redevelop the city on a scale never attempted before.

I will propose that the city acquire hundreds of acres of industrial property, at three separate locations not far from this spot. I will propose to completely redevelop this acreage for the highest quality commercial, institutional and residential uses. I believe that these three sites, once redeveloped, will rank among the most desirable locations in America for prime development. There is enough land at these locations to *double* the total amount of building space devoted to prime downtown uses in our city at this time. These projects will be the largest public commitment in the history of our city.

The development we have in mind is on such a scale that we call each of the development areas a "New City." Making the New Cities a reality will be important work for the next four years—important work for governmental, business, institutional and civic leaders of our state.

Where are these New Cities located? One is the old industrial waterfront—a sea of petroleum tanks, asphalt plants and other unsightly uses, stretching more than a mile along Allens Avenue. The industrial waterfront today contributes very little tax benefit to the city, and very little employment opportunity as well. In fact, the waterfront contributes only about $2 million in property taxes, or one percent of our total levy, and the petroleum industry employs fewer than 100 people.

We cannot, and will not, allow this situation to continue. The waterfront is the most important asset that the New Providence has. Now is the time to put that asset to work, for the good of our city and our state. We can bring about billions in new investment, create tens of thousands of new jobs, and generate tens of millions in new tax revenue for the city.

The second New City begins on the other side of the highway from where Providence Place is under construction. It flows along the banks of the Woonasquatucket River to the edge of Olneyville Square. The Woonasquatucket River Valley—once the center of our city's manufacturing might— is today an industrial cemetery, packed with block after block of deteriorated mills. With Providence Place rising in the distance, the time has come for sweeping change. The adjacent neighborhoods of Olneyville, Valley and Smith Hill will be major beneficiaries. I foresee bike paths, the reclamation of green space, and the creation of jobs and opportunity that will raise living standards in these neighborhoods.

The third New City is not land at all; it is the "air rights" on top of Route 95, extending from the Atwells Avenue bridge to the Broad Street bridge over the highway. The air rights would be completely decked over— just as the Mass. Pike is decked over to provide space for Copley Place in Boston. In Providence, we could obtain 12 acres of new development space, right in the center of the city. We would also block off the traffic noise and the polluting fumes created by 250,000 cars a day flowing through the city.

We envision that the dramatic development of the Route 95 air rights will speed the renewal of Atwells Avenue, the Armory District and Elmwood. It will reconnect these neighborhoods to downtown, link East Side to West Side, and create a unified and vigorous city once again.

Just as the railroad tracks and the Chinese Wall divided our city, so Route 95 has divided the city and contributed to the deterioration of neighborhoods, even though it is a vital link to the world of commerce beyond. What has happened? The railroad came down, the Chinese Wall came down, and now we have billions of new investment in the heart of our city. Now we must turn our attention to the highways: We must bridge the divide between east and west in our city; we must bring new hope and new opportunity to the people of Federal Hill, Elmwood and the West End; we must all be united once again.

In order to carry out these ambitious plans, we will have to raise hundreds of millions of dollars. We will have to sweep away the old, and create dramatic new settings for new construction. We will have to address the needs of employers for skilled labor. And we will have to ensure that the business taxes we charge are among the most highly competitive in America.

All of these things can be done. They can't happen in one year, or two or three; but we can begin today the great work of transforming our city. Remember that Capital Center was once a sprawling freight yard, a dying use in a dying city. We have so utterly transformed that deserted and disregarded real estate that the most prestigious department stores in America are making their way to our city. We are reclaiming our retail prominence when it was thought to be lost forever. We are succeeding where other cities have failed, because we had the will and the resources to totally change the city center.

Now it is our destiny to totally transform the riverfront of our city. In the nineteenth century, the rivers of Providence were used as a sewer. In the twentieth century, the rivers were channeled, covered up and forgotten. In the twenty-first century, the rivers of Providence will be the centerpiece of a revitalized and vigorous city. We will build a great city on the hills and the plains overlooking the rivers and the bay. We will reconnect our city, from east to west.

More than 350 years ago, Roger Williams rounded the bend at Fox Point in an Indian canoe, and saw before him the site of a new city, a new city he called Providence. What hopes and dreams he must have had for the city he would create out of a wilderness! Today we must share those same dreams, we must see the new city on the horizon, and we must never rest 'til the New Providence is ours!

4. Duluth 2001 and Beyond

Mayor Gary Doty

The urban renaissance of the 1990s and the beginning of the twenty-first century not only occurred in large cities like New York and Denver, but in a number of middle-sized cities like Providence and Duluth.

In 2000, Duluth was a city of 87,000 with a growth of only 1,500 people over the previous decade. It has depended for much of its history on the mining of iron ore and shipping. Like many middle-sized cities it has attempted to develop its tourism industry and seeks to develop high-tech and telemarketing industries to replace lost jobs in mining and factories.

Back in 1994, Duluth involved the community broadly in what was called the Duluth Vision 2001. In 2001, Mayor Doty reported on what had been achieved and what was still needed to create a positive future for Duluth. He argues that while Duluth is not a perfect community, its "getting closer all the time." It is a refrain that would be repeated by many mayors at the end of the twentieth and the beginning of the twenty-first century.

2001 . . . We're finally to the year that has had such significance for a long time. All around the country, of course, this year was emphasized decades ago in that famous movie called "2001: A Space Odyssey."

And while that film became a classic, we in Duluth produced our own 2001 hit many years later, called "Duluth 2001 and Beyond—A Vision for Our Future."

During my State of the City Address in 1994, I announced the formation of what at the time was called Duluth Vision 2001. I encouraged all Duluthians to take a role in helping shape our community for the twenty-first century. At that time, I said: "I am asking each of you to help us get there. We can either

SOURCE: Mayor Gary Doty, "2001 State of the City Address," January 8, 2001. Duluth Website. www.ci.duluth.mn.us. Reprinted by permission of the Mayor's office.

drift toward the next century without a plan, or we can set a well-defined course and reach our goals."

And even though 2001 was seven years off, thousands of you realized that this time would quickly fly by. So you took on this challenge to help improve Duluth. You exchanged great ideas at neighborhood meetings and public forums over a two-year period. And you came up with 26 recommendations for making our community better.

From preserving and enhancing the environment, to building a strong economic base, to investing in our people and neighborhoods, you dreamed big dreams and made them happen.

Before 2001 even arrived, 21 of those 26 recommendations for improving Duluth had already come to fruition, and the remaining few are well on their way to becoming reality.

So what do we do now? As a community, we set some lofty goals to achieve by 2001, and we've reached them. But the name of the process wasn't just called "2001," it was called "2001 *and Beyond*."

Our job now as a community is to keep building for the future. We need to continue to plan well, and we need to continue implementing those plans well, so that more dreams come true.

This year the biggest example of Duluth's continuing planning will be the creation of a detailed and thorough comprehensive plan, which will be the most in-depth roadmap this city has ever had for guiding its growth. . . .

But we're not putting the city on hold until that plan is completed. Not by a long shot. In the coming months the City of Duluth will implement new initiatives and development that crisscross our entire community.

Let's start with major construction projects, which during the past year and into 2001 have had the highest visibility in Duluth.

The Duluth Technology Village and the Great Lakes Aquarium both opened in the year 2000, greatly helping position Duluth as an international leader in two important areas.

The Tech Village is already home to 13 high-technology businesses, five non-technology companies and two schools of higher education. Its unique Soft Center concept has resulted in coverage by CNBC and *The New York Times*, among many other media outlets.

Similarly, the Great Lakes Aquarium is attracting rave reviews from all over the country, not to mention hundreds of thousands of visitors. Their interest in freshwater life and learning has put the aquarium far above attendance projections. . . .

The international attention being focused on Duluth is a major reason why this great facility we're in tonight, the Duluth Entertainment Convention Center, is in the midst of a 20 million-dollar expansion. Next month, the DECC will unveil 62,000 square feet of new conference and ballroom space, offering breathtaking views of Lake Superior, the Aerial Lift Bridge and the harbor.

This means that what was already the eleventh busiest complex in the entire nation will get even busier, the result being millions of dollars more in economic impact throughout the city each year.

But the DECC's improvements don't stop there. The DECC's improvements also include a much-needed, 600-car parking ramp. This year, the DECC is making $1.7 million in improvements to upgrade its facilities for the UMD men's and women's hockey teams, as well as for Duluth high school teams. These upgrades will help UMD to continue its 35-year hockey tradition in a first-class, waterfront location.

Of course, you can't say "waterfront location" without thinking of Bayfront Festival Park, and this coming August we will have a newly expanded and re-designed park ready for the public's use. New landscaping and pathways, new stages, restrooms and other additions are all being made possible. . . .

The development stories aren't just limited to downtown, though. Atop the hill Home Depot will open next month, but Duluth will get more than a new, privately funded home improvement store. We'll also enjoy a 33-acre nature preserve, which the Home Depot set aside when it built its facility.

United Health Care is also nearing completion of a 160,000 square foot com-plex that will house more than 1,000 workers. Only a few years ago, United Health Care employed just 50 people in Duluth. But with its new expansion, United Health Care will become Duluth's third largest private employer.

Development at Spirit Mountain continues this year with construction of a 20 million dollar, privately funded hotel and golf course, fulfilling the 25-year dream of having Spirit Mountain be a vibrant, year 'round facility. . . .

So far tonight I've talked a lot about economic development, which is of-ten seen in the form of new buildings. But it's what the buildings represent that is more important. Each new building in Duluth, or each expansion to an existing building, requires more people to work inside them. This means new opportunities for Duluthians. And hopefully more income to support their families. . . .

To help maintain that strength, we provide resources to help new and exist-ing businesses succeed. In the past five years, the City of Duluth and several other local partners have provided $29 million in assistance to more than 260 small- and medium-sized Duluth businesses.

It is this combination of small, medium and large companies that now pro-vide 62,281 jobs in Duluth. This is 778 more jobs than we had one year ago. And, it means that during the past eight years, more than 10,000 jobs have been added in Duluth.

Ten thousand new jobs in eight years is a great testament to how hard this community has worked to make Duluth better. But we can't rest on our lau-rels. We need to keep looking for even newer ways of improving our eco-nomic climate. . . .

One reason Duluth draws millions of visitors each year is because we have two advantages no one else has: many ways of accessing and enjoying Lake Superior, and a hillside location that provides incredible views of our lake from one end of town to the other. We will continue to do all we can to pre-serve and enhance these unique advantages for everyone's enjoyment. . . .

Duluth now has community police substations in ten neighborhoods, whereas just eight years ago we had none. In 2001 your police department will provide more training of officers in the successful DARE program, work-ing hard on drug issues in and around school zones. . . .

So 2001 will see many changes for the better in Duluth. But there are also some things that none of us ever wants to change about this great community.

Sometimes the term "quality of life" gets overused, but I know many around the United States who envy Duluth's neighborly people, safe and uncrowded streets and natural beauty. Each of us can add our own reasons to this list, because each of us has our own reasons for loving Duluth's quality of life.

Sure, this isn't a perfect community. But we're getting closer all the time. The reason is because we continue to dream big dreams. And we continue to pull together to make those dreams come true.

You don't have to be mayor to make a difference in Duluth. You don't have to be a City Councilor. You don't have to be a schoolteacher. You don't have to own a business.

The only requirement for making a difference in Duluth is wanting to. And I see it every day across this great city: we all do indeed want to make a difference. That's true in the year 2001 . . . and beyond.

Exercise
Discovering the Renaissance in Your City

For many, but not all urban regions, the 1990s were times of major economic growth and affluence. The purpose of this exercise is to determine what happened in your city and metropolitan region during this urban renaissance period. If this exercise is done by a class, different students may pick different cities around the country to study and then compare them.

If the largest city in your metropolitan region is not one of the cities included in these readings, you will want to discover what developments occurred or failed to occur during the 1990s and the beginning of the twenty-first century.

Begin by going to your city's Website, if you have one, and read the mayor's last inaugural address, turn of the millennium speech, or press releases at the time your city's 2001 proposed city budget was introduced. What programs or advances did the mayor announce during the renaissance period?

Alternatively, you may be able to get additional information from the convention and tourism bureau, city hall, the public library, and newspaper accounts. In some larger cities these documents will be available on Websites while in some smaller cities and suburbs these documents will have to be inspected in person. Either way, you should end up with a list of projects and expenditures to improve your city that were undertaken during the renaissance period or comments by public officials about the city's inability to make these improvements.

You may want to compare information from the urban renaissance period to the latest speeches, press releases, and news reports on the current state of your city and metropolitan region.

Chapter 2

Immigration, Urban Renewal, and Neighborhood Destruction

Social and economic conditions profoundly affect the politics and governance of cities, suburbs, and metropolitan regions. In turn, politics and government respond to social and economic problems and guide social and economic development. The people in the metropolitan regions and the conditions under which they work and live, along with the culture they bring with them, determine the shape of our cities just as the institutions of the metropolitan region mold and shape the people who live within them.

NEIGHBORHOODS AS CITY BUILDING BLOCKS

U.S. cities at the end of the nineteenth and the beginning of the twentieth centuries were centers of immigration. Manufacturing booms after the Civil War meant there were more jobs and money in American cities. So, like a magnet, these cities drew immigrants from abroad, especially as they were pushed out of their homelands by famine and war. And within the United States, cities drew men and women off the farms and out of the rural areas of the country, including former slaves from the South.

Nineteenth and twentieth century cities were filled with immigrants from all parts of Europe and Russia. They were soon followed by Blacks from the southern United States and Latinos from south of the border. By the end of the twentieth and the beginning of the twenty-first century, immigrants from the Middle East and Asia also flocked to American cities. Our urban areas continue to be a port of entry, a place where family, friends, and members of the same ethnic groups have already settled. Cities provide jobs and income for the newly arrived.

Cities and their neighborhoods are constantly being built, torn down, and rebuilt. To illustrate this process we focus on one neighborhood just west of downtown Chicago. We start with the account of Jane Addams, the founder of Hull House and one of the founders of the settlement house movement in the United States.

The Halsted/Maxwell area she describes at the beginning of the twentieth century was a polyglot with Italians, Germans, Polish, Russian Jews, Bohemians, French Canadians, and some more well-to-do English-speaking families. Its streets, according to Addams, were "inexpressibly dirty, the number of schools inadequate, sanitary legislation unenforced, the street lighting bad" and filled with overpopulated wooden houses and larger tenement apartment buildings, many with no water supply but a faucet in the back yard. Here immigrants often worked making clothes at low wages, or as street merchants, with their wives sometimes picking rags and their children shining shoes for extra money. Luckier immigrants got work in factories or in the stockyards where they worked long hours but received better pay.

This neighborhood was ruled over by a ward political boss, alderman, and saloon keeper named John Powers, or "Johnny De Pow" as the Italians called him. Despite attempts by Jane Addams and the Hull House workers to defeat him in elections, he remained in power.

Into a few of these immigrant communities, settlement houses like Hull House were established to provide some education and culture, relief services not run by the government but given out more humanely, and basic political organizing to improve conditions. The settlements also investigated and exposed neighborhood conditions, bringing them to public attention so that the worst of the problems could be ameliorated.

Such immigrant neighborhoods did not fare well at the hands of the government or large institutions. Fifty years after Jane Addams located Hull House at the Halsted/Maxwell Street neighborhood of Chicago, Mayor Richard J. Daley decided to locate a large university there in place of the poorer homes and businesses. This process of urban renewal would be repeated many times in many cities in the decades that followed: tearing down poor neighborhoods to make way for the new city.

Florence Scala, a feisty Italian woman who would later run for Chicago alderman against the political and criminal powerhouses of the First Ward, recounts how she grew up in the area around Hull House, taking part in its programs. Scala mobilized the neighborhood to fight the slum clearance program that would bulldoze her neighborhood to make way for the University of Illinois at Chicago. She tells, ironically, how the then middle-class Hull House Board of Directors sold out the neighborhood.

In her interview with oral historian Studs Terkel, Florence Scala tells of the uprooting of the neighborhood—how everything downtown near the Chicago Loop "is clearing and building and going up." She ends her story, telling about a Japanese elm in the courtyard of Hull House that was torn down and replaced by a new university campus which was walled off from what was left of the neighborhood.

The original construction of the University of Illinois at Chicago and the destruction of the older Halsted/Maxwell neighborhood occurred in the 1960s. At the beginning of the twenty-first century the university expanded again with the support of Mayor Richard M. Daley, the son of the original Mayor Daley. This time the university destroyed a unique set of historical sites and the commercial section of the old neighborhood. In an op-ed piece in a local community newspaper, *The Chicago Journal,* I wrote to protest my university's new expansion plan. This tearing down and rebuilding is a continuing story, not just of Chicago, but of the battle between powerful institutions and poorer neighborhoods throughout America.

By 2003, the city and the university finished destroying the Maxwell Street Market area, which had provided shopping for the working class in an open air market with street merchants and blues musicians for the last century. This slice of history was bulldozed away in order to provide student housing, new commercial shops, and high-priced condominiums on the private market. City neighborhoods are built, changed, recycled, destroyed, and reborn as a part of the shifting tides of social and economic change.

Destruction of the old Halsted/Maxwell Street neighborhood has brought some positive benefits to the city—a university that trains 25,000 city and suburban students from working-and middle-class families for productive and much better paying jobs than their ancestors from the neighborhood a century ago. The new neighborhood is now home to a series of world-class hospitals, modern housing, and wealthier residents as well. But we need to remember the human costs of these developments.

These accounts of the Halsted/Maxwell area, written over a hundred year period, encapsulate the changes that occur over time in most American cities. Some call it progress. Some call it the wanton destruction of our own history.

Neither immigration nor urban renewal has ended. By 1990, 17 million legal immigrants and as many as 4 million illegal immigrants resided in the United States.[1] More than 90 percent live in metropolitan areas. [2] These new immigrants are more often Latino, Asian, or Middle Eastern than in earlier years. Moreover, these immigrants have begun to live in suburban areas as well as in ethnic neighborhood enclaves in the central city.

The article by Gustavo Cano explorers the dimensions of the new Latino immigrant experience and the development of Latino political power in Houston and Chicago. It provides a sense of the complications of urban politics in the twenty-first century.

Immigrants and poorer citizens are also still displaced by expansions of major institutions like hospitals and universities, by downtown redevelopment plans, and, even more frequently, by gentrification as the older ethnic neighborhoods become more desirable to wealthier folks in the new service and global economy. Many suburbanites, downtown office workers, new couples, retirees, and single professionals have rediscovered the value of living in city neighborhoods. They have knocked down older buildings to build new condominiums, renovated and remodeled existing homes and small apartment buildings, and flocked to new high-rise buildings with the latest conveniences and best views. These wealthier residents have also demanded more amenities and cultural opportunities from their city.

Several important questions emerge from these readings. How should we provide the necessary services and amenities for immigrants and poorer neighborhoods in our cities and suburbs? The public school system is especially pressed hard to provide a good, modern education to the immigrant children who speak many different languages and come from many different cultures. How should our public education system be revised to meet these challenges?

Most of all, we need to discover how we can lessen the human costs of development and renewal in twenty-first century America. Buildings, institutions, and neighborhoods decay and need to be revitalized to fit modern needs. But should public housing residents always be displaced without finding new homes for them to live in first? Should entire communities be destroyed just to build or expand institutions or to provide new expensive housing that current residents can't afford?

FROM MANUFACTURING TO A GLOBAL ECONOMY

The final set of readings on social and economic conditions explore changes from the manufacturing and commercial economy, which previously character-ized American cities, to the new service and global economy, which is trans-forming them today.

American cities in the nineteenth and early twentieth centuries became great because they provided manufacturing jobs. Manufacturing plants, then located in U.S. cities, produced goods which were sold around the world. Now at the begin-ning of the twenty-first century, the old-fashioned, labor-intensive manufacturing economy has crashed.

Our urban manufacturing economy transformed into a service economy dur-ing the last decades of the twentieth century.

Manufacturing jobs moved from cities particularly in the Northeast and Mid-west to suburbs, rural regions, and the southwestern United States. Even more jobs moved abroad where land, labor, and taxes were cheaper. As a result, plants and factories began closing in many cities. Those manufacturing jobs that contin-ued in the restructured economy were no longer jobs requiring brawn and hard work but brains and high-tech computer skills. While manufacturing jobs in the previous century required little education, white-collar, well-paying service jobs are now available only for the well-educated. What is left for the poor and for new immi-grants are simple jobs at fast food restaurants, as janitors, or as landscapers—jobs that have low pay and no benefits. With welfare payments now ending after five years and our economy in recession, a crisis looms. Yet, with a strong economy up until September 11, 2001 and new "living wage" jobs there was some improvement during the last decade in the plight of the poor.

The ongoing change from a simple service economy to a global economy will bring more profound changes. Already in the major cities of the Northeast and the Midwest 36 percent of the jobs are in service while 10 percent more are in finance, insurance, and real estate.[3] Different cities and metropolitan regions sit differently in the pyramid of the global economy. Transnational corporate headquarters and the financial and legal service corporations that serve them tend to cluster in a few global cities like New York, London, and Tokyo. Second-level global cities like Chicago and Los Angeles mostly house national and regional corporate networks. Medium-sized cities like Cleveland and St. Louis are regional hubs.[4]

In *The Global City: New York, London, Tokyo*, Saskia Sassen explains that "the combination of spatial dispersal and global integration has created a new strategic role for major [global] cities . . . these cities now function in four new ways: first, as highly concentrated command points in the organization of the world economy; second as key locations for financial and for specialized service firms . . . third, as sites of production . . . in . . . leading industries; and fourth as markets for the products and innovations produced."[5] In short, some key global cities like New York, London, and Tokyo are sites for the production of specialized services for transnational corporations and financial innovations. They provide the services and financial products essential to the new global economy.

Since the original conception of global cities, the concept has been expanded to cover other cities. As Janet Abu-Lughod has written in her book, *New York, Chicago, Los Angeles: America's Global Cities,* "globalization is simply an ongoing process whereby larger and larger portions of the world become increasingly linked to one another. . . . [T]his process not only entails more 'integration' on the economic and political levels, but also permits more contact on the symbolic and cultural levels."[6] Almost all cities are drawn into the global economy and perform some specialized function in the hierarchy. But they have very different roles as "global cities."

Reference

Some of the topics in this section are further developed and elaborated in Judd and Swanstrom, *City Politics*, Chapter 6: "National Policy and the Divided Metropolis." Also in Ross and Levin, *Urban Politics*, Chapter 1: "The Urban Situation and Contemporary Los Angeles" and Chapter 10: "Suburban Politics and Metropolitan America."

Notes

1. "Immigration reform: Recent Trends and Legislative Responses, "*The Urban Institute Policy and Research Report*, Winter/Spring 1991, p. 12 and Rodman D. Griffin, "Illegal Immigration," *CQ Researcher*, Vol. 2, No. 16 (April 24, 1992), p. 364.
2. Dennis Judd and Todd Swanstrom, *City Politics*, New York: Longman, 2002, p. 147.
3. Judd and Swanstrom, p. 376.
4. Judd and Swanstrom, p. 377.
5. Saskia Sassen, *The Global City: New York, London, Tokyo*. Princeton: Princeton University Press, 1991.
6. Janet Abu-Lughod, *New York, Chicago, Los Angeles: America's Global Cities*. Minneapolis: University of Minnesota press, 1999.

5. The Halsted Street Saga

Jane Addams, Florence Scala, Studs Terkel, and Dick Simpson

1900–1920 by Jane Addams

Jane Addams and the settlement house she founded early in the twentieth century were major forces in American history. She was an important leader in the settlement house movement, the progressive movement in American politics, the fight by suffragettes for women's right to vote, and the peace movement. She and her colleagues at the Hull House Settlement helped to expose many of the problems of the inner-city poor of her day and to pass laws and to change government policies in ways that benefitted the poor. This is her description of the neighborhood in which she worked and lived in the early decades of the twentieth century.

Halsted street has grown so familiar during 20 years of residence that it is difficult to recall its gradual changes—the withdrawal of the more prosperous Irish and Germans, and the slow substitution of Russian Jews, Italians and Greeks.

Halsted street is 32 miles long, and one of the great thoroughfares of Chicago; Polk Street crosses it midway between the stockyards to the south and the shipbuilding yards on the north branch of the Chicago River. For the six miles between these two industries the street is lined with shops of butchers and grocers, with dingy and gorgeous saloons, and pretentious establishments for the sale of ready-made clothing. . . .

Hull House once stood in the suburbs, but the city has steadily grown up around it and its site now has corners on three or four foreign colonies. Between Halsted Street and the [Chicago River] live about ten thousand Italians—Neapolitans, Sicilians, and Calabrians, with an occasional Lombard or Venetion. To the south on Twelfth Street are many Germans, and side streets are given over almost entirely to Polish and Russian Jews. Still farther south, these Jewish colonies merge into a huge Bohemian colony, so vast that Chicago ranks as the third Bohemian city in the world. To the northwest are many Canadian-French, clannish in spite of their long residence in America, and to the north are Irish and first-generation Americans. On the streets directly west and farther north are well-to-do English-speaking families, many of whom own their houses and have lived in the neighborhood for years; one man is still living in his old farmhouse.

The policy of the public authorities of never taking an initiative, and always waiting to be urged to do their duty, is obviously fatal in a neighborhood where there is little initiative among the citizens. The idea underlying our self-government breaks down in such a ward. The streets are inexpressibly dirty, the number of schools inadequate, sanitary legislation is unenforced, the street lighting is bad, the paving miserable and altogether lacking in the alleys and smaller streets, and the stables foul beyond description. Hundreds of houses are unconnected with the street sewer. The older and richer inhabitants seem anxious to move away as rapidly as they can afford it. They make room for the newly arrived immigrants who are densely ignorant of civic duties. The substitution of the older inhabitants is accomplished industrially also, in the south and east quarters of the ward. The Jews and Italians for the finishing of the great clothing manufacturers, formerly done by American, Irish, and Germans, who refused to submit to the extremely low prices to which the sweating system, has reduced their successors. As the design of the sweating system is the elimination of rent from the manufacture of clothing, the "outside work" is begun after the clothing leaves the cutter. An unscrupulous contractor regards no basement as too dark, no stable loft too foul, no rear shanty too provisional, no

SOURCE: Jane Addams, *Twenty Years at Hull House*. Boston: Bedford/St. Martin's, 1999, pp. 80–89 and 98–100. Originally published 1910. From "Prologue: Florence Scala" in Studs Terkel, *Division Street: America* (New York: Random House, 1967), pp. 1–9. Reprinted by permission of Donadio and Olsen, Inc. And from Dick Simpson, "Watch Out for the Good Guys," *Chicago Journal*, Vol. 1, No. 1, October 19, 2000. Reprinted by permission of Chicago Journal.

tenement room too small for his workroom, as these conditions imply low rental. Hence these shops abound in the worst of the foreign districts where the sweater easily finds his cheap basement and his home finishers.

The houses of the ward, for the most part wooden, were originally built for the one family and are now occupied by several. They are after the type of the inconvenient frame cottages found in the poorer suburbs twenty years ago. Many of them were built where they now stand; others were brought thither on rollers, because their previous sites had been taken for factories. The fewer brick tenement buildings which are three or four stories high are comparatively new, and there are few large tenements. The little wooden houses have a temporary aspect, and for this reason, perhaps, the tenement-house legislation in Chicago is totally inadequate. Rear tenements flourish; many houses have no water supply save the faucet in the back yard, there are no fire escapes, the garbage and ashes are placed in wooden boxes which are fastened to the street pavements. One of the most discouraging features about the present system of tenement houses is that many are owned by sordid and ignorant immigrants. The theory that wealth brings responsibility, that possession entails at length education and refinement, in these cases fails utterly. The children of an Italian immigrant owner may "shine" shoes in the streets and his wife may pick rags from the street gutter, laboriously sorting them in a dingy court. Wealth may do something for her self-complacency and feeling of consequence; it certainly does nothing for her comfort or her children's improvement nor for the cleanliness of anyone concerned. Another thing that prevents better houses in Chicago is the tentative attitude of the real estate men. Many unsavory conditions are allowed to continue which would be regarded with horror if they were considered permanent. Meanwhile, the wretched conditions persist until at least two generations of children have been born and raised in them.

In every neighborhood where poorer people live, because rents are supposed to be cheaper, there is an element which, although uncertain in the individual, in the aggregate can be counted upon. It is composed of people of former education and opportunity who have cherished ambitions and prospects but who are caricatures of what they meant to be—"hollow ghosts which blame the living men." There are times in many lives when there is a cessation of energy and loss of power. Men and women of education and refinement come to live in a cheaper neighborhood because they lack the ability to make money, because of ill health, because of an unfortunate marriage, or for other reasons which do not imply criminality or stupidity. Among them are those who in spite of untoward circumstances, keep up some sort of an intellectual life; those who are "Great for books," as their neighbors say. To such the Settlement may be a genuine refuge. . . .

From the first it seemed understood that we were ready to perform the humblest neighborhood services. We were asked to wash the newborn babies, and prepare the dead for burial, to nurse the sick, and to "mind the children."

Occasionally these neighborly offices unexpectedly uncovered ugly human traits. For six weeks after an operation we kept in one of our three bedrooms a forlorn little baby who, because he was born with a cleft palate, was most unwelcome to his mother, and we were horrified when he died of neglect a week after he was returned to his home; a little Italian bride of fifteen sought shelter with us one November evening, to escape her husband who had beaten her every night for a week when he returned home from work, because she had lost her wedding ring; two of us had officiated quite alone at the birth of an illegitimate child because the doctor was late in arriving, and none of the Irish matrons would "touch the likes of her"; we ministered at the deathbed of a young man who during a long illness of tuberculosis had received so many bottles of whisky through the mistaken kindness of his friends, that the cumulative effect produced wild periods of exultation, in one of which he died.

We were also early impressed with the curious isolation of many of the immigrants; an Italian woman once expressed her pleasure in the red roses that she saw at one of our receptions in surprise that they had been "brought all the way from Italy." She would not believe for an instant that they had been grown in America. She said that she had lived in Chicago for six years and had never seen any roses, whereas in Italy she had seen them every summer in great profusion. During all that time, of course, the women had lived within ten blocks of a florist's window; she had not been more than a five-cent car ride away from public parks; but she had never dreamed of faring forth herself, and no one had taken her. Her conception of America had been the untidy street in which she lived and had made her long struggle to adapt herself to American ways. . . .

The Settlement, then is an experimental effort to aid in the solution of the social and industrial problems which are engendered by the modem conditions of life in a great city. It insists that these problems are not confined to any portion of a city. It is an attempt to relieve, at the same time, the overaccumulation at one end of society and the destitution at the other; but it assumes that this overaccumulation and destitution is most sorely felt in the things that pertain to social and educational privileges. From its very nature it can stand for no political or social propaganda. It must, in a sense, give the warm welcome of an inn to all such propaganda, if perchance one of them be found an angel. The one thing to be dreaded in the Settlement is that it loses its flexibility, its power of quick adaptation, its readiness to change its methods as its environment may demand. It must be open to conviction and must have a deep and abiding sense of tolerance. It must be hospitable and ready for experiment. It should demand from its residents a scientific patience in the accumulation of facts and the steady holding of their sympathies as one of the best instruments for that accumulation. It must be grounded in a philosophy whose foundation is on the solidarity of the human race, a philosophy which will not waver when the race happens to be represented by a drunken woman or an idiot boy. Its residents must be emptied of all conceit of opinion and self-assertion, and ready to arouse and interpret the public opinion of their neighborhood. They must be content to live quietly side by side with their neighbors, until they grow into a sense of relationship and mutual interests. Their neighbors are held apart by differences of race and language which the residents can more easily overcome. They are bound to see the needs of their neighborhood as a whole, to furnish data for legislation, and to use their influence to secure it. In short, residents are pledged to devote themselves to the duties of good citizenship and to the arousing of the social energies which too largely lie dormant every neighborhood given over to industrialism. They are bound to regard the entire life of their city as organic, to make an effort to unify it, and to protest against its overdifferentiation.

1940–1967 by Florence Scala

Decades after Jane Addams founded Hull House, Florence Scala, an Italian house-wife and later businesswoman and aldermanic candidate, describes the fight be-tween the Halsted/Maxwell Street neighborhood and city hall. It is a fight the neighborhood, like many urban neighborhoods, lost. Even the Hull House board of directors betrayed the neighborhood.

I was born in Chicago, and I've always loved the city. I'm not sure any more. I love it and I hate it every day. What I hate is that so much of it is ugly, you see? And you really can't do very much about it. I hate the fact that so much of it is inhuman in the way we don't pay attention to each other. And we can do very little about making it human ourselves.

What I love is the excitement of the city. There are things happening in the city every day that make you feel dependent on your neighbor. But there's detachment, too. You don't really feel part of Chicago today, 1965. Any more, I don't feel any [attachment].

I grew up around Hull House, one of the oldest sections of the city. In those early days I wore blinders. I wasn't hurt by anything very much. When you be-come involved, you begin to feel the hurt, the anger. You begin to think of people like Jane Addams and Jessie Binford and you realize why they were able to live on. They understood how weak we really are and how we could strive for something better if we understood the way.

My father was a tailor, and we were just getting along in a very poor neigh-borhood. He never had money to send us to school; but we were not impover-ished. When one of the teachers suggested that our mother send us to Hull House, life began to open up. At the time, the neighborhood was dominated by gangsters and hoodlums. They were men from the old country, who lorded it over the people in the area. It was the day of moonshine. The influence of Hull House saved the neighborhood. It never really purified it, you know what I mean? I don't think Hull House intended to do that. But it gave us . . . well, for the first time my mother left that damn old shop to attend Mother's Club once a week. She was very shy, I remember. Hull House gave you a little insight into an-other world. There was something else to life besides sewing and pressing. . . .

I always remember the neighborhood as a place that was alive. I wouldn't want to see it back again, but I'd like to retain the being together that we felt in those days.

There were Negroes living in the neighborhood even then, but there was not the tension. I've read about those riots in Chicago in the twenties—the race ri-ots. But in our neighborhood it never did come to any kind of crisis. We used to treat each other as neighbors then. Now we look at each other differently. I think it's good and bad in a way. What we're doing is not understanding, some of us, what it was like then. I think that the American-born—the first generation, the second generation—has not hung on to what his mother and father had. Accepting someone naturally as a man. We don't do that today.

I think that the man who came over from Europe, the southern European especially, who was poor, could understand and see the same kind of struggle and have immediate sympathy for it. He accepted the Negro in the community as a man who is just trying to make a way for himself, to make a living. He didn't look upon him as a threat. I think it was the understanding that both were striving. Not out of some great cause, but just in a human way. I'm convinced that the first and second generation hasn't any concern about the other person's situation. I think money and position are hard to come by today and mean an awful lot, and now they see the Negro as a threat. Though they may say he's inferior, they know damn well he's not. He's as clever as we are and does many things better than we can. The American-born won't accept this, the first and second generation family, especially among the Italians and Poles, and the Irish, too. . . .

Through my teens I had been a volunteer at Hull House. After the War, Eri Hulbert, Jane Addams's nephew, told me of a dream he had. The Near West Side, our area, could become the kind of place people would *want* to live in, close to the city. Did I think this was possible? I said no, people didn't care enough about the neighborhood to rebuild it. But he introduced me to the idea of city planning. He felt the only hope for big cities, in these communities that were in danger of being bulldozed, was to sit down and look and say we have a responsibility here. He convinced me that you could have a tree on the West Side, see?

That's where my life changed. I became involved with a real idea and talking to people like the banker, the social worker, and the Board of Trustees at Hull House. But I suddenly realized my inadequacy. I simply couldn't understand their language, you know? I had to go back to school.

This is where I began to lose the feeling of idolatry you have about people. I think that's bad. I idolized the people that were involved in Hull House. I thought they could never make a mistake. I was later to find out they were the ones who could hurt me the most. I feel that people have to be prepared always for imperfections in everyone, and we have to feel equal, really, to everyone. This is one of the things lots of slum kids, people who came out of poor areas, don't have. Not to be afraid to say something even though it may be way off base. I did this many times and I'd be embarrassed, realizing I had said something that had nothing to do with what they were talking about. But Eri Hulbert kept saying it makes no difference, just keep at it. You're as good as they are. . . .

In those days it was a new idea. You had to fight the politician who saw clearance and change as a threat to his power, his clout. He likes the kind of situation now around Maxwell Street, full of policy and hot goods being sold on the market and this kind of stuff that could go on and on without too much interference from authority because it's so oppressed. The rotten housing and no enforcement of codes and all that business. We had a tough time selling the Catholic Church, too. From '47 to '56 were rough years. It was tough selling people on the idea that they could do it for themselves, that it was the only way it could be done. Their immediate reaction was: You're crazy, you know? Do you really think this neighborhood is worth saving?

All the meetings we had were so much frustration. Eri Hulbert was trying to lead us in a democratic way of doing something about our city. The misunderstandings never came from the neighborhood people. It arose out of the Hull House Board's unwillingness to understand. He couldn't get his point across.

Eri Hulbert committed suicide before our plan was accepted by the city. His death, more than anything else, opened a door which I never dreamed could open. You know, there's a real kind of ugliness among nice people. You know, the dirty stuff that you think only hoodlums pull off. They can really destroy you, the nice people. I think this is what happened to Eri, the way he was deserted by his own. I think it really broke his heart. What disturbs me is that I was a grown woman, close to thirty, before I could see. Sometimes I want to defend the rotten politicians in my neighborhood. I sometimes want to defend even gangsters. They don't pretend to be anything but what they are. You can see what they are. They're not fooling anybody, see? But nice people fool you.

I'm talking about the [Hull House] Board of Trustees, the people who control the money. Downtown bankers, factory owners, architects, people in the stock market. The jet set, too. The young people, grandchildren of old-timers on the Board, who were not really like their elders, if you know what I mean. They were not with us. There were also some very good people, those from the old days. But they didn't count so much any more. This new crowd, this new tough kind of board members, who didn't mind being on such a board for the prestige it gave them, dominated. These were the people closely aligned to the city government, in real estate and planning. And some very fine families, old Chicago families. (Laughs.) The nicest people in Chicago.

Except for one or two of the older people, they made you feel that you had to know your place. You always felt this. That's the big argument about the poverty program today. You cannot have the nice rich people at the top passing on a program for the poor, because they simply don't understand, they can't understand. These people meet in board meetings once a month. They come by the main street into the building and out they go. They've never had anybody swear at them or cry or ask for help or complain the kind of way people do in our neighborhood. They just don't know.

In the early Sixties, the city realized it had to have a campus, a Chicago branch of the University of Illinois. (There was a makeshift one at the pier out on the lake.) There were several excellent areas to choose from, where people were not living: a railroad site, an industrial island near the river, an airport used by businessmen, a park, a golf course. But there was no give. The mayor [Richard J. Daley] looked for advice. One of his advisors suggested our neighborhood as the ideal site for the campus. We were dispensable. [This advisor] was a member of the Hull House Board. It was a strange thing, a very strange thing. Our alderman, he's not what I'd call a good man—even he tried to convince the Mayor this was wrong. But the Mayor was hearing other voices. The nice people.

The alderman alerted us to the danger. Nobody believed it. The priest himself didn't believe it. They had just opened the parish, a new church, a new school. Late in the summer of 1960 the community could have been touched off. But the people were in the dark. When the announcement came in 1961, it was a bombshell. What shocked us was the amount of land they decided to take. They were out to demolish the entire community.

I didn't react in any belligerent way until little kids came knocking at the door, asking me to attend a meeting. That's where the thing got off the ground. It was exciting to see that meeting, the way people felt and the way they talked and the way—they hurt—to hear our Italian priest, who had just become an American. This was in February, we had just celebrated Lincoln's birthday. He had just become a citizen, he couldn't understand.

Though we called the Mayor our enemy, we didn't know he was serving others. It was a faceless thing. I think he'd just as soon have had the University elsewhere. But the pressures were on. We felt it as soon as our protests began.

A member of the Hull House Board took me to lunch a couple of times at the University Club. The University Club—lunch—me! My husband said, go, go, have a free lunch and see what it is she wants. What she wanted to do, really, was to dissuade me from protesting. There was no hope, no chance, she said. I had had a high regard for her. I've been thinking she's probably one of those on the Board who would have fought the people's end. But she was elected to convince me not to go on. The first time I went, I thought this was a friend through whom we could work. But I could see, you know, that she allowed me to be just so friendly, and there was a place beyond which I couldn't go. There was a difference now. I stayed in my place, but I said what I wanted to say. There was a place beyond which she couldn't go, either. See? I was glad to experience it anyway.

I think I understand her. She had strong ties with old Hull House and she was really a good person who ought not have allowed this to happen and she knew it. When the lunches failed to bring anything off, I had no more contact with any of them on that level. We reached the letter-writing stage. We no longer used the phone. Our friendship died.

I shall never forget one board meeting. It hurt Miss Binford [a colleague of Jane Addams who had lived and worked at Hull House from 1906 until its destruction in 1965] more than all the others. That afternoon, we came with a committee, five of us, and with a plea. We reminded them of the past, what we meant to each other. From the moment we entered the room to the time we left, not one board member said a word to us. No one got up to greet Miss Binford nor to speak to her. No one asked her a question. The chairman came forward, he was a gentleman, and showed us where to sit.

Miss Binford was in her late eighties, you know. Small birdlike in appearance. She sat there listening to our plea and then she reminded them of what Hull House meant. She went back and talked, not in a sentimental way, about principles that must never waver. No one answered her. Or acknowledged her.

Or in any way showed any recognition of what she was talking about. It's as though we were talking to a stone wall, a mountain.

It was pouring rain and we walked out of the room the way people walk out who feel defeat. I mean we walked out trying to appear secure, but we didn't have much to say to each other. Miss Binford could hardly speak at all. The shock of not being able to have any conversation with the board members never really left her. She felt completely rejected. She knew then there would be no help anywhere. In the past, whenever there was a serious problem in the juvenile courts, she could walk into the Mayor's office and have a talk with him, whoever he was. Kelly, for instance, or Kennelly, or Cermak. And never fail to get a commitment from him. Never. But she knew after this meeting, she'd never find that kind of response again. And sure enough, to test herself, she made the rounds. Of all the people who had any influence in town, with whom she had real contact, not one responded. They expressed sympathy, but it was hands off. Something was crushed inside her. The Chicago she knew had died.

I don't think we realized the stakes involved in this whole urban renewal system. The money it brings in, the clout necessary to condemn land. . . a new Catholic Church was demolished, too. It had opened in '59, built near Hull House with the city's approval. The Church was encouraged to go ahead and build, so as to form the nucleus for the new environment, see? It cost the people of the area a half million dollars. The Archdiocese lends the parish money, but the parish has to repay. It's a real business arrangement.

Now the people of the area have learned a good deal, but it was a bitter education. The politicians' actions didn't bother us as much. We hated it, we argued about it, we screamed about it out loud. Daley gave the orders and the alderman followed it. This kind of thing we could understand. But we could never understand the silence of the others. A group wanted to picket the Archdiocese, but I felt it was wrong, because we were put into a position of fighting education, the University being built, you know.

Here we were in a big Roman Catholic city, we'd be looked upon as a bunch of fanatics. As I think back on it now, the instinctive responses of the people, who are thought of as being uneducated, were better than my own. I was very anxious we should not be looked upon as people from the slums, many of us Italians and Mexicans. We had to proceed in an orderly manner. We overdid that. We should have picketed the Archdiocese. We should have been tough with Hull House. We should have spoken the truth from the beginning. . . .

In an area like ours, the uprooting is of another kind. I lived on the same block for over forty-five years; my father was there before me. It takes away a kind of stability big cities need. Lots of the people have moved into housing no better than the kind they lived in. Some have moved into public housing. The old people have really had it worse. Some have moved into "nicer" neighborhoods, but they're terribly unhappy, those I've spoken with. Here, downtown in the Loop, everything is clearing and building and going up. And the social workers in this town, boy! I can hardly look at them with respect any more. The way they've knuckled down to the system themselves, because everybody wants a Federal grant or something. They don't want to be counted out. I'm sick of the whole mess and I don't know which way to go.

There are the little blessings that come out of struggle. I never knew Jessie Binford as a kid at Hull House. I used to see her walking through the rooms. She had such dignity, she just strode through the rooms and we were all kind of scared of her. In the past four or five years, we became close friends. I really knew the woman. It meant something to her, too. She began to know the people in the way she knew them when she first came to Hull House as a young girl. It really gave her life, this fight. It made clear to her that all the things she really believed in, she believed in all the more. Honor among people and honor between government and people. All that the teacher tells the kids in school. And beauty.

There was a Japanese elm in the courtyard that came up to Miss Binford's window. It used to blossom in the springtime. They were destroying that tree, the wrecking crew. We saw it together. She asked the man whether it could be saved. No, he had a job to do and was doing it. I screamed and cried out. The old janitor, Joe, was standing out there crying to himself. Those trees were beautiful trees that had shaded the courtyard and sheltered the birds. At night the sparrows used to roost in those trees and it was something to hear, the singing of those sparrows. All that was soft and beautiful was destroyed. You saw no meaning in anything any more.

There's a college campus on the site now. It will perform a needed function in our life. Yet there is nothing quite beautiful about the thing. They'll plant trees there, sure, but it's walled off from the community. You can't get in. The kids, the students, will have to make a big effort to leave the campus and walk down the streets of the area. Another kind of walling off . . .

To keep us out. To keep the kids out who might be vandals. I don't see that as such a problem, you know. It wasn't the way Jane Addams saw it, either. She believed in a neighborhood with all kinds of people, who lived together with some little hostility, sure, but nevertheless lived together. In peace. She wondered if this couldn't be extended to the world. Either Jane Addams brought something to Chicago and the world or she didn't.

2000–2003 by Dick Simpson

The story of the Halsted Street neighborhood didn't end with the creation of the University of Illinois at Chicago in the 1960s. It continued in the twenty-first century when university expansion, with the help of Chicago city government, destroyed the commercial market place and the last of the neighborhood's history. Some call the new student housing and private market upscale condominiums progress. Others decry the wanton destruction of neighborhoods in the constant rebuilding of the city.

The University of Illinois at Chicago is tearing down the remaining buildings of the old Halsted/Maxwell Market. Yes, a couple of buildings like the police station—which served as the set for the Hill Street Blues television program—will survive the wrecking ball. Yes, some building facades (apparently

even with the silhouettes of people drawn in the windows) may be glued to
new structures like the mammoth parking garage. And yes, in one old building
there may be a museum open to document a past that not only doesn't exist,
but which my university helped destroy.

Some call this progress. Others say it's inevitable. The cynical say it is just the
way for real estate developers with political connections to make a buck on the
backs of the poor. New housing and upscale shops will be built. The university
will expand its facilities to house more students and to provide better facilities
for some departments. Certainly teaching the students of Chicago, the suburbs,
and the world is a good service that we at the university provide. No one can be
against better education. But the university, the mayor, and local politicians
have conspired to expand university facilities in the worst way possible.

Today's policy of destruction began nearly 40 years ago when the university
began at its Halsted site. At the time Florence Scala, who led the fight against
destroying the Italian/Greek neighborhood which had been on the near West
Side for more than 100 years, said in an interview with Studs Terkel: "You
know there is a real kind of ugliness among nice people. You know, the dirty
stuff that you think only hoodlums pull off. They can really destroy you. . . .
[Rotten politicians and gangsters] don't pretend to be anything but what they
are. You can see what they are. They're not fooling anybody see? But nice people fool you. . . . Our alderman, he's not what I'd call a good man—even he
tried to convince [Mayor Richard J. Daley] this was wrong. But the Mayor
was hearing other voices. The nice people."

Now 40 years later, the collusion between the local ward politicians, the
university, and the new Mayor Richard M. Daley is even more blatant. The
former 1st Ward Alderman and the city's department of Streets and Sanitation
cut off service to the Halsted/Maxwell Market. Rather than reorganize the old
market with vendor licenses and fees and having the city clean up after the
Sunday open-air market, they let the filth accumulate. This Mayor Daley, like
his father, readily agreed to the university's expansion plan because it would
get rid of this historic eyesore for him and the developers.

Once the Mayor decided to ram the plan through, all creative alternatives
and efforts at compromise with the vendors, the preservationists, and the university were crushed. The fix was in: this was now a done deal.

So we will get a prettier Halsted/Maxwell area. The market has already been
moved and downscaled. It probably will be completely eradicated over time.

What is being lost? Bluesman Jimmie Lee Robinson, who like so many other
Bluesmen and women learned the Blues and perfected their craft performing on
Maxwell street, puts it this way in his guest column in *Streetwise*: "Maxwell
Street was a holy place. It was sanctified by the Jewish people and many Blues
and Gospel musicians and preachers of every religion. . . . [T]hese old buildings remaining on Maxwell and on Halsted Street are the temples of the Souls
of Chicago Past. The aura of the past is still in these buildings."

Poor people won't be able to buy cheap goods in the stores and at the
market any more. Street peddlers who have risen to business prominence
from humble Maxwell Street beginnings will not do so in the bright new
twenty-first century. And a university which claims to value its urban mission

has managed to kill yet another urban institution rather than creatively revitalizing it.

The destruction which the university and the city began 40 years ago is completed. Shame on us. We failed our urban mission.

Florence Scala was right. You expect Chicago politicians to sell the people out—but at least they are honest about what they do. It's the good people you have to watch out for.

6. Political Mobilization of Mexican Immigrants in American Cities

Gustavo Cano

Immigrants are not only important in our urban past but in the present. The largest immigrant group in U.S. cities today are Latinos. In many cities they have become a major population bloc. This article discusses the political mobilization of Latinos who are and who are not yet citizens. Since this article was written, both the city of Chicago and Cook County have recognized documents from the Mexican Consulate as legal papers of identity. This has been an important gain for Mexican immigrants.

A complete understanding of immigrant political mobilization must simultaneously focus on the relations of Mexican immigrants with relevant political institutions and processes in their "home" (in this case, Mexico) and "host" societies (the United States). Home state engagement with political mobilization in the host country has led to more, and not less political mobilization in the host country. This mobilization varies significantly based on the context of reception, including the local and state level political institutions. For the purposes of this research, Mexican immigrants are those persons who were born in Mexico, who live in the United States, and who are noncitizens.

In general terms, we can break down the process of mobilization into eight components: the issue or problem, the actors (who can be either the source or targets of mobilization), the message, the recipient, the perception of the message by the recipient, the action of mobilization, results of the action, and the ever-changing context in which mobilization takes place. The central focus of this study is the act of mobilization. The essence of the process is about how certain actors try consistently to persuade the recipient (the Mexican immigrant) to politically participate.

SOURCE: Gustavo Cano, "The Chicago-Houston Report: Political Mobilization of Mexican Immigrants in American Cities" a paper delivered at the American Political Science Association meeting in September, 2002. Reprinted by permission of the author.

THE STRUCTURE OF CITY POLITICS

One of the most important aspects that affect the way activists mobilize Mexican immigrants in cities like Chicago, Illinois and Houston, Texas is the fact that Chicago activists are influenced by their past and present experiences in dealing with the *political machine*. Whenever a problem arises, activists are inclined to deal directly with their alderman, and they try to solve the problem from a neighborhood-community perspective. As time passes by, activists and aldermen start to know each other, and a *quid-pro-quo* relationship may arise, in which a constant process of negotiation becomes the basic language of communication. It may also occur that the alderman does not pay attention to the demands of neighborhood organizations, then other contacts are developed within the local political structure with state legislators and/or Congressmen and U.S. Senators. However, the relationship with the alderman becomes the starting point to solve neighborhood-community problems, and the "other contacts" will be developed nevertheless. In any case, Chicago's city hall policies and politics are considered to be traditionally immigrant-friendly.

In Houston, organizations that deal with immigrants' issues are spread throughout the city. They rarely follow the neighborhood format, and they do not have the practice of dealing directly with a council member in order to solve their problems. Before the creation of the Mayor's Office of Immigrant and Refugee Affairs, there was practically no office within City Hall that could deal directly with immigrants' issues. Indeed, most organizations tend to deal directly with nongovernmental agencies that address immigrants' needs, which means that whenever trying to solve the set of problems that the community faces, these organizations have to spread efforts and address several issues with several agencies at the same time. This apparently has lead to the systematic proliferation of top-down organizations that deal with specific needs of the community as a whole, and may look forward to empower the community, but there are practically no traces of mobilization in the process.

Throughout time, bottom-up activists in Houston have become specialists in developing a wide open agenda of political action, which includes contacts with statewide and federal elected officials, and even out-of-state federal elected officials. For activists in Houston, Houston is only part of the agenda. Finally, one key difference between activists in Houston and Chicago, is that in Chicago some activists have accumulated electoral experience running against or with the machine, whereas in Houston, the possibility for an activist to become a politician is not that common.

Finally, local politics towards immigration issues in Houston and Chicago are changing rapidly because of demographics. Council members in Houston, and aldermen in Chicago are paying more attention to their immigrant constituencies because of their increasing numbers, as reported in the last U.S. census. Many city and state districts have dramatically changed their ethnic composition in the last twenty years and, in some cases, the Mexican-origin population has become the ethnic majority or even the majority of the district. Most politicians in these districts argue that regardless of whether their Mexican-origin constituency exerts their right to vote, they have the obligation to address the needs of their constituency. Moreover, some of them accept that they cannot ignore the voting potential of the Mexican-origin community.

The majority of these politicians recognize (1) the right of immigrant workers to defend their workers rights regardless of their migratory status, and (2) the right for undocumented immigrants to legalize their migratory status. Although there is a wide set of opinions about how to reach this last goal, the majority of these politicians agree that undocumented immigrants have earned the right to legalize their status because they pay taxes, because of their economic contribution to the city, and because of their consistent monetary contributions to the social security system of the country.

On the other hand, union and community-based organizations' activists are skeptical about politicians' intentions on the matter [in Chicago: *del dicho al hecho hay mucho trecho* (there is a long distance between saying and doing), and in Houston: *they talk the talk, let's see if they walk the walk*]. Activists assert that politicians' interest in their Mexican-origin constituency is also related to the influence that the undocumented members may exert on the voting members of the immigrant family. *El voto de rebote* (the rebounding vote) matters in local politics.

However, these city or state politicians are the minority in their respective political arenas in Chicago and Houston. In Chicago, most activists do not trust politicians (especially those who are identified as part of the *machine*), and they consider that there is very little that immigrant-based-constituency local politicians can do in the struggle for legalization. In Houston, the level of distrust towards these politicians is definitely lower than in Chicago; however, Houston's activists are deeply sensitive to the majority's moves regarding immigrant rights issues.

When dealing with local issues (mostly matters related to drivers licenses, workers rights, and education) in Chicago, city politics is considered an essential factor when deciding what to do and what not to do. In Houston, state-level strategic considerations generally overcome those of city politics, and mobilization strategies are mainly focused on coordinating efforts with activists in other cities. The aim is to exert coordinated pressure on the state legislature and the governor on issues. In Chicago, this also happens, but most mobilization efforts that are planned in the city start by a well-defined effort to form alliances at local levels (neighborhood, community, and sometimes interethnic).

Politicians and activists, mostly those whose constituency is formed by significant proportions of Mexican immigrants, know that after the World Trade Center's terrorist attack on September 11, 2001, many things have changed regarding U.S. immigration policies. Indeed, politicians in both cities expect that any important change regarding legalization of undocumented immigrants could now take years, even if this becomes an issue for the next presidential election. However, Chicago and Houston politicians are already experiencing a shift on the activists' targeting strategy. Before September 11, the leading forces behind legalization efforts were the Fox-Bush understanding on the issue and the collaboration of the U.S. Congress on the matter. After September 11, the U.S. Congress has a very different set of priorities, and congressmen who supported legalization measures apparently went from a growing majority to an isolated minority. This provides a great incentive for local activists to readdress their mobilization efforts, in order to target local politicians to obtain city and state resolutions supporting legalization of undocumented immigrants and to do positive legislative work on other immigrant-related issues.

ZONING AND ANNEXATIONS

In Chicago, the family is considered as the basic unit of mobilization among Mexican immigrants. In Houston, the individual and the family are the basic units. However, the transmission of the message flows more easily among Chicagoan families than among Houston's receptors. Mobilization among Mexican immigrants is about trust. The message is better perceived if it comes from somebody you trust, from the priest, from a member of your own family and, in some cases, your neighbor. From this perspective, we can say that there are higher levels of trust among Mexican immigrants in Chicago than in Houston.

Explanations about this difference have to do with the place of origin and immigration patterns of the Mexican migrants, and with the politics of annexation and zoning in their respective host cities. For trust to emerge among the community, three things are identified as sufficient, although not necessary conditions: families or individuals have to share the same physical space as neighbors during a long period of time, and they need to speak the same language and/or share similar habits. The longer we know the same neighbors, if they speak the same language we do, and they have the same habits that we have, the higher the chances are that a relationship of trust will emerge.

On the one hand, a significant difference between Mexican immigrants in Houston and Chicago is that Houston's immigrants are relatively close to their home-community, as an important segment of Mexican immigration comes from the states of Nuevo Leon, San Luis Potosi, and Tamaulipas. In some cases, their communities of origin can be reached in a matter of hours by bus, whereas in Chicago, the majority of immigrants come from a larger variety of Mexican states, and it is relatively harder for them to keep in touch with their community of origin, mostly because of the large distance between Chicago and Mexico. On the other hand, Houston is generally considered a port of entry to the U.S. job market in Texas, the Midwest, and more recently, the East Coast, whereas Chicago is generally considered by Mexican immigrants as their final destination. These conditions suggest that the floating immigrant population in Houston is higher than in Chicago, and that there are more incentives in Chicago for Mexicans to develop community life far away from home.

The city of Houston has a well-known tendency to constantly expand its city limits, whereas the limits of the city of Chicago have remained practically the same. Up to 1999, there have been no real restrictions to annexation policies in Houston. Free market rationale working at its best: city developers would buy important extensions of land, they would develop them, and the city would annex them mostly because those new pieces of developed land represent a fresh source of tax revenues. In the process, Mexican and Central

American immigrant labor was needed first as construction workers in developing the areas, and then they were hired to provide services to the newly developed and annexed areas. Considering that there are no zoning restrictions in Houston, an important portion of immigrant population ends up distributed through the whole city, following the job markets that are driven by the annexation dynamics of the place, and establishing themselves in a way that neighborhood life is not feasible.

In Chicago, an inactive annexation policy, a relatively efficient reinforcement of zoning rules, and more diversified sources of employment in the city (construction, services, and commerce), have lead Mexican immigrant populations to get established in "their own" neighborhoods for relatively long periods of time. Indeed, gentrification is the main issue in Chicago, which has led Mexican immigrants to either sell their properties and migrate to the suburbs (or simply migrate to the suburbs for those who do not own any property), or to stay in their neighborhoods, organize themselves, and mobilize people to fight for the community's right to stay in their neighborhood, sometimes successfully.

OTHER FACTORS

At a local level (in the last twenty years in Houston, and at least thirty years in Chicago), activists, organizations, and heads of immigrant families have gone through different mobilization experiences in order to fight for their rights. These experiences include, among the most important, (1) parents taking an active role in the local school's Parent-Teacher Association (PTAs) to effect their children's education; (2) activists mobilizing and lobbying to obtain the state legislature's support for immigrants to get their driver's licenses; (3) mobilizing and lobbying for immigrants' rights to continue with their college education, regardless of their migratory status; and (4) dealing with issues of gentrification.

These experiences have proved to be extremely useful through time, mostly because activists have become familiar with how the system works, who to trust and, most important of all, when and how to mobilize people. For activists and organizations in Houston, the most valuable experiences have been developed in the field of struggling for an open access of higher education for immigrants and getting driver's licenses for immigrants, both experiences at a state level. In Chicago, struggles against the effects of gentrification, and parents' involvement in PTAs have proved to be enriching experiences on political organization and mobilization.

At a national level, the Immigration and Naturalization Service (INS) misinterpretations of federal legislation regarding immigrants' issues (the amnesty of 1986, for example), or the action of certain government agencies [like the no-match letters that are currently being sent by the Social Security Administration (SSA) to employers whose employees have a social security number that does not match SSA records], have proved to be the triggering factor for immigrants to mobilize. Indeed, when the issue affects the immigrant at a national level, the tendency is that, at the beginning, the activist is the one who gets mobilized by the immigrant community, as the community demands solutions to the problem.

On the other hand, the INS experiences have proved to be a direct source of leadership renewal and organizational restructuring, as the current mobilization and organizational structures are not able to deal with the new problem. Houston's extremely well organized ARCA (Association for Residency and Citizenship of America) is the best example for this type of process. On the other hand, national issues, like struggling for legalization or a general amnesty for immigrants, make necessary the creation of coalitions at a national level. This has become a national challenge, as activists struggle to coordinate agendas, and to overcome the *who-gets-credit-for-what* rationale.

THE ROLE OF THE HOME STATE

The role of the Mexican consulate in the process of mobilization of Mexican immigrants is important from two perspectives. The first is related to a trust-building process between the Mexican consulate and the (mostly Mexican-born) leadership and the second is the role of the Mexican consulate in the formation and consolidation of state federations. A good relationship between the Mexican consul and the local Mexican-immigrant leadership is essential for the Mexican consulate in building bridges of communication and understanding with the community as a whole, and developing a strategic relationship based on trust. Here, every little detail counts: It is good if the consul welcomes the leadership into his office and listens to their demands; good if the consul attends periodically their celebrations and meetings; good if the consul eats and drinks the same stuff that the community eats and drinks; and good if the consul is available "24/7."

This relation-building process is extremely helpful for each party to understand each other whenever conflict arises. The leadership may not agree with the way the consul sees this or that problem, or with the solutions that the consul may offer to solve their problems, however, what really matters is that communication channels must remain as open as possible. Activists of Mexican origin definitely prefer to have the consul as a potential ally, rather than as a potential target. However, there are leaders in both cities that will always consider the Mexican consulate as the usual target and they will never initiate an alliance with the consul. On the other hand, if no communication channels are created, chances are very high that the Mexican consulate will be the target of mobilization.

In order to earn the community's trust, it is not enough for the consul to listen to their problems, or to attend most of their celebrations: his capacity to deliver is the most appreciated thing. The more the consul delivers, the higher the level of trust in the relationship. Indeed, from this continuous relation-building with the consul, the leadership is always processing basic information about the limits of action of the Mexican government. Leaders know in what kind of struggles they will count with the support of the Mexican consulate, and in what kind of struggles they will be on their own. This knowledge becomes essential when taking the decision to mobilize people for whatever the purpose.

How the Mexican consulate can "support" the cause, is generally up to the consul's discretion. The consul himself may become a facilitator by creating an informal network with local and state authorities in order to solve problems that can be solved through consular means. He can channel specific demands of the community through one of his subordinates or he can become an active player by intervening directly in the solution of the problem and personally supervising the implementation of the solution. Or he can do nothing, which is always an option, because there are issues in which the Mexican consulate cannot do anything. Finally, a consul who delivers, creates higher expectations of consular collaboration among the leadership whenever a new consul arrives.

In addition to building a trust-based relationship with the Mexican-immigrant leadership, some direct actions from the Mexican consulate are highly related to the mobilization process of the Mexican community in their host cities. The best example for this is the formation and consolidation of state federations. With the implementation of the "Program of Mexican Communities Living Abroad" (PMCLA) in 1990, the Mexican consulates in Chicago and Houston actively encouraged the formation of state federations. Some federations in Chicago assert that the Mexican consulate had nothing to do with their formation process (indeed, one organization already existed in the federation format even before the implementation of the PMCLA), and practically all of them attest that they organized themselves without any kind of support from the Mexican government. However, the majority of these organizations point out that it was through meetings that took place in the Mexican consulate in the early to middle nineties, that a number of leaders, representing hometown associations or families from the same state of origin in Mexico, met each other for the first time, triggering the formation process of the state federation.

Addressing the process of consolidation, the role of the Mexican Consulate in Chicago has been essential in negotiations to unify federations whenever a split on their membership leads to the emergence of two different federations for the same state. The Mexican Consulate has also played the role of mediator between the state federations and Mexican state governments when conflict arises. Finally, the implicit, and in some cases explicit, recognition that the Mexican Consulate extends to state federations is pointed out as one of the major contributions of the Mexican government to the consolidation process of state federations. Currently there are nine, and sometimes ten, active state federations in Chicago.

In Houston, the lack of formation and consolidation of state federations is pointed out as a consequence of the interaction of different factors. Mentioned among the most important are high levels of floating immigrant population, high levels of internal mobility of the immigrant population driven by local labor markets, the closeness of Houston to the Mexican border, and the lack of hometown associations. Also special emphasis is made about the lack of an established network of organizations that addresses the concerns of Mexican immigrants, like the "Protection Network," established by the Mexican consulate in Chicago in the nineties.

However, the only state federation that exists in Houston had the same origin as its counterparts in Chicago, which was an initial meeting in the Mexican consulate for leaders of hometown associations to meet with each other, and talk about the idea of forming a state federation. In addition to this state federation (the Zacatecas federation), there are people from other states willing to create new or bring back to life former state federations. However, the severe lack of hometown associations makes these projects look more like top-down organizational efforts, instead of the Chicago model, in which the majority of state federations are seen as the product of bottom-up organizational efforts.

Currently, state federations in Chicago (sometimes through coalitions, sometimes on their own), are increasingly developing a network of contacts in local politics at city and state levels, this in addition to a growing influence on their states of origin, back in Mexico. State federations are highly autonomous in their actions, and their potential of mobilization begins to be recognized and appreciated by other actors who deal with legalization and workers' rights issues. State federations in Chicago have become an efficient mode for the political incorporation of the Mexican immigrant community, as well as an active source of empowerment. Also the initiative of the Mexican consulate (mostly through its department of attention to communities), in the process of formation and consolidation of these organizations, has been decisive for them to become the role model of an evolving transnational organization in the political arena of a global city.

In Houston, the model of building a trust-based relationship between the leadership and the Mexican consulate still is an option for the consul. The intensity of such relationship depends on the consul's discretion, and this is highly related to the lack of the pressure that state federations may exert on the attention of the consul. Indeed, in the last twenty years, activists and Mexican-immigrant leaders in Houston only have present in their minds two consuls that "have voluntarily followed" the Chicago model. In Chicago, the consul apparently has no other choice than becoming a player. A demanding and organized community has implemented an informal system of checks and balances that is constantly reinforced by a relatively efficient and democratic renewal of leaders, who quickly learn the rules of the game in transnational and local politics.

This does not mean that in Houston nothing is happening, on the contrary, things are changing at a fast pace. A new generation of Mexican, and Central- and Latin-American-origin leaders are getting along very well with the traditional leadership. Traditional leaders appreciate that the new guys not only know how the system works in local politics, but that they bring in with them new and ingenious ideas about how to change things. They do not accept "no" for an answer.

A common trend in both cities, is that an increasing number of Mexican leaders have realized that it is not enough to know and play by the rules of Mexican politics. It is also necessary to know how the local system works. The quality of their meetings has remarkably improved by adopting democratic voting procedures that everybody accepts and exerts, regardless of the final outcome of the procedure. In the past, for example, whenever a conflict would arise in a meeting, a little screaming would be the more than enough for somebody to call the police and to bring the meeting to a weird end. Now, depending on the meeting, people may arrive with their lawyers, no need of yelling at each other, and if the police are called, lawyers deal directly with them. A good relationship with the Hispanic media is essential to capitalize mobilization efforts. However, new ways of entering into contact with mainstream Anglo press are currently being pondered.

MEXICAN POLICIES AND POLITICS

The explanation about the different levels of mobilization between Houston and Chicago is not complete if Mexican politics and policies are not included in the picture. There are some factors or events that affect in a similar way both places, and there are factors and elements that affect in a different way the Mexican community in these two cities.

Regarding the first category, two events in Mexican politics in the nineties have had a deep impact on political mobilization of Mexican immigrants: the Zapatista movement, and the Zedillo government's attempt to increase the monetary deposit for foreign vehicles entering Mexico, from $11 to a range between $400 and $800. In broad terms, the Zapatistas' abrupt entrance into Mexican politics in 1994, made people to get together in order to obtain information about what was really going on, and then to see what type of solidarity acts and/or protest measures they could all work out together. "Zedillo's cars" created a similar reaction (in terms of short-term mobilization) among the Mexican community, however, this time there was no ideological component in the discussions, and they were directed mostly to decide what kind of protest measures were the most effective. The simultaneous coordination of actions among several Mexican communities in different American cities became a fact in a matter of hours. Luckily for the Mexican consulates in these cities, Chicago and Houston included, the "Zedillo's cars" crisis lasted only a couple of days. It ended with the Mexican government canceling the measure.

In both cases, in both cities, people surpassed the leadership's capacity of response at the beginning of the events in terms of mobilization. In the long term, new leaders, activists, and organizations emerged as an outcome of those initial meetings. Some of the people who met for the first time in those meetings, are currently leading activists in legalization and immigrants' rights issues, or are the driving force behind the creation of local coalitions of organizations that deal with immigrants' issues. On the other hand, some organizations have embraced several aspects of the Zapatista philosophy, as they found many similarities with the Zapatista movement in their everyday struggle for the dispossessed. The Zapatista movement still remains present in the minds and words of some Mexican leaders and activists in both cities. Indeed, both mobilization experiences opened new views about how to deal with the Mexican authorities in times of crisis.

In the second category, the right for Mexicans to vote abroad, and the relationship between Mexican state governments with their communities abroad, both affect in a different way certain aspects of immigrant mobilization in both cities. In Houston, both issues generally get very little attention from activists. When a governor of a Mexican state comes to Houston, generally the

Mexican consulate is the main reference when planning the governor's agenda. Regarding the right of Mexicans to vote abroad, most activists show solidarity with the subject, but the topic on its own is not an issue for the mainstream Mexican immigrant community. However, when it comes to legalization issues, Houston's activists have strategically developed (more implicitly than explicitly) a working agenda with several members of the Mexican Congress, generally representatives and senators from border states.

In Chicago, both issues are related in a very specific and curious manner: both function in a way that they generally have not required any major mobilization efforts on the part of the activists. Up to now, the struggle for the right to vote has absorbed large quantities of time and human resources, mostly among the leaders that are involved in the issue. After more than five years of letters, national activism on the subject, information campaigns, and meetings with electoral authorities and members of Congress in Mexico, the outcome has been extremely disappointing. The main idea is not only for Mexican immigrants to obtain the right to vote in Mexican elections while working and living in the United States, but to elect their own representatives in order to get direct representation in the Mexican Congress, which is much more complicated than simply casting their vote for presidential elections every six years.

The Chicago leadership, along with other Mexican leaders in the United States, currently considers taking the next and extremely challenging stage: mobilizing people. It is challenging because nobody really knows to what extent Mexicans can be mobilized to get the right to vote and elect representatives of their own in the Mexican Congress. It is also challenging because there is no way to know to what extent the Mexican political parties and the federal government, will react after a successful mobilization campaign of Mexican immigrants in U.S. territory. There is no way to foresee any possible outcome after mobilization efforts have been made. Finally, it is challenging because the success of mobilization does not depend on a single city. This effort requires a national coordination and, with the exception of Los Angeles and Chicago, most Mexican communities in other major American cities are not that aware of the struggle as a whole.

However, there are different types of mobilization that are being considered by some leaders: a campaign of signatures, which could be extremely successful, but ineffective in the short term. Also a well coordinated boycott against the consumption of Mexican products, or coordinated blocking actions of the Mexican consulate in several cities, and even a boycott of the remittances that are regularly sent to Mexico. These last three actions seem more feasible in a symbolic mode than becoming authentic measures of pressure. In these actions, the activist makes the mobilized to choose between sacrificing a part of his or her (and his or her family's) well-being in order to enhance the probabilities for them to get the right to vote in Mexican elections. Some activists assert that there is no way for that to happen, that Mexican immigrants came to the United States to work, and that the voting issue is completely secondary to the problems that they face on arrival and in everyday life. Although, they also recognize that "you really never know" what the response of the immigrant will be if serious mobilization efforts take place.

Finally, Mexican state governments have increasingly replaced the role of the consulate in the consolidation process of the state federations in Chicago. The practice of state federations being officially recognized by their respective home state government practically eliminates any potential creation of a parallel organization. On the other hand, if the state government enters in conflict with the state federation, for whatever the reason and regardless of the final outcome, chances are high that the state federations will end up better organized and more united.

On the other hand, the simultaneous contact of state federations with politicians of their homeland (governors, city mayors, representatives, and senators) allows them to have a transnational vision of certain problems that affect the Mexican immigrant. They find themselves in the privileged position of choosing allies or targets in the Mexican or American political arenas, depending on the issue and the timing. However, up to now, state federations have not seen themselves in any need to mobilize their constituency.

CONCLUSION

Mobilization efforts of Mexican immigrants in Chicago have been linked more to Mexican state's organizing efforts in the United States and to ethnic machine politics in the city. Mobilization efforts of Mexican immigrants in Houston have been less linked to Mexican state efforts and, to a certain extent, more linked to mainstream, "Anglo" assimilatory processes of *political incorporation*. Mexican immigrants in Chicago are experiencing a process of segmented assimilation, and expectations are that full political incorporation of Mexican immigrants can be reached through a major legalization of undocumented immigrants. In any case, most actors consider that political mobilization of Mexican immigrants is already a way of incorporating this population into the political system of the city.

In Chicago, machine politics is an essential factor to understand the political incorporation of minorities by the local political system. Although Mexicans generally have been considered the last of the "major-league players" in the process, the political structure of the city in the last fifty years has shaped their slow integration into local politics. Moreover, Chicago is one of the most segregated cities in the country and this is a potential source of political mobilization.

The majority of Chicagoans have lived in neighborhoods with strictly delineated *de facto* borders, giving the inhabitants and each neighborhood an impression of being permanently isolated from the rest of the city. Such isolation enhances nationalist feelings and group consciousness among ethnic groups whenever the community has to solve a problem. This leaves the doors open in developing a process of segmented political assimilation, as ethnic community leaders dealt with their community-neighborhood problems by consulting first their respective aldermen. In theory this works if the alderman shares the ethnic identity of their constituency, although this is not always the case, and even if it were the case, the fact that the alderman has a Mexican-origin ethnic background does not mean that the results will always favor the interest of the Mexican community.

In Houston, assimilatory tendencies work with practically no middle-of-the-road points in the process. Although legalization is seen as an essential component in the process of political incorporation, it seems that Mexicans get involved in a winner-takes-all dynamic, in which the winner goes from being a Mexican immigrant to becoming a U. S. citizen who lives in Texas, and then the individual is incorporated into political life. This generally happens with second generation immigrants. There is no hard evidence about systematic or institutionalized processes of political mobilization of Mexican immigrants in Houston. Low levels of political mobilization among Mexican immigrants have led to low levels of political incorporation and participation. In Texas, citizenship does matter.

However, things are changing fast in Houston. On the one hand, some local politicians consider that regardless of their citizenship status, Mexican immigrants are "citizens of the city" of Houston. They represent more than ten percent of the total population, and they are a component of the city's economy that cannot just be ignored. They represent tax revenues for the city and the state, and they require the most elemental services from the city as well. From this perspective, mainstream local politicians cannot afford anymore to ignore the presence of Mexican immigrants, mostly when it comes to the allocation of city resources in order to address their constituency's needs.

On the other hand, recent organizational and mobilization efforts among immigrants have proved to be extremely successful at a local level. ARCA's ingenious dealings with the INS regarding late amnesty cases, and the Coalition for Higher Education for Immigrant Students' efforts to grant higher education to the immigrant population, are examples reinforcing the idea that through the process of nonelectoral mobilization, political incorporation is definitely a reachable goal for noncitizens in Texas. Through the whole process of mobilizing and organizing immigrants in order to reach their objectives, the leadership of these organizations has built strong links with local, state, and national level politicians. They single out these links as essential in accomplishing their aims, although they also point out that hardly anything can be done without a good mobilization plan and well developed organizational skills.

The Switch from the Manufacturing to the Global Economy

There is a direct relationship between the social conditions and the economic transformations that are occurring. Cities are primarily places of economic opportunity. People move to the city because of the jobs that are available there. Since the mid-nineteenth century, U.S. cities have been places with manufacturing and commercial jobs that were not available in rural areas. But now manufacturing is decreasing in the cities as plants move to the suburbs and, more frequently, overseas. By the 1970s, cities were transforming from a manufacturing and commercial economy to a service economy. This is a trend that has accelerated into what is known today as the global economy. If we are to understand the modern American cities, we have to understand these economic transformations and what they mean for the people who live in these cities.

To understand modern American cities we first have to understand the loss of manufacturing jobs and the switch to the service economy. The change began to be obvious in U.S. cities by the 1980s. The city of Chicago, for example, lost 250,000 manufacturing jobs from 1970 to 1985. This recession in the 1980s, would have been worse if nearly 200,000 new jobs—mostly in the service sector—had not been created. The problem with this job replacement was that the average wages in services are one-fourth lower than manufacturing jobs and retail wages are less than half the manufacturing wages.

The service sector itself is a two-tiered economy. Some service jobs such as top bankers, stock brokers, and corporate lawyers earn more than a $100,000 a year with good health benefits, pensions, and expense accounts. At the lower tier of the service economy are part-time jobs with no health and pension benefits and an average wage of less than $15,000 a year—which means that many service workers are the working poor who earn below the official poverty level in the United States.

There are many causes for the loss of manufacturing jobs and the switch to the service economy. One is factories moving out of the cities to manufacturing centers overseas which pay very low wages and have no labor unions to insure worker safety and benefits. The moving of billions of dollars of capital and millions of jobs out of U.S. cities by transnational or global businesses has caused deindustrialization and unemployment problems here at home. These job losses have resulted in human tragedies for individuals and families—lost homes, failed marriages, spousal abuse, suicides, health and financial crises.

These economic changes encouraged cities to follow new strategies for economic revitalization at the beginning of the twenty-first century. Cities have tried to build up their downtown business centers, to encourage new service industries to locate there—especially the legal, financial, computer software, and Internet companies. Cities have also tried to lure wealthy and middle-class families to homes in the city again—even if it has meant urban removal of the poor, private high-rises or gated communities, and gentrification. These same cities have made big investments in tourism and entertainment—in sport stadiums, museums, performance centers, casinos, and tourist attractions to build a tourism and entertainment base to their economies.

The article by investigative reporter Merrill Goozner documents the effects of the loss of manufacturing jobs and the switch to the service economy. The problem is that service jobs—many of which were part-time with neither health insurance or pensions— pay too little to lift their workers into the middle class as the lost manufacturing jobs had done. Service jobs pay at least 22 percent less than manufacturing jobs and retail jobs pay more than 50 percent less. So the per capita income in the Chicago metropolitan region dropped in the 1980s to $14,655 from a high of $15,328 in the 1970s. This differential continues today as the middle class in the United States appears to be shrinking in the new economy.

Professor David Ranney in his latest book, *Global Decisions, Local Collisions*, traces much of the problem to transnational investment in plants overseas. Cities simply can't prevent decisions in the private sector made by transnational corporations from closing plants and ending jobs. According to Ranney, in Chicago alone in the 1980s, there was a loss of 128,986 manufacturing jobs; nearly 100,000 more jobs were lost as a result of these plant closings as the loss of those plant employees as customers affected restaurants, hardware stores, and grocery stores.[1] This is one of the more obvious effects in cities of the switch to the service and global economies.

The switch to high-tech jobs has not saved metropolitan regions from economic turmoil either. Reporter Jim Yardley documented job layoffs in the high-tech sector in Austin, Texas. When the high-tech companies collapsed at the start of the twenty-first century, cities like Austin were helpless to stem the job losses.

Some cities have almost no contact with the global economy. They continue to supply goods and services only in their metropolitan area or the state in which they exist while Global Cities like New York are tied directly to the international trade and finance. Thus, each city fits into the global economy and is affected by it differently.

While the transition to the service and global economy has caused major problems, it is important to realize as well that our cities still produce more products and wealth than most countries of the world. Chicago and its suburbs, for instance, generate more wealth than countries like Argentina, Thailand, and Switzerland.

Despite this level of business and production, real economic problems for U.S. cities continue. Reporter Carla Rivera summarizes a study that shows that the Los Angeles metropolitan region does not have enough jobs for everyone who is unemployed and those on welfare who need to work. Currently, there are 5.4 job seekers for each new job offering in Los Angeles—and most of the available jobs are in the low-paying service sector. Like other American cities and suburbs, Los Angeles County lost nearly 500,000 jobs between 1990 and 1994 and had regained only a quarter of them by the end of the 1990s. At the turn of the millennium, more than 300,000 people remain unemployed in this single metropolitan county alone.

Robert Reich, former Secretary of Labor in the Clinton administration, has warned of the growing wealth gap in America and argued that "education is the fault line dividing winners from losers."[2] He argues that we must equip all Americans to succeed in the new economy by investing in education. But in many states, spending for prisons is outstripping spending for education. The cost of providing the education needed for all citizens to succeed in the new economy is beyond the ability of cities alone to pay.

One small step that some U.S. cities have taken to overcome the worst of the economic gap is passage of a "living wage ordinance." This ordinance guarantees better salaries for employees of firms that do business with the city. As reporter Nancy Cleeland asserts, for these employees it can mean the difference between sleeping on flattened cardboard boxes or having their own apartment; taking public transportation or having a car; being hungry or having enough to eat. Living wage ordinances are small steps, but for affected workers they can be important.

All evidence points to the fact that urban and suburban economies are changing. New jobs and new structures are being created. The issue is whether people will be able to control these economic transformations or whether they will be victims of changes they can't control. Globalization gives the promise of new wealth and prosperity for some, but it also impoverishes other people and communities if there are not some controls over it. The effects of the new global economy upon our cities and suburbs are still unfolding.

Notes

1. David Ranney in Dick Simpson, ed., *Chicago's Future in a Time of Change,* Champaign, Il: Stipes, 1993, pp. 88–98 and *Global Decisions, Local Collisions: Urban Life in the New World Order.* Philadelphia: Temple University Press, 2003.
2. Robert Reich, "Secession of the Successful," *New Perspectives Quarterly,* Vol. 13, No. 2, Spring 1996, pp. 18–19.

7. What Ails Post-Industrial Chicago

Merrill Goozner

The 1970s saw the loss of manufacturing plants and jobs in major cities. By the 1980s the change from a manufacturing to a service economy was well underway as documented in this article on Chicago by *Crain's Chicago Business* reporter, Merrill Goozner. Those trends have only accelerated in the new global economy.

Harvey Anderson, a computer programmer at the Federal Reserve Bank of Chicago, and his wife, Myra, a temporary office worker, consider themselves fortunate. Unlike some of their neighbors, they haven't suffered from the collapse of manufacturing on the city's South Side.

By purchasing a personal computer and taking computer science courses at Roosevelt University, he was able to move up the ladder at the bank into his current position. She enjoys the flexibility of her part-time job.

The Andersons, with a combined household income of $30,000 a year, consider themselves middle class. Yet their income isn't sufficient to replace their 1979 Oldsmobile Cutlass, much less dig out from $10,000 in consumer debt.

Mr. Anderson, 33, hopes to buy a house someday, but "a decent home in Beverly or Dolton is just too much. Right now, it's out of my reach," he says. Does he think he's on a path to acquiring that traditional symbol of middle-class status? "I doubt it. I don't think I'll be making a whole lot more money in the next few years," he says.

In Chicago's surging service economy, Mr. Anderson has one of the good jobs. Yet he isn't benefitting from the recent economic expansion, which has slowed dramatically in the past year. Indeed, he's worse off now than he was five or six years ago.

He's not alone. Many young families are having a difficult time attaining the standard of living their parents enjoyed. Established members of the middle class are seeing their real incomes erode.

Whole groups of the semiskilled and poorly educated, who once could turn to the manufacturing sector to attain a middle-class lifestyle, now are seeing that dream slip from view. And for the working poor, it's becoming harder and harder to make ends meet.

The local economy generated nearly 200,000 new jobs since the trough of the last recession. A downtown construction boom is underway. High-tech and office corridors are burgeoning in Lake and DuPage Counties. Yet many people are experiencing economic decline.

Why? The lion's share of new jobs being created in Chicago are in services or in retail trade. Thousands of these employees—waitresses, fast-food workers, security guards, cashiers and clerks—earn very low or part-time wages. Their incomes are insufficient to achieve middle-class status.

Even in the finance sector and in business services—the fastest-growing service categories—many of the new jobs are not comparable in pay to the manufacturing jobs that once dominated the local scene.

In other fast-growing industries, especially professional services, the new jobs provide extremely good incomes for some employees, while a core workforce makes do with less-than-average wages.

Some business leaders, economic development specialists, and public officials point with pride to the new service economy. Ignoring critics who warn that the region can't prosper without a healthy manufacturing base, they argue that the Chicago area will thrive if it attracts its share of service jobs.

SOURCE: Merrill Goozner, "What Ails Post-Industrial Chicago," *Crain's Chicago Business*, Vol. 9, Nos. 43 and 44, (October 27–November 9, 1986). Copyright © 1986 by Crain Communications Inc. All rights reserved. Reprint permission conveyed through Reprint Management Services.

These officials have all but given up hope of rebuilding manufacturing, which declined by 135,000 jobs in the six-county area between 1979 and 1985 and fell to 25 percent from 31 percent of all jobs.

But a three-month study by *Crain's Chicago Business* of the new economy being structured here reveals a far different picture. Every statistical measure of personal and job income shows the average Chicago-area resident is worse off today than a decade ago.

Interviews with dozens of displaced manufacturing workers, workers in the emerging service industries and sociologists who are studying patterns of poverty, work and consumption indicate the emerging service economy could result in a permanently lower standard of living for many area residents.

This conclusion raises disturbing questions for the region's economic planners and public officials. Is it acceptable to pursue an economic development strategy that requires a portion of the population to permanently make do with less? Can the region afford such a strategy if it leads to the permanent impoverishment of sections of the inner city and some older blue collar suburbs?

MANUFACTURING'S DECLINE

For the most part, these are the neighborhoods whose residents once depended on manufacturing for their well-being. But manufacturing, the traditional wellspring of wealth in this area, continues its inexorable decline as companies shift production to outside suppliers, either to low-wage areas in the United States. or abroad. The recent fall of the dollar is affecting that process very slowly, if at all.

In some cases, the boom in services is nothing more than a statistical shuffling of jobs from manufacturing as employers turn to outside contractors for a wide range of services they once performed in-house. A byproduct of these efficiencies is a sharp reduction in workers' income.

Some economists and policy analysts argue further that the emerging service economy and concomitant decline in manufacturing is widening the gap between the region's haves and have-nots. They raise the specter of a declining middle class.

"A lot of the new jobs are temporary, high-turnover jobs with few benefits and low pay. Then, there are relatively high-paying jobs for some service workers. There's not much in between," says Gary Orfield, director of the University of Chicago's Committee on Public Policy Studies, which recently completed a study of federal job-training programs for the U.S. House Subcommittee on Employment Opportunities.

Says Barry Bluestone, a professor of political economy at the University of Massachusetts in Boston who has studied the problem at the national level, "Both the high end and the low end are growing at the expense of the middle. Overall, the income distribution among families is more unequal today than it was in 1947."

Chicago-area data on this point won't be available until the next census. But nationally, the proportion of families earning less than $15,000 per year grew to 23.5 percent last year from 21.4 percent in 1979, according to the

Census Bureau's most recent national survey. Meanwhile, the proportion of families earning more than $50,000 rose to 18.3 percent from 16.8 percent.

The "declining middle" thesis is hotly debated. Neal Rosenthal, chief of the Bureau of Labor Statistics' division of occupational outlook, argues that the percentage of workers in the lowest-paying occupations actually is falling. "Services are not all low-paying jobs," he says, "Computer programmers, systems analysts are high-paid people."

Earning Power Eroded

But in terms of real earning power, many of those jobs don't measure up to the high-paying manufacturing jobs that disappeared. For people like Harvey Anderson, they offer insufficient income to attain the traditional benefits of middle-class life.

Just as important, the skill levels needed to get those jobs are beyond the reach of thousands of displaced manufacturing workers—the less-than-college educated, high school graduates and dropouts, all of whom once had access to decent-paying jobs in manufacturing but who now face a bleak economic future.

"The availability of middle-income jobs for low-or semiskilled people is disappearing," says Thomas Bailey, an economist at Conservation of Human Resources, a manpower think tank at Columbia University in New York.

"Those jobs existed because of the interaction of unionization and protected markets," conditions that no longer exist, he says. These are the people being pushed out of the economic mainstream.

While economists engage in a national debate over the existence and extent of downward mobility, the effects of the changing economy on manufacturing-dependent Chicago are plain.

- Average household income has risen only slightly during the current economic expansion, and remains below the mid-1970s peak, despite the massive influx of women into the labor force and the rise in two-income families.
- Earnings per job have fallen even faster, with some of the greatest declines registered in industries with the greatest growth.
- Key poverty indicators remain stubbornly high. A recent Chicago-area survey showed that two years of economic expansion changed the nature, but not the extent, of economic hardship.

In addition, key components of middle-class life are moving beyond the reach of many working families. The rate of home-ownership, for instance, is falling with the greatest drop concentrated among young families. Nonexistent and inadequate health care coverage is emerging as a major issue for a growing number of people who have jobs.

Despite these demographic portents, the upper echelons of Chicago's business leadership and many economic development specialists say the service economy can usher in a new era of prosperity for the region. . . .

Income Level Lacking

However, replacing one job with another doesn't necessarily mean replacing the income. The average wage in services is 22.4 percent below the average manufacturing wage, according to the Illinois Department of Employment Security. The average retail-trade wage is less than half.

Clearly, a high proportion of the new jobs in the area are in industries with extremely low average wages, especially compared with the declining manufacturing sector. In some of those industries, wage scales are pegged to the federal minimum wage, which hasn't been raised since 1980. . . .

"You have to add three jobs in restaurants to make up for a job lost in steel," says Mr. Bluestone of the University of Massachusetts. "As jobs have changed to lower-wage jobs, you need more people working just to keep up, and even then, families aren't keeping up."

Part-time Jobs

Further, the economy is generating an increasing number of part-time jobs. Some fast-growing service industries, such as restaurants and retail sales, traditionally generate a lot of part-time employment to cope with surges of business on a daily, weekly or seasonal basis.

But an increasing number of corporate offices, business services, colleges and distributors are supplementing their core workforce with part-time workers to cut down on benefit costs and increase flexibility in case of another downturn.

Temporaries Utilized

"Today, the largest companies are looking at the use of temporary staff as a support mechanism for their regular staff," says Mitchell Fromstein, chief executive of Manpower, Inc., the Milwaukee-based temporary employment firm, whose business has more than doubled since the end of the 1982 recession. "The core work staff in many cases is much smaller than it was before."

Adds Eddie Smith, a direct-compensation consultant for Lincolnshire-based Hewitt Associates, "When you go into a recession, permanent employees are very expensive. The longer you take to hire a permanent employee, the better off you'll be." . . .

Figures Doubled

According to unpublished statistics from the Bureau of Labor Statistics—which defines part-time as fewer than 35 hours per week—the number of people in the Chicago area who were employed part-time involuntarily doubled to 149,000 between 1979 and 1985. In fact, more part-time jobs—and the commensurate low level of wages and benefits—were added to the economy than full-time jobs, which increased by only 52,000 during the period.

Not all service jobs are low-paying, of course. The average wages in some burgeoning industries conform to the image of a high-paying service economy—computer and data services, legal and accounting service, for instance. Upon closer inspection, however, the picture isn't so rosy.

Many of the prestigious so-called new-collar jobs simply don't measure up in terms of real purchasing power, especially when compared with high-paying manufacturing jobs that dominated the local scene a decade ago.

Employers, in an effort to cope with the heightened competition caused by the globalization of the economy, a strong U.S. dollar, and changing market-places, have succeeded in forcing workers to lower their long-term expectations as well as their current standards of living.

Successful Stance

At Philip Morris, Inc.'s Oscar Mayer & Co. plant at 1241 North Sedgwick, for instance, blue-collar workers last summer successfully defended their $10.67-per-hour wages in the face of company demands for a wage concession. Still, they haven't had a raise since 1980, a reduction in real income of 32 percent.

Decreased Earnings

Moreover, when manufacturing workers lose their jobs through plant closings, a frequent occurrence in recent years, many face years of decreased earnings. They often wind up in the service sector at a permanent reduction in income.

For instance, it was mostly women workers who lost their jobs at the Playskool, Inc. plant at 4501 West Augusta Boulevard when Rhode Island-based Hasbro, Inc. decided to shut it down in 1985. Today, "they are universally paid less in their new jobs," says Judith Wittner, a Loyola sociologist who surveyed the impact of the shutdown.

Severe income drops also occur when corporations turn to outsourcing to cut costs. The trend has been well documented in such high-paying fields as steel, construction machinery, and autos. But it's also happening in low-wage manufacturing industries like apparel.

"As our [union] labor price escalated, we became less competitive with manufacturers in this area who did not have to pay the same price we did," said Sheldon Mann, president of Henry-Lee Co. One of the few remaining dress manufacturers in the area, the company employs about 75 people in designing, cutting, and office work.

He once employed about 400 people in sewing. "I now give my work out to subcontractors who provide the labor," he says. Most of the subcontracting firms are run by entrepreneurs in the Hispanic and Asian communities, who generally pay much less than union-scale wages.

Often, manufacturing workers displaced by outsourcing have witnessed the transformation of their jobs, as if by magic, into service jobs—usually at much lower pay.

When the outside contractor provides janitorial and cleaning services, the avoidance of union wages can cut labor costs in half. When the major manu-

facturer turns to an outsider for sophisticated maintenance work, the wage reductions are less dramatic, but still significant.

For instance, USX Corp. (formerly U.S. Steel Corp.) sold its machine shop
at South Works to Metalkrafters of Illinois, Inc. That firm, whose 60 person
workforce is made up almost entirely of ex-South Works employees, now does
machinery repair work for the remaining operations at South Works and
other steel mills in South Chicago and Northwest Indiana.

Machinists there earn $10 an hour, $2.25 an hour less than they earned at
U.S. Steel. Their fringe benefit package also is inferior under their new employer, although the workers there are glad to have the work.

Lower Living Standard

Clearly, this downward pressure on wages is lowering the average local resident's standard of living in the three-county metropolitan area (Cook, Du-
Page, and McHenry Counties), per capita income peaked in 1978 at $15,325
(1984 dollars). Despite a rebound in 1984, per capita income remained
4.4 percent lower, at $14,655, according to the U.S. Department of Com-
merce's Bureau of Economic Analysis.

Household income also is declining. In constant dollars, the Census Bureau
reports, the average for the Chicago area fell to $24,292 in 1983 from
$27,332 in 1975. Both were recession years.

The 11.1 percent decline in household income over the past decade is even
more startling when the massive movement of women into the workforce is
taken into account. Nearly 300,000 women entered the job market between
1976 and 1985, bringing the area total to 1.6 million. With 55.6 percent of all
women older than 16 now in the labor force, women constitute 43.5 percent
of all workers, up from 40.9 percent a decade ago.

"What the American consumer first did to fight declining income was send
his wife out to work," says A. Gary Shilling, a New York City-based economic consultant: "It slowed the decline but didn't stop it." . . .

How Service Economy Strains Social Fabric

A college-educated couple hesitates to buy the house they want for their 2-year-
old daughter because the commitment demands that both parents remain
steadily employed. A middle-aged divorcee prays she won't get sick because
her job doesn't provide health insurance. A Hispanic office worker who has
struggled to upgrade her skills finds every effort to get a decent job—$5 an
hour in her eyes—lands her back on the unemployment line. Five years after
losing his job, a displaced manufacturing worker finally lands a good job. In
real terms, he's paid half of what he earned before. These people have one
thing in common. They work in the fastest-growing segments of the Chicago-
area economy: services, finance, and real estate.

Beyond the data, sociologists and social service providers are beginning to
attribute a host of social problems to changes in the economy. Family life is
coming under increasing stress as young parents attempt to juggle their desire

for children and homes with the painful realization that both parents must work full time to achieve their goals. An increasing number of young people from white- and blue-collar homes are having difficulty finding a niche in the economy. Bouncing from one low-paying job to another, they often wind up back in their parents' homes, one sociologist dubs the phenomenon "young adult return syndrome." Perhaps the greatest effects of the shift from manufacturing to services, are being felt in the Black and Hispanic communities, which have depended on manufacturing for access to middle-income jobs. With those jobs disappearing, a large segment of the minority population is being forced back toward poverty status. . . .

Insurance Lacking

Locally, about 20 percent of all city residents have no medical insurance or are underinsured, according to the Chicago Health Systems Agency. Its suburban counterpart, the Suburban Cook County/DuPage County Health Systems Agency, says the suburban rate is about 14 percent. "It's growing," says Richard Sewell, executive director of the suburban group. "Employers are creating a number of part-time jobs or cutting back in coverage as a way of cutting costs."

For many employees, that means doing without health insurance coverage. "I can't afford it," says Sandra Hamilton, a 45-year-old temporary office worker from Glen Ellyn. "I just pray I stay healthy."

A recent study of changes in economic hardship in the city and suburbs confirmed that inadequate health insurance coverage is a growing problem. The study, which compared 1985 to 1983, found that fewer people were doing without food or shelter but more families experienced problems with access to medical and dental care.

"There was some improvement, but not what you'd expect, given the upturn in the economy," says Christopher Jencks, professor of sociology at Northwestern University's Center for Urban Affairs and Policy Research and an author of the report. "I suspect the jobs that are being created don't put as much money in people's hands."

That theory was confirmed in a companion study conducted at the University of Illinois at Chicago, in which researchers interviewed 89 families in South Austin, Little Village, and on the East Side in 1983 and again in 1985.

Took Available Jobs

"More people were working, but they were working for lower wages," says Charles Hoch, a professor in the School of Urban Planning and Policy. Further, "there was a much lower level of health insurance" as people abandoned their dependency on welfare and took the available low-wage and part-time jobs.

These studies confirm Census Bureau data showing little drop in the overall poverty rate despite a drop in unemployment during the past several years.

The poverty rate nationwide fell to 14.0 percent in 1985 from 14.4 percent the previous year. But in the Midwest, the rate fell to 13.9 percent from 14.1 percent, a decline deemed statistically insignificant by the Census Bureau.

These studies also suggest that poor people constantly are looking for work, only to find the available jobs inadequate to lift them out of poverty.

"The jobs people had were fairly temporary. There was tremendous turnover," says Mr. Hoch of the families surveyed in the three Chicago blue-collar neighborhoods.

The jobs were like those 28-year-old Katherine Otero could find after completing her high school equivalency exam and improving her office skills in 1984. This past year the Wicker Park mother of two was abruptly laid off from office jobs with Group W Cable and S. A. Maxwell Co. (Last week, Ms. Otero found a job as a receptionist for a North Side construction company.)

"It seems like every time I get one foot on the ladder, something knocks me off", she says.

SLIPPING BACK

Many don't succeed. "Many of these people are slipping back into poverty," Julius Wilson, chairman of the University of Chicago's sociology department says. "But it's not fair to characterize them as an underclass. These families have a long work history."

Pearl Alexander is one such worker. At 32, she had 10 years' experience at the Playskool plant at 4501 West Augusta Boulevard when Hasbro, Inc. decided to close the plant nearly two years ago. Her $6.70-an-hour assembly line job allowed her and her husband, James, to dream of owning their own home.

Now, James struggles on his $25,000-a-year job as a resident counselor at Joliet Community Corrections Center to repay her credit card bills and maintain the household as she desperately searches for work.

The only jobs she can find, though, are washing dishes or cleaning houses, positions that pay two-thirds of her previous income. She calculates that after paying for day care for her 2-year-old son and carfare, those jobs are not worth taking. "I've been working all my life," she says. "It's hard to sit at home."

Blue-collar families aren't the only ones who find the new service economy inadequate. Many new-collar workers—computer programmers, technicians and back office personnel—find that their incomes provide a tenuous hold on middle-class status.

With two incomes needed to make ends meet, many families—especially those with young children—confront a host of new problems. "The first major questions they confront is child care," says Bernice Weissbourd, president of Family Focus, Inc., which runs parent-aid centers in Evanston and Lincoln Park.

"Another issue is time management—trying to do it all. There are emotional questions. You feel guilty for wanting to stay home. Budgeting becomes a constant issue," she says. . . .

Many Affected

Clearly, the changing job and wage structure of the economy is affecting more and more people, including many who consider themselves middle class. There are more and more workers earning less and less money. People are running faster and faster, but not keeping up. "Despite the influx of two-wage earner families, people aren't getting ahead of where they were," says Mr. Levy of the University of Maryland. "It's that sense of gaining year after year—a new car, moving from an apartment to a new home in the suburbs— that's getting harder and harder to do."

8. High-Tech Fall in Austin, Texas

Jim Yardley

By the turn of the twenty-first century, the bubble had burst in the high-tech sector of the economy. The collapse of once mighty corporations in the high-tech and communications sectors only worsened after the terrorist attacks of September 11, 2001 and the general economic recession that followed. This is the story of how those job losses affected one city, a story common to many cities after 2001.

Fresh out of Stanford University in 1994, Alexa Lange came here expecting sagebrush and prairies and instead found lakes and greenery and a technology boomtown not unlike what she left behind in Silicon Valley. She soon had her own headhunting firm and a social schedule filled with launching parties for one startup after another.

Ms. Lange, 29, is still going to parties, but they are for layoffs, not launchings.

"We're nurses now," she said of the calls from job seekers. "People call us every single day. They call us for support: 'What's new? Is the market going to turn around?'"

In all of the nation's technology capitals, whether Boston or Seattle or Silicon Valley, the giddiness from the not-too-distant boom times has disappeared. But the pain is just as acute in Austin, which before the booming '90s had been centered on the University of Texas and the state government. Then the technology economy transformed the city so quickly that many people began to believe the good times would never end.

"There was a kind of naive idea that we had created a new paradigm," said Mark Hazelwood, president of the Greater Austin Chamber of Commerce, who as a former petrochemical executive endured the ups and downs of the volatile oil industry.

In recent months, nearly 15,000 people have been laid off here as some companies have closed or streamlined. There is a glut of high-end houses and no shortage of sports cars with "For Sale" signs. The most obvious symbol of woe is what is now called the Intel shell, the unfinished downtown building on which Intel halted construction when it ran into financial problems.

Mr. Hazelwood and other officials are quick to point out that most cities would ache to have Austin's problems. Though the city's unemployment has roughly doubled since December, it still stands at a paltry 3.3 percent. This city of 643,000 people, called Silicon Hills, has benefited from a huge influx of new wealth.

From 1994 to 1999, roughly 17,000 "millionaire households" were created, according to a consulting firm. A $94 million performing arts center is under construction and a once-moribund downtown is very much alive. Only a year ago Forbes magazine ranked Austin as the best city in the nation in which to do business.

And yet a year seems almost like a lifetime. Last year, the central issue at the Greater Austin@Work conference sponsored by the Chamber of Commerce was how employers could find enough qualified workers. At the conference in June the question was how the city could keep its talented but increasingly unemployed work force from moving away.

"I would just encourage people to maintain the faith," Mr. Hazelwood told a television reporter who asked about the economy.

The day after the conference, almost 800 people showed up for a high-tech job fair. The available technology jobs were fairly slim. But one funeral home passed out a pamphlet assuring prospects "It's Not Morbid" to "consider joining the most successful company in the death care industry!" Other companies looking for workers included restaurant chains.

"I just didn't think I would ever get laid off," said Stella Papadakis, 24, who was looking for a job after being one of about 4,000 workers laid off this year by Dell Computers.

"I just thought it would be blue-collar workers. I'm thinking I should have taken an economics class because I had no idea what the real world was like. I guess I was oblivious to the facts of what the up-and-down economy meant."

Ms. Papadakis, who grew up in Indiana and hopes to stay in Austin, was among the waves of newcomers drawn to the city in the 1990s when the metropolitan area ranked second only to Phoenix among the nation's fastest-growing regions.

A decade ago, Austin had a population of 460,000. It was best known then for its live-music scene and easy access to the Texas Hill Country, and for providing a good quality of life for middle-income earners.

The origin of the city's technology economy goes back to the 1960s, and with each successive decade that economy grew larger. The University of Texas also played an essential role.

But nothing compared with the 1990s, when the hometown Dell Corporation became a dominant player in the personal computer market and gave rise, through stock options, to a generation known here as "Dellionaires."

Then the dot-com craze of the late 1990s ushered in a new surge of wealth. Venture capitalists began pouring money into scores of start-ups that promised riches off the developing online economy. One of the best-known ventures, Living.com, raised $68 million to sell furniture over the Internet. (It closed last year.) The amount of venture capital invested in Austin rose to $2.3 billion last year from $329 million in 1998.

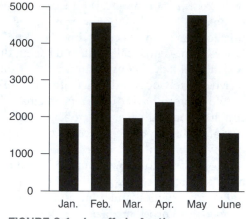

FIGURE 3.1 Layoffs in Austin
Since the beginning of the year 2001, Austin, Texas, has had 16,990 layoffs.
Source: Research AngelouEconomics

And a lot of people got rich. John Hime, one of those known as "angel investors" for making an initial investment to help a company organize, turned one $62,000 loan to a software startup into $2.4 million after only 15 months.

The Austin American-Statesman ran a feature on a purple-haired 37-year-old software millionaire who spent $100,000 on a stereo. Some college graduates began demanding six-figure salaries and stock options.

Disposable income took on a new meaning. People bought getaway ranches in the Hill Country and seven-figure limestone mansions began rising on the hills west of the city. A local steakhouse began a weekly wine tasting at $25 to $50 a glass.

"Things went crazy," said Kathy Warbelow, business editor of The American-Statesman. "It lasted long enough that people began to believe that this is how it is going to be."

But the city's middle class, including teachers and government workers, felt increasingly squeezed by escalating property values and taxes and frustrated by choking traffic. Residents in the poorer neighborhoods in east Austin fell even further behind.

Now the economic growth rate in Austin is the lowest in a decade as it adjusts to the collapsed Nasdaq and the rest of the struggling national technology economy.

There is finger pointing over blame between the venture capitalists who poured money into companies and the entrepreneurs who started them. The optimists say that Austin will continue be a technology capital and the pain it is feeling represents a sort of success.

"What that proves is that Austin has kind of accomplished what it was trying to accomplish in the last 10 years, which is to be a legitimate part of the technology economy," said John Thornton, head of Austin Ventures, the city's largest venture capital firm. "So we feel it when these cycles go up and down."

Mr. Hime, the investor who worked for years in Silicon Valley, says that the local technology economy remains fundamentally solid but warns that more problems are probably ahead. "In Austin," he said, "there has never been a lot of experience with cycles."

Ms. Lange, the Stanford graduate and high-tech headhunter, said that at the height of the boom her company turned away business. Now she has stacks of résumés and no jobs to match them with.

"I still have this gloomy film over my eyes," she said. Then a wave of optimism overcame her.

"What's the next big thing?" she asked. "What's the next big thing in technology?"

9. Too Few Jobs Imperil Welfare Reform Plan in Los Angeles

Carla Rivera

The economic recession following 2001 not only hit the high-tech sector and well-paying jobs in the global economy; unemployment increased in all cities and at all levels. Unfortunately, this occurred just as welfare recipients under the federal welfare reform laws of the 1990s ran out of their life-time amounts of five years of welfare payments. Now, there weren't enough jobs for them even if they had the skills, will and circumstances to allow them to take them. This is the story of Los Angeles.

An independent study offered a sober assessment of welfare reform in Los Angeles County on Tuesday, concluding that the region does not have enough jobs for everyone who needs to work.

The study by the Economic Roundtable, a nonprofit public policy research group, concluded that policymakers will have to revise some strategies if reform efforts are to succeed.

SOURCE: Carla Rivera, "Too Few Jobs May Imperil Welfare Reform Plan," *Los Angeles Times*, May 20, 1998, p. A-1. Copyright © 1998 Tribune Media Services International; Los Angeles Times. All rights reserved. Reprinted by permission.

The success of those efforts could have vast social repercussions, affecting the standard of living for millions of Los Angeles residents, the study said, and influencing the viability of the region's still shaky economic recovery.

The report, obtained by *The Los Angeles Times,* shows that the number of aid recipients seeking jobs in coming years will vastly outnumber the jobs available—an average of 2.5 job seekers for every new opening. When unemployed job seekers are added to the mix, the ratio increases to 5.4 job seekers for each new opening.

It also offers one of the most detailed accounts of the occupations and industries in which welfare recipients are finding work.

Most are concentrated in a few service occupations—janitors, housekeepers, cooks, waiters and sewing machine operators.

The report, called "By the Sweat of Their Brow, Welfare to Work in Los Angeles," concludes that these workers rotate in and out of the same low-wage, low-skill jobs over the course of their working lives, earning no Social Security, unemployment or disability benefits.

The report was financed in part by the Arco Foundation and the Liberty Hill Foundation.

One leading economist, however, painted a rosier picture of the ability of the local economy to absorb welfare recipients and contended that current statistics are not keeping up with the region's barreling recovery.

"I think we are a little better off than they estimate," said Jack Kyser, chief economist for the independent Los Angeles Economic Development Corp. "The employment numbers don't give us a complete picture of what's going on right now."

The Economic Roundtable report provided this rundown on the Los Angeles County economy to help explain the difficulty of finding jobs for the roughly 150,000 welfare recipients expected to be seeking work under the new welfare reform program.

- Los Angeles County lost 436,700, or 10 percent, of its jobs between 1990 and 1994 and by 1997 had regained only 168,800.
- Despite the beginning of an economic recovery, unemployment in the county still averages close to 300,000 people.
- The true level of unemployment may be as much as 200,000 to 300,000 higher than official figures because many workers have become discouraged and dropped out of the labor market.
- Although 20 percent of single mothers in the county's welfare caseload have strong employment prospects, 60 percent face formidable odds because of a lack of education, spotty work histories and other factors.

"Regardless of how we view welfare dependency, the reality is that a majority of aid recipients do work and are part of the low-wage work force," the report states. "We share an important practical interest in seeing welfare recipients successfully employed because the social fabric of the region will be damaged in ways that affect everyone."

The report is one of the most comprehensive studies to date of the challenges in implementing federally mandated welfare-to-work legislation in Los Angeles County, which has the nation's largest public assistance caseload.

The new welfare laws place a five-year lifetime limit on aid, with exemptions allowed for 20 percent of the caseload. Current welfare recipients in Los Angeles County have two years to find work; those who applied for aid after April 1 must find work within 18 months.

In addition, 50 percent of single parents in California's welfare caseload must be engaged in some kind of work activity for at least 32 hours a week by 2002, or the state faces steep financial penalties.

The report recommends that state and county officials should set aside local funds to provide for those who can't find work.

The authors note that welfare reform "raises the prickly question of what mix of understanding, support and pressure is needed to move welfare recipients into employment." They concede that many other working families are "scrambling to keep the wolf from their own doors" without the benefit of special treatment.

But all Los Angeles residents will derive practical benefits from seeing welfare recipients succeed, they insist.

"We all have a stake in this," said Daniel Flaming, president of the Economic Roundtable and one of the report's authors. "I own a home and have roots here in Los Angeles, and I would like to see this be a region that works. If we have growing numbers of destitute families, it's worse for all of us."

Flaming suggested that the county will need to revise policies that treat welfare recipients as a single population, taking into account their diversity of needs and tailoring programs individually.

In particular, the report urges that Greater Avenues of Independence, or GAIN, the county's main welfare-to-work program, should be reviewed. The GAIN program emphasizes jobs over education and skill development, but "it is likely that many recipients are returning to the same jobs in which they previously worked," the report notes.

However, county officials say many welfare programs to enhance job opportunities for recipients are too new to be counted as successes or failures.

Welfare recipients are finding jobs at a rate of 4,000 per month and projections are optimistic, said Department of Public Social Services Director Lynn W. Bayer.

"Everyone recognizes that we have a tremendous challenge ahead. But we've tried to build a program to keep flexibility in place and as for looking at different policies, we're not there yet," she said. "We anticipate placing the vast majority of people into meaningful jobs."

Bayer said preliminary results of an ongoing study of the GAIN program show a more promising outcome than projected by the Economic Roundtable report. But she agreed that the county must develop long-term strategies to boost economic development and job creation.

10. Lives Get a Little Better on a Living Wage

Nancy Cleeland

More than 25 cities and counties across the country, primarily under pressure from labor unions and community action groups, have passed a "living wage" ordinance. These ordinances require private firms contracting with the city or county government to pay a wage sufficient to provide an annual income above the poverty level. For instance, in California in 1997 the state minimum wage was $5.75 an hour while the "living wage" was set at $7.25 an hour. This article traces the difference for real workers between the two standards. It is particularly important because local governments have been "privatizing" services like janitorial services to save money. Thus, in larger cities and counties these ordinances can affect several thousand workers.

Let the academics, politicians and labor leaders debate the definition of a living wage. For airport janitor Jose Morales, it means two concrete things—a bed and a car.

Two years ago, Morales was sleeping on flattened cardboard boxes in a Compton garage. Every morning before dawn, he stumbled to the corner bus stop for the start of a two-hour commute to his job at Los Angeles International Airport.

Twice on that corner he was mugged. Without health insurance, he considered himself particularly lucky to escape unhurt.

Now Morales stretches out at night on a soft double bed. With his commute time cut in half by driving, he can sleep until 5. He no longer feels vulnerable to predawn assaults. And if he was to be hurt, his medical expenses would be covered by insurance.

What has made the difference is a 1997 "living wage" ordinance that boosted pay for the LAX janitor, and some 2,000 other bottom-rung workers in Los Angeles, by nearly $2 an hour.

Now in exchange for eight hours of sweeping, dusting and dumping trash, the 36-year-old immigrant earns $59 a day, plus health benefits. Still far from princely, it's a 36 percent raise over his old pay, and enough to qualify for what Morales calls a *salario digno*.

"Everyone thinks that working here at the airport, we must earn a lot of money," said Morales, chatting in a closet-sized room where he and 45 other Terminal 2 janitors pick up mops and change into navy blue uniforms. "It's not true. But at least now with the living wage, we can hold our heads up high."

The ordinance is part of a wave of living wage legislation pushed by labor unions and community groups and adopted by more than 20 local governments, including Pasadena, during the past four years. Dozens more are considering similar laws.

From Boston to Portland, the movement has drawn attention to the growing gap between rich and poor, a division that has accelerated sharply in the last decade as wages have stagnated for the nation's janitors, food servers, parking lot attendants and other low-skilled workers.

It has also prompted dueling studies on the economic impacts of boosting pay for those low-wage workers.

Business groups depict the law as job-killers that hurt entry level workers the most by denying them a toehold in the market. Organizations such as the Greater Los Angeles Chamber of Commerce have argued that they add to an unfriendly business climate that drives away development. In general, said Carol Schatz of the Center City Assn., "it's more difficult to do business here, more expensive to do business here, and there's more social engineering here."

Backers say the laws help revitalize poor communities because the extra dollars ripple through local economies. And because low-wage workers in Los Angeles are predominantly Latino immigrants and African Americans, proponents cast the law as a matter of social justice.

For all the hoopla and hand-wringing, however, the mandated living wages, which range from $6.25 an hour in Milwaukee to $9.50 in San Jose, have affected relatively few workers. Most apply only to companies with city contracts or subsidies. And they take effect slowly, as contracts are renewed. Although nearly 2 years old, the Los Angeles ordinance is just beginning to benefit large numbers of workers. It is expected to raise pay for only 5,000 to 10,000, concentrated at the city's airports, sports venues and government offices.

"The actual numbers are small, and the fact that they are small is part of the reason [living wage ordinances] are winning," said Robert Pollin, a political economist at the University of Massachusetts at Amherst. "But for those few people, it's a lot of money. It's going to improve their living standards."

For the estimated 2,000 workers who have received raises in Los Angeles so far, the living wage can be measured in immediate and tangible terms. Co-workers of Morales include a single mother who quit her second job to spend more time with her children; a newlywed who moved with his wife from shared housing to an apartment of their own; a man in his 50s who started paying off a hospital debt that stemmed from a bus stop beating.

For Morales, the step up from $5.45 to $7.25 an hour (increased to $7.39 a year later) moved him from a chronic state of crisis to a more manageable level of poverty. He still counts pennies. He still scans the garbage he dumps for discarded treasures. He still considers a rare fast-food meal to be a dining-out experience.

He has learned over the last year and a half that there is nothing magic about the city-mandated living wage. It is just an arbitrary number, with no more meaning in the real world than the slightly higher federal poverty line, or the much lower minimum wage.

But with $1,000 a month in take-home pay, the janitor is able to afford some minimal comforts.

Two purchases changed his life: a bed and a '93 Mazda sedan. Both items, along with matching love seats for the living room and a small dining room table, were purchased on credit—a luxury he could not previously afford. Now Morales finds himself in a juggling mode familiar to many consumers.

"Sometimes I have to be late with a payment," he said, spreading a file of bills on the new table. "The next month, I always pay that one on time."

Like many low-wage workers in Los Angeles, Morales, who emigrated from Guadalajara 18 years ago, has survived by pooling resources with friends and family members. For several years, he shared a converted garage with his sister, her husband and the couple's two young sons. Too poor to buy furniture, they scavenged cardboard boxes from a nearby supermarket and spread them on the floor to make a communal bed.

But Morales' raise allowed the extended family to move to more spacious quarters—a two-bedroom house that rents for $615 a month—and to slowly begin furnishing it.

Still far from palatial, the house measures about 800 square feet and is covered with peeling beige paint and security bars. Inside, the rooms are dark and stuffy, and sister Angelica Hernandez rarely ventures outside at night. She earns $80 a week baby-sitting two children, in addition to caring for her own two young sons and running an informal market out of her kitchen. Her husband takes occasional construction jobs and earns cash fixing cars for neighbors and friends. As the only family member with a full-time job, Morales is the major breadwinner.

And so he pays the largest share of the rent—$315, including utilities. In turn, his sister prepares most of his meals. His other regular monthly expenses include: $200 for credit cards—$50 each to J.C. Penney, MasterCard, Target and a furniture store; $280 for car and insurance payments; and $12 for a pager, which he deems necessary for his union activism.

That leaves less than $200 a month for gas, incidentals and rare nights out at a disco with friends—a tight squeeze by any measure.

"The truth is, it's not a very livable wage," said Morales.

"But it's a big change for the better," he said. "We have health insurance, and for families that means a lot. I think for this moment, it is a fair wage. And maybe later," he added, "we can get it a little higher."

Morales dreams of a day when his pay approaches that of the few airport janitors who remain directly employed by the city. Those Civil Service jobs, which rarely come open and are highly competitive, start at more than $8 an hour, and can climb to $15 an hour with full benefits.

The enormous pay gap grew out of the city's outsourcing of most janitorial services to private contractors at the airport, the Central Library, the zoo and other municipal facilities. Outsourcing has saved the city millions, primarily because private contractors were able to dramatically cut labor costs by paying workers the state minimum wage, now $5.75 an hour.

But living wage advocates argued that labor had paid too high a price, and that the city had an obligation to push wages for those outsourced jobs to a livable level.

The amount arrived at in 1997—$7.25 an hour—was just below the federal poverty line for a family of four. It was bumped up to $7.39 by a cost-of-living increase last year.

Eventually all airport workers should earn the living wage under a strengthened amendment passed by the council in November.

Last month, about 700 airport concession workers employed by Host Marriott, including bartenders, food servers and cashiers, signed a new contract that brought their wages up to $7.39 an hour or higher, plus benefits.

Living wage proponents are now focusing their efforts on security baggage screeners, who are attempting to affiliate with the Service Employees International Union.

The long-term effect of the wage hikes won't be known for some time, but UCLA law professor Rick Sander, who has monitored the living wage law for the city, said the impact so far has been small.

"We estimate the city is bearing about half the cost of living wage increases," Sander said. Companies eager to do business with the government are absorbing the other half, he said. There has been little shrinkage of the work force to compensate for higher wages, Sander added.

Living wage advocates clearly hope their local successes will be bolster arguments for a higher minimum wage at the state and federal levels, where proposed legislation has failed in recent years.

If nothing else, the issue has stirred debate about what it takes to make a decent living these days.

Higher-wage advocates say true living costs are even greater than the hourly wages of $7 to $9 set by most of the 25 cities and counties with living wage laws.

In a recent study for Los Angeles County, Sander estimated basic living expenses for a family of three at $20,000, or about $10 an hour.

"If you look at surveys of peoples' expenditures, that's pretty close," Sander said. "People who make $8,000 a year spend a lot more than that. How do they do it? With credit cards, personal loans, extra informal income. However they can. Until people make close to $20,000, their spending usually exceeds their income."

For hundreds of thousands of Los Angeles workers, it may come as little surprise that the city's "living wage" doesn't cover the basics. But those who benefit are grateful for what they can get.

"If it wasn't for the law, I would be making $5.90 an hour now," said Morales. "At least I'm up to the poverty line. That's a big step for me."

Exercise
Studying Immigration and Economic Gaps in Your City

The purpose of these exercises is to determine key social and economic patterns in your metropolitan region. When you have completed them, you will know which racial and ethnic groups make up your city and whether your local economy has changed from a manufacturing-based economy to service or global economy.

You may have to modify the exercise depending upon the ease of obtaining this information at your university and in your community. But you should be able to generally answer the questions in the exercise for your metropolitan region.

IMMIGRATION AND RACIAL PATTERNS

Begin with a visit to your university library. Most school libraries have a special section called government documents. In some major cities like Chicago, there are special publications like the *Chicago Community Fact Book* published by local universities that compile the data for you by community area. With the help of the documents librarian, you can obtain the best version of the census data for your metropolitan region compiled by community area.

Alternatively, you may locate the information on the Internet at **http://www.census.gov.** Use any of the major Internet engines such as **http://www.google.com** or **http://www.yahoo.com** to help you find additional Websites such as city or local government sites with census data and other relevant information. If you go to **www.google.com** you may also type in "the name of your city, race/ethnic population, 2000, map" to get the information.

At the **www.census.gov** site follow the prompts. Depending on how the site continually changes you should be able to click on census 2000 for current census data, click on search by address and enter an address in the search text box. At the next screen choose Metropolitan Statistical Area and click go. It will take a few minutes for the data to be sorted. Then you can scroll down and choose options on the types of data or maps you want.

In any case, using census data from whichever source, determine the percentage of African American, White, Latino, and Asian people in your city. You should also be able to determine any major immigrant groups in the city. If possible, plot the concentrations of these different groups on a map to see where they live.

ECONOMIC ACTIVITY

Go back to the census data to find information about employment in your city. Look at the data from 1990 in terms of the number of manufacturing and service jobs and compare that to the 2000 census data.

How many manufacturing jobs has your city lost from 1990 to 2000? How many service jobs has your city gained?

Probe for more information on your city's economy. This may be found by searching your city's largest newspaper or its business or city magazines. Look for news stories during the last year about (1) job losses and layoffs, (2) new companies moving in, (3) corporate headquarters arriving or leaving, and (4) globalization and trade. If you have access through your school or local library to Lexis-Nexis, you can quickly locate the stories by searching the database. If you don't have access to Lexis-Nexis, most newspapers in major cities have a search engine function to help you at their own Website. (You may have to pay, however, to print out entire stories from the publication's archives.) You can also search manually through bound hard copies of newspapers and key magazines at most libraries and most of them provide an annual index to news stories related to the economy.

Based upon the census data and newspaper stories about your city what do you conclude about jobs being gained or lost? What is your city's role in the global economy? Are new manufacturing plants moving into or out of your city? Is your city growing economically or losing ground? What plans or programs have business groups or local governments created to improve the economic situation in your city?

Chapter 4

Racial Conditions

The following articles provide a focus on race and poverty in the city. Since the 1960s, U.S. cities have come to be characterized by racial regions in which Whites, Blacks, and Latinos live separately. Older ethnic neighborhoods, while they still exist, are no longer the defining characteristic of our cities. Frequently, conditions in the Black and Latino ghettos are no better than the tenement neighborhoods of the previous century. Today's poorest neighborhoods are filled with decrepit high-rise public housing projects and low-rise slums that surround them. Whether the new federal program of destroying high-rise public housing will disperse these racial ghettos remains to be seen.

Since racial segregation was the law of the land until the late twentieth century, it is not surprising that racial regions would replace ethnic neighborhoods as the defining social characteristic of American cities. These racial divisions made the original division between suburbs and inner city more than a simple geographical boundary on a map. Until the last decade, minorities and the poor tended to be locked into the inner city while Whites frequently fled to the suburbs. The 2000 census demonstrates that some minorities have now also moved to the suburbs — only sometimes to find themselves resegregated into all-Black or all-Latino communities once again.

Affordable housing is in short supply, particularly in the suburbs. Compounding the problem in some metropolitan regions, one of every four families are spending more than 30 percent of their income on housing while racism prevents the building of affordable housing in suburban communities nearest available jobs.[1]

Racial housing segregation has inevitably led to educational segregation and job discrimination. In the past, elementary school boundaries in residential areas were drawn small enough that children could walk to neighborhood schools. The boundaries for high schools simply combined a number of geographically contiguous elementary schools, which meant that most of them were also segregated. So if a city was residentially segregated, as nearly all were, they were *de facto* educationally segregated into separate but unequal schools. Busing, magnet schools, and other solutions applied in response to the Civil Rights movement mostly failed to overcome segregation in schools. For instance, a recent *Chicago Tribune* study found that of the 179 failing Chicago public schools that made the worst score on standardized reading and math tests, 178 were virtually all-Black or all-Latino. Only one had a White majority.[2]

Entry-level jobs at manufacturing plants originally were located in the poorer neighborhoods and not in the rich or pretty parts of town, and certainly not in the pristine suburbs with their large lawns and single-family homes. When the factories began to close in the 1960s and 1970s to relocate to the suburbs, rural areas, and overseas for cheaper land, lower wages, and lower taxes, the poor—who were often, but not exclusively, Blacks and Latinos—were left behind. Thus, residential segregation led to employment discrimination as well. While policies of affirmative action have attempted to mitigate discrimination in the workplace, they have only partly succeeded.

A number of demographers and sociologists have demonstrated the link between race and poverty in the cities. For instance, demographer Pierre de Vise demonstrated that the richest communities in the Chicago metropolitan region were and continue to be in all-White suburbs while the desperately poorest communities were and continue to be in all-Black inner city ghettos around public housing.[3] The result of these housing patterns on the lives of urban residents is devastating. As de Vise duplicated these findings in all the decades since his original study in the 1960s, he demonstrated that the color gap has became greater, despite official national policies of ending racial segregation.

Perhaps one of the best historical accounts of the development of race and inequality is Thomas Sugrue's study of Detroit entitled, *The Origins of the Urban Crisis*. Sugrue argues that racial tensions that led to two race riots and the decline of Detroit as a city can be traced to a capitalism that generated economic inequality and to African Americans who, because of segregation and discrimination, were forced to bear the impact of that inequality disproportionately. Particularly Northern industrial cities after World War II were overwhelmed "by the combination of racial strife and economic restructuring." While Detroit received significant federal funding in the 1960s and 1970s, it was insufficient to overcome the patterns of race and poverty in the inner city. Since the 1970s, "industrial and population flight have drained the city [like many others] of resources necessary to maintain infrastructure. . . . Celebrated public-private partnerships, including the Ford-financed Renaissance Center hotel and office project, and the General Motors Poletown plant, have done little to enlarge the city's employment base, and have drained city coffers of more tax money."[4]

Some racial progress has been made over the last 40 years—not all African Americans and Latinos are poor, not all minorities live in the inner city, and not all Whites are rich. For instance, Stephen and Abigail Thernstrom in their article in the *New Republic* cite evidence of advances in race relations and the continued commitment of most Blacks and Whites to an integrated society.[5] But the racial gap remains a fundamental problem with which American cities still struggle and these racial divisions are central to understanding metropolitan regions today.

As scholars continued to study the racial divide in American cities, they concluded that not only is there a racial and economic gap in American cities today, but it has lasted generations—that is to say, in the words of William Julius Wilson, there is a permanent underclass which simple antidiscrimination laws alone cannot cure. This permanent underclass in the central city and inner-ring suburbs creates huge subregions of the rich in the privileged quarter and the poor in the underprivileged quarters of the metropolitan region. The poor are locked into the inner city and the poorer, most segregated suburbs in the immediate ring adjacent to the city. Many poor Blacks, who are locked into public housing, welfare programs, and poor schools, live their lives in these ghetto conditions and so will their children after them. The fact that some poor Blacks, Latinos, and Whites escape to the middle class and that some working-class members through education, opportunity, and hard work rise to be wealthy does not change the basic situation. Generally speaking, in our nation of abundance, the rich have gotten richer and the poor have gotten poorer and race is a major factor in who gets richer and poorer. It is discouraging that from 1990 to 1995, the poverty rate increased in cities and suburbs in all regions of the country and the gap between the rich and the poor widened despite the booming economy.[6]

Franklin James in his research suggests that poverty is not the same for all groups and that the underclass theory does not fit Latinos as well as it does African Americans. Nonetheless, poverty—if not the complete ghetto, underclass experience— is a serious problem for many Latinos. Since they are the fastest growing racial/ethnic group in U.S. cities, this means that we all need to pay more attention to their issues and concerns. The civil rights and affirmative action laws which address the problems of African Americans may be insufficient to improve the lot of Latinos in our cities and suburbs.

Residential segregation also differs among cities and suburbs across the country. The 2000 census data shows that Midwestern cities are the most segregated in the country and that some Western cities are the most integrated. But residential segregation remains too high in all U.S. cities and suburbs.

We are a nation of ghettos in which rich neighborhoods and suburbs have dug a deep moat around themselves, isolating themselves from the poor with fears and rumors. It is important to see that there are rich ghettos as well as poor ones and how artificial both can be. Evan McKenzie underlines this point in his account of "gated communities" that create barriers between the rich and the poor. As he puts it, "The upper classes withdraw to a privatized world of self-segregation built of gated communities, private police forces, heavily surveilled shopping malls, and guarded office buildings. . . . Inside their walls, the affluent give up their liberties in order to obtain the security they cherish. And outside the walls, the poor are demonized and often brutally repressed as unrestrained police violence becomes commonplace."

Two theories have developed about what should be done about the obvious disparity between races and classes which runs counter to the American ideal. Conservatives define the problem as social programs like public housing and welfare payments, which, in their view, create and maintain the permanent underclass. In their analysis, all that needs to be done is to destroy public housing and to end welfare. Once there is no government safety net, the poor, according to this theory, will raise themselves by their bootstraps into the promise of the American dream. It is true that some welfare programs created dependency and did not encourage the poor to raise themselves from poverty through their own work and education. But simply abolishing public housing and public welfare programs will not automatically eliminate the underclass.

The other theory developed by liberal scholars, journalists, and politicians is that government and business need to do more to supply education, jobs, day

care, and better health care to the residents of the inner city and the poorer suburbs. This theory holds that, if residents are provided real jobs paying good wages
and the education necessary to further themselves, they can then make their own
way. However, young children, the mentally ill and addicted, and the elderly cannot
be lifted from poverty by better public welfare payments, job training or education
programs. Even the working-age poor, given all the problems they face, may require decades of government support before they or their children can leave
poverty behind. In the meantime, the reality of the "color gap" and the "permanent
underclass" remain.

Undeniably race problems still exist in U.S. cities (witness the race riots in
2001 in Cincinnati). But there are also efforts at revitalizing the racial ghettos and
improving race relations (witness the successes of the neighborhood organization
in the Dudley Street area in Boston).

Notes

1. Tom McCann, "Low Income Housing Push is Set," *Chicago Tribune,* July 22, 2002 Section 2, p. 2.
2. Michael Martinez, Stephanie Banchero, and Darnell Little, "Race, Poverty Define Failing Schools," *Chicago Tribune,* July 21, 2002, p. 1.
3. Pierre de Vise, "Chicago's Widening Color Gap," in Dick Simpson, ed., *Chicago's Future in a Time of Change,* Champaign, IL: Stipes, 1993, pp. 45–62. Originally published as Chicago: Interuniversity Social Research Committee, Report No. 2, 1967.
4. Thomas J. Sugrue, *The Origins of the Urban Crisis: Race and Inequality in Postwar Detroit,* Princeton: Princeton University Press, 1996, pp. 5–6 and 270–271.
5. See Stephan and Abigail Thernstrom, "We Have Overcome: The Good News About
   Race Relations," *The New Republic,* October 13, 1997, Vol. 217, No. 15, pp. 23–28 or
   their book, *America in Black and White* (New York: Simon and Schuster, 1997).
6. U.S. Bureau of the Census, USA, *Counties Database* (www.census.gov-statab-
   www/county.html). Cited in Dennis Judd and Tood Swanstrom, *City Politics,* New
   York: Longman, 2002, p. 436.

11. Poverty, Joblessness, and the Social Transformation of the Inner City

Loïc J. D. Wacquant and William Julius Wilson

Sociologists like William Julius Wilson have discovered that there are fundamental
patterns of poverty in the ghettos in which the poor live in our cities. These patterns have changed over time. We now have what Wilson has named the permanent underclass in which families are locked into cycles of poverty for generations.
The ghettos themselves have changed now that they have lost the institutions that
make for a complete community. Wilson maintains that more than laws outlawing
racial discrimination will be needed to change these patterns and overcome the
problems of the inner city.

The conspicuous problems of inner-city poverty and welfare cannot be understood, and therefore successfully tackled, in and of themselves: They do not emerge, develop and eventually dissolve in a social vacuum. Rather, they are the outcome of the historical interplay of forces and struggles that cut across the field of politics and public policy, the economic field, and the field of class and race relations.

Nonetheless, the public debate on welfare tends to pay scant attention to the basic societal processes that produce and sustain poverty in the first place. As a result, the malady is often ill-identified and the cure prescribed ends up falsely putting the blame on the victims (the poor) or on the programs of assistance designed to help them (welfare). The underlying causes for the emergence and ongoing crystallization of a Black underclass, for instance, have typically been obscured by an excessive concern for alleged individual deficiencies—behavioral, moral, or cultural—of those who compose it, or worse yet, unfounded claims that such an underclass is one of the "counterintuitive" effects of welfare programs.

Drawing on a detailed examination of Chicago, we show how the class and institutional transformations undergone by central city ghettos in recent decades have further exacerbated the effects of the broader economic changes.

CHICAGO'S INNER CITY: FROM INSTITUTIONAL GHETTO TO PHYSICAL GHETTO

The extent to which conditions in the inner city have deteriorated and the ways in which such deterioration fuels the expansion of welfare can best be ascertained by probing the transformations of the social and economic fabric of these decaying urban areas. Because of the long-standing importance of smokestack industries in its economy, together with its extreme levels of racial segregation and trends in the concentration of poverty that parallel those of other Rustbelt metropolises, the city of Chicago offers a particularly favorable terrain for unraveling these changes.

Table 4.1 offers a synoptic overview of the spectacular rise of social dislocations in Chicago's inner city. In a period of only ten years, conditions worsened dramatically in the Black communities of the South and West Sides, increasing the schism between poor Black neighborhoods and the rest of the city (not to mention its suburbs). In 1970, the citywide percentage of families living under the poverty line in Chicago was around 12 percent; in the ghetto, these rates were already in the twenties and thirties for most neighborhoods. A decade later, the city's poverty rate had risen by less than 5 percent, but shot up an average of 12 percentage points in its poorest sections. In eight of the ten community areas that make up the historic core of the Black Belt, upwards of four families in ten were mired in poverty. Accompanying the rise of poverty was a proliferation of single-parent families: on the South Side, more

SOURCE: Wacquant, Loïc Journal, D., and Wilson, W. J. (1989). *Poverty, Joblessness, and the Social Transformation of the Inner City.* In Phoebe H. Cottingham and David T. Ellwood (eds.), *Welfare Policy for the 1990s* Cambridge (MA): Harvard University Press, 70–102.) Reprinted by permission of the authors.

TABLE 4.1   Selected Social and Demographic Characteristics of Chicago's Ten Poorest Inner-city Neighborhoods 1970–1980

	% Families Below Poverty Level		% Families Headed by a Female		% of Adults (aged 16 or over) Not in Labor Force		% of Population on AFDC-GA		% Change, 1970–1980		
	1970	1980	1970	1980	1970	1980	1970	1980	Population	Net Migration	Number of AFDC-GA Recipients
South Side											
Near South Side	37.2	42.7	41.0	76.0	55.2	62.4	22.4	72.8	-17.4	-28.0	+166.6
Douglas	31.1	42.6	43.0	70.0	48.9	57.0	24.3	36.6	-13.5	-33.0	+30.6
Oakland	44.4	60.9	48.0	79.0	64.3	76.0	38.4	60.5	-8.4	-25.6	+44.1
Grand Boulevard	37.4	51.4	40.0	76.0	58.2	74.5	30.4	45.6	-32.9	-37.6	+0.7
Washington Park	28.2	43.2	35.0	70.0	52.0	67.1	23.2	48.2	-30.6	-35.7	+50.5
Englewood	24.3	35.8	30.0	57.0	47.7	61.9	21.8	41.1	-34.2	-46.2	+25.0
West Side											
Near West Side	34.7	48.9	37.0	66.0	44.6	64.8	26.9	44.4	-27.2	-37.9	+20.1
East Garfield Park	32.4	40.3	34.0	61.0	51.9	67.2	32.5	42.7	-39.5	-53.8	+20.6
West Garfield Park	24.5	37.2	29.0	58.0	47.7	58.4	24.6	40.4	-30.1	-46.7	+14.8
North Lawndale	30.0	39.9	33.0	61.0	56.0	62.2	32.2	40.6	-35.1	-50.1	+18.0
Chicago	12.2	16.8	29.7	27.0	41.5	44.8	8.5	16.9	-10.8	-17.3	+78.1

than 70 percent of all households were headed by women in 1980, compared to a level of about 40 percent ten years earlier and to a citywide figure of less than 27 percent in 1980. Even more spectacular was the growth and spread of public aid receipt. Despite heavy population losses due to voluminous outmigration (from one third to one half of the residents of these areas deserted them in those ten years), the number of recipients of AFDC and general assistance increased throughout the ghetto to reach unprecedented levels.

It is well established in the sociological literature that economic hardships adversely impact the formation and stability of families. Research has consistently demonstrated, for example, a direct relation between the timing of marriage and economic conditions: the more encouraging the latter, the earlier young people tend to marry. Once married, the higher income of the couple, the lower their chance of divorce, and so on. In this connection, the weak employment status of a large and growing number of Black males has been hypothesized as the main reason for the fact that Blacks marry considerably later than Whites and have much lower rates of remarriage, each of these phenomena being closely associated with the high incidence of out-of-wedlock births and female-headed households that has gripped the ghetto in recent years. Indeed, Black women generally, but especially young Black females residing in large cities, are facing a shrinking pool of "marriageable" (that is, economically secure) men.

And this problem is particularly acute in the ghetto areas of the inner city. For example, in Oakland, Grand Boulevard, and Washington Park, three areas which compose the heart of Chicago's Black ghetto, the aggregate ratio of employed males over adult females has decreased sharply and continuously since 1950 (see Figure 4.1). At that time, there were between six and seven employed males for every ten adult women in these neighborhoods, a ratio close to the citywide figure of 73 percent. Thirty years later, this proportion had dropped to 56 percent in Chicago, but plummeted to 24 percent in Grand Boulevard, 29 percent in Washington Park, and a mere 19 percent in Oakland. No other group in urban America has experienced such a rapid and near-total depletion of the pool of marriageable men.

This argument involves no presumption that the marriage rate will rise automatically once a sufficient number of employed males are present in a neighborhood, for clearly a host of other factors are involved in the process of family formation, such as the cultural meaning of marriage, the balance of power between genders, the cultural acceptability of cross-racial or live-in unions, the age considered proper for mating, together with the differential age composition of gender groups, and so on. But, other things being equal, a minimal pool of securely employed males is a necessary, if not a sufficient, condition for the smooth functioning of a stable marriage market. It is hard to deny that a large demographic deficit of such partners, as evidenced by Figure 4.1, places severe structural constraints on marriage processes, irrespective of the cultural idiom of the population in question. As Blau aptly puts it, "whether our choices are fully determined by our constitution, background, and experiences or whether we are entirely *free* to marry anyone who is willing to marry us, we cannot marry Eskimos if there are none around." When aggregate ratios of women (of all ages) per employed men drop to such lows as one for

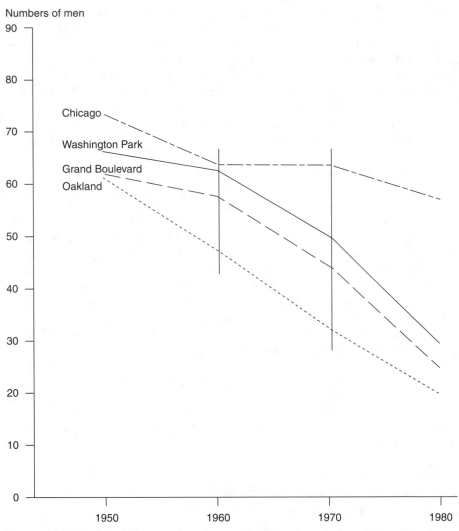

Numbers of men

FIGURE 4.1 Employed Men per 100 Women in Chicago and Three Inner-city
Communities in Chicago

seven, it seems warranted to conclude that joblessness hinders family formation in the inner city.

The sharp drop in the pool of "marriageable" men is a reflection of a cu-
mulation of economic and social dislocations that have fundamentally altered the social fabric of inner-city communities. Today's ghetto neighborhoods are not only very different from other urban neighborhoods, they
are also quite different from what they were twenty or thirty years ago. The
evolution of the class structure of the ghetto testifies to an increasing segregation of the most deprived segments of the Black community. This is most
clearly seen in the skyrocketing rates of labor market exclusion. The number of working adults in the inner-city neighborhoods of the South Side

dropped by 50 percent in the decade from 1970 to 1980 alone. Whereas a majority of adults residing in Oakland, Grand Boulevard, and Washington Park were gainfully employed in 1950, by 1970, 57 percent of them did not hold a job, and in 1980 that figure had risen to a staggering 73 percent. By comparison, the employment rate for the city as a whole remained above the 55 percent throughout this 30-year period. As might be expected, the most severe losses occurred among blue-collar workers. In 1950, more than 35,800 residents of these three communities were laborers and operatives, and a full 6,600 were foremen and craftsmen. By 1980, these occupations added up to fewer than 6,200, a drop of more than 85 percent. The number of managers, professional, and technical staff living in these areas also dropped, from 5,270 in 1950 to 2,225 in 1980; the number of clerical and sales employees, from 10,300 to 5,200. These middle class occupations represented at most 10 percent of the adult population of these ghetto neighborhoods at any time; by contrast, their proportion more than doubled among Black adults in the entire city over that period to exceed 17 percent by 1980.

The fate of the Black community of North Lawndale on the city's West Side vividly exemplifies the cumulative process of social and economic dislocation that has swept through Chicago's inner city. After a quarter-century of uninterrupted deterioration, North Lawndale resembles a war zone. Nearly half of its housing stock has disappeared since 1960; what remains is, in most cases, run-down and dilapidated. A recent survey of the area found that only 8 percent of its buildings were in good to excellent condition, with 10 percent on the verge of collapse and another 40 percent in need of major rehabilitation. The physical decay of the neighborhood is matched only by its social deterioration. Levels of crime in North Lawndale have reached astronomical proportions: in 1985, its murder rate was twice that of the city and six times the national figure. Police contacts with juveniles, for instance, were 20 times more frequent there than in the White neighborhoods on the North Side of town, with 5 percent of all youths referred to court in the year 1980 alone. While infant mortality has dropped both nationwide and in Chicago, it has continued to climb in North Lawndale. In 1985 it peaked at 28 deaths per 1,000 live births, almost three times the national figure. According to recent counts, a full 70 percent of all babies born in this community are born out of wedlock. And half of all births are currently to mothers 21 years or younger, with one in seven to girls aged less than 17. The proportion of households headed by women doubled in the last decade, reaching 61 percent or twice the city average in 1980. At the same time, the percentage of those receiving welfare assistance, including Food Stamps and no-grants medical assistance, rose from one-third to one-half of the entire population.

This staggering explosion of social woes is closely related to a string of plant and store shutdowns that have gradually turned North Lawndale from a lively industrial and commercial hub into one of the most destitute ghetto communities of the city. Chicago still had more than 8,000 factories in 1970; by 1982, this figure was down to 5,200, a net loss of more than 35 percent. Because North Lawndale, like many inner-city neighborhoods across the country, depended heavily on smokestack industries for low-skilled jobs and steady income, it has shouldered more than its share of the costs of this deindustrialization. In its good days, the economy of this West Side community was anchored by two huge factories, the famous Hawthorne plant of Western Electric with over 43,000 jobs, and a Harvester plant employing some 14,000 workers; the world headquarters of Sears, Roebuck, and Company was also located in its midst, bringing another 10,000 jobs. Lorean Evans, a resident of North Lawndale and head of a local economic development group, recalls how the whole area was "just a conglomerate of stores then. We had an auto center and banks, a York's department store, a Woolworth's. We had all kinds of specialty shops." There were, among others, a Zenith and a Sunbeam factory, a Copenhagen snuff plant, an Alden's catalogue store, a Dell Farm food market and a post office bulk station. But things changed quickly: Harvester closed its gates at the end of the sixties and is now a vacant lot. Zenith, Sunbeam, and Alden, too, shut down their facilities. Sears moved most of its offices to the downtown Loop in 1973, leaving behind only its catalogue distribution center, with a work force of 3,000, until last year, when it was moved out of the state of Illinois. The Hawthorne factory gradually phased out its operations and finally closed down in 1984. As the big plants went, so did the smaller stores, the banks, and countless other businesses dependent for their sales on the wages paid by large employers. To make matters worse, scores of stores were forced out of business or pushed out of the neighborhood by insurance companies in the wake of the 1968 riots that swept through Chicago's West Side after the assassination of Martin Luther King, Jr. Tens of others were burned or simply abandoned. It has been estimated that the community lost 75 percent of its business establishments from 1960 to 1970 alone. Today North Lawndale has 48 state lottery agents, 50 currency exchanges, and 99 licensed bars and liquor stores, but only one bank and one supermarket for a population of some 50,000.

During the decades since the fifties, the easing of racial strictures on housing and the rapid improvement of economic opportunities for educated Blacks in the corporate and public sectors, spurred by the civil rights movement and affirmative action legislation, led many Black middle-class and stable working-class families to leave the ghetto. From 1970 to 1980, the number of poor families in North Lawndale decreased by one-tenth, but the number of non-poor families dropped by more than a third. The heavy bleeding of industrial jobs—the number of North Lawndale residents employed in manufacturing and construction declined by two-thirds, from 15,200 in 1960 to less than 5,200 20 years later—combined with the accelerating exodus of working families to produce a quadrupling of the official unemployment rate and an even sharper drop in employment rates. In 1980, a large majority of all adults (62 percent) living in North Lawndale did not hold a job, compared to only four in ten in 1950, when the neighborhood enjoyed the same employment ratio as the rest of the city. These job losses resulted in a sharp drop in the median family income from 74 percent of the city average in 1960 to less than half in 1980. By then, 7 of the 27 census tracts that comprise North Lawndale had poverty rates in excess of 50 percent, while the overall poverty rate peaked at 43 percent, up from 30 percent only ten years before.

Needless to say, the heavy loss of entry-level jobs in industrial plants across the city and the accompanying outmigration of middle-class and stable working-class families were not the only factors involved in the growing social dislocations of Chicago's inner city. The "urban renewal" policy of the last 30 years contributed very directly to entrenching the underclass by concentrating massive public housing projects in the most segregated and poorest neighborhoods of the city. Moreover, inner-city schools have declined along with the other institutions of the ghetto. Far from offering an avenue of upward mobility, or even of integration into the working class, let alone into the middle class, the public education system now serves to further solidify the social and economic isolation of the underclass. Of the 39,500 students who enrolled in the ninth grade of Chicago's public schools in 1980 and should have graduated in the spring of 1984, only 18,500 (or 47 percent) did so, and a mere 6,000 (15 percent) of them were capable of reading at or above the national twelfth-grade average. And educational failure was even more likely for those Black and Hispanic students who attended nonselective segregated public high schools (as opposed to integrated or selective academic schools) and who represented two-thirds of the original class of 1984. Of their cohort of 25,500 ninth graders, a full 15,900 (63 percent) never finished their secondary schooling. Of the 9,600 who did graduate, 4,000 read at or below the junior level and a meager 1,900 or 7.6 percent read at or above the national average. In the early 1980s, then, the probability that a youngster living in Chicago's inner city will successfully complete his or her high school education is of the order of 1 in 14, compared to a national chance of more than 1 in 3 (and 6 in 10 in selective academic high schools of the Chicago area).

Looking beyond high school, the fate of those privileged few who did graduate from inner-city high schools proves no brighter. Of the 16,000 graduates tracked by a recent study, only 31 percent held jobs and 32 percent were reported as unemployed. The paucity of school resources, the grossly skewed class and racial composition of its public the severely limited chances of mobility it affords and the absence of a perceptible connection between educational and occupational success, all add up to make the school a mechanism of exclusion for the children of Chicago's ghetto residents. As a former superintendent puts it, inner-city public schools have become "reserves for the poor."

Changes in North Lawndale typify the social transformation of inner-city neighborhoods in Chicago. They reveal a shift from what we may, in ideal-typical terms, described as an "institutional ghetto," largely duplicating the activities and organizational texture of the larger society, to a physical ghetto incapable of offering even the most basic resources, services, and opportunities. Our analysis of the increasing concentration of poverty, joblessness, and welfare receipt in other Rustbelt central cities, as well as of the bleeding industrial jobs on which the urban poor have traditionally relied most, suggests that this bleak picture of Chicago's inner city is not unique. It indicates, rather, not only that life-conditions have dramatically worsened in the ghettos of the country's large metropolises, but also that these racial enclaves now harbor unprecedented concentrations of the most underprivileged segments of the urban poor.

12. Midwest Cities Among Nation's Most Segregated

David Mendell

Residential segregation in U.S. cities has not ended with our entrance into the twenty-first, century. African-American segregation persists, although it has declined somewhat, while Latino and Asian segregation remains high in many cities. Residential segregation is better in some cities and in some parts of the country, but it remains a major characteristic of urban America today.

T he United States has endorsed the ideal of racial and ethnic integration, championed by Rev. Martin Luther King, Jr. as America's moral imperative, but the nation's heartland remains stubbornly segregated.

As the rapidly growing South and West became more integrated during the 1990s, Midwestern cities continued to represent the bulk of the most segregated large metropolitan areas, according to a new analysis of 2000 census data.

Detroit, Milwaukee, Chicago, Cleveland, Cincinnati, St. Louis, and Indianapolis all ranked among the 10 metropolitan areas with the most Black-White segregation, the Los Angeles Times analysis found. And Hispanics in Chicago, Cleveland, and Milwaukee live in more pronounced segregation than Latinos in any other major metropolis.

Decades ago, Chicago and big urban centers in the Midwest were destinations for Blacks fleeing racial oppression in the South. But today, these cities stand as vivid case studies in the plodding progress to achieve a national landscape in which individual communities reflect the diversity of the whole.

"Clearly there is something in our collective histories throughout the Frost Belt that breeds a pattern of racial isolation," said Marc Levine, director of the Center for Economic Development at the University of Wisconsin-Milwaukee.

Though the causes of segregation are complex, social scientists point to several reasons for the Midwest's glacial movement toward diversity: entrenched attitudes about where people of certain races should live; economic disparities between Whites and minorities; and a housing industry rife with institutionalized racism.

High-growth cities such as Dallas, Phoenix and Las Vegas, experienced high levels of integration for some—but not all—minority groups over the decade. Demographers believe the many new residents of these regions were less influenced by preconceived notions of where minorities should live.

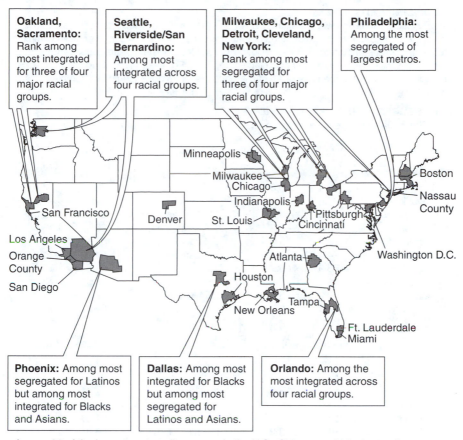

Oakland, Sacramento: Rank among most integrated for three of four major racial groups.

Seattle, Riverside/San Bernardino: Among most integrated across four racial groups.

Milwaukee, Chicago, Detroit, Cleveland, New York: Rank among most segregated for three of four major racial groups.

Philadelphia: Among the most segregated of largest metros.

Phoenix: Among most segregated for Latinos but among most integrated for Blacks and Asians.

Dallas: Among most integrated for Blacks but among most segregated for Latinos and Asians.

Orlando: Among the most integrated across four racial groups.

Among 33 of the largest metropolitan areas in the U.S., Chicago ranks in the top five for segregation among Blacks, Latinos, and Asians, according to the dissimilarity index. Although Black segregation in Chicago decreased over the past decade, the city saw increase in Latino, Asian and White segregation.

FIGURE 4.2 Chicago Metro Area One of the Most Segregated in United States

The analysis used a "dissimilarity index," a common tool of demographers and sociologists that gauges segregation. The index tracked block-by-block housing patterns by race and ethnicity in 33 of the largest metropolitan areas.

Every big city in the country, including Chicago, took some strides toward diversity in the 1990s, the analysis found. But change in the Midwest was so small that some researchers considered it negligible and ultimately damaging to the country's racial climate.

The index highlights an issue that has long bedeviled civil rights advocates and demographers: National efforts to end segregation, such as fair housing laws and affirmative action, have narrowed only slightly the prevailing racial and ethnic divide in many middle-American metropolitan regions.

Despite a decade of unbridled economic prosperity, the vast majority of Blacks in many Midwestern population centers still lived in primarily Black communities in 2000.

THE DISSIMILARITY INDEX

The dissimilarity index shows the distribution of one racial/ethnic group against all others across a metro area. It is the percentage of that group that needs to move to achieve complete integration. Scores of 40 and below show low segregation. Moderate segregation ranges from 40 to 60. A score of 60 or higher shows high segregation. For example, Chicago's index of 79.8 for Blacks means that percentage of African Americans must move to achieve complete integration.

MOST SEGREGATED BY RACE AND ETHNICITY

KEY: Chg. equals change in segregation 1990–2000

BLACKS Metro Area	Index	Chg.	LATINOS Metro Area	Index	Chg.
1. Detroit	85.4	−8.6	1. Chicago	62.6	+4.1
2. Milwaukee	82.6	−0.1	2. Milwaukee	59.1	−3.9
3. Chicago	79.8	−8.5	3. Cleveland	57.9	−2.5
4. Cleveland	78.6	−7.3	4. Philadelphia	56.8	+13.0
5. Cincinnati	76.9	−2.2	5. Orange Co.	55.1	−2.9
6. Miami	74.5	−7.2	6. Boston	54.9	+11.6
7. St. Louis	73.9	−6.7	7. Dallas	52.5	+5.3
8. Nassau County	72.9	−5.8	8. Los Angeles	52.5	+3.5
9. Indianapolis	72.2	−5.4	9. New York	52.3	−1.2
10. Philadelphia	72.1	−5.8	10. Phoenix	52.2	+2.1

ASIANS Metro Area	Index	Chg.	WHITES Metro Area	Index	Chg.
1. Pittsburgh	54.7	+1.3	1. Detroit	74.6	−1.1
2. Detroit	54.0	+1.3	2. Milwaukee	71.1	+0.1
3. New Orleans	53.5	+4.8	3. Cleveland	70.3	−4.1
4. New York	53.3	+0.5	4. Cincinnati	68.2	−5.0
5. Chicago	51.7	+1.4	5. New York	67.3	−4.1
6. Dallas	51.2	+3.2	6. Philadelphia	66.6	−4.4
7. Houston	50.8	+4.2	7. New Orleans	64.9	+0.6
8. Los Angeles	48.5	+6.1	8. Indianapolis	63.6	−6.8
9. Philadelphia	47.5	−0.1	9. Baltimore	63.5	+2.9
10. Boston	47.4	−0.3	10. St. Louis	63.1	+1.2

FIGURE 4.2 Chicago Metro Area One of the Most Segregated in United States (*Continued*)
SOURCE: U.S. Census Bureau/Los Angeles Times

In Chicago, the African-American population fell by about 20,000 over the 1990s and now stands at 1 million. At least some of these Blacks appeared to have moved to southern suburbs already populated with Blacks, such as Harvey, South Holland and Matteson. Coupled with Whites moving to mostly White suburbs, that left the region still extremely segregated.

In Milwaukee, migration of Blacks to the suburbs is almost imperceptible. The census showed that the suburban Black population of Milwaukee County rose only 2 percent over the last decade, with 96 percent of all Blacks living within the Milwaukee city limits.

"Even as you have this growth of integration in the south and west, you still have very little breakup of these large racially isolated ghettos elsewhere," said demographer Roderick Harrison of the Joint Center for Political and Economic

Studies in Washington. "In many parts of the country, we seem to be crossing into some new dynamics between the races, or at least a moderation in the dynamics. But not everywhere."

RACIAL INEQUITY

In Cincinnati, where Blacks make up 43 percent of the population, activists suggested that segregation played a key role in riots this spring after a White police officer shot and killed an unarmed Black teenager.

"You have all these White police officers who live out in the White suburbs and the only time they ever see a Black person is when they're arresting him," said Karla Irvine, executive director of a fair housing agency in Cincinnati and a member of the local NAACP board. "We also have concentrated public housing in certain neighborhoods away from White populations, and it makes for very little interaction between Blacks and Whites."

In Milwaukee, many middle-class Blacks have settled in mostly Black city neighborhoods on the north side.

That trend follows a history of racial inequity in the Milwaukee area. Until the civil rights era, some suburbs enforced laws that forbade Blacks to buy homes in their communities or to walk the streets after 10 p.m.

Recent studies have shown that Blacks with incomes similar to Whites in Milwaukee are four times more likely to be denied home loans. In the robust 1990s, unemployment for Blacks in the region hovered in the double digits.

"This is a city where the lines of demarcation are strictly adhered to, and the messages sent are undeniable," said Bill Tisdale, president of a Milwaukee-based fair housing group.

Chicago's legacy of segregated neighborhoods is similar to those of other Midwestern cities.

In the 1960s and 1970s, real estate profiteers played on White fear to make a quick dollar as Blacks kept arriving from the South. In the evenings, White residents in some integrating neighborhoods were besieged with anonymous phone calls announcing, "They're coming! They're coming! Sell now! Sell now!"

As a result, many South Side neighborhoods, such as Roseland and Englewood, changed from nearly all White to nearly all Black almost overnight.

"When we moved in more than 30 years ago, you'd say to people who were living here, 'Hi neighbor.' And he'd look at you kind of strange and then you'd never see him again—he moved out," said Cass Hood, owner of a construction company in Roseland.

Amid this "White flight," property values plummeted, contributing to the impoverishment of many Black families. In addition, those new Black neighborhoods suffered disinvestment by financial institutions.

Neighborhoods were redlined into zones bereft of economic activity: No loans were granted. City services were cut. Businesses and groceries, like the White residents, were gone.

Eventually, the initial Black settlers with a measure of wealth moved away, leaving behind the poor.

To stem this tide, Congress passed civil rights legislation aimed at ending conditions that exacerbated segregation.

REDLINING OUTLAWED

In 1977 redlining was officially outlawed by the Community Reinvestment Act, which requires banks to lend money throughout regions they serve, including poor neighborhoods, without taking undue risks. In 1988 the Fair Housing Amendments Act strengthened the enforcement of local open housing laws and steeply increased damage awards for housing discrimination.

Still, historic housing patterns had been set. Even today, it could take generations to heal old wounds, experts predict.

A 1997 study by the non-profit Leadership Council for Metropolitan Open Communities found segregation persisted in Chicago because of continued racial steering by real estate providers, a general social environment hostile to minorities, zoning that discourages the construction of moderate-income housing, and decisions by minorities not to expose their families to potential hostility in "certain traditionally exclusionary communities."

The report, called "Black, White and Shades of Brown," didn't name names. But it concluded there had been a failure of regional leadership to confront racism.

"In so many communities, economic development is prominent in the minds of the elected officials, but ultimately, it is human relationships that make communities strong," said John Lukehart, vice president of the Leadership Council.

"BLACKFISH BAY" MILWAUKEE

Perhaps no community reveals more about the Midwest's flagging progress toward integration than a neighborhood some African-Americans call "Blackfish Bay." The nickname is derived from its stark racial contrast to the affluent, nearly all-White lakeshore suburb of Whitefish Bay.

For decades, Whites have been leaving the small, leafy neighborhood wedged tightly between large tracts of urban blight. As Whites have departed, middle- and upper-income Blacks have moved into the stately homes that overlook lush green lawns on the city's north side.

The area is more commonly known as the Sherman Park neighborhood or Historic Grant Boulevard District. Several Black residents said they have no interest in being pioneers of suburban integration.

Willie Buchanan, 66, a retired welder, bought a two-story, brown-brick house there three years ago. Digging a bed for new sod in his front yard recently, he said he moved where he felt most comfortable. Buchanan's choice is indicative of many middle-class Blacks who shun White areas.

"You like to live around people who you feel want to be your neighbor," said Buchanan, who is Black. "I just know if I would move out to the suburbs, there would be a few people who didn't want me around, a few people who probably would say things behind my back they'd never say to my face."

"I don't think prejudice is as bad as it used to be. But it's still around, so I just decided to move here."

A 1999 study by the non-profit Woodstock Institute found that Blacks in the Chicago area overwhelmingly chose to buy homes in Black areas. African-Americans tend to purchase houses on the Far West Side, Far South Side, in a cluster of western Cook County suburbs and in suburbs in southern Cook County east of Interstate Highway 57.

WHITE PIONEERS

Milwaukee's Earl and Elaine Klabunde are pioneers of another sort—White Grant Boulevard residents who stayed put.

They still live in the house they bought in 1958, as neighborhoods on all sides have turned from nearly all White to mostly Black.

The Klabundes said they considered moving, especially after their nearby church followed its congregation to the suburbs.

"We adopted a Black girl and raised her, and perhaps that helped us keep a different attitude about Black people," said Earl Klabunde, 71, a retired public school music teacher.

But later, Klabunde said changes in nearby neighborhoods have unsettled him too. Crime was high years ago, he said, and a neighbor was mugged on Klabunde's front lawn. Those incidents have subsided, although he lamented that pockets of nearby poverty seem intractable.

"You watch CNN and see the problems in the Third World countries, but you can go just a couple of blocks over and see things here that are just unbelievable," he said.

Today, a small number of Whites have begun moving back into the neighborhood.

LATINOS ALTER PATTERNS

In the Chicago area, the tide of Hispanic immigrants and fast rise in the number of Asians are changing the dynamics of segregation. Latinos soon will outnumber Blacks as the region's most populous minority. As more Latinos, particularly Mexicans, come to the United States, they become more segregated, researchers said.

Census data show Latinos and Asians are far more likely than Blacks to settle in historically White suburbs that offer plentiful jobs. That has led to a demographic paradox:

Segregation for Latinos is greater in Chicago than in any other major metropolitan region in the country. At the same time, Latinos in Chicago live in less segregated neighborhoods than Black residents.

Much like the flood of European immigrants of the early 20th Century, Latinos are creating ethnic enclaves of their own, where Spanish is the predominant language. In the 1990s, Cicero joined Stone Park as a majority Hispanic suburb, and Berwyn and Melrose Park should soon follow suit as White populations in those inner-ring western suburbs dwindle.

Researchers will closely watch these immigrants to see if they shape America's composition or if America shapes them, Harrison said.

"This country has tremendous assimilative pressures, and I think the question is what happens to these young generations of immigrants," he said. "For all the talk of valuing one's heritage and language, youths tend to be the consumers of mass culture and be shaped by the culture. Will they hold on to their history and Spanish language, or will they give in to America's culture like most of the European Anglo immigrants early in the 20th Century?"

The answer certainly will help determine where Americans of all colors—in the Midwest and elsewhere—choose to call home.

13. Cincinnati One Year Later
Public Broadcasting System News Hour

In the twenty-first century, U.S. cities continued to struggle with race relations and race riots continued to break out. In Cincinnati, race riots occurred in April 2001. This report was given the following year and tells of the progress being made and the long distance still to go.

JIM LEHRER: Finally tonight, Cincinnati, one year later. Attorney General Ashcroft today signed an agreement to improve policing in Cincinnati. The city was torn apart by race riots last April. Betty Ann Bowser reports on what has happened since.

DEMONSTRATORS: I ain't gonna let nobody turn me around. . . .

BETTY ANN BOWSER: People took to the streets in Cincinnati to mark the first anniversary of the police shooting of an unarmed Black man. But this year they were singing instead of shouting. (Singing gospel) The city's police department was practically invisible. There was no violence, and there were no arrests.

DEMONSTRATORS: Put the gun down! Put the gun down!

BETTY ANN BOWSER: This was in sharp contrast to one year ago, when the city exploded into three days of riots. (Gunfire) It started after a White policeman shot and killed 19-year-old Timothy Thomas. People were angry because Thomas was not the first Black man killed by the cops, but the fifteenth since 1995—a period in which no White suspects died at the hands of the police. (Sirens) One hundred and twenty-five state troopers were called in; a state of emergency and dusk-to-dawn curfew were declared.

SOURCE: PBS Online News Hour, "Cincinnati One Year Later," http:www.pbs.org/newshour/bb/race_relations/jan-june02/cincinnati_4-12.html. Reprinted with permission from MacNeil-Lehrer Productions.

When things finally did calm down, Cincinnati's poor neighborhoods were devastated. More buildings were boarded up, more businessmen moved out, the riots had cost millions. The trauma of those days in April were a call to action for leaders in both the Black and White communities. So the mayor says they started with something they had never done before, something very basic.

MAYOR CHARLIE LUKEN, Cincinnati: One of the things that I think Cincinnati has done for the last year is engaged in an unprecedented, community-wide dialogue. Thousands of people, churches, community groups, police, talking to one another. And my real hope is that that is going to lead to an understanding and more trust in our community. But it's . . . we're just a work in progress.

BETTY ANN BOWSER: So you would say there's a lot more work to be done?

MAYOR CHARLIE LUKEN: Absolutely. I think we might be at the foot of the hill, but it took us a long time to get there. Now we have to climb it.

BETTY ANN BOWSER: While people were talking, there was still more controversy. The violence triggered two investigations of police behavior by the U.S. Justice Department. And Black leaders pressed forward with a lawsuit— filed before the riots—that charged the police with racial profiling. Of all the issues that confronted Cincinnati, this was the most contentious, because police refused to admit they had ever engaged in racial profiling in any way. Nevertheless, after marathon negotiating sessions, this week the lawsuit was settled, avoiding a long, expensive court battle.

SPOKESMAN: There are thousands of people of good will in our community who are working hard to make Cincinnati a better place. (Singing gospel)

BETTY ANN BOWSER: Reverend Damon Lynch is pastor of a church in the neighborhood where the riots took place, and a major party to the suit.

REV. DAMON LYNCH, New Prospect Baptist Church: We do think it's a landmark agreement. We do think it will bring accountability to the city . . . to the police force in our city. It will put a citizens review panel overseeing how policing is done. The Justice Department has come in, and it will change how force is used in our city. The police division will be held accountable by the citizens, and the citizens will hold themselves accountable for how we treat police and how we act among ourselves.

BETTY ANN BOWSER: For the settlement to work, all parties had to agree to it, including the Fraternal Order of Police But its members felt if they signed off, they were admitting to racial profiling. After much debate and pressure from city hall, the FOP grudgingly approved it with this reservation.

ROGER WEBSTER, Fraternal Order of Police: Our membership at the FOP in no way, shape, or form, ever agrees or has agreed that we have committed racial profiling or that we racial profile. We don't do it, we haven't done it, we will never do it.

BETTY ANN BOWSER: Another officer said even with a settlement, he doubts city hall will back police up when they are the ones who are harassed.

KEITH FANGMAN, Fraternal Order of Police: Now God knows, my fellow officers and I do not trust the city of Cincinnati to represent our best interest.

And when police officers use reasonable, justified force because somebody is violently resisting arrest and that person who fights us gets hurt, then our critics need to come to our defense and support the officer. We've never had that in this community. Never. Hopefully with this agreement, we will have that.

MAYOR CHARLIE LUKEN: I'm not crazy about what they said today. I don't like hearing them go off on the city. I'm used to it, but I don't like it. The good news is they're in the process. We're moving forward, and I think part of the problem in Cincinnati is that there is a lack of trust between the community, the police, city hall. That's what all of this is designed to begin to address.

BETTY ANN BOWSER: Officer Scotty Johnson, who heads the Black Sentinels police organization, says his department can restore trust by treating African Americans with more respect.

SCOTTY JOHNSON, Sentinel Police Association: The old timers and those young clowns that don't want to see any change, have to get rid of the old mindset and say "look, there's got to be a different way to do business. There's got to be a different way that we work hand in hand in the community." And I've got to be honest, those that don't want to see change, it's time, definitely, for them to go find a new job.

BETTY ANN BOWSER: City officials aren't just concerned about police community relations. They also worry about a 39 percent increase in violent crime at a time when police have been making fewer arrests. Rev. Lynch says police are doing less to control crime in the city to get even for the racial profiling suit.

REV. DAMON LYNCH: And the problem that I see with that is it's a matter of policing in extremes. Either you let us police the way we want to, which results in chokings and shootings and abuses, or we will just not police at all. And we cannot afford policing in extremes in our city. Police need to properly do their jobs and there has to be a working relationship between police and community that will abate the crime.

BETTY ANN BOWSER: FOP President Webster says there's no official slowdown; cops are just being cautions.

ROGER WEBSTER: In the guys' minds out there on the street, they're not sure what they can and cannot do. And I think they're reserving themselves and not responding like they normally would have. I just think that they're afraid of the public scrutiny, and they're not sure, they're not being given any direction on where to go and what they can and cannot do.

BETTY ANN BOWSER: The mayor thinks the police are doing the best they can.

MAYOR CHARLIE LUKEN: And I think the police department is trying very hard to reduce crime in city neighborhoods, but—and I will never understand the relationship—but this has always been and remains one of the safest cities in America. But why after the riots did violent crime in our community went like this and continues there, I don't know if there's a relationship, but it has happened here.

BETTY ANN BOWSER: And you have confidence in the police department's ability to control it?

MAYOR CHARLIE LUKEN: Yes.

BETTY ANN BOWSER: But some of the shoppers who come to the Findlay Market every Saturday morning don't share the mayor's confidence. The market is a 150-year-old Cincinnati landmark located in the neighborhood that was devastated by the riots one year ago. Mike Ewing is a carpenter. He's worried that police are so intimidated by charges of racial profiling, that they will let criminals go.

MIKE EWING: The violent portion and the drug dealers, you know, right now I think they have got a free pass because the cops are afraid to do too much of anything.

BETTY ANN BOWSER: Are you worried that the police are going to be too timid now because of some of the rules that have been laid down in this agreement?

MIKE EWING: I think that the people that are supposedly being helped by all these changes are going to be hurt even more, because, yes, I think police are going to be more timid.

BETTY ANN BOWSER: Vernon Kelley is father of five children. He's lived in the neighborhood where the riots occurred most of his life, and he says a settlement to the lawsuit won't change how the police do their jobs.

VERNON KELLEY: Some just are still going to have that brutal mentality. So when they first appear when they see a Black male in a car, they harass you hard. Instead of "May I see your drivers license?" It's "don't move, shut up"—this and that, this and that. So it's not a "sir, I need to see your driver's license," because they don't give you that type of opportunity, so they make the Black male react.

BETTY ANN BOWSER: Not only are there continuing problems between the police and the public, Cincinnati is still reeling from an economic boycott staged by the Black community after the riots. Big name Black entertainers and at least one convention have canceled appearances, costing the city more than $20 million in lost business. The mayor has been criticized for referring to the boycott as economic terrorism.

MAYOR CHARLIE LUKEN: I've also said that I regret that remark. I regret it to the extent that it implies that anything going on here is of the same scope of what's going on in the country. The point I'm trying to make is that the boycott has innocent victims. The innocent victims are the cab drivers and the people who work in hotels and the valets and those folks—many of whom, if not most—are African American.

SPOKESMAN: The moment African Americans assert their human rights and their civil rights, then we are charged with, "you're hurting the Black shoeshine man." There will be sacrifices and struggles we all have to take, because our goal is to save lives, our goal is to bring about systemic change. And we are more than willing to work with any business that may be hurting.

SPOKESMAN: We will not turn our backs on the parents who have lost their sons. . . .

BETTY ANN BOWSER: Lynch and other leaders in the Black community say they will continue the boycott until something is done to discipline those officers who have killed 15 African Americans in the last seven years. They also want the city to live up to its promise to pour more than $200 million into impoverished neighborhoods.

Just a few days before hundreds of demonstrators gathered downtown to mark the one-year anniversary, the mayor hired Cincinnati's first Black city manager, and a citizens group said a rescue plan for poor neighborhoods was coming soon. It may not be the justice these demonstrators talk about, but for many people in this Ohio River city, it represents a beginning.

14. The Renaissance of Dudley Street, Boston
Jay Walljasper

Some of the most important aspects of neighborhood empowerment are the activities of community organizations. This is the story of the Dudley Street Neighborhood Initiative and its partnership with a local foundation and city government to transform a neighborhood in Boston.

The neighborhood surrounding Dudley Street, an avenue winding through Boston's Roxbury district, is one of the poorest in Massachusetts, with per capita income half that of Boston as a whole and unemployment at least twice as high. Thirty-five percent of families live below the poverty line, and it's not hard to spot crack dealers slinking past shabby apartment buildings on the side streets. But you also see giggling kids walking home from school, old ladies tending flower patches in their side yards and neighbors chatting over fences behind tidy White wood-frame houses. The town common hosts a farmer's market and a bandstand.

Nearby is Davey's Market, which serves as a gathering spot for anyone seeking the latest neighborhood news. Conversations may be in Spanish, Cape Verdean or the melodious accents of the Caribbean, but you still sense something of the idealized America found on Norman Rockwell's *Saturday Evening Post* covers.

What's going on here? The answer can be found just down the street from Davey's Market in the cramped storefront office of the Dudley Street Neighborhood Initiative (D.S.N.I.). During the afternoon, it stands in for the corner soda fountain as kids wander in to say hello and see who else might be

SOURCE: Jay Walljasper, "When Activists Win: The Renaissance of Dudley Street," *The Nation*, May 3, 1997, pp. 11–17. For subscription information call 1-800-333-8536. Portions of each week's Nation magazine can be accessed at http://www.thenation.com.

around. The busy staff usually finds time to talk and joke with them, and when there really is a reason for the kids' visit, they listen carefully. One afternoon when I was there. Ros Everdell, a D.S.N.I. organizer, counseled 16-year-old Jason Webb about an algebra class with no regular teacher. "Get all the kids in the class to go with you and say you need a real teacher, and that you need to make up all the material you've already missed."

The Dudley Street Neighborhood Initiative has been at work in this corner of Roxbury since 1985, pursuing local residents' vision of their community as a safe, lively and close-knit urban village. Dudley Street residents will tell you they've seen significant changes in their neighborhood, achieved against considerable odds. "It's been slow," says Olivio Teixera, co-owner of the Ideal Sub Shop right on Dudley Street, "but that's because it's big work. It's so much nicer around here now."

Besides the usual problems of inner-city neighborhoods—poverty, redlining, unemployment, racism, inadequate public services, pollution, poor schools, crime, drugs, neglect by government officials—Dudley Street has faced some unique challenges. Many landlords in the neighborhood had reacted to plummeting property values by torching their houses for the insurance money, killing several people and leaving the area pockmarked with vacant land. More than 20 percent of the lots in the one-and-a-half-square-mile Dudley Street neighborhood were empty. These soon became dumping grounds, not only for midnight drop-offs of old refrigerators and construction debris but for illegal garbage transfer stations that operated in the light of day. The neighborhood also had to overcome problems associated with an ethnically fragmented population, including many immigrants with a limited command of English.

African Americans make up 40 percent of the neighborhood's 24,000 residents, with Latin Americans, mostly from Puerto Rico and the Dominican Republic, at 30 percent. Cape Verdeans, from islands off the coast of West Africa that were a Portuguese colony until 1975, account for another 24 percent of the population, and Whites, mostly elderly Irish and Italians who've lived here since the fifties, make up 6 percent.

The revitalization of Dudley Street began when La Alianza Hispana, a local social service agency, interested a small Boston-based trust in taking on the neighborhood as a major program. But when the Riley Foundation unveiled its plans at a community meeting in St. Patrick's Catholic Church on Dudley Street, it was greeted with skepticism. Distrust of outsiders ran strong in Dudley Street because many residents had been forced out of the adjacent South End neighborhood in the seventies by city-sponsored gentrification. Only a few seats on the proposed twenty-three-member board were slated for residents. Che Madyun, a mother of three with a background in the performing arts and a commanding presence, stood up, stared straight at the assembled panel of redevelopment experts and, as she recalls, "I asked how many of the people up there lived in the neighborhood. Not one. And then I asked, How can you say the residents are going to be represented when there are only three of us on the board?" Other voices quickly joined her. Robert Holmes, a trustee of the Riley Foundation and an attorney with the prestigious downtown Boston law firm of Warner and Stackpole, remembers: "Che scared the

daylights out of me. I was looking at the door at the back of the room, thinking about how do I leave."

Reeling from its reception at the meeting, the Riley Foundation decided to
fund improvements in the Dudley Street neighborhood without maintaining
direct control of the project—a show of support rarely seen in philanthropic
circles. "We allowed the neighborhood process to happen on its own."
Holmes says. "Some people thought we were crazy. They thought we were
throwing away our grant money."

Residents made up a majority on the D.S.N.I. board and were joined by representatives from area social service agentcies. churches and businesses. The
board then hired Peter Medoff, a savvy community organizer who had grown
up in Boston, to head the project. Medoff, firmly committed to residents controlling the process yet with surprisingly good contacts at City Hall, proved an
excellent choice. Emphasizing that D.S.N.I's foremost goal was organizing the
neighborhood as a political force rather than becoming another developer of
low-income housing or broker of social services, he and the board launched
several campaigns that resulted in immediate success: restoring rail service to
an abandoned commuter train stop on the edge of the neighborhood and improving safety conditions at the hazardous intersection of Dudley Street and
Blue Hill Avenue. By setting achievable goals, D.S.N.I. kept the level of participation high even though the bigger things like getting the dumps out of Dudley
Street and providing affordable housing were slow in coming.

The organization's active membership has grown steadily over the past
decade, and now numbers 2,500. Its biggest accomplishment has been imbu-
ing Dudley Street residents with the sense that things are looking up. From the
start, the group's members devoted considerable time and energy to envision-
ing what they wanted for Dudley Street. More than 150 people met to plot
out the future of their neighborhood in an eight-month series of meetings that
were conducted in Spanish and Cape Verdean as well as English. They came
up with a wide-ranging plan that emphasized building community spirit as
much as erecting new houses. Bike paths, apple orchards, outdoor cafes, community gardens, fountains, art programs and a town common with concerts
were identified as goals alongside pressing economic needs like jobs.

"The only way to make things happen is to dream," explains Gertrudes Fi-
dalgo, who participated in the original visioning process as a youngster and became a D.S.N.I. organizer after college. "Dreams are your best resource." This
visioning process has gone on for ten years, and results from the latest round
are taped to the wall in D.S.N.I.'s conference room, testifying to people's powerful yearning for community—and ice cream. An ice cream parlor figures in
many of the scenarios of Dudley Street's future that were jotted down on big
sheets of paper, along with dreams like this: "People Walking. People Talking.
People Laughing. Saying Hello to Everyone We Meet." Another reads: "I want
affordable housing and schools with beautiful green playgrounds."

"A lot of these urban programs do only housing," notes Gus Newport, the
former Berkeley, California, mayor who succeeded Medoff as executive director
of D.S.N.I. from 1988 to 1992. "I think planners take it for granted that poor
people don't need culture, vital businesses or beauty. If you had those things in

inner cities, you'd have a lot less crime. You have to get inside the heads of people who live here, see what they want. They want more than houses. Beauty—no matter how small it is, just a few flowers—is what matters most."

Newport, who now lectures and consults on urban issues around the country and is still involved with D.S.N.I., notes that the concept of urban villages has become fashionable recently among progressive architects and planners. "But these people didn't get the idea from academics," he says. "What you have here are a lot of people who grew up in the rural South and the Cape Verde Islands and the Caribbean. They want to work with the land. They want open spaces for kids to play in. They don't want to live in tall buildings. They want to know their neighbors. They understood all by themselves that they wanted to get back to the village."

Standing in the way of these dreams of a thriving urban village, however have been some very real problems, beginning with dozens of wrecked cars abandoned on the neighborhood's streets each week and regular shipments of other people's garbage, including rotten meat. "You had to hold your nose when you drove down the road," remembers Che Madyun, who became D.S.N.I.'s board president in 1986. "It was terrible." Madyun and Medoff guided the Don't Dump on Us campaign, which strong-armed Boston Mayor Raymond Flynn to do something about all the illegal dumping. Flynn, who had campaigned for mayor against African-American activist Mel King as a populist representative of Boston's neighborhoods in 1983 but had virtually no support in minority communities, was looking for ways to boost his popularity in Roxbury. He immediately saw the political advantages of siding with a scrappy neighborhood group and offered some city resources to assist D.S.N.I., going so far as helping Madyun padlock the gates of one illegal garbage transfer station before rolling TV cameras. "People were galvanized in seeing that they could change things," remembers Ros Everdell.

The next question was what to do with the empty land. The city had acquired about half of it through tax delinquency and, after some prodding, Flynn agreed to deed it over to D.S.N.I. The rest, however, was owned by individuals, among them real estate speculators, who hoped that some giant urban renewal scheme would net them a handsome profit. Redevelopment plans were hindered by the checkerboard pattern of land ownership. D.S.N.I. then decided to boldly go where no community group has ever gone before, to undertake a controversial move: eminent domain.

This is the legal tool that has been used to devastate many urban neighborhoods, where people are forced to sell their homes and businesses to make way for freeways, convention centers and other megaprojects. Could it be used to help rebuild a neighborhood? After convincing City Hall to grant it that power and four years of challenges in courts, D.S.N.I. gained the right to buy any empty land in the neighborhood.

The time tied up in court wasn't wasted because the organization still needed to come up with funding to buy the land. The Riley Foundation's support of D.S.N.I. has been limited, amounting to $1.4 million through the years. (Riley contributed more than $1.5 million to social service agencies in the neighborhood as well as making arrangements for considerable pro bono legal work on the eminent domain case and other matters.) Other local and national foundations have contributed smaller amounts. But it would take a sizable chunk of cash to purchase the land. Since banks and other conventional lenders steer clear of projects like this in poor neighborhoods, finding the money was a formidable task. Finally, the Ford Foundation agreed to make a $2 million loan.

Besides working to build affordable housing, D.S.N.I. has been busy with numerous other projects and partnerships. An annual neighborhood cleanup was launched, dozens of community gardens planted and a multicultural festival and a network for family daycare providers established. When drug dealers set up shop at the playgrounds in Mary Hannon Park, the community retook the park by establishing regular youth activities and sports programs. Working with planning professionals, residents translated the ideas of a sociable, walkable urban village into a master plan that was accepted by the city. More than 300 units of housing in the area have been rehabbed. A special effort was made to draw young people into the project, including designating youth seats on the board and bringing on a special organizer. State and municipal money was secured to construct the lovely town common, which opened last June, and plans are under way to remodel an old municipal building into a community center. Renovations for the nearby Orchard Park public housing project (childhood home of soul singer Bobby Brown) have been announced by the Boston Housing Authority, with much of the money coming from Washington. Playgrounds will be built by the authority for residents of the development, and an old cabinet factory on Dudley Street was acquired and will eventually house D.S.N.I., along with a new charter school and a small furniture manufacturer.

Leveraging money from municipal, state and federal authorities as well as foundations has been a key ingredient of D.S.N.I.'s success. Starting with Medoff, who had critical ties into City Hall, and then Newport, who had a national reputation as an urban advocate, on through current director Greg Watson, who served as Commissioner of Agriculture under Michael Dukakis and current Republican Governor William Weld, the organization has made the most of its political and philanthropic connections.

Winning a few early campaigns and publicizing them also positioned Dudley Street as a "success story." Foundation officials, politicians and government agencies—weary of what felt like the intractable problems of urban ghettos—were more than eager to join enthusiastic inner-city residents on what looked to be a winning team. Newport says, "Once you have people who are positive and working toward a goal themselves, then it's easy to get pro bono services and other kinds of support. Make things happen in the neighborhood and you can make things happen other places, too."

D.S.N.I. also got involved with some projects outside the Dudley Street area, joining protests against redlining by Boston banks and sponsoring regular classes for groups who wanted to rehab apartment buildings and low-income people who wanted to buy houses. One of the people signing up for the home-buying class was Debra Wilson, a 39-year-old caseworker for the welfare department. That's how she heard about Dudley Street's Winthrop Estates, which comprises the first 38 of 225 new housing units rising from what was vacant land. Wilson now lives there with her two teenage sons and grandmother. Walking me through her town house, which is modeled on traditional New England houses with clapboard-style siding and a bay window that looks out on one of the new parks, she says. "When I first came here it was all overgrown with weeds, old tires, abandoned cars everywhere. I couldn't imagine this as a neighborhood like it is now. It still surprises me."

Winthrop Estates was developed by D.S.N.I. with funding from various foundations and government programs. The houses can be bought by families with incomes as low as $18,000, in part because the land is owned by a trust. The adjacent Stafford Heights development offers co-ops for families with incomes as low as $15,000. Although only three years old these houses already feel like a rooted neighborhood, and not just because of newly fashionable old-fashioned touches like front porches and wooden columns at the doorways. Winthrop Estates and Stafford Heights avoid the suburban look of many urban redevelopment projects by emphasizing classic city features like sidewalks, compact lots and narrow streets. Because residents guided the planning process, the usual cookie-cutter subdivision designs were tossed out in favor of plans that fit their vision of an urban village. You see kids racing in front of the houses and hear folks calling out to one another.

The new neighborhood has already pulled together several times to deal with problems in the area: a nearby crack house, speeding drivers, noise from a 24-hour gas station. Thanks to prodding from residents, police drove the crack dealers out. In response to residents' petitions, the city made several streets one-way to discourage drivers from taking shortcuts through the neighborhood. And picketing pressured the gas station owner to quiet his customers. "All of us here realized that this is the first time we had ever spoken up," Wilson says. "We didn't know things could change."

Wilson is involved with a D.S.N.I. committee promoting economic development. "We just had a meeting about what we wanted on the Main Street. In two or three years we'll see the business coming back—places to eat outside, a bakery, restaurants where you can take the family."

Promoting small businesses is one of the strategies adopted by residents to increase employment in Dudley Street. So far the construction and rehabbing projects have provided a few jobs for local people, and the reopening of the commuter rail stop provided better access to opportunities downtown, but economic development has lagged behind other D.S.N.I. goals. "It's a much tougher nut to crack," admits D.S.N.I. organizer Everdell. "The answer is not just jobs in the neighborhood but all over the metro area."

So what is it that's brought a new sense of hope to a place whose poverty and deterioration once marked it as a lost cause in the eyes of the city officials and even many residents? "There's a tremendous core here, it's not just two or three heroic people" explains journalist Holly Sklar, author, with Peter Medoff (who died in 1994), of a history of the Dudley Street project, *Streets of Hope* (South End Press). She adds that D.S.N.I.'s efforts were effective because they transcended racial and ethnic differences and reached out to young people. "The foundations and government agencies became partners, not patrons," she says. "And the residents are really the leaders."

But Sklar goes on to offer a cautionary note: "Some people will say this shows you don't need government programs. If every neighborhood was just good enough, we wouldn't need government. But you can't duplicate this around the nation on the basis of foundation money. There's millions of dollars of federal, state and municipal money here. You can't do this instead of changing U.S. policies, instead of raising the minimum wage, instead of full employment policies, instead of improving the education system. No village is an island. Even here they're going to be hit hard because of changes in the welfare bill and the immigration bill."

Dudley Street's significance as a symbol of hope for America's hard-hit urban neighborhoods is not that it represents a magic way to mend problems without spending taxpayers' money. Rather it points to what can be done to make sure that both public and private money invested in low-income areas truly makes a difference in people's lives. Much of the backlash against social spending in inner cities stems from middle-class people's doubts that it does any good. Billions of dollars have streamed into ghettos since the sixties, and poverty and hopelessness persist. The most important message from Dudley Street is that conditions in inner-city neighborhoods can actually improve if revitalization efforts inspire the enthusiastic involvement of people who live there.

Urban revitalization plans are usually cooked up in a foundation office or government agency, and then neighborhood residents are invited to participate in the process—almost as an afterthought. Because many inner-city residents are poor, undereducated, immigrants, minorities or plain out-of-luck, some planners assume they have little to offer. Yet, in one sense, they are the real experts on inner-city life. Gus Newport notes, "This doesn't mean that you can't use professionals. But you must remember that community people know a lot. Here in Dudley Street, they looked over everything that came from the planners and analyzed it. They asked a lot of good questions and offered a lot of good ideas."

Politicians go on about "personal responsibility" as the key for inner-city residents in turning around their lives. The success of Dudley Street proves this true, but not in exactly the sense that Bill Clinton or William Weld means it. Because residents were in complete charge of the planning process for D.S.N.I., they assume responsibility for where the neighborhood was headed and they tapped unrecognized resources. Local teenagers, for instance, volunteered to help the architects on designs for housing. Che Madyun and a number of other residents proved to be talented leaders. This would never have happened with a top-down project, even a more lavishly funded one. Some housing might have been built and some services provided but there would have been no boost for the neighborhood's sense of itself. As a result of this experience, folks in Dudley Street began to view politics differently: as a way to get things done, not just as something that does things to them. That, as much as the foundation and government money, made a difference in this corner of Roxbury.

Of course, Dudley Street is not safe from the storms of federal policy and the global economy. What happens in Washington and Wall Street directly affects this neighborhood. But the lasting impact of a project like D.S.N.I. is that it strengthens the neighborhood's ability to withstand such assaults. They have more resources to figure out how to deal with the effects of the draconian welfare bill and anti-immigrant legislation. These policies will hurt people on Dudley Street but not as much as they would if D.S.N.I. wasn't there. Community-based organizing is not a substitute for the hard political work of pulling America back from its rightward course. But the success of this project strengthens the case for progressive policies by showing that public concern and taxpayer money can make a real difference.

There are unique elements of Dudley Street's story that limit its applicability to other urban neighborhoods—empty land strewn with garbage but also providing a catalyst for redevelopment, immigrants struggling with language skills but still enjoying the strengths of extended families, a local foundation willing to invest in a neighborhood rather than just a project. But the overriding theme of Dudley Street applies anywhere: The people living in a neighborhood were called on to make the decisions about its future. And they responded with enthusiasm, outrage, hope, creativity, patience and lots of energy.

15. Gated Communities

Evan McKenzie

Segregated enclaves occur not only in the form of racial ghettos for the poor but in gated communities for the rich and the upper-middle class. Gated communities are one of the most common forms of housing development in cities and suburbs today. They provide a private world for the privileged and a withdrawal from the city or suburb where they are built.

W hy are so many people choosing to live in gated communities? A group of scholars, myself included, spent two days talking about that question earlier this month at the University of California at Irvine. This isn't just an American issue—the panelists included experts on Brazil, France, Turkey, the Philippines, and South Africa, in addition to the United States.

SOURCE: Evan McKenzie, "Walls Do Not Make Good Neighbors," *Chicago Journal*, June 21, 2001, pp. 5–6. Reprinted by permission of Chicago Journal.

The conference produced insights that people in Chicago should consider, given that gated communities are popping up around downtown and all over the metro area.

The gated community phenomenon is occurring in cities all around the world, and it has something to do with the relationship between violence and democracy. Fear of violence—often fanned beyond reason by the media's irresponsible addiction to portrayals of crime—undermines liberal democracy by eroding support for everything public, including public spaces and public institutions, and the very notion of "the public" itself. Things that are public become associated with danger. And those who can afford the price tag then opt for things that are private, which become associated with safety and security.

The result is a segmented society. The upper classes withdraw to a privatized world of self-segregation built of gated communities, private police forces, heavily surveilled shopping malls, and guarded office buildings. They have their own private governments that administer a full array of what used to be public services. The lower classes inhabit the public realm and are dependent on increasingly impoverished public institutions. And in both of these worlds, liberal democracy and civil liberties suffer. Inside the walls, the affluent give up their liberties in order to obtain the security they cherish. And outside the walls, the poor are demonized and often brutally repressed as unrestrained police violence becomes commonplace.

These trends are easiest to see in the developing nations of the southern hemisphere, because there the contrasts are sharpest. While these nations have, by and large, adopted democratic procedures and hold regular competitive elections, respect for civil liberties sometimes has not kept pace with the electoral reforms. In some cases, democratization seems actually to have produced increased repression.

In Sao Paolo, Brazil, the police are widely perceived as murderous and corrupt. Television news has shown videotapes of police summarily executing suspected criminals on the spot, and apparently they are trusted by no one. So, people buy as much private security as they can afford. The rich have walls, spiked gates, and security guards, and the middle classes emulate them on a smaller scale. Even the poor erect makeshift gates outside their improvised hovels.

In Turkey, private enclaves for the rich are being constructed that closely resemble the ones you could see in southern California, the Las Vegas Valley, or the Chicago collar counties. One of these is north of Istanbul, and was designed by the trendy American New Urbanist architectural firm of Duany/Plater-Zyberk. There seem to be remarkable similarities in design and marketing between this compound and the instant communities DPZ designs for Americans. These include Celebration in Florida, the Disney-built, "neo-traditional," pseudo-small town technoburb that set the mainstream media atwitter a few years ago. Of course, there are differences between the Turkish and American versions of the New Urbanist utopias. For example, the promotional literature for the Turkish fortress enclave features pictures of guards wearing colonial-style uniforms, complete with pith helmets. Ah, to be back in the good old days, when the poor knew their place. . . .

In the so-called developed world, we see the French increasingly terrified by immigrants from North Africa, many of whom are housed in public housing projects on the outskirts of Paris. And here in the United States the last three decades have witnessed the abandonment of many social welfare programs, a massive expansion of the prison population which now includes truly incredible numbers of African Americans and Latinos, and the spread of a quarter of a million private communities, many of them gated and walled.

The cities of Chicago, New York, and Los Angeles regularly pay multi-million dollar settlements and jury awards to the families of citizens shot to doll rags or beaten to a pulp by police officers. Perhaps we are just returning to an older form of social organization. In ancient times, the Latins and Etruscans demarcated their cities, including Rome, by yoking a bull and a heifer to a plow and circumnavigating the city. They would mark this furrow with stone pillars called cippi and consecrate it. This sacred boundary was called the "pomerium," a symbolic wall that illuminated the line between civilization and barbarism, order and anarchy, civil peace and war. Often a real wall was built near this sanctified line, but its real significance was symbolic. The pomerium is a line drawn around the spiritual city. Everything good is inside; everything bad is outside.

These cities were pre-liberal. That is, they were built before the modern notions of liberal democracy and universal humanism were invented. But I wonder sometimes whether we have entered a post-liberal era. As you travel around downtown Chicago, I think you can trace the lines of our pomerium. It includes the Loop and all the tourist attractions—the stadia, the theaters, the museums, the restaurant areas. It includes the gated security condominiums along the lakefront, the gentrified areas in the north side, and the new South Loop townhouse corridors. It is being extended around the redevelopment areas where the worst Chicago Housing Authority buildings are being demolished, with the former residents sent wherever their housing vouchers happen to take them.

But sometimes it seems that large parts of this city are, and will remain, outside the pomerium, and this is a tragedy. I think the greatest challenge facing American cities, including this one, is to knock down the imaginary wall that divides us and find ways to promote integration rather than segregation. This means, for example, strengthening public institutions, especially schools; making public places safe for everybody to use; and building an honest, efficient, and humane police department, a competent court system with laws based on wisdom rather than moral panic, and an enlightened city government.

We also have to find ways to keep the affluent from seceding. The top one or two percent of the income distribution have always had their own institutions. But what we are toying with here is something quite different. Ask yourself what happens when the top one-third have seceded. Then we are speaking, truly, of Post-Liberal America, and this, I suggest, is not a place to which we want to go.

Chapter 5

Changes in Racial
and Cultural Politics

Social and economic conditions, particularly as revealed by the 2000 census, provide a framework for what is happening politically today. It is clear that beyond mere numbers of population, there are major changes in racial and cultural politics in the metropolitan regions. Population size, political leadership, and voter mobilization matters. The purpose of the following articles is to highlight some of the greatest changes in racial and cultural politics in American cities to date.

There has been a massive growth in African-American and Latino public officials. Based on data from the Joint Center for Political and Economic Studies and the U.S. Bureau of the Census we can construct the following table:

Year	Total Number of Black Elected Officials	Total Number of Hispanic Elected Officials
1970	1,469	NA
1975	3,503	NA
1980	4,912	NA
1985	6,056	3,147
1990	7,370	4,004
1995	8,419	5,459
2000	9,040	NA

SOURCE: Joint Center for Political and Economic Studies, *Black Elected Officials: A National Roster, 1984-2001,* (available at *www.jointcenter.org*). p.17 and Manthi Nguyen, ed., *Hispanic Americans: A Statistical Abstract.*(Palo Alto, CA: Information Publications, 2003), p. 95.

But the increase in elected representatives by minority groups by itself does not guarantee that there will be a real increase in political power or an ability to adopt governmental policies that will most benefit the minority group.

Valerie Johnson describes Black suburbanization and the struggle for greater power in the Maryland suburbs of Washington D.C. She reports that as African Americans grew more numerous in the suburbs, they gradually elected more minorities to political office. We have seen this trend earlier in larger cities, but it is now true of suburbs as well. However, African Americans, even as they gained more elected representatives, were not necessarily able to gain the power to affect public policy in key areas like education and housing in ways that would benefit them most. Moreover, splits emerged between upper-class and poorer Blacks, as well as between various political factions in the African-American community. This made it hard for the African Americans to agree on a common political agenda and to achieve the power to carry it out.

The issues of Black and minority politics in the twenty-first century are not simply numerical representation among elected and appointed officials, but unifying their group's voting strength and getting their interests as a community reflected in public policy-making. There is also, of course, the serious question of what is the interest of any community or racial group—is it defined by the upper class, the middle class, the lower class or some other interest that transcends class? Later research has shown that even if minority communities represent a large percentage of a city's total population, a number of elected officials of their race, and a widely accepted group goal such as affirmative action programs, political power of other racial groups and coalitions may still prevent them from achieving their goals of equality.[1]

One reason for this as Edward Lebow, in his story about Phoenix City Council elections, indicates, is that African Americans and Latinos are often pitted against each other in the struggle for representation and political power. In many U.S. cities, White males continue to dominate in key policy-making positions. So both Blacks and Latinos are engaged in a struggle for power, and frequently, this leads to a struggle between them (as it has in Phoenix).

The good news about racial politics is that there has been a change in voting patterns in local elections. There are frequent examples of candidates overcoming racial prejudices and winning votes from other races than their own. We are witnessing more subtle racial politics in the twenty-first century. Cities like Houston, Dallas, San Francisco, Denver, and Minneapolis—all with African-American populations below 30 percent—have Black mayors, while majority Black cities like Baltimore and St. Louis have White mayors. Candidates more than ever have to campaign for votes in every racial community. As Rob Gurwitt reports, "Slowly but noticeably, Cleveland voters have begun dismantling their habit of looking at everything through the filter of race." Gurwitt concludes that race is still a factor in urban politics, but no longer the only factor.

Beyond racial conflict and the usual economic development debates in urban politics there are highly charged issues of "culture wars." How do issues like gay rights, abortion, and pornography get handled in urban politics? In different situations public officials play very different roles from instigating these "culture wars" at the local level to repressing the groups who are trying to get these issues on the local policy agenda. These issues of social conflict are as important as economic development in understanding urban politics today. Social conflict has to be managed in a way that satisfies the voters if local public officials are to stay in power and if a local governing regime is to be seen as legitimate. If social conflict is not channeled productively, it can lead to violence and turmoil.

In looking at urban politics, the role of gender in local political regimes is often neglected. Since more than 4,000 women serve as local public officials and "women's issues" make up an important part of the urban policy arena, it is important to understand the effects of gender on urban politics. Some famous women have, of course, won highly visible public offices—like Chicago's Mayor Jane Byrne or San Francisco's Mayor and now-Congresswoman Diane Feinstein.[2] But many more women serve at the local level in the day-to-day business of governing our cities and suburbs.

In the same way that Blacks and other minorities have a right to representation and political incorporation, women have that same right. While the literature on the effect of women in politics at all levels of government is still developing, the empirical evidence gathered so far is that having women in positions of power does matter.[3] It leads to attention to neglected policy questions and changes the focus of local government.

The following articles explore the ways in which minority groups affect local government and politics in cities and suburbs; how conflict between minority groups emerges in local politics; how "culture wars" occur; and the role that women play in local government. They are indicative of the broader trend of constant changes in politics at the local level, which then ripple up to transformation at the national level. Politics and government are constantly changing in subtle ways and the changes often occur first in our cities and towns.

Reference

See Judd and Swanstrom, Chapter 6: "National Policy and the Divided Metropolis"; Ross and Levine, Chapter 9: "Women and the Gendered City" and Chapter 10: "Suburban Politics and Metropolitan America."

Notes

1. Ola Adeoye, Ph.D. Dissertation, "Dynamics of Urban Politics and Block Power: The Set-Aside Program in Chicago and Other Cities" (1980–2000) University of Illinois at Chicago, Chapters 5–8.
2. For the biography of one woman mayor, see Bill Granger and Lori Granger, *Fighting Jane: Mayor Jane Byrne and the Chicago Machine*. New York: Dial Press, 1980.
3. See, for example, Susan J. Carroll, ed., *The Impact of Women in Public Office*. Bloomington, Ind.: Indiana University Press, 2001.

16. Black Suburban Mobilization

Valerie Johnson

One of the major changes occurring in America today is the movement of African Americans, Latinos, Asians, and immigrants from the Middle East to the suburbs. The challenge in integrating suburbs is to incorporate these minority groups into the existing power structure and to produce new public policies that best serve the interests and needs of these newer residents.

Prince George's County is a suburban enclave of the nation's capital. In 1960, the county was 91 percent White. By 1980, the White population had declined to 59 percent and Prince George's had become the suburban county with the largest percentage of Black residents in the nation. By 2000, Prince George's Black population had increased to 63 percent of the population.

The demographic transformation of inner-ring suburbs was not unique to Prince George's County. Suburban communities across the nation saw significant Black migration in the 1970s and continued growth in subsequent decades. During the 1970s, the number of Blacks living in the suburbs increased by 50 percent. By 2000, 38.9 percent of Black people living in metro areas lived in the suburbs, up from two-thirds in 1990. Other metropolitan areas with high percentages of Black suburbanization include Atlanta, Richmond-Petersburg, New Orleans, and Fort Lauderdale. As Table 5.1 depicts, during the 1990s, Blacks moved to the suburbs more often than other racial and ethnic groups.

THE HISTORICAL CONTEXT OF BLACK SUBURBANIZATION

Despite growth over the past 30 years, Black suburbanization is not new. Although the latest stage of Black suburbanization is markedly different from previous periods, Blacks have lived in suburban communities since the 1920s. During the 1920–1970 period however, Black suburbs were either poor or working-class jurisdictions.

Poor Black suburban communities were underdeveloped and often unincorporated areas on the city's periphery with a limited tax base for adequate schools and government services. These communities typically lacked adequate water and sewage infrastructure, and were more similar to poor Black urban communities than to White suburban communities. As J. John Palen notes, "while such small communities were technically in the suburbs, socially and economically they were not of the suburbs."

Solidly working-class Black suburbs were one step above poor Black suburbs. Examples of this type of suburban community include Robbins and Harvey in the southwest suburbs of Chicago. Although different, both types of early Black suburb stood in direct contrast to the typical image of White middle-class homogeneous suburban communities.

Although the word "suburb" continues to evoke images of economic, social, and racial homogeneity, suburbs are just as diverse as the cities that they surround. This is particularly true for Black suburbs. As Harrigan notes, Black suburbs vary in socioeconomic status from those comprising old previously rural communities, to those that are affluent, and those that are mere extensions of inner-city communities that they border.

The reception that Blacks received in the suburbs was chilly at best. The same factors that drove mass White migration away from the city were re-

---

SOURCE: Adapted from Valerie C. Johnson's Ph.D. Dissertation, *The Political Consequences of Black Suburbanization in Prince George's County, 1971–1994*. University of Maryland, 1995. Reprinted by permission of the author.

TABLE 5.1	**Suburbanization During the 1990s**		
	1990	**2000**	**% Increase**
Total	61.2%	62.2%	1.0%
Black	34.2%	38.9%	4.7%
Asian	50.2%	54.3%	4.1%
Hispanic	45.7%	48.8%	3.1%
White	68.6%	70.6%	2.0%

SOURCE: U.S. Census Bureau, American Demographics Analysis.

newed as Blacks moved to predominantly White suburban communities. As it had been in urban jurisdictions, the integration of public schools again became a contentious issue. As Blacks settled in inner-tier suburbs like Prince George's County, they immediately sought political influence within suburban governing coalitions. And as they had previously in the city, Blacks also began to attack barriers to socioeconomic opportunity in the suburbs.

As Blacks have migrated away from the inner cities and into the suburbs, the political consequences of their migration are becoming increasingly important. As Prince George's County attests, increased Black suburban migration will no doubt have implications on suburban governing structures and political arrangements.

As this process occurs with greater frequency, it is important to assess the openness of political institutions as Blacks seek political influence in suburban jurisdictions. This is the story of the Black community's struggle to become a central force in suburban Prince George's County's governing coalition over a 30-year period (1971–present), and the factors that impeded their ability to gain political representation commensurate to their numbers in the population.

The beginning point of the analysis (1971) is significant because of the rise of Black political representation and activism in the educational arena, an arena that significantly affected White residential patterns in the county. In 1971, a group of Blacks joined with the local chapter of the NAACP to file suit in Federal court challenging the county's system of segregated schools. As Table 5.2 depicts, school integration correlated with a tremendous decline in the White population.

If achieving political influence were simply a matter of representation on policy-making bodies, it would surely seem that Blacks in Prince George's County are well on their way. Currently as 63 percent of the population, African Americans represent 47 percent of key policy-making positions (positions on the County Council, the Board of Education, and the county's delegation to the state legislature). Although Black representation is not commensurate with the population of Blacks, it is closer to parity than it has ever been.

Nonetheless, political influence is much more than representation on policy-making bodies. It also entails the ability to initiate and implement policy that promotes the interests of a particular constituency—becoming an integral part of the policy-making coalition. Although representation on its face

TABLE 5.2   Black/White Population Trends Prince George's County (1970–2000)

Year	White	% Change	% of Total	Black	% Change	% of Total
1970	561,482	73.0	85.0	85,873	177.1	14.0
1980	393,550	−30.0	58.4	247,888	188.7	37.0
1990	314,616	−20.0	43.0	369,791	49.0	52.0
2000	216,729	−31.1	27.0	502,550	35.9	62.7

SOURCE: Bureau of the Census; Decennial Censuses 1970–2000.

does not guarantee influence in the policy-making arena, it is an important prerequisite to political incorporation and speaks to the level of group unity.

In their seminal study of minority political incorporation, Browning, Marshall and Tabb illustrate the significance of cohesiveness and unity in the African-American quest for electoral representation:

> We were able to establish the agreement that if one African-American candidate was selected by the caucus, the others would not run, since there would be White candidates in the field. More than one African-American candidate would practically insure the election of no African-American candidates.

According to Browning, et al., group electoral mobilization proceeds other strategies. And, "if successful, it leads to representation and some level of group incorporation into city government."

As numerous urban case studies attests, the quest for political incorporation on the part of newly emerging groups typically encounters resistance, and often entails working in coalition with other groups to change the existing governing coalition to one that is more amenable to power and resource sharing. Yet, the extent to which Blacks may alter existing governing coalitions is based on their ability to mobilize and exhibit electoral unity. Therefore, increasing Black representation and policy influence is largely predicated upon mobilization and electoral unity within the Black community.

Blacks have been instrumental to the monumental political changes that have taken place in the governing coalition in Prince George's County. A striking example of the degree of political change is the success of archconservative George Wallace in the 1972 Prince George's County Presidential primary, and the subsequent success of liberal Reverend Jesse Jackson in the 1984 Prince George's County Presidential primary. Because each candidate represented distinctly different ideological positions, within the span of a decade the political climate in Prince George's County had shifted dramatically.

In 1980, Blacks represented 37 percent of the total population in Prince George's County. By 1990, the Black population had increased to 52 percent. Although, in both decades Black representation on key policy-making bodies were not commensurate to the Black population, Blacks were able to act in concert with liberal Whites in order to alter the balance of power away from conservative elements in the Democratic Party. This in turn had an impact on their ability to increase their representation.

Black organizations and individuals have attempted to organize and mobilize the Black population in Prince George's County since the mid 1950s. Despite early mobilization efforts, electoral mobilization and unity have been relatively elusive as a result of divisions within the Black community. The foundation of this division lay in the diverse socioeconomic makeup of the Black community in Prince George's County. In addition to being a premiere Black suburb, Prince George's County has the distinction of being "the only suburban county ever to become richer as it became blacker." In 1989, the median income of Black families in Prince George's County was $45,198 or 85 percent of White median family income. Nationally, the median income of Black families was $22,429 or 60 percent of White median family income. Currently, Prince George's County is the largest concentration of Black affluence, as well as the largest and most affluent Black county in the country.

All however, is not rosy in suburban Prince George's County. Although Prince George's County has an affluent Black population, it is also home to a significant poor Black population, residing primarily in close proximity to the county's Washington, D.C. border. Like many predominantly White suburbs, affluent Blacks in Prince George's County place emphasis on preserving property values. In the predominantly Black Woodmore Highlands community of Prince George's County, the homeowners association has established strict building guidelines that deter the migration of poor people. Houses must be a minimum 3,000 square feet and located on at least one acre of land. Practices such as these, while expected, are out of step with early efforts toward Black unity.

BLACK ELECTORAL POLITICS: 1950–1970

The Independent Democrats, organized in the mid 1950s, is the earliest of many organizational efforts that attempted to foster Black inclusion in local governmental affairs in Prince George's County. Although this effort did not culminate in the election of Blacks, it was instrumental in electing liberal Whites as well as influencing Black appointments.

Prior to the establishment of the Independent Democrats, Black political participation was confined to lobbying the county government and private businesses to include Blacks. Early accomplishments included the establishment of a Human Relations Commission for county government, and the hiring of Cora Rice as the first Black teller at Suburban Trust Savings Bank.

Later efforts resulted in Black appointments to the State Attorney's office, the Human Relations Board, and the Board of Elections. According to former County Council member Deborah Marshall "these concessions were given to the various 'leaders' who weren't in charge enough to be elected—but who the White folks went to for the votes."

The small Black population in Prince George's County in the 1950s— 12 percent of the total population—would have rendered the election of a Black candidate unlikely without tremendous backing. Marshall's remark addresses the nature of political interactions between the Black and White communities. As had been the experience with the Republican Party during the late nineteenth century, Black voter participation was only courted when it was in the interest of White political power brokers.

According to the late community activist, Cora Rice, "they [machine members] use to send pigs feet, chitterlings, whiskey, and beer into the Black community the night before the election and the next morning the Black people would vote for them." The power of the powerful Sasscer machine in Prince George's County "lay in the political indifference of the unconcerned."

By the 1960s, as the Civil Rights Movement was galvanizing Blacks across the country, Black Prince Georgians were becoming more interested in politics in the county. A significant mobilization effort designed to effect Black political inclusion was the establishment of the Prince George's Cosmopolitan Democratic Club. The organization focused its efforts on getting Blacks involved in local politics. Forums led by officials, administrators, and department heads from county government were a prominent activity designed to familiarize Blacks with the workings of local government in Maryland.

The Black Ad Hoc Committee grew out of the Cosmopolitan Democratic Club. Its goal was to unify and run Black candidates for political office. Its members included prominent Blacks and early Black political leaders, including Arthur King, who became Prince George's County's first Black delegate to the state assembly. Arthur King was elected to the state assembly in 1966.

At the close of the decade of the 1960s there were three Black officials in county government. Only two, King and Warr however, occupied primary policy-making positions. Although minuscule, the sudden growth in Black representation paralleled the 1962–1966 decline and overthrow of the Sasscer organization by the more liberal and reform minded.

BLACK ELECTORAL POLITICS SINCE 1970

In 1974 with the encouragement of Central Committee Chair Tom Farrington and the Democratic organization, [Black politician Tommie] Broadwater was slated by the [Democratic Party's] Blue Ribbon Selection Committee. The problem for Black community leaders, however, was that they slated him to run against King to be the first Black senator from Prince George's County.

Broadwater accepted the nomination despite the fact that Arthur King, who had already served two terms in the State House of Delegates, had already declared his candidacy. The political battle between King and Broadwater became the first major political division within the Black community, and unwittingly laid the foundation for the evolution of Black politics in Prince George's County.

The race between Broadwater and King illuminates points of disagreement regarding optimal strategies and alliances in the quest for Black political empowerment, as well as disparate leadership styles based on socioeconomic differences.

With the aid of the Democratic Party, Broadwater defeated King in the 1974 primary election by a three to one margin (3,279 votes to 1,281 votes), and laid claim to any spoils of machine politics allocated to the Black community. According to Broadwater, the key to his success was his "coalition with White folks." Broadwater's brash style provided tangible rewards (especially in the area of appointments) to the Black community. However, his leadership style and association with the White Democratic Party power structure was a bane for many who sought a power base independent of the Democratic Party structure.

Many Black leaders in the community recognized Prince George's growing Black population as a potential voting bloc and made attempts to maximize their strength. For them, Broadwater's political style was subversive to their agenda, and pursued personal interest and political ambitions over that of the community's. Further, it was thought, that Broadwater provided Black support to the organization at a minimal return to the Black community. Thus, for Black leaders, the Democratic Party structure's recruitment of Broadwater was viewed as an attempt to receive Black community support without the attendant requirement of offering Blacks full partnership within the governing coalition.

As the lone Black state senator, Broadwater became the intermediary between the Democratic Party power structure and the Black community. As state senator, Broadwater was effective in pushing Black appointments to various governmental boards. In return, the Democratic Party structure received the balance of power to elect its leaders to office. In 1974 with the help of Tommie Broadwater, the Black community provided liberal leaders the additional votes necessary to win key elective offices.

With the death of Sasscer in 1964, new leaders of the Democratic Party emerged who were more liberal and inclusive of Blacks. This new breed like their predecessors, fashioned what some perceived to be a political machine nonetheless. According to the Reverend Perry Smith, a key leader in early Black mobilization efforts, "we thought that we were helping to destroy the machine . . . [but] we essentially helped to create another machine." The difference between the two organizations was the degree to which they were oppressive to the Black community's agenda. According to Reverend Smith, "the Sasscer machine was overtly oppressive, you knew what they felt. This [liberal machine] was oppressive as well, just more covert at it."

The new machine, was quite different from the Sasscer machine, or common conceptions of machine politics. The new machine was merely a club-like organization, and as has been described, an alliance of the "in group." Patronage was limited to appointive positions; however, the strength of the machine was in many ways just as subversive of Black political ascendancy as a typical machine. The strength of the new reform oriented organization was its ability to provide formidable resources for the candidates that they tapped for political office. The Democratic Central Committee, along with their campaign resource arm, the Blue Ribbon Selection Committee, was very effective in garnering support for their slate through voter education and registration drives, and fund raisers.

Although the days of the Sasscer machine had now ended, there was a new "boss" in the county—one that operated as a reform-oriented organization. There were key differences, however. Tommie Broadwater, as the boss of Black politics in the county, was able to further encourage Black inclusion on the Party's slate and push through Black appointments. According to Broadwater, this was a constant battle. Therefore, while Broadwater was in the fold, it was difficult to force concessions from the Party structure.

In addition to Broadwater's election as the Black state senator, Blacks obtained other elective positions during the 1970s. In the span of a decade, the number of key Black officials jumped from two (4 percent) to six (12 percent) at the close of the decade. In 1979, the Black population had again grown tremendously, and had increased from 14 percent of the population in 1969 to 37 percent. Despite an overwhelming increase in the Black population, the lack of Black voter participation became an obstacle confronting the Black community. Where predominantly White districts had a 50 percent voter registration rate, Black precincts (dominated by apartment dwellers), had registration rates hovering at 25 percent. The decade of the 1980s posed additional challenges for the alliance of Black elected officials.

At the beginning of the 1980s there had been two elections where two strong and popular Black candidates had opposed one another. In both races, Broadwater received the support of the influential Democratic Central Committee, and won by large margins. Broadwater's Black opponents had run against the Democratic Party machinery. Both candidates cited Broadwater's ties to the Democratic Party organization as problematic and subversive to Black political interests.

Cora Rice and other Black community activists did not view Broadwater's ability to slate Blacks as a major victory. According to Rice, "we got this big gift of putting some Black people on a ticket from the Black community when they didn't need a ticket in the first place."

In 1983, Broadwater's reign as Black political boss came to a screeching halt when he was convicted for fraud for obtaining $70,000 in food stamps from an undercover federal agent posing as a thief. Broadwater subsequently processed the food stamps for cash through his Fairmount Heights supermarket. Broadwater served four and a half months in prison and spent four years on probation. A court ruling in 1989 however, allowed him to run for office again. Broadwater's daughter, who was also implicated in the food stamp scheme, was given probation instead of a jail term. Broadwater lamented that he cashed in all of his cards for his daughter, and subsequently had to pay the piper by serving time himself.

The 1984 Democratic primary was the biggest rallying point and mobilization effort of Blacks in Prince George's County. During the primary season a number of Black elected officials and community activists organized for Jesse Jackson's bid for the Democratic nomination. This effort, while initially divided, ultimately joined Blacks who were previously unable to reach consensus.

The Jackson candidacy also served as a countywide rallying point for the first Bowie State College Convention of Black People, held in March of 1984. The convention was attended by 300 Black participants from diverse backgrounds and socioeconomic levels, and provided workshops on police protection, political empowerment, the Black family, economic development, and education. The efforts of the participants of the convention and the Black community resulted in Jesse Jackson winning Prince George's County with 43 percent of the vote.

As a result of Jackson's success in Prince George's County, Black elected officials, for the first time felt their potential power, and began to lobby the White-controlled power establishment for a place on the ticket for a county-wide seat. The White establishment, also realizing the newfound political power in the Black community, dropped the former State's Attorney from the ticket in 1986 and replaced him with a Black attorney. By 1990, Blacks represented 52 percent of the county population and 26 percent of the key elected offices in the county.

Despite the unity that provided some electoral success, disunity among Black elected officials and within the Black community persisted, and was met by an increasingly guarded Democratic Party structure. In early 1990, Cora Rice, then-president of the NAACP, led a demonstration against County Executive Parris Glendening, criticizing him for failing to consult with Black community leaders when he engineered a lucrative employment contract to retain School Superintendent John A. Murphy. Glendening sought to persuade Murphy to stay amidst dissatisfaction with the school superintendent within some portions of the Black community. An earlier rift between the Black leadership involved Glendening's selection of a new police chief without public discussion or consultation with Black leaders despite continuing Black complaints of police brutality.

Another example of the continued disunity within the Black community, involved a demonstration led by a group of 200 Blacks from Prince George's County against the county's Black delegation to the state legislature, in Annapolis in February of 1990. Responding to the acrimony, state senator Decatur Trotter lamented "we [Black people] fight just like White people fight. We have our differences. That's growth, that's healthy. " This type of growth however, potentially diluted the Black vote at a time when Blacks had finally obtained the numbers necessary to win.

The 1998 elections saw an increase in the number of Blacks elected to office. As a result of gains, Blacks represented 47 percent of the county's key elective positions in 2000. Despite gains, however, Black representation again, was not commensurate to their numbers in the population, which had by 2000 grown to 63 percent of the total population. Nonetheless, it reached the greatest level of parity than it ever had.

CONCLUSION

In a matter of 30 years, suburban Prince George's County, Maryland has undergone revolutionary changes. In addition to monumental changes in the population, there has also been tremendous change in the county's governing coalition.

However, several factors contributed to Black electoral divisions. One key factor was the socioeconomic divisions within the Black population. Although in 1970, the majority of Blacks resided in communities in close proximity to the Washington, D.C., upper-class Blacks had begun their trek to communities deeper into the county. Early on, Black leaders were billed as either the representatives of middle-class Blacks or as representatives of poorer Blacks. Thus, electoral mobilization and unity was thwarted.

Another key factor, and perhaps most significant, was the White liberal wing of the party's ability to divide the Black community by selecting Black leaders who were not the dominant choice of key Black leaders. Although the Black community won concessions as a result of these leaders' alliances with the then dominant governing coalition, many believed that it was subordinate to the level of influence Blacks would have received had they first developed internally.

Despite their ability to establish alliances with liberal Whites, Blacks were not equal partners in the Democratic Party organization. Instead, Black officials have divided their support behind the leading White power brokers in the county organization, and have been unable to reach consensus in electoral efforts.

If Black representation on policy-making bodies alone determined political influence, then it could be said that Blacks in Prince George's County are on their way to becoming a force to be reckoned with. However, political influence is determined by a group's ability to have its interest met within the political system. And this is where the impact of Black divisions proves to be most significant. The same socioeconomic divisions that have influenced Black representation have likewise impacted Black policy positions on a wide variety of other issues, including education, housing and key appointments.

The question facing Blacks of diverse socioeconomic status migrating to suburban communities becomes: which interests constitute Black interests. This question becomes most salient when middle-class Blacks migrate to suburban communities where a working-class or rural Black population already exists. Although Blacks are most likely to unify behind issues and policies relating to civil rights, they are unlikely to mobilize behind issues pertaining to socioeconomic status. This creates a dilemma for Black suburban political representation, and subsequently impacts the level of political incorporation that can be obtained.

Although socioeconomic diversity played a role in Black political divisions, neither faction within the Black community benefited. The key to Black suburban political incorporation is for Blacks to build on their strength in numbers in order to gain representation commensurate to their numbers. The lesson of Prince George's County is that mobilization toward equal representation must precede Black class interests if Blacks, no matter the faction, are to become an integral component of suburban policy-making coalitions.

17. Primary Colors in Phoenix City Council Elections

Edward Lebow

This article explores the pitting of Hispanic hopes of better representation against Black history and struggles for empowerment in a Southwestern city in which both groups have been traditionally under represented. In Phoenix, White males have ruled for most of the twentieth century Now, as we begin the twenty-first century, that is changing.

Carolyn T. Lowery—African-American neighborhood gadfly, city council candidate and ice pick in the toes of just about every authority—has a penchant for sometimes spouting outrageous candor. So while others attending a June forum for candidates at the Saint Catherine's School on south Central Avenue aired platitudes about the richness of the district's ethnic diversity, she reached into a damp cove of community psyche and vented the angst aroused by the surge of newcomers to District 8, in south and central Phoenix.

Peering out from under the wide, shadowing brim of a straw summer hat, she wagged a microphone at her chin and intoned soulfully from the stage: "I remember the times we could ride down funky, funky Broadway. And I could drive in there and flirt with some of the men and get a hamburger without even paying."

She drew a breath without breaking her preacherly flow.

"Then I would go on down to the service station and let the men fix my tires, just show 'em a little leg and that was all. Now I don't have nowhere I can stop, because I don't see my people nowhere, man, you know what I'm saying?"

A scattered chorus of "uh huhs" from the African Americans and ripples of uneasy laughter from the Latinos in the crowd of about 100 confirmed that everyone knew *exactly* what she was saying. And they didn't need an official U.S. government census to know it.

In the past ten years, the Hispanic population in District 8 has jumped from 48 percent to 64 percent; it's even higher in some parts of the district. Numerous older Latino and African-American neighborhoods are filled with young Hispanic families, many of them recent immigrants.

In a city accustomed to fretting about historical divides between Whites and every other human color, these changes have exposed significant rifts between African Americans and Hispanics, and among diverging groups of Latinos themselves.

"We have a big conflict with the new," says state Representative Leah Landrum-Taylor, an African American who has represented part of the district since 1999, "and it's not just new Hispanics coming in here. It's the new people. How do you mix in the new without feeling like you're knocking out the old and established?"

"It's a pressure cooker right now," she adds. "And we've got to find a way to release some of that air."

Nowhere is this pressure more apparent than in south Phoenix politics.

For more than a generation, District 8 has been the only African-American seat on the Phoenix City Council, a secure bully pulpit for the city's relatively small Black population. Cody Williams has held the seat for the past eight years, and Calvin Goode for 21 years before him.

The spot has been theirs even though the Black population in District 8 has been slowly falling off, from 17.7 percent to 13.6 percent in the past decade.

SOURCE: Edward Lebow, "Primary Colors," *Phoenix New Times*, August 30, 2001, http://www.phoenixnewtimes.com/issues/2001-08-30/feature.html/page1.html. Reprinted with permission of New Times.

Now, the boom in the Latino population, the drop in the number of Blacks and Williams' forced departure due to term limits are giving Latinos their best shot in years to put one of their own on the council.

A Hispanic voice on the governing body of the nation's sixth largest city is long overdue. Latino population has exploded citywide, especially in core districts. Since 1990, the number of Hispanics has tripled to 32 percent in District 4, which covers a swath north of Thomas Road in the heart of town. It has doubled to 21 percent in District 6, an area that dog-bones down from east Phoenix to Ahwatukee. It's jumped from 19 percent to 48 percent in west Phoenix's District 5, and from 50 percent to 72 percent in southwest Phoenix's District 7.

Despite these dramatic gains, Hispanics have not held a seat on the Phoenix city council in five years. The last Latino city councilman was the ineffectual Salomon Leija from District 7. He lost the job in 1996 to Doug Lingner, who has since beat back a strong Hispanic challenger despite his district's overwhelming Latino majority.

Some observers attribute Lingner's survival to his political savvy in dealing with the Latino community. Others contend he's marshaled the dwindling number of Anglo voters into an effective minority bloc.

The likelier explanation is that Latinos are a mess politically, their power sapped by pitifully low numbers of registered voters, abysmal voter turnouts, and—within their communities—profound social and cultural differences which belie the notion of ethnic unity.

That's clearly the case in District 8, where nine candidates—two Latinos, three African Americans and four Anglos—are vying for the council seat.

In an attempt to prevent the fracturing, a coalition of some 50 Latino community leaders earlier this year endorsed Feliciano Vera, a Harvard-educated community organizer who grew up in the district.

But the coalition's efforts to unify Latino support haven't produced the intended solidarity. A significant number of coalition members split off and, along with some Hispanic elected officials, are backing Abedón Fimbres, a social-services administrator.

In recent months, the two campaigns have become mired in political finger-pointing that reveals more about fundamental rifts and differences among Hispanics than it does about common ground.

The wedge being driven into Latino solidarity could leave an opening for Mike Johnson, a retired city police officer and strong Black candidate, to squeeze through. Even though he's also a political novice, Johnson has been endorsed by outgoing councilman Williams, county supervisor Mary Rose Wilcox (one of the city's more prominent Latinas) and a number of other established leaders. Wilcox is friends with Johnson, but she's also never won an election without solid Black support.

A split in the Latino vote between Vera and Fimbres could send the election into a November 6 runoff with Johnson and perhaps Trace Vencenza, an Anglo who is president of the Roosevelt Neighborhood Association and has strong support in the in the upscale historic areas on the edge of the district.

This upheaval would seem to favor Johnson because the Black community usually votes as an overwhelming bloc. In the last council election in the district, in 1997, some heavily African-American precincts powered Cody Williams' win with 80 percent to 98 percent of the vote.

"What you've got in District 8 this year," says attorney Daniel Ortega, who's part of the coalition backing Vera, "is basically a free-for-all. Right from the beginning we felt that having two Hispanics run was going to cost the other. Now we've got a situation where they're clearly going after the same voters."

"You could potentially wind up with a situation where you don't have an Hispanic in the runoff at all."

◆   ◆   ◆

From a trail halfway up the north face of South Mountain, most of District 8 lies within a single sweeping view. Down the dusty, scrub-covered hills and washes below the mountain, it extends north in patterns of red and tawny walls and rooftops toward the dry, sand-trap river that splits the district. It tilts uphill across the Salt and passes beyond the first rung of glittering high rises downtown. Off to the right, it reaches the easternmost end of the runways at Sky Harbor Airport.

On a map, the area seems a unified, if ragged rectangle stretching from the mountain to Thomas Road, and west from the Tempe border at 48th Street to 19th Avenue. But in the neighborhoods of south and central Phoenix that unity gives way to a jolting array of urban contrasts—perhaps the most diverse in the city.

In some areas, expensive homes and pricey urban amenities are just across the street from landscapes of abject poverty, crime and neglect. In downtown itself, the gleaming commercial and governmental towers, theaters, museums, stadium and arena are just a short walk from the crack-fed blight of neighborhoods engulfed by homeless people—many on drugs, many mentally ill—drifting from one social service or splash of shade to another.

This alternating current of rich and poor, old and new, hasn't always fueled the district's image.

For many years vast portions of District 8 were dumping grounds for the unlucky or undesirable. In the era of more formalized segregation, discriminatory property deeds and banking practices, it was the only place where African Americans and Hispanics could own homes. For much of the past generation, its neighborhoods have been burdened by poor schools, poor commerce, lousy shopping, crumbling and non-existent infrastructure, a decaying stock of affordable housing and high rates of poverty and crime.

The banks of the Salt River, at the heart of the district, have been taken over by grimy car-crushing and recycling businesses, sand- and gravel-mining operations and toxic waste dumps.

These malignancies have kept property values preposterously low. Yet in what seems an inevitable turn of events in a city pressurized in the past decade by booming growth and a sound national economy, the low values have made the district one of the city's hottest destinations for an incongruous mix of impoverished immigrants, real estate speculators and developers.

Across the formerly rural southern breadth of the city, acres of cotton fields, commercial flower gardens and citrus orchards have given way to suburban-style boulevards lined with industrial parks and high-end housing developments, outfitted in a few instances with golf courses.

Cody Williams gets much of the credit for attracting this influx of private wealth and business, and for cheerleading the area's proximity and significance to a downtown that badly needs the abundance of low-wage service workers that District 8 has traditionally housed.

Still, some fault Williams for what they say are his cozy relationships with developers. They contend that this has prompted him to support wiping out poor and neglected areas, rather than providing them with the basic services and improvements that would help to reverse their decay.

Some even say he has forgotten his own deep roots in the area.

His father, Travis, was a contractor who built homes—many for African Americans—in south Phoenix, laying some of the groundwork for communities that, despite periods of trouble, have remained some of the tightest in the city.

"These are people who have been here for a long, long time," says Mike Johnson. "They raised their families here. They stayed through the bad times. And they always stuck together."

The same is true of many older, predominantly Hispanic neighborhoods.

"There's always been a sense of community here," says state Representative Carlos Avelar, whose south Phoenix home is surrounded by generations of his family. "We don't all live on the same block. But a block directly west of me is the street where my sister lives. A block south of me another sister lives. My kids, my daughter and her husband are there. I like going to Fry's or Food City. Getting a gallon of milk isn't a 15-minute thing. Because you're bound to run into somebody you know."

About a year and a half ago, Avelar attended a swank reception at the Legacy golf community, a splashy new development between Southern Avenue and Baseline. He was standing by the pool, gazing southward past the golf greens and posh homes at the crag of mountains, when a woman sidled up to him and commented, "Now this is the kind of development we've needed down here for a long time."

Avelar agreed, but wondered aloud when south Phoenix will have had enough of high-end development:

"We've got the Raven (golf course). We've got the Legacy. Thunderbird is going to be turning into another gated community. What's going to happen to those people who've been here for generations, what's going to happen to our senior citizens who are just paying taxes. Are they going to be forced out by assessment? And the cost of housing skyrocketing?

"Without blinking, she says to me, 'What about relocation?' "

The sentiment doesn't resonate well with longtime residents who drive past these glitzy new communities on their way to neighborhoods that have never had even basic niceties.

"One of the things that's happening," says Johnson, "is that the more people see these new places and what they have, they're going to start comparing that with what they don't have. They're going to want the little amenities like the sidewalks, the curbs, the real nice parks."

In a neighborhood near 20th Street and Broadway, he turns down a street of hardscrabble yards strewn with trash and broken beer bottles. He slows in passing the torched hulk of a house and an abandoned duplex, then points out one small well-kept white house with a yard of young trees.

"A lot of times, people living in places like this have just given up," he says. "They don't have no hope. But you've got good people over here who are trying to maintain and improve their property. But there's great odds against that."

A few years ago, Phoenix City Manager Frank Fairbanks attended a meeting at a central city neighborhood, near 7th Avenue and Buckeye, to talk about improving services. The area is one of the most beleaguered in the district, the product of years of public and private neglect.

"We were talking about development of things like street lights, stop signs, sidewalks, streets—basic stuff that has been historically neglected in many of District 8's older neighborhoods," recalls Feliciano Vera. "And he said that south Phoenix is never going to be Paradise Valley. What struck me was how disconnected the idea of these basic needs was from the idea of Paradise Valley."

"Some of the problems our neighborhoods have," he says, "can be traced to the fact that too many people here just don't vote. They don't vote because they're not taken seriously."

Touring the blocks west of 7th Avenue, Vera pulls his truck to the corner of 11th Avenue and Pima, barely a 20 minute walk from City Hall. He stares through the windshield at an obliterated neighborhood of broken houses amid a trash-strewn expanse of dirt lots, the kind of scene he hopes to do something about if elected.

"This is pretty typical for down here. These neighborhoods languish because the decision over time has been to leave them be. There's not the political will to work at stabilizing them.

"There aren't many votes here. There's no money that comes out of these neighborhoods. Their median income is probably $10,000 a year. But they're sitting on prime real estate. So the owners of these lots are just sitting on them, waiting for the big bucks to come by.

"The investment hasn't been here," he continues. "The investment has gone to the outlying reaches of the city, to the newer developments where people haven't given up."

Voting trends help to explain why.

Though District 8's population has grown by more than 26,000, to nearly 152,000, in the past decade, its number of registered voters has declined by about 4,000, this despite a successful effort in south Phoenix last year by the Southwest Voter Registration Education Project that enrolled about 2,900 new voters.

Other inner-city districts suffer from similar disparities between population and voting: District 7 has gained more than 46,000 people while losing 4,700 voters; District 5, 52,000 while losing 7,000 voters.

Not surprisingly, predominantly non-Hispanic White outer districts—2 and 3 and parts of 6—have gained both population and voters.

In a system where money and votes are twin pillars of influence, this drain of votes has stunted the power of inner-city areas, which are booming with Hispanic-driven growth, to get the city's attention and services.

This growing powerlessness is compounded by the failure of politicians to discuss the impact these shifts are having on neighborhoods in and around District 8.

"There's not a lot of honesty about this," says Vera, "because politicians are looking to save their skins. They won't and can't talk about it because it is political dynamite."

"You've got multiple communities in the same physical space," he says, "but they don't interact with each other. You've got immigrant communities that exist in a shadow world. They support our real estate industry. They support our service sector. They have largely supported the growth, but they're not citizens. They don't have the full rights. We're a city in denial about these kinds of issues."

But immigration is a major issue facing the city of Phoenix, and in the neighborhoods of District 8, it is the most basic of debates, affecting the living conditions of immigrants and citizens alike.

Immigrant families are doubling and tripling up in houses and apartments built to hold fewer people. Alleys mount with trash. Shacks are added to already dilapidated houses, and detached garages are closed in to accommodate more newcomers.

The failure of city officials to meet these pressures has only heightened frictions between old timers, who see their neighborhoods going down the tubes, and newcomers who are scrambling to get a foothold.

Yet the divisions go beyond those separating the old and new.

"As Latinos, Chicanos, or whatever you want to call us," says Carlos Avelar, "we are as different from the newly-arrived Mexican in terms of our linguistics, our culture and our religion as a Mexican is from a Colombian, or an Argentinean. We may have some of the same roots, some of the same likes and dislikes. But we're very different. There are differences between Americans and Englishmen. The myth is that we're one monolithic group."

"It's nice to be united but get real," says immigration attorney Emelia Banuelos, a Vera supporter. "I say something and the Salvadorans get pissed off at me. I say something else and the Cubans get pissed off at me. Guatemalans, it's another matter."

That makes it hard for Hispanics to line up behind a single candidate.

And Avelar notes that unnecessary rifts have arisen from too many Hispanic candidates running in the same race.

That occurred in 1996 when Tommy Espinoza challenged Mary Rose Wilcox for the County Board of Supervisor's slot now held by Wilcox.

"People are still feeling the pain over that race," says Luis Ibarra, president of Friendly House, a Latino-oriented social-service agency. "Here we had two people who are pretty high in esteem in the community and they're running against each other."

The larger Latino failure is getting eligible voters to the polls. The Black community is much more successful.

"The reality is, if you look at voter turnout, it's very low in Hispanic communities," says Avelar, who is backing Fimbres.

In the last District 8 election, in 1997, turnout in some largely Hispanic precincts was a paltry 5 percent. Key Black precincts reported voter turnout of 15 percent. The city's average turnout that year was 20.5 percent.

Hispanic leaders say this weakness at the polls is a combination of apathy and a sizeable contingent of recent immigrants, legal and illegal, who cannot vote. The Hispanic population also tends to be younger.

African Americans are far more politically entrenched.

Though they amount to less than 20 percent of District 8's residents, Blacks have flexed their political might by voting more consistently and more often as a unified bloc than any other group.

"We've been effective because we communicate well," says Heather Jenkins, a young African American who serves as Feliciano Vera's campaign manager. "It's been proven over time that African Americans can put certain personal issues and differences aside when it comes to these elections. We know how to come together."

Still, Jenkins is a friend of Vera's and says she is helping him because she believes he is a young leader who isn't bogged down by the profound differences at play in the district.

She and others say the effectiveness of Black voters stems partly from the involvement of clergy and churches. Churches historically have been the centers of African-American political and social action, nurturing leaders like Dr. Martin Luther King, Jr. and the Reverend Jesse Jackson. That role comes alive in the weeks leading up to elections as churches gear up to turn out the vote.

"You have every preacher in African-American churches the Sunday before the election telling them that it's their duty to go out and vote," says Avelar. "That has a tremendous impact."

But in the Hispanic community, he says, "about 90 percent of Latinos are Catholics. The Catholic Church is scrupulous about not getting involved. So, if we're lucky, they'll make an announcement that Tuesday is an election day."

Hispanics also lack the shared crucible of the civil rights movement and the struggle to gain the right to vote.

Leah Landrum-Taylor, who supports Mike Johnson, says the diligence of Black voters was forged by that experience.

"It was so important in my family," she says, "that one of the rites of passage when I turned 18 was we got our voter registration form. This was a major major thing."

"On the way down to the polls," she says, "my mom and dad explained to me the history of how we got this right, that when I was born, this was something that was still being fought."

The emerging political competition between African Americans and Hispanics in District 8 is also playing out in other arenas.

The Roosevelt Elementary School District, located within city council District 8, was for years controlled by African Americans. In the past five years, the struggle for control of the school district has been a well-publicized donnybrook.

Latinos rose to power on the school board following the 1996 dismissal of administrator Charles Townsel, an African American. Townsel, who is now running for the city council seat, had misued school district funds. Ward-style political infighting continues, particularly among the Latinos, including board member Carlos Avelar.

The reversal of Black political fortunes at the school board level was just one more reminder that Hispanic power is on the rise in District 8.

And now, after years controlling the local politics, Blacks are talking openly about being left behind.

"People feel unheard and invisible sometimes," says Leah Landrum-Taylor.

Reverend Oscar Tillman, head of the Maricopa County NAACP, recently told a meeting of the state's redistricting commission, which is preparing new congressional and state legislative districts, that the new political maps are being drawn solely to benefit Hispanics.

"If you're talking about working together," says Tillman, "you don't stand there and talk about adding all these Hispanic groups and not talk about including other groups. That sent a message."

◆ ◆ ◆

In this complex landscape, voters must decide who's best suited to get the district the attention it needs at City Hall.

At 25, Vera is the youngest candidate in the race. Opponents call him "the kid." But there's nothing kid-like in his grasp of district and city issues. A Harvard graduate, who was born and grew up in south Phoenix, he can't resist turning the discussion of every topic into an Ivy League oral report. He talks about "multi-modality," "unidimensional measures," "implementation perspective," "pro-active strategies," and "empowering relationships."

"I'm always telling him to use a nickel word," says Luz Gutierrez, who is part of the Latino Political Action Coalition that supports Vera.

Vera sees the totality of Phoenix. An irrepressible policy gadfly, in the past few years he's been a member of the South Mountain Village Planning Commission and a researcher and intern at the Phoenix City Manager's office. He's dived into community debates over illegal dumping, affordable housing, transit and homelessness in his own district as well as throughout the city. He was among the coalition of neighborhood leaders who fought the expansion of Innovative Waste Utilization, a toxic-waste facility in south Phoenix.

Vera is concentrating on creating a coalition of progressive Anglos, Blacks and Hispanics. His prime issues include better affordable housing, essential services and economic development for the district's have-not neighborhoods, building on the progress that Williams made in attracting new development, and solving the bad land-planning and zoning patterns that have made a mess of many older neighborhoods in the district.

Fimbres, 33, is Vera's chief Latino rival, and he portrays Vera as the hand-picked candidate of the older, washed up Hispanic leadership. He sees himself as the new voice of the district's rising Latino masses.

Born in the Golden Gate community that was erased by the expansion of Sky Harbor Airport in the 1980s, he studied at ASU in the 1990s. He served on the Arizona Board of Regents as a student, and now works for a social service agency administering state-funded anti-tobacco programs.

Fimbres has a parochial view of diversity and a generally poor grasp of city concerns.

Despite the booming cultural and religious diversity of the region, he sees and talks about a world and district devoted to "Judeo-Christian values."

His priorities are to develop more affordable housing, improve basic city services, pass a paid holiday recognizing Cesar Chavez, see to it that more minorities are hired at City Hall, and make sure the city's upcoming redistricting effort doesn't dilute minority power.

However, he knows nothing about two issues that matter not just to his district but to the city as a whole: the current Maricopa County proposal to consolidate downtown homeless services in a single campus, and efforts to revitalize the beleaguered neighborhoods around the Matthew Henson public housing project, west of Seventh Avenue at Buckeye Road.

Fimbres is campaigning hard to get out the vote in south Phoenix's Latino-dominated neighborhoods where the Southwest Voter Registration Education Project had such success last year. His signs have been visible all over the district for several months.

Yet Mike Johnson is counting on the African American bloc—and the weakness of the two other Blacks in the race, Carolyn T. Lowery and Charles Townsel—to give him the advantage. If past elections are any guide, the 47 year-old Johnson, stands to gain from whopping majorities in heavily Black neighborhoods, where turnout typically runs twice that of heavily Hispanic precincts.

Johnson's priorities don't differ much from those of his chief opponents. He cites the need to upgrade city services and infrastructure, add affordable housing and fight the blight that plagues many areas. His 22 years with the Phoenix Police Department, some of it in community affairs work, engrained in him the need for more comprehensive youth programs.

"We create problems," he says, "when we create programs that take kids only up until the age of 15 to 16 years old, then we just put them out there on the street."

Johnson, who now runs a security company, has lived in the district for three years. And he says that in his time on the force—working from Maryvale to Buckeye to South Mountain—he came to know the city and district well enough to understand the conflicts of its increasing diversity.

Though long considered the city's forgotten quarter, south and central Phoenix is hardly that now. If Census trends continue—and there's no reason to think they won't—District 8 is a preview of what more of Phoenix will look like in years to come.

"This district's got to be about looking at people as people," says Johnson. "Not trying to make one better than another, pit the old against the new. It's going to take a strong person to do that and be fair."

18. Subtle Racial Politics in the Twenty-first Century

Rob Gurwitt

The 2001 mayoral election in Cleveland illustrates changes in racial politics. While African Americans still vote most often for Black candidates and Whites most often vote for White candidates, anyone running for public office now has to campaign in all communities. Racial issues by themselves are no longer the deciding ones in all elections. Voting patterns are changing and, consequently, so are local political campaigns. In November 2001, former County Commissioner Jane Campbell, a White woman, was elected the 55th Mayor of Cleveland on a platform of making Cleveland a safer, healthier, more livable city with a stonger economy.

There is an election for mayor this fall in Cleveland. Nearly a dozen people are running, and, as you might imagine, it is a free-for-all. Packs of politicians are appearing at union halls, churches, sidewalk rallies. Any candidate is likely to turn up in any corner of the city. White aspirants are stumping in the Black community. Black hopefuls are working hard for White votes. It is difficult to single out a racial or ethnic standard-bearer anywhere in the bunch.

It's normal urban politics, you might say, except that it's not normal at all in Cleveland. More than 30 years ago, this was the first major city in America to elect a Black mayor, and it has been fixated on its racial divisions ever since. For decades, major municipal elections in Cleveland have been about race and very little else. The last time City Hall was genuinely up for grabs, in 1989, the city split straight down the color line, even though the two major contenders were both African American. A blurred racial landscape like the current one represents dramatic political change for Cleveland.

But it is not a change unique to Cleveland. This relaxation of racial politics has been taking place for some time around the country. Cities everywhere seem eager to confound old expectations. There are now nearly 500 Black mayors in the United States, a substantial increase over the 314 a decade ago. And of the 11 Black mayors in cities with more than 400,000 residents, most were not chosen by Black majorities.

Houston, Dallas, San Francisco, Denver and Minneapolis—none with a Black population greater than 30 percent—all have Black mayors. Baltimore, about two-thirds Black, voted in 1999 for Martin O'Malley, a White city councilman, to replace the African-American Kurt Schmoke. St. Louis, which is 51 percent Black, this year elected a White mayor, Francis Slay, after a cam-

SOURCE: Rob Gurwitt, "Black, White, and Blurred: The Subtle Urban Politics of the Twenty-first Century," *Governing* (September, 2001), pp. 20–24. Copyright © 2001 by Rob Gurwitt. Reprinted by permission of the author.

paign that was far less racially charged than the 1997 contest between two Black candidates, one of whom had the overwhelming support of White voters.

In Philadelphia last year, John Street—who first made his political name in the 1970s as an activist within the African-American community—became mayor after a contest against a White opponent in which race hardly figured as a subject at all. And this past summer, Los Angeles elected James Hahn, a White candidate who won in large part because of his solid support in the Black community. It isn't difficult to make the case for the headline on a story in the *Christian Science Monitor* a while back, "Racial politics subside in cities."

There is a difference between subsiding and disappearing. In both St. Louis and Philadelphia, the campaigns may have been free of racial opportunism, but the voters themselves split mostly along racial lines; the winner was the one who got more crossovers. And as the Los Angeles mayor's race suggests, it doesn't take much to inflame racial sensitivities: The White candidate won in Los Angeles because of solid support among Blacks and moderate and more conservative White voters, which he consolidated by tying his Latino opponent to the cocaine trade, in one of the more blatant racial stereotyping ads in a recent campaign.

So it's not so much that racial politics have abated in America's big cities, it's that they've changed, taken on a new format and new language. Cleveland is as good an example as any. During the tenure of the outgoing mayor, Michael R. White, city government made great progress in discarding its old racial prisms. Still, poverty, unemployment, low-performing schools, an aging population, housing segregation and other urban ills continue to hamper the city, and these are matters that community leaders and city residents do not wish to have forgotten down at City Hall. What they haven't been able to decide yet is whether the race of the person occupying the mayor's office matters in getting the problems solved.

It took this year's campaign in Cleveland an inordinately long time to get started. That is because the entire city had to wait upon the decision of Mayor White, who became the city's second African-American mayor in 1989 and now, after three terms, is the longest-serving mayor in its history. It was initially assumed that there was a Black heir apparent—Stephanie Tubbs Jones, who used to be the county prosecutor and now represents much of Cleveland in the U.S. House.

But Tubbs Jones decided not to run, and her decision served to accentuate the racial blurring. There are two announced Black candidates, state Representative John Barnes, Jr. and Raymond Pierce, a former mid-level official in the Clinton administration, but neither has much of a political base in the city. Barnes won legislative office largely on the strength of voter loyalty to his father, a former city councilman; his only attention-getting role has been as chairman of a roving statewide Commission on African-American Males. Pierce, though he has won respect as a good speaker and hard campaigner, remains essentially unknown to much of the city.

That has left three White candidates free to scramble for Black votes, largely on the basis of their history of concern for inner-city social welfare issues. Cuyahoga County Commissioner Jane Campbell, a liberal Democrat, won broad popularity for her oversight of the county's transition to welfare reform and, as a former state legislator, has long-standing ties to the city's East Side, where most African Americans live. Tim McCormack, another county commissioner, also has made a name for himself as a child welfare advocate. Bill Denihan, a public administrator who had been director of public safety under White and director of natural resources at the statewide level, became head of the county's child welfare department in 1999. He won broad respect in that position for setting the politically troubled department on a more even keel.

In the last days before the October 2 primary, no one is quite sure what role race is likely to play in determining the outcome. But the suggestion that racial issues may be just a sideshow is a striking development in Cleveland's political history. To understand how it came to this juncture, it is important to know something about Mike White's 12 years in office.

When White first ran for mayor, no promise he made carried more weight than his insistence that he would treat the city's east and west sides equally—or, as he put it, that he would say the same things on the East Side that he said on the West. For generations, Cleveland was, in essence, two cities separated by the Cuyahoga River. The west side was White and ethnic, the east African American, except for some neighborhoods along its fringes. Not surprisingly, after Carl Stokes was elected as the first Black mayor in 1967 and city government began opening up—before Stokes, City Hall had pretty much been off limits to the African-American community—struggles over allocation of the city's resources took on the convenient shorthand of east versus west.

When White first ran in 1989, his opponent in the general election was the African-American president of the city council, George Forbes. Forbes—who now heads the NAACP in the city—was an autocratic leader, and both on the council and in his regular radio show he displayed little interest in treating the concerns of West Siders diplomatically. So when it came time to vote that year, White voters were drawn to White on more than the strength of his argument that there was no place for racial division in running City Hall; it was also, simply put, the fact that he was not Forbes. As Norman Krumholz, a professor of urban affairs at Cleveland State University and the city's former planner, puts it, "People on the West Side were waiting in the weeds to vote against George Forbes."

A starkly race-based election such as that could not happen these days in Cleveland. And this is due in no small part to White's years in office. He demanded solid performance from his employees, and if they didn't deliver, he came down hard on them, regardless of their race. When issues arose that had the potential to push racial hot buttons, White did the unexpected. He lobbied to end the city's long and debilitating experiment with court-ordered school busing, and even allowed the Ku Klux Klan to hold a rally in downtown Cleveland.

As a self-described moderate-to-conservative, White was part of a generation of mayors—along with counterparts such as Steve Goldsmith of Indianapolis, John Norquist of Milwaukee and Dennis Archer of Detroit—who shared a belief in running city government efficiently and with a broad public in mind, rather than using it to broker the demands of competing identity groups. This was a collection of politicians who understood, as Swarthmore College political scientist Keith Reeves puts it, that "when you look at folks in these cities, African Americans and Latinos and the Whites who are coming back into the cities, at the end of the day they want to make sure their cities are safe, their kids are taken care of, they're going to get a quality education, and the quality of services are such that they believe their tax dollars are well spent." From the beginning, White spoke of Cleveland as a single city and focused his attention on issues with broad appeal: developing its downtown, redeveloping its neighborhoods and fixing its schools.

The result is a place that looks quite different from the one he took over. There is, of course, the famous downtown makeover: new sports stadiums, the Rock and Roll Hall of Fame, a revitalized warehouse district. There is also progress on the school front. In 1998 White gained power to appoint the school board—fighting off charges that he was undermining African-American voters by doing so—and three years ago brought in a new administrator, Barbara Byrd-Bennett, from New York; Byrd-Bennett is now widely considered one of the most effective and popular public officials in the city.

Just as important, there are signs that some of the city's neighborhoods are regaining their health. Since 1992, says Community Development Director Linda Hudecek, private lenders have put $4.3 billion into Cleveland's neighborhoods, thanks in part to pressure from City Hall, and the results are evident on both sides of the river: New housing developments dot the city, some of them scatter-site, some of them much like suburban tracts, and they in turn are beginning to spark commercial revitalization.

Not surprisingly, all of this has begun to transform the city's politics. When a city council coup in 1999 ousted President Jay Westbrook and replaced him with Mike Polensek, a council veteran from a once solidly White ethnic ward on the far East Side, the central issue was whether the council had been too compliant in going along with White, whose strong personality and my-way-or-the-highway attitude had alienated other politicians. Race was essentially irrelevant: Each side was racially mixed.

Slowly but noticeably, Cleveland voters have begun dismantling their habit of looking at everything through the filter of race. The progress is subtle: When White ran for his last term in 1997, he did well citywide but lost most of the White precincts on the West Side. "He was dismayed," says his pollster Bob Dykes, "because in some of those areas, in the worst areas for him, he got, say, 30 percent of the vote, while his opponent (a White city council member) got 70 percent. I pointed out to him that when Carl Stokes ran in 1967 and 1969 there were whole wards of the city where he only got 10 percent, and there were a bunch of Black precincts where he did not lose a single vote. Not a single one! That's how racially polarized this city was 30 years ago. So is race still a factor in politics? You better believe it. But it's a factor, not *the* factor."

Despite all the physical signs of renewal, the 2000 Census was not encouraging for Cleveland. It showed the city losing 28,000 residents during the 1990s, a 5.4 percent drop that took it to 478,000 people; of the 243 cities and counties around the country with more than 100,000 residents, only 17 lost population more rapidly. "One of the fastest-growing groups moving out of the city is the

Black middle class," says Mike Polensek. "Which should send shock waves, because this city cannot afford to lose the Black middle class. And Hispanics on the West Side are moving south and west. Why do people move? Better schools, better housing opportunities, safer streets—all the historic reasons that 'White flight' took place. What we have come to realize is it's not White flight, it's economic flight. So this is our decade of decision: We rebuild, we stabilize our neighborhoods, or Cleveland will be the hole in the doughnut."

The truth is, there are two ways of looking at where the city is these days. You can get a sense of this if you drive around the Hough neighborhood, which sits in the middle of the East Side, and was where the 1968 riots began. Hough is one of the more remarkable experiments in neighborhood revitalization anywhere in America. Developers have scattered enormous suburban-style homes—mini-mansions, really—around the neighborhood; they sell for as much as $700,000 and are filled with upscale African-American families. There is a suburban-style shopping center, Church Square, right next to Beacon Place, a market-rate townhome development that is entirely sold out and—without any special efforts having been made—racially mixed.

"The other day," says Mike Cox, Cleveland's parks and recreation commissioner, "I get to 79th and Church Square and there's this young White female walking her dog at 6:30 in the evening. Who would have expected to see that in this part of the city?"

Yet all around the new development is the Hough that Clevelanders have known for decades: miles of beaten-down blocks with boarded-up homes, cratered brick industrial buildings, glum-looking garden apartments with kids playing in weedy, abandoned lots next door, and young men gathered aimlessly on the corner. It is all a suggestion of how far Cleveland still has to go. Charles See, who runs a program for ex-offenders based on the near West Side, probably puts the city's dilemma best when he says, "If I have a thousand-pound weight on my foot and you remove 500 of those pounds, I still feel that remaining 500 pounds quite intensely."

This is the ground on which the mayor's contest is being fought, and many people who have surveyed it, White and Black, insist that in many respects race is simply irrelevant. Our highest unemployment rates," says Ed Rybka, a White city councilman, "are in the African-American community—we need to develop job training, day care facilities, the ability to transport people to where the jobs are—but as glaring as the needs are there, the people who need to have this addressed are Black, White and Hispanic."

The Reverend Marvin McMickle, one of the city's most politically active Black ministers, says that mayoral candidates sometimes bring up racial issues with him, and he tells them to talk about something else. "That's not the issue," says McMickle, whose Antioch Baptist Church sits in the midst of a mixed poor and lower-middle-income Black neighborhood not far from Hough. "There's no other race to relate to if you live in this neighborhood. These neighborhood residents want to talk about jobs, medical care, functional public education, things like that. When was the last time the curbs were replaced here? When was the last legitimate time a small business went in along the main street through Hough? What will it cost to keep neighborhood business owners who are trying to stabilize neighborhoods one block at a time? These issues are citywide."

Yet it's also true that McMickle worked hard to persuade Stephanie Tubbs Jones to run for mayor, and was one of about 100 African-American community leaders who met to plot strategy just after she'd announced she didn't want to leave Washington. To understand this, it helps to see the results of a Gallup Poll Social Audit released in July. That survey of 2,000 people across the country found Whites to be considerably more optimistic about race relations than Blacks, and Blacks growing more pessimistic about progress in such areas as equal housing and equal educational opportunity. In Cleveland itself, there remains an intense awareness among Black politicians that there is a limit to how high they can aspire—there are 10 city council positions, a few seats in the state legislature, Tubbs Jones' seat in Congress, and the mayoralty of Cleveland. Winning countywide is difficult, and statewide, they believe, impossible.

It should be no surprise, then, that some African-American leaders still have an abiding conviction that a Black mayor will, quite simply, be more attuned to Black sensitivities. "What's at stake is not just the prestige of a Black mayor but also the power of that mayor to appoint," McMickle says. "It's not just the one position of mayor that's at stake but the many places where the hand of the mayor reaches."

Even these, however, are ambiguous currents. When Tubbs Jones withdrew as White's heir apparent, some Black leaders were troubled that there would be no Black candidate of citywide stature. On the other hand, they had trouble reaching a consensus on how to proceed, other than by listing a set of issues they wanted addressed—improving emergency services, restoring an inner-city trauma center, creating youth programs, developing a biomedical technology program. A group of White, West Side ministers could have come up with pretty much the same list.

It is a fact of political life in Cleveland that whoever does replace Mike White will have to do it on his or her own. There is no White-run political machine in town, and the one attempt to build a political organization in the Black community—begun by former Congressman Louis Stokes—petered out after he retired. White himself is a political loner, and never groomed a replacement—as McMickle points out, "I think Mike could say, 'I won this office the hard way, and whoever does it next will have to do the same.'"

As the October 2 primary approaches, there's no question that all the candidates are looking forward to a stronger showing among voters of their own race than across racial lines. But they aren't looking forward to it with anything like the certainty they would have felt just a few years ago. As Charles See puts it, "Of course race matters. But folks rise to a level of sophistication at a time like this: They want to know what is the likelihood of a candidate delivering on what he or she promised. Everyone knows what to *say* these days. We want to know where you've *been*."

19. Culture Wars and City Politics

Elaine Sharp

Much of city and suburban politics is focused around economic development or specific policy areas like public safety. The problems and costs of basic city services also are at the center of many urban government conflicts. However, the city is also the focus of highly charged culture wars issues—these include gay rights, pornography, Nazi marches, and abortion clinics. This article explores local government's role in these social conflicts.

In communities across the United States, strident social conflicts are posing thorny problems for local governance. In some communities, these stem from controversy over abortion and the efforts of the pro-life movement to disrupt the functioning of abortion clinics. In other communities, controversy surrounds gay rights initiatives as struggles emerge over ordinances to provide civil rights protections for gays or efforts to ban such protections. In still other communities, episodes over book banning and antipornography crusades, sometimes spearheaded by public officials, have sparked controversy over free speech, women's civil rights, and the community's efforts to enforce moral standards. And, in a number of communities, the efforts of authorities to deal with the emergence of neo-Nazi groups or with particular hate crimes directed at religious minorities have been embedded in controversy. In contemporary America, such controversies reflect a new era of conflict, and they have, on many occasions, placed city governments in the eye of a firestorm.

URBAN SCHOLARSHIP AND CULTURE WARS

Scholars of urban politics have largely overlooked this category of conflict. There are exceptions, of course. There are some relevant case studies, several of which will be referred to often in this article. However, relatively few of these case studies are written by urban scholars or approached with a focus on local government's role in the controversy. There is also a substantial body of work on racial and ethnic conflict and protest activity in U.S. cities. However, the culture wars that are the focus of this analysis are arguably distinct from racial and ethnic conflict, even if there are some important commonalities between the two. And, if anything, contemporary treatments of protest over racial issues are moving toward rational self-interest explanations rather than explanations that emphasize the cultural bases and nonmaterial stakes that underlie the controversies of interest in this article.

SOURCE: Elaine B. Sharp, "Culture Wars and City Politics," *Urban Affairs Review*, Vol. 31, No. 6, (July, 1996), pp. 738–758. Copyright © 1996 by Sage Publications. Reprinted by permission of the publisher, Sage Publications.

There are several likely reasons for urban scholars' lack of attention to the sorts of social conflict at issue here. For one thing, police, prosecutors, and the local judiciary are likely to play a relatively central role in these controversies because decisions are made about parade permits, arrest tactics for protesters, enforcement of hate-crimes statutes, changes in human rights ordinances; changes to and prosecutions stemming from pornography laws, and the like, yet these institutions are among the least well integrated into mainstream theories of urban politics and are less often incorporated in urban research.

Lack of attention may also stem from the ideological complexity of the issues in contemporary culture wars. In the 1960s, activism was associated with the Left, and studies of social protest and civil rights agitation attacted the research interest of sympathetic intellectuals. However, the *status quo challengers* in contemporary culture-war controversies include activists such as abortion clinic protesters and pornography crusaders as well as gay rights activists and feminists.

The character of this issue domain is an obstacle to scholarly attention in another way as well. The elevation of *interests* over *values* as the focus of inquiry in political science leaves the matter of morals-based social conflict on the periphery of the intellectual enterprise. For example, there has long been an assumption that groups based on expressive and solidary values are unstable and less likely to be of relevance to policy formation than are materially based interest groups, and the groups at issue in these culture wars are expressive and solidary groups par excellence. Furthermore, the very intensity that makes these conflicts attractive to the media marginalizes them as a topic for urban scholarship:

> The events themselves tend to be presented as flashes of political insanity— spasmodic symptoms of civic maladjustment—against the routine conduct of public affairs. Such events are rarely related to one another, but appear to be merely "disparate" outbursts by disparate (and sometimes "desperate") individuals and groups. Commentators make little effort to explain and interpret these stories and the issues that underlie them, to place them in a broader frame of reference.

To the extent that the social conflicts emerging from contemporary culture wars are viewed as irrational flashes of political insanity on the fringes of the normal life of the community, they are also distanced from the mainstream of urban political theory in particular. . . .

Culture-war conflicts are critical aspects of urban governance, however, for several reasons. Although Congress, the federal courts, and state governments are significant institutions in the ongoing development of policy regarding abortion, pornography, hate crimes, and the like, city governments are critical to the policy process as well, in initiating policy change and in implementing federal and state policy. With respect to policy initiation, for example, a number of cities have enacted local ordinances that offer civil rights protections for homosexuals, and others are grappling with the issue. City governments have also been on the front line in attempting to deal with the potential, and in some cases the reality, of violence around abortion clinics. The concept of a buffer zone around abortion clinics clearly emerged from the difficulties that local police experienced in handling this potential for violence—experience that led to congressional passage of the Freedom of Access to Clinic Entrances Act in 1993.

It is important to note that social conflict and the implementation of policies addressing it involve local government in a web of intergovernmental relations that are at least as important, and as complex, as are intergovernmental relations surrounding policies with material stakes. The rights-based federal laws that are at issue in the social regulatory realm affect large numbers of individuals, often receive minimal federal enforcement attention, and often are implemented by state and local authorities, "who are permitted much discretion." In the case of pornography, the primary regulatory is "state and local government with the principal emphasis at the municipal level" because of the Supreme Court's ruling that "community values" must shape the regulation of pornography.

Culture-war controversies are also important phenomena from the local government perspective because of the substantial consequences that such controversies can have for local officials and the communities they serve. The dollar costs of maintaining social order in the face of strident social conflicts can be quite high, and the outcomes of local elections can turn on the dynamics of these culture-war issues. Furthermore, because the emergence of these explosive issues often draws national media attention, local governments find themselves in the spotlight, with the reputation and image of the community at stake. To the subtleties of image, one can add the realities of lives saved or lost, and injuries and property damage suffered or averted, depending upon local government's handling of the explosive issues in the culture-war domain.

CASE SELECTION

The purpose of this article is to explore the various roles, both proactive and reactive, that city governments may play in emergent social conflicts. Ultimately, theoretical development in this area will require explanation of variation in city government responses. Because of the limited attention that these conflicts have received and because of the lack of urban theory concerning them, however, my goal here is more modest—that is, to develop a theoretically rich typology of city government roles in such conflicts. To enhance its theoretical potential, the typology will be based in part on application of concepts from social-movements, political-entrepreneurship, and agenda-setting theory.

However, the typology should also be empirically grounded. In this analysis, that empirical grounding consists of analyzing cases of community controversy involving abortion clinic protest, gay rights, regulation of pornography, protests against judicial handling of sexual assault, and controversy over neo-Nazis. Table 5.3 lists the cases that will be used. The cases were chosen based upon the availability of published accounts of community controversies and because they most clearly epitomize the issues of sexual morality and religion that are at the heart of contemporary culture wars. The cases constitute a con-

TABLE 5.3   **Cases of Community Conflict Over Culture War Issues**

Issue Area	Case Coverage	Source(s)
Abortion clinic protest	Conflict concerning Operation Rescue activities in Brookline, Massachusetts, late 1980s	Hertz (1991)
Abortion clinic protest	Controversy concerning an abortion clinic in Fargo, North Dakota, 1980s	Ginsburg (1989)
Pornography regulation	Conflict concerning an antipornography ordinance with a feminist, civil rights orientation, Minneapolis, Minnesota, 1983	Downs (1989)
Pornography regulation	Events concerning the city's adoption of an antipornography ordinance with a feminist, civil rights, orientation, Indianapolis, Indiana, 1984	Downs (1989)
Gay rights	Conflict concerning a drive for gay rights legislation in New York City, 1970–1971	Marotta (1981)
Gay rights	Conflict concerning the adoption of a gay rights ordinance in Wichita, Kansas, 1977	Various journalistic accounts, assembled by the author
Gay rights	Emergence of a politically mobilized gay community in San Francisco (1960s) and the adoption of a gay rights ordinance in 1977	D'Emilio (1983) and Shilts (1982)
Hate-group regulation	Conflict concerning plans by a Chicago-based Nazi group to march in Skokie, Illinois, 1977	Downs (1985)
Judicial handling of rape	Effort to recall Judge Simonson, Madison, Wisconsin, after his bench comments during a rape case, 1977	Woliver (1993)
Judicial handling of sexual assault	Effort to recall Judge Reinecke, Grant County, Wisconsin, after his bench comments concerning the sexual promiscuity of a five-year-old sexual-assault victim	Woliver (1993)

venience sample rather than a representative random sample. However, the purpose of the analysis is not hypothesis testing and generalization but exploration of the potential diversity of city government roles in social conflicts. Fortunately for this purpose, not only were there cases in each issue area, but the cases involve large and small communities and conservative and liberal-progressive communities; there were cases that received national attention, and cases that did not. The time frames for the cases vary as well, in line with the cycles of activism that have occurred in each issue area.

Finally, there is variation both across the cases and within the cases (i.e., across the various phases of each case) in the amount of conflict and controversy evoked by the issue. Brief descriptions of each of the cases illustrate these variations in level of conflict. In the case of abortion clinic protests in Brookline, Massachusetts, there were disruptions over several months as Operation Rescue repeatedly descended upon local abortion clinics, blocking entry when possible and attracting street-side shouting matches between rescuers and pro-choice opponents. Local police were forced to provide extra coverage at a cost of at least $17,000 per day in overtime pay. In the Fargo, North Dakota, case, controversy over the scheduled opening of the community's first abortion clinic was initially confined to low-key prayer vigils; then a new pro-life group emerged, which "introduced a confrontational style" of protest, bringing ABC television coverage of the activities of the militant group, and a local reaction to the group, culminating in a variety of legal actions against them.

In Minneapolis, Minnesota, the city council passed a controversial ordinance that prohibited "discrimination [against women] by trafficking in pornography" and allowed a woman to sue for damages against the purveyors of pornography if she could show a causal link between an assault she suffered and a particular piece of pornography. The ordinance was vetoed by the mayor, but a revised version was enacted at a meeting featuring the arrest of 24 women "for disrupting the council's proceedings." In Indianapolis, Indiana, an antipornography ordinance modeled on that of Minneapolis was enacted with much less controversy, despite opposition from the Indianapolis Civil Liberties Union, the city's Urban League, its equal opportunity board, and its legal staff.

In Madison, Wisconsin, Judge Archie Simonson's comments about the dress of women clashed with the rape reform efforts of women's groups attempting "to change the public's perception of rape from a crime of passion to a crime of violence" and evoked protests and a campaign to recall Simonson. With the support of many governmental organizations, politicians, and groups, Simonson was successfully recalled from the bench. In the Grant County, Wisconsin, case, parents organized to recall Judge Reinecke after his bench comments about the sexual permissiveness or promiscuity of a five-year-old victim of sexual assault. This recall effort was more divisive than that involving Judge Simonson, because law enforcement officers, the county prosecutor, the local bar, and local newspapers rallied to support Judge Reinecke. In a recall election, Reinecke retained his judgeship, capturing 51 percent of the vote.

Of the cases involving proposed gay rights legislation, two exhibited considerable controversy. The New York City case featured a series of high-profile protest actions by the Gay Activists' Alliance, at least one of which turned into a melee between local police officers and gay activists. The proposed gay rights ordinance ultimately stalled in committee. In Wichita, Kansas, the proposal for a gay rights ordinance split the community and the city council, which, after heated hearings, passed the ordinance on a split vote. With the support of the local district attorney, a petition drive was mounted to force the ordinance to a referendum, in which it was defeated overwhelmingly. By contrast, a gay rights ordinance was enacted in San Francisco in 1977 on a 10–1 city council vote with only minimal criticism. The ordinance, the "pet project" of Harvey Milk, the first openly gay municipal official in the United States, reflected the substantial electoral muscle of the gay community. The sole vote against the ordinance came from Councilman Dan White in an ongoing feud with Milk that culminated in White's assassination of both Milk and Mayor Moscone.

In the Skokie, Illinois case, the National Socialist Party of America (NSPA) planned a march in the community, home to large numbers of Holocaust survivors, after the Chicago Park District prevented their demonstration in Marquette Park. In response to threatened violence by the Holocaust survivor community, Skokie officials got an injunction to prevent the march and enacted a series of ordinances to deter the activities of such organizations. With help from the American Civil Liberties Union, the NSPA filed several suits, which were eventually decided against Skokie.

A TAXONOMY OF LOCAL GOVERNMENT ROLES IN SOCIAL CONTROVERSIES

Exploration of these cases yields evidence of a variety of different roles that local governments play in social controversies. This section delineates six distinctive roles that were so identified: evasion, repression, hyperactive responsiveness, responsiveness, entrepreneurial instigation, and unintentional instigation.

Initially, it might be expected that local politicians would avoid the volatile issues that evoke culture wars or, when they are raised by citizen activists, evade them as much as possible by referring them to task forces or using other responses that provide access or agenda responsiveness while evading policy responsiveness. After all, the intense minorities that are typically involved in culture-war conflicts can pose problems for political officials, whose constituencies may be alienated by extremist actions or policies that evoke strident protest from opposing single-issue groups. The evasion approach is indeed evident in several of the cases. Skokie officials initially planned to allow the Nazi march, reasoning that it would be best to keep it routine and hope that the event would pass unnoticed and without disturbance. This was precisely the meaning of the "quarantine" policy that major Jewish organizations espoused as a way of preventing anti-Semitic groups from attaining the publicity that they desired. As I will discuss later, this intentionally low-key approach ultimately backfired for Skokie officials. Evasion also characterizes the response of key New York officials in the case of the failed drive for gay rights legislation in New York in 1971. Although a bill was introduced and many council members gave encouraging responses to activists pressing for the legislation, then-Mayor Lindsay delayed making a public announcement in favor of the ordinance, and without his public support, the legislation remained bottled up in council committee.

Evasion is characterized by symbolic politics and other low-key efforts to maintain the status quo. But, at other times, local governments take more overt and aggressive action to maintain the status quo in the face of challengers.

During an intense culture controversy, especially one that imposes substantial costs on local government, local officials may respond in ways that approximate Tarrow's definition of repression—that is, action to "either depress collective action or raise the cost of its two main preconditions—the organization and mobilization of opinion." In Brookline, for example, city officials filed suit against Operation Rescue under the provisions of the Racketeer Influenced and Corrupt Organizations Act (RICO), ostensibly to recover the roughly $75,000 in police overtime costs that had resulted from the organization's "rescue" effort. However, the repressive purpose of filing the suit is clear from the case. None of the Operation Rescue leaders had monetary resources that the town could have recaptured, and the town counsel did not pursue the litigation once suit was filed. However, the chair of the town council explained that "the RICO suit had done its job, that it had scared off potential rescuers and was largely responsible for the group's dwindling number."

Concerned Citizens for Children in Grant County also found itself subject to repression. Judge Reinecke's supporters included law enforcement officials, and the husband of an activist was nearly run off the road by a county police officer in what was considered a "life-threatening situation." There was also a more subtle form of tacit repression, as Woliver. explained: "People active in the recall recounted their fears for their families, businesses and futures in Grant County because of their involvement in a controversy against one of only two local judges."

In Fargo, court decisions and city council action generated repressive responses to a relatively militant pro-life group, Save-A-Baby, especially when that group received national television attention. The group, which had established a women's clinic to compete with the community's abortion clinic, had been sued by the abortion clinic for using an imitative clinic name and false advertising to lure women with unwanted pregnancies who presumably had been seeking abortion services. The district court issued a preliminary injunction against the pro-life center, mandating "that they change their name and publicity, and inform callers that they do not perform abortions." Ultimately, a county district court jury assessed $23,000 in special damages against the pro-life clinic. The abortion clinic had also sued a leader of the Save-A-Baby group for harassment after he went into the abortion clinic dressed as Santa Claus. The Court ruled in the abortion clinic's favor on this as well, sentencing the Save-A-Baby leader to "two days in jail, a $200 fine, and a year on probation during which he could not be near the abortion clinic." Meanwhile, the city council passed a ban on the picketing of private residences in direct response to the activities of the Save-A-Baby group. Ginsburg argued that these official responses "drew authoritative limits to the range of acceptable behaviors that would be tolerated in the battle over the abortion clinic."

Tarrow argued that even relatively low-level action, such as a requirement for parade permits, should be conceptualized as a form of repression, because "it gives officials an easy way to keep tabs on their [protestors'] organization and encourages them to resort to legal means." By such standards, the Chicago Park District's requirement that the Nazis obtain $250,000 in liability insurance before being allowed to demonstrate in any Chicago park is clearly an example of repression, as were the Skokie ordinances banning the distribution of hate literature or the wearing of military regalia and the Skokie government's effort to get an injunction barring the neo-Nazis from demonstrating in the community. These efforts to repress an organization whose hate message was offensive to the community were all declared unconstitutional by either the Illinois Supreme Court or the federal district and appeals courts.

There are, in short, substantial legal constraints on the repressive responses that local governments can use, even in dealing with the most disruptive culture-war situations. However, there has also been a wave of innovation in the use of the law in these situations, especially as an instrument to repress hate groups. City governments may, for example, take a cue from civil rights attorney Morris Dees, who pioneered in "bankrupting White extremist groups with extraordinary civil judgment."

But local governments do not necessarily act in ways opposed to the challengers of the status quo. Even when vocal minorities are promoting relatively radical changes, local governments can and do play several kinds of roles in support of status quo challengers; and, sometimes, local officials initiate the movement for radical change.

A number of the cases provide evidence of overt and aggressive action in support of status quo challengers. The hyperactive responsiveness to the agenda of an intense minority is a far cry from the stereotype of local officials studiously hiding from the explosiveness of culture-war issues. Characterizing a response as hyperactive is, of course, a normative judgment, suggesting that officials have gone too far or acted rashly. In several of the case studies, however, evidence is presented to suggest such a characterization—evidence suggesting official action that (a) was relatively precipitous, (b) bypassed normal procedures, (c) disregarded obvious legal or constitutional issues, or (d) was some combination of these. For both the Minneapolis and the Indianapolis cases, Downs provides evidence that antipornography ordinances were rushed to enactment, some normal procedures that would have provided input from a broader array of stakeholders were bypassed, decision making was swayed by emotional, one-sided hearings, and the constitutional concerns of city legal staff were overlooked. As a result, Downs' interpretation is that the two cases represent "something all too common in political life—the reluctance of elected officials to be found on the wrong side of an emotionally charged issue which partisans have framed as a matter of good versus evil."

The case of abortion clinic protest in Fargo presents another example of government officials making a relatively precipitous decision, apparently as a result of being swept up in the intense emotions of the issue, without due consideration of constitutional issues, at least until their hyperactive responsiveness was reversed by the action of another official. Shortly before the city's first abortion clinic was to open, a local pro-life organization tried to block the clinic's opening by petitioning the city council to revoke its building permit. With the mayor out of town, the remaining city commission members hurried a vote in favor of the petition, but upon his return, the permit was reinstated by the mayor, who declared that the clinic was a legal enterprise and that the use of local regulations to discriminate against it would embroil the city in pointless litigation.

Local politicians can be responsive to the policy demands of status quo challengers without being hyperactive. This straightforward form of responsiveness is nowhere better illustrated than in the case of Wichita, where the city council passed a gay rights ordinance in 1977. In contrast to the precipitousness, disregard of constitutional issues, and short circuiting of normal procedure that characterize hyperactive responsiveness, city officials in this case took excruciating pains over the ordinance. Before passing the ordinance, Wichita council members heard public comment from both sides at a council meeting, delayed action for a month in order to obtain an opinion from the Kansas attorney general stipulating that the ordinance would not conflict with state law, and had nearly seven hours of hearings on the issue before voting 3–2 in favor. After the positive vote on first reading (in Wichita, an ordinance must be endorsed twice), council delayed action on the second reading to get another ruling on the issue of whether the ordinance would affect the school board and other governmental units.

Local politicians are, of course, not limited to responding to culture-war-style conflicts. They can, and sometimes do, play a role in instigating the conflicts, in one of two ways. Conflict can be intentionally instigated if public officials take on the role of issue entrepreneurs, mobilizing the public on symbolic or morals issues. This entrepreneurial instigation is especially evident in the cases involving pornography crusades. In Minneapolis, a veteran city council member, Charlee Hoyt, served as an entrepreneur for the issue of fighting pornography by using the new weapon of an ordinance defining pornography as a violation of women's civil rights—an innovative approach that was being promulgated by feminist theorists Andrea Dworkin and Catharine MacKinnon. In Indianapolis, both Mayor Hudnut and the local prosecutor, Steven Goldsmith, were issue entrepreneurs for the city's crusade against pornography. Goldsmith had won the prosecutor's office in 1979 on a campaign emphasizing pornography problems and had immediately initiated pornography raids on local establishments. In the early 1980s, Mayor Hudnut pushed the antipornography issue and directed the local police to escalate their crackdown. When Hudnut learned of the innovative ordinance with which Minneapolis had experimented, he established communication between the Indianapolis council and the city council member in Minneapolis who had championed the issue, and he maintained visible and vocal support for passage of the ordinance in Indianapolis.

Entrepreneurial instigation sometimes occurs when local officials, who are elected on platforms stressing pornography, gay rights, or abortion-related issues, follow through with policy initiatives in the culture-war genre. In the Indianapolis pornography case just described, for example, electoral politics positioned prosecutor Goldsmith for a role in promoting an aggressive response to pornography. With respect to gay rights, the same is true of Milk, who won election to a San Francisco council seat as a champion of the gay community and made a ban on gay discrimination his first legislative initiative.

The category entrepreneurial instigation is meant to be reserved for those instances in which public officials serve as the initial promoters of a culture-war issue, in the process mobilizing citizen groups behind the issue. In practice, it may be difficult to distinguish entrepreneurial instigation from another familiar category—co-optation. Although the term is commonly used to refer to the neutralization of the independent agenda of citizen groups by government, McCarthy and Wolfson emphasized the possibility that the apparatus of the state can be co-opted by a social movement. The example of entrepreneurial instigation in the Minneapolis case could be interpreted as co-optation of the state by nonstate activists, in this case, Dworkin and MacKinnon. Although there was a history of antipornography efforts in the community, the radical legal departure represented by Dworkin and MacKinnon's ordinance was made possible when Councilwoman Hoyt "opened her office and all its resources to Dworkin, MacKinnon, and their followers"—a relatively clear-cut statement of co-optation of a segment of the state. Although it may be empirically difficult to make a clear distinction between issue entrepreneurship that is literally initiated by public officials and issue entrepreneurship that public officials take up as a result of being co-opted by activists within a social movement, the distinction itself may not be conceptually important, because both involve entrepreneurial instigation. As Tarrow argued, "protesting groups create political opportunities for elites . . . when opportunistic politicians seize the opportunity created by challengers to proclaim themselves tribunes of the people."

At other times, local officials appear to instigate controversy unintentionally—typically by taking actions that spark the emergence of local protest groups and frame a heretofore nonissue in rights-oriented terms. This unintentional instigation is especially apparent in the early history of the gay rights movement. In San Francisco in the 1960s, the emergence of a politically mobilized gay community was in large part the unintended consequence of aggressive police action against the gay community. The San Francisco police "had a long history of harassing gay bars," and a major scandal in 1959 had revealed that the police had been shaking down a number of gay bar owners for payments, in exchange for which they would be allowed to continue to operate. Aggressive police crackdowns on gay bars continued even after this "gayola" episode, and when a group of Protestant clergy instituted a new organization to work with the gay community, local police attempted to force the cancellation of a benefit dance organized by the group. Failing to stop the dance, the police made an aggressive show of force outside the dance and arrested lawyers for the organization who were challenging the police action. But the ministers and lawyers "provided a legitimacy to the charges of police harassment that the word of a homosexual lacked." More generally, political agitating for gay rights in San Francisco "came alive through the attacks mounted against it by a hostile city administration and police force."

The case of Judge Simonson's recall in Madison provides yet another example of unintentional instigation if one is willing to construe the concept to include catalytic action for a social movement that is already organized. That is precisely the interpretation offered by Woliver, who noted that "A critical mobilizing event, like Simonson's remarks, can actually help an incipient social movement. Whether mobilization occurs, though, also often depends on the facilitation provided by a preexisting social movement."

TABLE 5.4   **A Typology of Local Government's Role in Culture Wars**

	Supportive of Status Quo Challengers	Not Supportive of Status Quo Challengers
First order	Hyperactive responsiveness	Evasion
	Responsiveness	Repression
	Entrepreneurial instigation	
Second order	Unintentional instigation	Unintentional instigation

Yet another version of unintentional instigation is exemplified by the dilemma of Skokie officials, whose choice of a minimalist strategy in response to a planned Nazi march turned out to be a miscalculation. Skokie officials had not understood how strong the response of Holocaust survivors would be. Their anger and threats of violence placed officials unexpectedly in the eye of a firestorm, even though evasion was intended to prevent just such controversy.

This transformation of our interpretation of Skokie's response from one of evasion to unintentional instigation suggests a problem with the typology. If a single behavior or set of behaviors, such as Skokie officials' adoption of a quarantine policy, can be classified in one of two different categories, the typology is not mutually exclusive. The answer to this dilemma lies in recognizing the fact that Skokie officials' unintentional instigation of controversy hinges upon the reaction of nongovernmental groups to local government's action. Similarly, it may be that some local government efforts at repression may instead turn out to be unintentional instigation—for example, if overly aggressive efforts to prevent protest activity by pro-life groups actually sparked a determination on the part of such groups to target the city for high-profile activity. In short, the typology of local government's role in local culture wars perhaps should be conceptualized as including both first-order and second-order responses (see Table 5.4). First-order responses, such as repression, evasion, responsiveness, and intentional instigation, are primarily based upon the intent of the local decision makers who take the action. A second-order response, such as unintentional instigation, hinges upon the interactive effects of governmental actions and the actions of nongovernmental groups that are a party to the controversial issue. As the foregoing examples suggest, unintentional instigation can either be supportive or nonsupportive of status-quo challengers depending upon who is inadvertently mobilized by governmental action.

20. Local Elected Women and Policy-Making

Janet Boles

According to the Center for American Women and Politics 1,670 women served in state legislatures in 2000 and 4,513 women served as mayors or city council members in 1994. As more and more women serve in public office, particularly at the local level, two major questions arise: Does having women rather than men elected to office make any substantive difference? And do women generally accomplish more on "women's issues"—those policy areas in which women hold opinions and focus more concern than the majority of men?

This study examines the impact of women officeholders by looking at the policy-making role of local legislators, male and female, in Milwaukee. The research focuses on changes in six policy areas of special interest to women: sexual assault, domestic violence, child care, displaced homemakers, library services for children, and childbirth in public hospitals.

The purpose here was to answer the following questions: Do male and female elected officials place different priorities on women's issues? Are there differences between male and female elected officials in providing leadership on these issues within local legislative bodies? And has the presence of women in local office affected in other ways the actions and operations of these institutions? Finally, if local female legislators do have a distinctive impact on legislation related to women's interests, are these officials acting as feminist trustees or as delegates from the women's movement? In particular, what role do women's policy networks play in the local decision-making process?

Milwaukee, the site for this study, provides a setting where women's political participation has been extensive and relatively effective. In 1998 there were ten (of twenty-five) female county supervisors; three (of seventeen) alderwomen on the Common Council; and three (of nine) female members of the Milwaukee School Board. These percentages meet or exceed the national average of female representation in that local office. If there is a "critical mass" in terms of numbers and proportions of female colleagues that is a requisite for a distinctive impact by female officeholders, then presumably Milwaukee meets that criterion.

Milwaukee-area women continue to support a wide variety of women's rights organizations. There are two chapters of the National Organization for Women (NOW) and local affiliates of the National Women's Political Caucus (NWPC) and 9to5. *The Milwaukee Area Women's Resource Directory* (1998)

SOURCE: Jane K. Boles, "Local Elected Women and Policy-Making: Movement Delegates or Feminist Trustees," in Susan J. Carroll, ed., *The Impact of Women in Public Office*, Bloomington, Ind.: Indiana University Press, 2001, pp. 68–86. Copyright © 2001 Indiana University Press. Reprinted by permission of the publisher, Indiana University Press.

lists a number of groups and services relevant to this study, including three domestic violence shelters; an abuse hotline and task force on domestic violence; an older women's network; a sexual assault treatment center and two counseling services; a child care resource and referral group; and a nurse-midwifery service. Parallel groups exist on the state level as well: the Wisconsin Women's Network (with 90 member organization) and coalitions on domestic violence, sexual assault, childbirth alternatives, and displaced homemakers.

Interviews were conducted in 1990 with the sixteen women who had served on the Milwaukee County Board of Supervisors or the Milwaukee Common Council since 1966. The same number of men, chosen from districts that closely resemble those represented by their female colleagues, were also interviewed. Although some attempt was made to include both veteran and newly elected officials, the average term for the male sample was twelve years, compared with eight years for female officeholders. Women continue to be comparative "new girls" in local politics.

In addition, thirteen city and county administrators or officials of community-based organizations holding government contracts to deliver services and fourteen leaders of women's organizations were interviewed. All were chosen because of their involvement with one of the six focal policy issues or their concern with women's rights generally.

Most interviews were conducted by the author in the office or home of the interviewee; most lasted 30 to 40 minutes; and all but six respondents allowed taping. Three interviews with former elected officials were conducted by telephone, and one took place in the author's office.

ACTIVITY ON WOMEN'S ISSUES

In general, women officeholders reported activity on more and a broader range of women's issues than did men. Women placed a greater importance on these issues and were more likely to have provided leadership on the Board or Council when related policies were considered.

Initially, the local officials were asked to list any women's issues on which they had worked during their period of service. The mean number of issues on which men were active was 2.06; women, on average, reported activity on 3.69 issues. These figures reflect that women not only were active on more women's issues than were men, but they also defined a "women's issue" differently and more broadly. Whereas male respondents mentioned a total of eleven issues (three dealt with different dimensions of affirmative action), women officeholders recalled 27 different issues, including welfare payments, child support, women in local jails, family recreation programs, homeless families, AIDS, and gay rights.

The role of male and female officeholders on the six focal issues—sexual assault, domestic violence, child care, displaced homemakers, library services for children, and childbirth in public hospitals—was studied in three ways. Each indicated in writing the extent to which that issue had been if special importance to him or her. All were also asked to recall whether those issues had been addressed by the Board or Council during their period of service. Finally, each was questioned about policy outcomes and those colleagues who were most actively involved on each issue.

Although, in practice, both the city and county governments have some programs in each policy area, it is a common perception that one level of local government is "more" responsible for a particular service than is the other. For example, county government in Wisconsin is the primary administrator of social services, including what was then Milwaukee County's only public hospital (but the city's Health Department provides means-tested pre- and postnatal care). Local libraries are a part of municipal government (but the County Federated Library System assures an open borrowing policy for all residents).

To allow for any officeholders who might consider "important" only those issues closely associated with her or his own level of government, respondents were given the option "not a Council/Board issue" in reporting their priorities on the six women's issues. As Table 5.5 indicates, women in city and county office placed a higher level of importance on all six issues than did their male colleagues. This also remains true after those "opting out" of the ranking are dropped from the analysis, even though women were less likely to perceive these issues as "not my job." (Fifteen percent of all responses from women were of this type, compared with 29 percent for men.)

There was no similarly clear-cut pattern differentiating the ability of male and female officeholders to recall examples of policy-making on the six issues. On three of the issues (day care, domestic violence, and sexual assault), there were high levels of awareness of activity among local legislators. Only on the three remaining issue areas did alderwomen (children's library services and displaced-homemaker programs) and female supervisors (childbirth in public hospitals) exhibit markedly greater knowledge of policy-making.

Women officeholders have played an important but not dominant role in shaping policy on day care, domestic violence, and sexual assault. This was confirmed in interviews with urban administrators. Ten (of thirteen administrators) recalled direct contacts with elected officials on one of these policies.

TABLE 5.5 The Priorities of Milwaukee Legislators on Women's Issues

Issue	Common Council		County Board	
	Men	Women	Men	Women
Day care	2.44	1.89	2.00	1.14
Domestic violence	2.33	2.22	1.86	1.14
Sexual assault	2.33	1.67	1.86	1.29
Displaced homemakers	4.00	2.89	2.86	1.86
Children's library services	3.22	2.44	4.29	3.14
Childbirth in public hospitals	4.00	3.00	2.43	1.86

All figures are mean scores: 1 = high/top priority; 2 = important but not a top priority; 3 = some importance; 4 = not at all important; 5 = not a Common Council/County Board issue.

And although roughly equal numbers of male ($n = 9$) and female ($n = 10$) officials were mentioned at least once by a bureaucrat, contacts from women (regarding one of the six issues) made up a larger percentage (63 percent) of the total responses. This is particularly striking in that women constitute a much smaller percentage of elected officials.

It is in qualitative terms, however, that women's leadership on these issues differs most from that of men. Rarely did men volunteer information beyond the policy adopted (e.g., the formation of the Task Force on Sexual Assault and Domestic Violence as a part of city government, the establishment of a sexual assault counseling unit within the District Attorney's office). For several women on the Board or Council, however, the politics of each decision was recalled in vivid and full detail: the funding of the first women's shelter in Milwaukee, despite a motion by a male colleague to deny the request ("I looked at the alderman and said, 'Could I ask you to withdraw your motion before we may need a home for a battered man?' At which point, he did withdraw his motion"); the negotiations with the Chief of Police to establish a special sexual assault unit ("he was backed into a corner by the city's Finance Committee, who held his purse strings . . . he did have to do certain things"); an expanded prosecution unit in the District Attorney's office to handle a greater number of domestic violence cases arising from a new local mandatory arrest policy ("many of your colleagues are attorneys . . . and many of these attorneys feel that it's going to reflect badly on some of their clients if all of a sudden they wind up getting arrested . . . it was held in committee and held in committee . . . ").

Women were more likely to take the lead in initially raising the issue and in establishing new programs and bureaucracies. In the area of day care, for example, women coordinated the first day care needs assessment in both city and county government. Women were key to the establishment of an on-site day care center in the County Courthouse, an (unsuccessful) attempt to open a center in City Hall, and an after-school latchkey program offered through the County Parks System. Male legislators were active in other important but more technical ways: manipulating the committee system to get a day care proposal on the agenda; establishing a voucher system for day care services in the community and a payroll deduction for county employees; expanding the supply of private day care through granting zoning variances; and (unsuccessfully) requiring developers to provide space for day care in exchange for a building permit.

A core group of three female legislators was viewed as leaders on all three visible issues, which would seem to indicate a general advocacy position on behalf of women's issues. Male leaders often played a leadership role on only one issue as a part of some other official position (i.e., Council President, Board Chair, or chair of the Finance, Public Safety, or Judiciary Committee). Exceptions here were men who linked their activity with district interests (e.g., funding for a shelter or day care center) or a general concern for social services. Female officials were somewhat more aware of available grants and services for displaced homemakers. Two of the women had also served as advisers to displaced homemakers' organizations.

Children's library services were also more salient to female legislators. Two related the issue to their own backgrounds as professional educators; two others noted their service on the Library Board, including one (the acknowledged leader) who reported regular meetings with children's librarians to plan the summer reading program. Four others gave examples of their efforts to expand or preserve branch library services in their districts. Interestingly, only one man acted as district ombudsman on library services; the only other specific policy noted (by two men) was the audiovisual library maintained for school use by the County Public Museum—a service the Board eliminated from the 1990 budget.

Childbirth in public hospitals was associated with a number of maternal and infant policies by both men and women. Women again had a higher awareness and a broader knowledge base. For example, two female supervisors knew that the Board had just authorized the modernization of County Hospital's obstetrics unit to include birthing rooms and a more family-oriented style of childbirth. And only women reported personal involvement here in blocking a required drug test for pregnant women receiving welfare ("all that means is that women who are doing cocaine are going to have their babies at home; they're not going to get prenatal care"); dealing with teen pregnancy and associated insurance problems; preserving midwife services at a hospital serving a poor neighborhood; and canceling county prenatal care contracts with those providers not informing their clients about their eligibility for WIC food supplements. . . .

DISCUSSION AND CONCLUSIONS

With certain qualifications, the importance of having women officials in strategic decision-making positions was again confirmed. Female elected officials in Milwaukee have clearly made a difference for women. Over the ten to twenty years that women's issues have been on local agendas, a relatively small number of female officials have disproportionately provided strong and consistent leadership on these issues. Although not every woman played a leadership role, ten of the sixteen women to serve in local public office since 1966 were recalled by one or more colleagues as having been a leader on at least one of the six policy areas considered in this study. As a group, women officials were active on more and a broader range of women's issues and placed a higher priority on them.

Women's leadership is also qualitatively different from that of men. Women are more active in agenda building and the design of major new policy programs men are more likely to advance the women's agenda through incrementally changing existing programs or by using bureaucratic procedures such as zoning and contracting. But whereas men appear to provide leadership as a part of some other role—as district advocate, legislative leader, or committee chair, or out of welfare liberalism generally—the representative role of female officials is less straightforward.

The influence of a formal caucus of female supervisors, alderwomen, or elected women in Milwaukee or nationally does not underpin these distinctive roles. Instead, women rely on informal cooperative relations as each issue arises.

Nor is there sufficient evidence of female officials' participation in a local women's policy network to support an instructed delegate role. These women do maintain closer ties to local women's groups in terms of conference attendance, formal memberships in such groups, and group-initiated contacts. And many were very positive about women's networks. But women officials, like their male colleagues, were quite divided concerning the exact nature of such a network in Milwaukee. This uncertainty appeared to be linked with a rather low level of activity and visibility of women's groups in local legislative politics, as well as some perceived problems of agenda-setting and strategic effectiveness.

Fortunately for women, Milwaukee elected women act on their own initiative as feminist trustees to represent women's interests. This role is rooted in both the nature of urban representation generally and the character of local feminist groups today. From the San Francisco Bay Study, conducted in the late 1960s, to the most recent studies of urban elected officials, local legislators have been found to adopt a trustee representative focus. As a result, elected representatives resolve most issues on the basis of their independent judgments, even though these decisions generally tend to be consistent with the preferences of affected citizens. In the case of local elected women, feminist concerns can be addressed by these friendly allies within city and county government with only minimal contacts between representative and issue constituency.

In contrast to the legislative policy-making that dominates on the national and state levels, however, the primary responsibility of city and county governments is the delivery of services within their own jurisdictions. Therefore, in seeking to advance the feminist agenda on the local level, feminist groups rationally have concentrated on bureaucracies and the service-delivery system. And here again, local female officials play a role as advocates for women before the bureaucracy.

In summary, local elected women in Milwaukee, acting as feminist trustees, have served as internal catalysts for change by raising women's issues, sensitizing their male colleagues and urban administrators to these issues, and bringing those officials into active or passive support of concrete policies. Many may also be willing, but underutilized, delegates for local women's rights groups who support these same issues.

Exercise
Race and Gender at City Hall

The purpose of this exercise is to determine the connection between race and poverty in your city and the racial, ethnic, and gender balance among the most powerful local elected officials. Comparing the characteristics of your officials to the characteristics of the general population, you can determine if men, women, African Americans, Latinos, Asians, and Whites are represented fairly. You can also ask if there are legitimate reasons for any discrepancies in racial, ethnic, and gender representation. The exercise also draws your attention to any racial or gender conflicts that are occurring and any changes in racial or gender-related public policies that have been adopted.

RACIAL GAP

Once again you can begin either with a visit to your university library or the Internet to get census data. If you use the **http://www. census.gov** site, follow the prompts. Click on census 2000 for current census data, click on search by address, and enter an address in the search text box. At the next screen choose Metropolitan Statistical Area and click go. It will take a few minutes for the data to be sorted. Then you can scroll down and choose options on the types of data or maps you want.

You now want to compare community areas in your metropolitan region or city. A community area is a census area that compiles block data into "communities" of, say, from 2,500 to 25,000 people. Note that in the case of suburbs, "community area" will correspond to suburban towns. Once you have found the community level census data, look for data on median family income and rank order the communities from 1 to 250 (or the total number of communities in your metropolitan region).

Next, take a map of the community areas or zip codes (from the census information) and mark in the ten richest communities (1–10) on the map. You may use a color or cross-hatching to designate them. Then mark the ten poorest communities (240–250) in another color or with another symbol. Look at the map. Where are the richest and poorest neighborhoods physically located?

Now go back to the census data for the ten richest communities and the ten poorest communities and compile data on the race of the residents. Perhaps on a second map of the communities make symbols representing 10 percent or less African American, 50 percent African American, and more than 90 percent African American. Looking at your two maps what do you

(continued)

(continued)

conclude about the connections between race, wealth, and poverty in your own metropolitan region?

RACE AND GENDER AMONG PUBLIC OFFICIALS

Now from city and county government records obtain a list of city council and county board members. (This may be a published document available at your library or city hall, a list published on your city government's Web page, or a news story in your local newspaper published in hard copy or archived on the newspaper's Web page.) From this list, from your own direct knowledge, or from newspaper accounts, determine how many are White, African American, and Latino. (If other ethnic divisions are particularly important such as Irish, Italian, or Polish, determine the number of aldermen from each ethnic group as well.) Now compare the percentage of city council members from each racial group to their percentage in the population. Do all racial and ethnic groups have approximately the same level of representation in the city council and county board as in general population? Now consider the race of the last three or four mayors for your city. Do they represent the same or different racial groups? Does any one racial group have predominant political power?

Next consider the gender of the officials at city hall. Are the same number of men and women serving as city council members? How many women have served as mayor in your city? Are publically announced homosexuals serving in any key governmental bodies? What laws provide for equal rights for women? What laws such as Human Rights Ordinances provide for gay rights? Gather the same information on the county board commissioners and the county board president (or county executive). Does the county government differ from the city government in its makeup or in its laws regarding racial and sexual balances?

Finally, going to newspaper stories once again, what have been the principal racial and gender conflicts in local politics and government over the last ten years? What are the trends of any changes that may be occurring—such as greater representation of minorities and women, conflict between minority racial groups, or a gradual change in the racial or gender policies of your local government?

Chapter 6

The Struggle for Power

Politics is the struggle for power to determine governmental outcomes. This struggle takes place at many levels, including the most local levels of politics and government. Urban politics is diverse because U.S. cities differ in their size, racial and ethnic composition, economic base, and history. Although American cities present a variety of politics, they are constrained by a shared national history. Local struggles for power can tell us much about politics and government at higher levels as they provide a laboratory in which new ways of governing can be tested.

In the late nineteenth and early twentieth centuries, urban politics was defined by a fundamental conflict between machine and reform politics. Before the Civil War and for some years afterwards, larger cities of the Northeast and the Midwest were ruled by commercial and business elites who were most often Yankees (White Anglo-Saxon Protestants who had been in America for the longest time).[1]

These men (and they were only men because women did not hold these offices until the mid-twentieth century) served as the first mayors and city council members. They wanted their cities to be healthy places to live and to grow and prosper economically. Since they were most often in businesses like real estate and law, which depended upon the growth of the city for their prosperity, these first urban leaders created pro-growth policies, combined with low taxes and minimal public services.

As the number of immigrants grew, power shifted to ethnic politicians who first became members of local city councils representing their ethnic wards. Later in the twentieth century, ethnic politicians amassed enough power and votes to become mayors. To gain their power, they invented the urban political machine.

Thus, the first reading describes machine politics and why it persisted from the mid-nineteenth to the late twentieth century. Many writers claim that the death of Richard J. Daley in 1976 marked the end of big-city machine politics.[2] George Washington Plunkitt described machine politics as it existed in the classic Tammany Hall of New York City in the beginning at the turn of the twentieth century.

As soon as the political machine was created, it was opposed by reformers who believed that machine politics led to waste, corruption, and bad government. They wanted to create honest, efficient local government in which the nepotism, patronage, and corruption would be eliminated. The original reform rallying cry was that government should be run like a business. The reform, "progressive" movement in the first decades of the twentieth century successfully sponsored

153

many reforms such as the direct election of U.S. senators, installation of city managers to run city bureaucracies, development of settlement houses, and other social reforms to assist the poor. Some urban areas, especially in the West and
Southwest, never had political machines and adopted reform structures and ideals
from their beginnings as cities. Most suburbs also developed a reformist system of
government, although some like DuPage County Illinois and metropolitan New Orleans parishes developed Republican and Democratic machines.

As the case of Mayor Samuel Jones of Toledo illustrates, there were social reformers as well as good government structural reformers.3The social reformers
sought to gain municipal ownership of utilities, cheaper transit fares, higher wages
for workers, and improved public education. So urban political wars between machine politicians and both good government and social reformers waged throughout the nineteenth and twentieth centuries.4

MODERN URBAN POLITICS

Although it is necessary to understand the great battle of machine and reform politics that dominated urban politics for more than a century, modern urban politics is
more complicated. First of all, while elected officials like mayors and aldermen still
play a central role, bureaucrats heading separate agencies like Robert Moses of
New York, businessmen who advise various mayors, and lobbyists like those in Miami have a powerful effect upon their cities.

Second, even where one might argue that a machine still exists, as in the case
of "the new machine" of Mayor Richard M. Daley of Chicago, it is a machine that is
very different from that of his father Richard J. Daley. While remnants of the old machine may remain, the politics and government of cities like Chicago are thor-
oughly modern—just not the modern cities that reformers had advocated.

Third, it appears that all cities and suburbs are governed by "regimes" or community power structures that include "the informal partnership between city hall
and the downtown business elite."5 In some small towns, suburbs, and cities with
homogenous populations or in larger cities early in the nineteenth century, the
regime was simply some business and political insiders who "exercised tight-fisted
control."6 In larger cities today, the balance of power among business, civic, and
political leaders varies greatly. In Atlanta, Black political leaders and mostly White
businessmen constitute the regime.7 In Pittsburgh, the civic and nonprofit sector
has great influence.8 In San Francisco, the city's many racial, ethnic, political, business, and ideological groups create a pluralistic regime.9 While in Chicago the political leaders usually dominate their business partners.10

Beyond the regime labels and formal governmental structures, it is important to
remember that leaders of today's cities are people—with their individual quirks and
idiosyncrasies. Some are saints, some are sinners, some are self-serving politicians
and some are seeking the public good. Most are a combination of these traits. These
readings attempt to give you a sense of the differences between urban leaders.

The exercises in this section let you map the "power structure" or "regime"
that governs in your city or suburb.

We begin with a discussion of political machines. Political machines were
more than an alliance between shady businessmen and corrupt politicians. They

were a political party whose goal was control of local government. Such a "ma-chine" was characterized by patronage precinct captains with jobs at city hall, backroom slate-making of party candidates for public office, city contracts to busi-ness benefactors, political favors for voters who supported the party, and straight-ticket voting. These machines created an economic reward system fueled by self-interest rather than by the qualities of candidates or abstract public policies.

In such a system, government patronage jobs created precinct workers to con-tact the voters door-to-door, political favors to convince the voters to support the party's candidates, and policies like curbing police raids and providing government contracts to insiders who gave money to fund the campaigns. These patronage workers, favors, and policies benefitting particular interests, combined to elect the party's candidates who controlled the government so that they could dispense pa-tronage jobs, political favors, favorable policies, and city contracts necessary to oil the different parts of the political machine.

As Tammany's most eloquent spokesperson, District Leader George Washing-ton Plunkitt put it, "people ain't in politics for nothing, they want to get something out of it." Party workers want a city job if they are going to do precinct work, citi-zens want government services if they are going to vote for a candidate or a party, and businessmen want a city contract if they are to give lavish campaign contribu-tions. The political machine was a mechanism to distribute just these spoils. A strong machine like Tammany Hall was best able to control the many fragmented local governments so as to deliver rewards to their supporters.

One side effect of the political machine was inevitably political corruption—politicians who took outright bribes to pass certain laws, policies, zoning changes, or to provide city contracts to cronies or contributors. Plunkitt makes a distinction between "honest" and "dishonest graft," which is no longer recognized under fed-eral law. Illegal corruption today is any use of one's public position to gain personal profit, such as taking a bribe to provide a zoning change or a liquor license to a business. The distinction between honest and dishonest graft was always difficult to grasp. If party workers legally exchanged city services for votes from con-stituents and got their jobs at city hall in exchange for working their precincts, it was always hard for them to distinguish between cashing in on their inside knowl-edge of government, which was legal in the past, and taking a cash bribe to get government to do something, which was always illegal. As a result, in Chicago since 1971, 26 members and former members of the 50-member city council have been convicted of corruption. So have politicians in many American cities that are as different as Miami and San Diego. Machine politics fostered corruption which, in turn, fueled cries for reform.

Plunkitt derides reformers as "Mornin' Glories" and argues that at the turn of the twentieth century, none of the reform organizations lasted more than a couple of years. "They were mornin' glories—looked lovely in the mornin' and withered up in a short time, while the regular machines went on flourishin' forever, like fine old oaks." However, while individual reform organizations and individual reformers may have faded, others replaced them and slowly defeated the machines one by one, city by city.

Some who favored machine politics argued that it was worth putting up with a little corruption to have a city that worked—in which government provided needed services and socialized the many immigrants moving to the cities. But machine politics also brought autocratic control by party bosses.

Party bosses like Plunkitt were constantly challenged by reformers. Lincoln Steffens, one of the best known muckraking journalists of the early twentieth century, blamed the citizenry for the continuation of machine rule. He argued that politicians are political merchants and that they will supply any demand that the public creates. He wrote, "All we have to do is to establish a steady demand for good government."[11] More often, however, the people were fooled, bought, intimidated, or simply apathetic. Reformers appealed to patriotism and good government, but often this was not enough to bring change. Eventually, when society changed, machines no longer served their purposes and disappeared.

In city after city, the population shifted and the old political machines that had organized the immigrants gradually faded away. In many regions of the country, they were replaced by reformers and by progressive governments. In the last years of the twentieth century, White ethnic mayors were often replaced by Blacks, Latinos, and "progressive" mayors. By the beginning of the twenty-first century, urban politics seems to be shifting again to give power to managerial or administrative mayors and, perhaps, to a new machine that incorporates elements of both the old machine and the reformer's good government agenda.

The machine also faced legal setbacks. In 1979, the *Shakman Decree* declared political patronage to be unconstitutional.[12] The court ruled unconstitutional both patronage hiring and firing under the First and Fourteenth Amendments. This ruling was reaffirmed by the U.S. Supreme Court in *Rutan v. The Republican Party of Illinois* in 1990.[13] Not only is corruption illegal (as it always has been), but now patronage—the backbone of machine politics—is illegal as well.

Most early reformers simply wanted to achieve honest, efficient, effective city government. In short, they wanted their city government to be run like a good business. They sought what might be called structural or good government reforms. Other early reformers, like Samuel M. "Golden Rule" Jones of Toledo, Ohio, however, were social reformers who sought not just honest and effective local government but more fundamental reforms like lower transit fares or publicly owned utilities. Thus, the fight was not just against party bosses but against many of the private businesses that were taking advantage of the working class and the poor to make an unfair profit. The transit fight in Toledo (and in many U.S. cities) pitted the mayor against the "traction" or transit business monopolies. Jones and his successor in Toledo finally forced the street car lines to operate under permanent public control, providing good service and cheap fares for citizens. These fights have echoes in American cities today where providing public transportation systems with inexpensive fares continues as an ongoing political battle.

An often forgotten stream of urban politics was American socialism. For instance, Milwaukee's socialist Mayor Daniel Hogan from 1916 to 1940 was a different kind of social reformer. He ran an efficient, honest, and quiet radical government, which sets the expectations of Milwaukee citizens for clean government even today. In his book, *City Government*, he argued against the usual claims that the business community demanded clean government.[14] Mayor Hogan claimed that what most businessmen want is for governments to be servile to their individual and class interests. He said that businessmen often "do not seek a government for the benefit of all the people. . . . " Mayor Hogan argued that it is the worker who "is very vitally and actively interested in clean government" and supports fights "for lower tax rates, better conditions, good recreational facilities, ideal health conditions, and good public school educa-tion."[15] Finally, according to Hogan, the middle class as well as civic and service groups can play a "vital part in the battle for better government." However, mo-bilizing the working and middle classes as well as the civic organizations re-quires leadership and vision.

The Municipal Platform of the Socialist Party of Milwaukee in 1932 under Hogan's leadership included not only the usual reformist measures fighting graft and corruption, but a demand of a shorter working week to a six-hour day and five-day work week, freeing small homes of workers from taxation, the extension of public ownership of utilities, and state handling of light wines and beer. Changes at the local level were seen by socialists as an important component in a larger politi-cal transformation of the nation and the world.

The diversity of urban history is demonstrated by regions of the country like the Southwest and the West that were never controlled by political machines. Since their cities developed later in American history, they were always "reform cities" ruled by a business elite on behalf of the middle class. Amy Bridges tells how in these cities reformers were not the "Mornin' Glories" described by Plunkitt, but the dominant politicians for most of the twentieth century. In the Southwest these reformers replaced partisan elections with nonpartisan ones, gave power to a civic elite composed of businessmen, empowered city managers, and brought most of the progressive reforms proposed in the 1920s to practice. In these cities, "Reform regimes governed a political life of low participation and little public dis-sent." They were governed primarily by a group of relatively small, affluent, Anglo leaders. "The results," according to Bridges, "were a small, contented political community that had good government and knew it was good, and political leaders well insulated from such popular discontent as might exist." However, by the 1990s the central institutions of "big-city reform" in the Southwest had mostly been dis-mantled. The future of the Southwestern and Western cities like those in the rest of the nation is still to be decided in the twenty-first century.

Reference

See Judd and Swanstrom, Chapter 3: "Party Machines and the Immigrants" and Chap-ter 4: "The Reform Crusades." In Ross and Levine see Chapter 4: "Formal Structure and Leadership Style," Chapter 5: "Machine Politics," and Chapter 6: "Reform Politics."

Notes

1. Robert Dahl, *Who Governs,* New Haven: Yale University Press, 1961, pp. 11–88 and Dick Simpson, *Rogues, Rebels, and Rubber Stamps: The Politics of the Chicago City Council from 1863 to the Present,* Boulder: Westview, 2001, Chapter 1. See also Gabriel Al-mond, *Plutocracy and Politics in New York City,* Boulder: Westview, 1998, pp. 15–16.
2. See for instance, Dennis Judd and Todd Swanstrom, *City Politics,* New York: Long-man, 2002, p. 53.

3. Simpson, *Rogues, Rebels, and Rubber Stamps,* Chapter 2.
4. For an account of the civic wars in the nineteenth century see Mary P. Ryan, *Civic Wars: Democracy and Public Life in the American City During the Nineteenth Century,* Berkeley: University of California Press, 1997.
5. Clarence Stone, *Regime Politics: Governing Atlanta, 1946–1988,* Lawrence: University of Kansas Press, 1989, p. 3.
6. Judd and Swanstrom, *City Politics,* p. 9.
7. See Stone, *Regime Politics.*
8. Barbara Ferman, *Challenging the Growth Machine: Neighborhood Politics in Chicago and Pittsburgh,* Lawrence, University of Kansas Press, 1996.
9. Richard DeLeon, *Left Coast City: Progressive Politics in San Franscisco, 1975–1991,* Lawrence: University of Kansas Press, 1992.
10. See Simpson, *Rogues, Rebels, and Rubber Stamps.*
11. Lincoln Steffens, *The Shame of the Cities,* New York: Hill and Wang, 1957, p. 5. Originally published in book form by McClure, Phillip and Company, 1904.
12. "Patronage: *Shakman v. Democratic Organization of Cook County* and *Rutan v. Republican Party of Illinois*" in Dick Simpson, ed., *Chicago's Future in a Time of Change,* Champaign, IL: Stipes, 1993, pp. 147–153.
13. "Patronage," p. 154.
14. Daniel Hogan, *City Government,* New York: Harcourt, Brace and Company, 1936. See especially, pp. 57–64.
15. Hogan, p. 61.

21. Honest and Dishonest Graft

George Washington Plunkitt

George Washington Plunkitt was a Tammany Hall political boss and elected official in New York City in the early years of the twentieth century. He was blunt in his defense of machine politics. These three excerpts are from his talks with reporter William Riordan and some of his talks on the radio. Machine politics was dominant in Northeastern and Midwestern cities from the late nineteenth century until the mid-twentieth century and remnants of machine politics still persist in diminished form in some cities and suburbs today.

Everybody is talkin' these days about Tammany men growin' rich on graft, but nobody thinks of drawin' the distinction between honest graft and dishonest graft. There's all the difference in the world between the two. Yes, many of our men have grown rich in politics. I have myself. I've made a big fortune out of the game, and I'm gettin' richer every day, but I've not gone in for dishonest graft—blackmailin' gamblers, saloonkeepers, disorderly people, etc.—and neither has any of the men who have made big fortunes in politics.

SOURCE: From William L. Riordon, *Plunkitt of Tammany Hall: A Series of Very Plain Talks on Very Practical Politics* (New York: Dutton, 1963), pp. 3–6, 17–20, and 25–28.

There's an honest graft, and I'm an example of how works. I might sum up the whole thing by sayin: "I seen my opportunities and I took 'em."

Just let me explain by examples. My party's in power in the city, and it's goin' to undertake a lot of public improvements. Well, I'm tipped off, say, that they're going to lay out a new park at a certain place.

I see my opportunity and I take it. I go to that place and I buy up all the land I can in the neighborhood. Then the board of this or that makes its plan public, and there is a rush to get my land, which nobody cared particular for before.

Ain't it perfectly honest to charge a good price and make a profit on my investment and foresight? Of course, it is. Well, that's honest graft.

Or supposin' it's a new bridge they're goin' to build. I get tipped off and I buy as much property as I can that has to be taken for approaches. I sell at my own price later on and drop some more money in the bank.

Wouldn't you? It's just like lookin' ahead in Wall Street or in the coffee or cotton market. It's honest graft, and I'm lookin' for it every day in the year. I will tell you frankly that I've got a good lot of it, too.

I'll tell you of one case. They were goin' to fix up a big park, no matter where. I got on to it, and went lookin' about for land in that neighborhood.

I could get nothin' at a bargain but a big piece of swamp, but I took it fast enough and held on to it. What turned out was just what I counted on. They couldn't make the park complete without Plunkitt's swamp, and they had to pay a good price for it. Anything dishonest in that?

Up in the watershed I made some money, too. I bought up several bits of land there some years ago and made a pretty good guess that they would be bought up for water purposes later by the city.

Somehow, I always guessed about right, and shouldn't I enjoy the profit of my foresight? It was rather amusin' when the condemnation commissioners came along and found piece after piece of the land in the name of George Plunkitt of the Fifteenth Assembly District, New York City. They wondered how I knew just what to buy. The answer is—I seen my opportunity and I took it. I haven't confined myself to land; anything that pays is in my line.

For instance, the city is repavin' a street and has several hundred thousand old granite blocks to sell. I am on hand to buy, and I know just what they are worth.

How? Never mind that. I had a sort of monopoly of this business for a while, but once a newspaper tried to do me. It got some outside men to come over from Brooklyn and New Jersey to bid against me.

Was I done? Not much. I went to each of the men and said: "How many of these 250,000 stones do you want?" One said 20,000, and another wanted 15,000, and other wanted 10,000. I said: "All right, let me bid for the lot, and I'll give each of you all you want for nothin'."

They agreed, of course. Then the auctioneer yelled: "How much am I bid for these 250,000 fine pavin' stones?"

"Two dollars and fifty cents," says I.

"Two dollars and fifty cents!" screamed the auctioneer. "Oh, that's a joke! Give me a real bid."

He found the bid was real enough. My rivals stood silent. I got the lot for $2.50 and gave them their share. That's how the attempt to do Plunkitt ended, and that's how all such attempts end.

I've told you how I got rich by honest graft. Now, let me tell you that most politicians who are accused of robbin' the city get rich the same way.

They didn't steal a dollar from the city treasury. They just seen their opportunities and took them. That is why, when a reform administration comes in and spends a half million dollars in tryin' to find the public robberies they talked about in the campaign, they don't find them.

The books are always all right. The money in the city treasury is all right. Everything is all right. All they can show is that the Tammany heads of departments looked after their friends, within the law, and gave them what opportunities they could to make honest graft. Now, let me tell you that's never goin' to hurt Tammany with the people. Every good man looks after his friends, and any man who doesn't isn't likely to be popular. If I have a good thing to hand out in private life, I give it to a friend. Why shouldn't I do the same in public life? Another kind of honest graft. Tammany has raised a good many salaries. There was an awful howl by the reformers, but don't you know that Tammany gains ten votes for every one it lost by salary raisin'?

The Wall Street banker thinks it shameful to raise a department clerk's salary from $1,500 to $1,800 a year, but every man who draws a salary himself says: "That's all right. I wish it was me." And he feels very much like votin' the Tammany ticket on election day, just out of sympathy.

Tammany was beat in 1901 because the people were deceived into believin' that it worked dishonest graft. They didn't draw a distinction between dishonest and honest graft, but they saw that some Tammany men grew rich, and supposed they had been robbin' the city treasury or levyin' blackmail on disorderly houses, or workin' in with the gamblers and lawbreakers. As a matter of policy, if nothing else, why should the Tammany leaders go into such dirty business, when there is so much honest graft lyin' around when they are in power? Did you ever consider that?

Now, in conclusion, I want to say that I don't own a dishonest dollar. If my worst enemy was given the job of writin' my epitaph when I'm gone, he couldn't do more than write: "George W. Plunkitt. He Seen His Opportunities, and He Took 'Em." . . .

REFORMERS ONLY MORNIN' GLORIES

College professors and philosophers who go up in a balloon to think are always discussin' the question: "Why Reform Administrations Never Succeed Themselves." The reason is plain to anybody who has learned the a, b, c of politics. I can't tell just how many of these movements I've seen started in New York during my forty years in politics, but I can tell you how many have lasted more than a few years—none. There have been reform committees of fifty, of sixty, of seventy, of one hundred and all sorts of numbers that started out to do up the regular political organizations. They were mornin' glories—looked lovely in the mornin' and withered up in a short time, while the regular machines went on flourishin' forever, like fine old oaks. Say, that's the first poetry I ever worked off. Ain't it great?

Just look back a few years. You remember the People's Municipal League that nominated Frank Scott for mayor in 1890? Do you remember the reformers that got up that league? Have you ever heard of them since? I haven't. Scott himself survived because he had always been a first-rate politician, but you'd have to look in the newspaper almanacs of 1891 to find out who made up the People's Municipal League. Oh, yes! I remember one name: Ollie Teall; dear, pretty Ollie and his big dog. They're about all that's left of the League.

Now take the reform movement of 1894. A lot of good politicians joined in that—the Republicans, the State Democrats, the Stecklerites and the O'Brien-ites, and they gave us a lickin', but the real reform part of the affair, the Committee of Seventy that started the thing goin', what's become of those reformers? What's become of Charles Stewart Smith? Where's Bangs? Do you ever hear of Cornell, the iron man, in politics now? Could a search party find R. W. G. Welling? Have you seen the name of Fulton McMahon or McMahon Fulton—I ain't sure which—in the papers lately? Or Preble Tucker? Or—but it's no use to go through the list of the reformers who said they sounded in the death knell of Tammany in 1894. They're gone for good, and Tammany's pretty well, thank you. They did the talkin' and posin', and the politicians in the movement got all the plums. It's always the case.

The Citizens' Union has lasted a little bit longer than the reform crowd that went before them, but that's because they learned a thing or two from us. They learned how to put up a pretty good bluff—and bluff counts a lot in politics. With only a few thousand members, they had the nerve to run the whole Fusion movement, make the Republicans and other organizations come to their headquarters to select a ticket and dictate what every candidate must do or not do. I love nerve, and I've had a sort of respect for the Citizens' Union lately, but the Union can't last. Its people haven't been trained to politics, and whenever Tammany calls their bluff they lay right down. You'll never hear of the Union again after a year or two.

And, by the way, what's become of the good government clubs, the political nurseries of a few years ago? Do you ever hear of Good Government Club D and P and Q and Z any more? What's become of the infants who were to grow up and show us how to govern the city? I know what's become of the nursery that was started in my district. You can find pretty much the whole outfit over in my headquarters, Washington Hall.

The fact is that a reformer can't last in politics. He can make a show for a while, but he always comes down like a rocket. Politics is as much a regular business as the grocery or the dry-goods or the drug business. You've got to be trained in the business and trained to conduct it or you're sure to fail. Suppose a man knew nothing about the grocery business and tried to conduct it according to his own ideas. Wouldn't he make a mess of it? He might make a make a splurge for a while, as long as his money lasted, but his store would soon be empty. It's just the same with a reformer. He hasn't been brought up in the difficult business of politics and he makes a mess of it every time.

I've been studyin' the political game for forty-five years, and I don't know it all yet. I'm learnin' somethin' all the time. How, then, can you expect what they call "business men" to turn into politics all at once and make a success of it? It is just as if I went up to Columbia University and started to teach Greek. They usually last about as long in politics as I would last at Columbia.

You can't begin too early in politics if you want to succeed at the game. I began several years before I could vote, and so did every successful leader in Tammany Hall. When I was twelve years old I made myself useful around the district headquarters and did work at all the polls on election day. Later on, I hustled about gettin' out voters who had jags on or who were too lazy to come to the polls. There's a hundred ways that boys can help, and they get an experience that's the first real step in statesmanship. Show me a boy that hustles for the organization on election day, and I'll show you a future statesman. That's the a, b, c of politics. It ain't easy work to get up to y and z. You have to give nearly all your time and attention to it. Of course, you may have some business or occupation on the side, but the great business of your life must be politics if you want to succeed in it. A few years ago Tammany tried to mix politics and business in equal quantities, by havin' two leaders for each district, a politician and a business man. They wouldn't mix. They were like oil and water. The politician looked after the politics of his district; the business man looked after his grocery store or his milk route, and whenever he appeared at an executive meeting, it was only to make trouble. The whole scheme turned out to be a farce and was abandoned mighty quick.

Do you understand now, why it is that a reformer goes down and out in the first or second round, while politician answers to the gong every time? It is because the one has gone into the fight without trainin', while the other trains all the time and knows every fine point of the game. . . .

STUDY HUMAN NATURE AND ACT ACCORDIN'

There's only one way to hold a district: you must study human nature and act accordin'. You can't study human nature in books. Books is a hindrance more than anything else. If you have been to college, so much the worse for you. You'll have to unlearn all you learned before you can get right down to human nature, and unlearnin' takes a lot of time. Some men can never forget what they learned at college. Such men may get to be district leaders by a fluke, but they never last.

To learn real human nature you have to go among the people, see them and be seen. I know every man, woman, and child in the Fifteenth District, except them that's been born this summer—and I know some of them, too. I know what they like and what they don't like, what they are strong at and what they are weak in, and I reach them by approachin' at the right side.

For instance, here's how I gather in the young men. I hear of a young feller that's proud of his voice, thinks that he can sing fine. I ask him to come around to Washington Hall and join our Glee Club. He comes and sings, and he's a follower of Plunkitt for life. Another young feller gains a reputation as a baseball player in a vacant lot. I bring him into our baseball club. That fixes him. You'll find him workin' for my ticket at the polls next election day. Then there's the feller that likes rowin' on the river, the young feller that makes a name as a waltzer on his block, the young feller that's handy with his dukes—I rope them all in by givin' them opportunities to show themselves off. I don't trouble them with political arguments. I just study human nature and act accordin'.

But you may say this game won't work with the high-toned fellers, the fellers that go through college and then join the Citizens' Union. Of course it wouldn't work. I have a special treatment for them. I ain't like the patent medicine man that gives the same medicine for all diseases. The Citizens' Union kind of a young man! I love him! He's the daintiest morsel of the lot, and he don't often escape me.

Before telling you how I catch him, let me mention that before the election last year, the Citizens' Union said they had 400 or 500 enrolled voters in my district. They had a lovely headquarters, too, beautiful roll-top desks and the cutest rugs in the world. If I was accused of havin' contributed to fix up the nest for them, I wouldn't deny it under oath. What do I mean by that? Never mind. You can guess from the sequel, if you're sharp.

Well, election day came. The Citizens' Union's candidate for Senator, who ran against me, just polled five votes in the district, while I polled something more than 14,000 votes. What became of the 400 or 500 Citizens' Union enrolled voters in my district? Some people guessed that many of them were good Plunkitt men all along and worked with the Cits just to bring them into the Plunkitt camp by election day. You can guess that way, too, if you want to. I never contradict stories about me, especially in hot weather. I just call your attention to the fact that on last election day 395 Citizens' Union enrolled voters in my district were missin' and unaccounted for.

I tell you frankly, though, how I have captured some of the Citizens' Union's young men. I have a plan that never fails. I watch the City Record to see when there's civil service examinations for good things. Then I take any young Cit in hand, tell him all about the good thing and get him worked up till he goes and takes an examination. I don't bother about him any more. It's a cinch that he comes back to me in a few days and asks to join Tammany Hall. Come over to Washington Hall some night and I'll show you a list of names on our rolls marked "C. S." which means, "bucked up against civil service."

As to the older voters, I reach them, too. No, I don't send them campaign literature. That's rot. People can get all the political stuff they want to read—and a good deal more, too—in the papers. Who reads speeches, nowadays, anyhow? It's bad enough you gotta listen to them. You ain't goin' to gain any votes by stuffin' the letter boxes with campaign documents. Like as not you'll lose votes, for there's nothin' a man hates more than to hear the letter carrier ring his bell and go to the letter box expectin' to find a letter he was lookin' for, and find only a lot of printed politics. I met a man this very mornin' who told me he voted the Democratic State ticket last year just because the Republicans kept crammin' his letter box with campaign documents.

What tells in holdin' your grip on your district is to go right down among the poor families and help them in the different ways they need help. I've got a regular system for this. If there's a fire in Ninth, Tenth, or Eleventh Avenue, for example, any hour of the day or night, I'm usually there with some of my election district captains as soon as the fire engines. If a family is burned out I don't ask whether they are Republicans or Democrats, and I don't refer them to the Charity Organization Society, which would investigate their case in a month or two and decide they were worthy of help about the time they are dead from starvation. I just get quarters for them, buy clothes for them if their clothes were burned up, and fix them up till they get things runnin' again. It's philanthropy, but it's politics, too—mighty good politics. Who can tell how many votes one of these fires bring me? The poor are the most grateful people in the world, and, let me tell you, they have more friends in their neighborhoods than the rich have in theirs.

If there's a family in my district in want I know it before the charitable societies do, and me and my men are first on the ground. I have a special corps to look up such cases. The consequence is that the poor look up to George W. Plunkitt as a father, come to him in trouble and don't forget him on election day.

Another thing, I can always get a job for a deservin' man. I make it a point to keep on the track of jobs, and it seldom happens that I don't have a few up my sleeve ready for use. I know every big employer in the district and in the whole city, for that matter, and they ain't in the habit of sayin' no to me when I ask them for a job.

And the children—the little roses of the district. Do I forget them? Oh, no! They know me, every one of them, and they know that a sight of Uncle George and candy means the same thing. Some of them are the best kind of vote-getters. I'll tell you a case. Last year a little Eleventh Avenue rosebud, whose father is a Republican, caught hold of his whiskers on election day and said she wouldn't let go till he'd promise to vote for me. And she didn't.

22. Early Reformers: Mayor Samuel M. "Golden Rule" Jones of Toledo

Melvin G. Holli

Samuel Jones was a social reform mayor in Toledo at the end of the nineteenth and the beginning of the twentieth century. As Plunkitt was an exemplar of machine politics, Jones was an exemplar of progressive reform politics of the time.

One of the most tempestuous and enduring urban political issues between 1890 and 1920 was the fight between reform administrations and the street railway companies over operating rights on the public streets and the price of streetcar fares. In this pre-automobile age, urban workers

SOURCE: Samuel M. "Golden Rule" Jones, 1897–1904 in Melvin G. Holli, *The American Mayor: The Best and The Worst of Big-City Leaders*, (University Park, Pennsylvania: Pennsylvania State University Press, 1999), pp. 44–52. Reproduced by permission of the publisher.

and their families were transit-dependent, and the cost of transportation was a critical part of the budget and therefore a volatile and sensitive issue. The fight generally pitted the mayor and the city's straphangers against the traction monopoly. The street railway companies sought to extend their exclusive privilege to operate on the city streets for twenty-five years or longer—the effect of which would drive up the value of their faltering bonds and enable them to sell more securities at higher prices and greater profit to the owners.

In exchange for these monopoly privileges, reform mayors sometimes sought three-cent fares, universal transfers, and concessions from the company, such as street paving between the tracks, and sometimes contract provisions that provided for eventual municipal ownership of the utility. In Detroit one student of traction called it the "thirty-year war"; in Cleveland, Tom Johnson called it the "battle against privilege"; and Toledo's Mayor Samuel M. Jones also fought for three-cent fares and eventual municipal ownership of the lines. A mayor's chief weapon in these battles was his ability to wield the veto to stop corrupt ordinances or franchises that he believed were not in the public's interest.

One of the classic confrontations between the mayor and the traction company occurred in Toledo in 1903, when Mayor Sam "Golden Rule" Jones began what would be his last term. The Toledo Rail & Light Company had just pushed through the city council a twenty-five-year franchise extension, which the mayor opposed and vetoed because it did not offer three-cent fares, tax revenue for the city, and other concessions that could lead to municipal ownership. The council called a meeting to override the mayor's veto, and that in turn prompted the city's famous "petition in boots," in which agitated citizens, civic groups, labor unions, and ethnic fraternal lodges marched en masse to city hall to support their mayor. The small gallery intended to hold one hundred was packed with four hundred of the mayor's hooting and boisterous supporters, with additional hundreds gathered noisily on the streets below the chamber.

The steely showdown was between the street railway interests man, Barton Smith, and the Golden Rule mayor. Amid hisses and jeers, Smith taunted the mayor, saying: "I suppose this is the kind of government we can expect when the Golden Rule comes into full force." The mayor shot back, "Mr. Smith, this is the kind of government we have when the rule of Gold is in full force." Smith then needled the mayor with a rejoinder: "How much gold did it cost you to get them in here?" It was a sneering reference to the unruly assemblage supporting Jones. The mayor took umbrage and upbraided Smith for his "slandering reference to the Golden Rule," and the gallery erupted with a crescendo of hisses and jeering. The "petition in boots" had made its point: Smith withdrew his company's demand for the ordinance, and the council, cowed by the public protest, tabled their resolution to override the mayor's veto. That was a classic display of Toledo's Golden Rule mayor in operation, triumphing over what he called the "rule of Gold."

One of the most widely noted and written-about fin-de-siècle mayors, Samuel M. Jones was born in Wales and came to America as a three-year-old immigrant with his family, who settled on a tenant farm in New York State.

Jones, who had less than three years of formal schooling, took up the drudgery of a farm laborer at the age of ten, later working for a while for a steamboat operator. By age nineteen he had drifted into the oil fields of Pennsylvania, where he learned that business; then he moved on to Lima, Ohio, where in 1885 he founded an oil company that soon sold out to the John D. Rockefeller interests. From there Jones went to Toledo, Ohio, where in 1894 he established the Acme Sucker Rod Company to manufacture an oil well pump he had invented. A life of penury, scrimping to get by, forced saving, and a streak of inventive luck were finally rewarded as great fortune came to the immigrant oil-field roustabout.

A successful inventor, entrepreneur, and now a wealthy factory owner, Jones in his writings and speeches seemed to repudiate the system that had made him rich. He was repelled by the savage competition of a coldly functional economic system and its deification of private ownership of property. The Golden Rule, that one should do unto others as one would have them do unto him, seemed increasingly to define his philosophy of life. . . .

Jones had the Golden Rule tacked up on a wall at his factory. A benevolent employer, he tried to apply his brotherhood-of-man philosophy in his factory by paying above the prevailing wage, implementing an eight-hour day (when a ten-hour day was common), and giving his employees a one-week vacation with pay and a Christmas bonus. He abolished the job of factory timekeeper, for each man was to keep his own time; he established a jointly supported insurance program; and he distributed sermonettes on brotherhood in pay envelopes. Hot meals at cost were also part of the Golden Rule factory regimen, and in 1901 he set up a profit-sharing plan in which employees could become shareholders. All these benefits, granted freely by Jones, addressed the very issues industrial workers and their unions would spend the first third of the twentieth century fighting to attain. Jones's company welfarism was not the corporate welfarism of the 1920s, which had been intended to head off unionization. It was a genuine reflection of what Jones believed was the right thing to do. And in fact, he encouraged his workers to join unions and even marched with them in Labor Day parades because he hoped that unions would become instruments for fostering his concept of the brotherhood of man.

Outside the factory gate, Jones turned an open field into Golden Rule Park, which had playgrounds and places where his workers' "Golden Rule Band" could serenade the proletariat with instruments paid for by Sam Jones. His private philanthropy carried over into public policy when in 1899 he developed the Toledo park system and a year later established public playgrounds for children. For the winter season, he established a "Golden Rule House," where he often preached on his favorite subjects or invited such social reformers as Governor Hazen Pingree, settlement-house founder Jane Addams, or social gospelers Washington Gladden or Josiah Strong to speak. On the coldest nights, he could be seen in the poorest sections of the city giving aid where it was needed. Although he condemned charity as evidence of the weakness of the capitalist system, he later gave up his full salary as mayor to the poor.

When Jones decided to run for mayor or Toledo, the overwhelming popularity of the lovable and eccentric capitalist followed him to the polls and elected him in 1897. A fortuitous split and an internal squable among the Republican political bosses had given Jones the nomination, and the election put him in city hall. When party bosses subsequently presented the new mayor with a list of faithful followers to be appointed to patronage jobs, His Honor balked: he refused to fire good people who were already on the job simply because of party disloyalty. He told his Republican backers that he had been elected by the people and was not beholden to the party.

As a result, the same Republican machine that had nominated Jones turned fiercely against him in his first reelection try in 1899, and in a wild and woolly city convention he was denied renomination. That suited Jones just fine. The galleries, packed with Jones's nonvoting delegates, hissed at the party stalwarts and shouted, "Down with the traction company!" Jones boldly thumbed his nose at the Republican stalwarts and used the convention platform to announce his independent candidacy for mayor. Thereafter, the maverick mayor became increasingly anti-party and later described himself as "a man without a party, a free untrammeled soul, owing allegiance to nothing less . . . than the whole human race." Jones easily won reelection and was ecstatic that he carried the working-class and labor union vote. He boasted to a correspondent: "The only union in the city which failed to endorse me was the Ministers' Union." . . .

When it came to law and order, Jones believed brotherly love should prevail. He tried to humanize the jails by turning their focus from punishment to rehabilitation and by exposing inmates to sermons on brotherhood. Jones took away truncheons from the police and substituted canes, and in exchange gave them a shortened workday of eight hours. He also went along with the city council's repeal of Sunday saloon closings and thereafter followed a lax policy of letting them stay open seven days a week. "It is not true that the saloons are run wide open on Sunday," Jones sputtered in defense of his policy. "Most of them have their back doors and side doors open, but the front doors of all saloons are closed and the curtains are down on Sunday." That Jonesian sophistry persuaded no one, however, and certainly not the city's venerable clergy, who were shocked and unleashed thunderous sermons from the pulpit against the reign of sin unleashed by the misguided Golden Ruler. Jones then defended himself more persuasively by saying that he considered the saloons to be poor-men's clubs and that the workers should no more be impeded from getting to their social recreation than the rich should be denied access to brandy and billiards at their private clubs.

The moral guardians of the community were even more shocked when Mayor Jones, in his capacity as police magistrate, began to preside at the police court on Monday mornings when the judge was absent. Jones released drunkards, disorderly persons, and prostitutes—sometimes merely with a sermon on goodness and the brotherhood of man, and occasionally with an attack on the "system"—but always without a fine. Drunkenness was not the cause of poverty, Jones declared, but poverty was the cause of drunkenness. He regularly condemned the competitive system as the source of the parade of misery he saw in police court, and he once assured worried good citizens: "Do not take alarm. I am not going to abolish the courts. I can't. But love will one day abolish them and judge and jury, sheriff and policemen, warden and guard will find sweet release from their hideous jobs and be permitted to join the great army of useful workers to set up the real Kingdom of Heaven here and now." So furious were the city's clergy that the Ministers' Union refused to observe National Golden Rule Day in 1901 because it might have brought favorable press to their mayor, who, they believed, had misappropriated the sobriquet "Golden Rule." "Jones's utopian program and his erratic noncon-formist behavior," Jack Tager notes, "brought down upon his head the wrath of the institutional forces of society."

Jones's relaxed attitudes toward law enforcement, and his refusal to enforce the Sunday "blue laws," provided an opportunity for his now-fierce oppo-nent, city boss Walter Brown, to undercut the influence of this perceived nemesis of morality. Brown, with his connections to the state legislature, pushed through a "police-ripper" bill that would have deprived the mayor of control over Toledo's police board and hand it over to the Republican gover-nor. The act also sought to stop the mayor from acting as occasional police magistrate. Jones defiantly refused to recognize the state-appointed police board and took the occasion to challenge special local legislation, or "rip-perism" as it was called. His newly found aide and legal adviser, Brand Whit-lock, skillfully steered the case into the Ohio Supreme Court, which struck the "ripper bill" from the books and overturned the whole system of "specific leg-islation" that state lawmakers had used to meddle in city affairs. The signifi-cance of the court decision was that it denied the legislature the right to pass bills applicable to only one city and required that measures be applied to a class of cities or to all cities. It also forced the state assembly to pass a new municipal code that advanced the cause for municipal home rule.

Unorthodox in his political campaigns, as in most things, Jones campaigned for office by occasionally using his son to blow trumpet blasts to assemble his auditors, but more often he carried a portable piano on the campaign trail with him so that after the speech the assembled could join the mayor in singing hymns he himself had written. Success at the polls, and his defeat of the Repub-lican Mark Hanna machine in Toledo, elevated Jones's stature in Ohio political circles and led to a run for the governorship in 1899. He was defeated in the Re-publican nominating convention by Hanna operatives, and when Jones tried to run as an independent he lost the election. Jones did well in two of the state's largest urban counties, which included Toledo and Cleveland, indicating that those cities were ready for reform. His fame grew rapidly after his first term, and he was called on to speak all over the nation. In addition to his urban reform nostrums, he opposed the Spanish-American War and the American occupation of the Philippines. In a rare departure from his anti-partyism, he endorsed anti-imperialist presidential candidate William Jennings Bryan in 1900 and was used by the Democrats as a kickoff speaker in the New York State campaign for the silver-tongued orator. Although Bryan lost, some benefit accrued at home for Jones: it added Democratic voters to his independent column on election day, and Jones drew a sizable bloc of Bryan's partisans in his 1901 reelection.

The anti-party Jones had nothing resembling a political organization to support him, only an unorganized electorate, because he refused not only to punish his enemies but also to reward his friends. The anti-party mayor re-fused to endorse candidates for the city council and as a result often lacked the support of that body. Nevertheless, he did bring many reforms to Toledo and prepared the ground for many more to follow under his friend and successor, Brand Whitlock. Jones fought to eliminate politics from the police and fire departments and placed them under civil service, and he sought to instill in law enforcers a concept of friendly service—Toledo's early version of "officer friendly." He also implemented the eight-hour day at the waterworks and in other city departments and boosted the low pay of municipal laborers. He pressed hard for other issues, established free public baths, and helped persuade the school system to introduce free kindergarten. To beautify Toledo, he sought measures to force overhead power lines into underground conduits, and he found useful ways to help the unemployed by putting them to work cleaning the city's streets and al-leys. And it was Jones who began the fight for home rule, which would be realized under Whitlock in 1914.

On one of the hottest political issues of his age—the traction problem—Jones campaigned vigorously for low-cost "workingmen's fares" (so-called because they were to be offered during commuting hours), the approval of franchise extensions only by popular referendum, and if possible, munici-pal ownership of all utilities, including traction, gas, and electric light plants. Most state constitutions and city charters prohibited public owner-ship of the utilities, as did Toledo's, but by wielding the veto pen and his fa-mous "petition of boots," Jones was able to stop giveaways to streetcar companies and win from them fares lower than five cents. One of his goals—three-cent fares during workingmen's hours—was achieved by Whitlock in 1913.

Jones defined and focused public attention on the critical issues of his city and his time. For the next fifteen years, the traction question was the central issue in Toledo politics. It was also the issue that carried Jone's successor, Brand Whitlock (1906–13), into office. Jones and Whitlock played key roles in educating the public about the complexities of the traction problem and how stock-watering, bad management and lack of public control could bring high fares and bad service. "So powerful was the influence of his [Jones's] democratic principles and policies that he injected three great issues into Toledo politics that dominated public discussion for a generation after his death," wrote historian Randolph Downes. "These were (1) the Independent movement; (2) home rule; and (3) the campaign to bring the streetcar com-pany under strict public control." The Golden Rule mayor's steely is show-down with traction's "Rule of Gold" was brought to a satisfactory conclusion in 1920 when the streetcar lines agreed to operate under permanent public control and a cost-of-production basis.

Mayor Jones has been judged one of the best of our big-city mayors, be-cause he had defined for his city the key issues of the Progressive Era, and he was an impetus for reform that went on for a generation after. In addition, Jones had trained his successor, reform mayor Brand Whitlock, who carried many of Sam "Golden Rule" Jones's proposals and programs to completion.

23. Reformers in Southwestern Cities

Amy Bridges

Urban political history is not uniform in the United States. Historian Amy Bridges tells the story of the development of "reform" cities in the Southwest. They had their own weaknesses and flaws, different from those cities under machine control in the twentieth century. This alternative urban history still affects these cities in the twenty-first century.

I n one of his most famous remarks, George Washington Plunkitt dismissed municipal reformers as "morning glories" who "looked lovely in the mornin' and withered up in a short time, while the regular machines went on flourishin' forever, like fine old oaks." Plunkitt recalled New York's People's Municipal League of 1890, the Committee of Seventy of 1894, the Citizens' Union, the good government clubs; none had lasted more than a few years. New York was hardly exceptional. Although the municipal reform movement eventually had profound effects on city politics everywhere, in the large cities of the Northeast and Midwest, municipal reformers celebrated few victories at the polls, and when they did win, their time in office was in most places fleeting. So Plunkitt found "college professors and philosophers . . . are always discussin' the question, 'Why Reform Administrations Never Succeed Themselves.' "

In the Southwest municipal reformers enjoyed a different history. In the Progressive Era, and again in the 1940s, municipal reformers celebrated political victories across the region. Just as the big cities of the Northeast and Midwest were commonly governed by political machines, and the cities of the South by Bourbon coalitions, so the cities of the Southwest have in the twentieth century been governed by municipal reformers. Had Plunkitt investigated the morning glory, this possibility might have occurred to him. Plunkitt, of course, was talking about the flowers, which open in the morning and fade as the sun goes down. By contrast, its roots and vines (as anyone with morning glories in the garden has the misfortune to know) are invasive and tenacious. Nowhere is this more true than in the Southwest. There the vigor of the morning glory is so great that other plants are smothered by it. In Arizona the morning glory is considered an agricultural pest, the sale of morning glory seed is banned, and import of plants of its genus (*Ipomoea*) illegal. Likewise, the growth of municipal reform in the Southwest choked out its opponents, replacing parties with nonpartisanship, party politicians with a civic elite, mayors with commissioners and managers, competition with political monopoly. . . .

SOURCE: Amy Bridges, *Morning Glories: Municipal Reform in the Southwest*. Princeton: Princeton University Press, 1997, pp. 3–9, 14–16, 23–25 and 29. Copyright © 1997 by Princeton University Press. Reprinted by permission of Princeton University Press.

The textbook history of reform is a truncated one. Students of city politics are familiar with the mugwumps and party bosses of the late nineteenth century, the muckrakers and progressives of the first generation after 1900, the Seth Lows, Tom Johnsons, Carter Harrisons, and George Washington Plunkitts. These actors dominate the history of their eras as they dominated the politics of the nation's big cities. In later periods municipal reform suggests the profound effects the movement eventually had on local politics everywhere: the decline of corruption, the replacement of patronage with civil service, the introduction of professionalism and expertise to city government, the growth of ungovernable bureaucracies.

By the middle of the twentieth century, reform governance was, in the textbooks, relegated to the suburbs. In *City Politics,* Edward Banfield and James Q. Wilson explained the "reform ideal" and sketched the kind of community in which it was "nearly realized in practice":

> An example is Winnetka, a suburb of Chicago the residents of which are almost all upper middle class Anglo-Saxon Protestants. Winnetkans are in fundamental agreement on the kind of local government they want: it must provide excellent schools, parks, libraries, and other community services and it must provide them with businesslike efficiency and perfect honesty. Politics, in the sense of a competitive struggle for office or for private advantage, does not exist. No one offers himself as a candidate for office. Instead the civic associations agree upon a slate of those "best qualified to serve" which the voters ratify as a matter of course. Members of the city council leave "administration" entirely in the hands of the city manager.

Robert C. Wood's *Suburbia* had shown that the style of politics found in Winnetka was typical of suburbs, where, it seemed, good government advocates had found their greatest success.

The institutionalization of reform politics in the suburbs is presented as the denouement of the history of the municipal reform movement. Contemporary city politics textbooks have shared this reading, Judd and Swanstrom report in *City Politics, Private Power and Public Policy* that city-manager government was "rarely instituted in the big cities, [although] it became common in smaller cities around the nation." Harrigan writes in *Political Change in the Metropolis* "reform-style city government is most likely to be found in suburban cities." The same textbooks discuss the bias of various reform arrangements (citywide elections, for example) but do not offer a portrait of reform governance. Historians have shared this reading; even urban historians as wise as Roger Lotchin and Charles Glaab agreed that "the city manager system 'did not significantly influence big city government and politics' after World War II."

Yet at the moment Banfield and Wilson were writing *City Politics,* Dallas, Austin, Phoenix, San Antonio, San Jose, Albuquerque, and San Diego were governed by nonpartisan city-manager regimes, with city council members elected citywide. In 1960 they were small cities, only Dallas ranking in the largest dozen of the nation's metropolises. In 1990 the same cities were all among the nation's largest dozen cities and still boasted nonpartisan city-manager governments (although city councils were by then mostly elected from districts). If the suburbs are home to the denouement of municipal reform, the movement's greatest achievements were the governments of the big cities of the Southwest.

BIG-CITY REFORM

The nineteenth-century history of machine politicians and municipal reformers is the prologue to this account of big-city reform. Machine politicians and municipal reformers were the fraternal twins of the antebellum United States, their simultaneous birth beginning a struggle for control of the nation's cities. Hardly had the first party boss appeared in local politics when a municipal reform movement was organized to dethrone him. Baltimore, Boston, Philadelphia, New York, Pittsburgh, Springfield (Massachusetts), and Cincinnati had municipal reform movements before the Civil War. For the rest of the century, and in some places much longer, party politicians and municipal reformers competed for control of city governments.

The rhetoric and much of the program of municipal reform were nineteenth-century inventions. Reformers saw the ills of local government as a consequence of machine rule. "Nothing can be more true than that that modern and monstrous instrument known as the political party machine . . . is the source of these evils." Machines drew their strength, reformers argued, from the unquestioning partisanship of working class, especially immigrant, voters bought with the dispensation of favors and patronage. The corruption inherent in such a system was both shameful and expensive. Were machine politicians to remain in control of city government, Boston's Citizens Ticket feared "a load of municipal taxation and debt more intolerable than the British tyranny, from which our fathers revolted."

Reformers' program followed directly from this analysis. Largely negative, the proposals of municipal reformers were meant to dismantle machines by loosening the ties between voters and officials. The key was depriving politicians of patronage and other resources. First, reformers championed nonpartisanship to erode the ties of party. In Boston the *Daily Advertiser* hailed the election of a reform mayor as "a victory of citizens without distortion of party against a corrupt and proscriptive partisan rule." Similarly, New York's reformers boasted that their candidates were "untrammeled by party pledges." Second, in place of party politicians, reformers offered government by the city's "best men." Reformers would, if elected, replace the rule of muscle with government by men of "spotless integrity, close judgement, and sterling common sense." Reform candidates promised businesslike efficiency in place of extravagance, as when New York's reformers declared, "Retrenchment is the twin of reform." Philadelphia's reform administration claimed credit for lowering taxes and replacing the "evil-minded, vicious, and depraved in office with men of probity and good business capacity." Later, civil service and competitive bidding for government contracts were proposed to deny the resources of favors, patronage, and corruption to municipal officeholders.

Municipal reformers were often politically allied with nativists, and later, with proponents of eugenics and white supremacy, sharing with them antipathy to immigrants and people of color, and so a desire to tighten controls on voting. From the middle of the nineteenth century through the Progressive Era, reformers and nativists proposed voter registration, literacy testing, extending the residency period required for voting, and the poll tax. Banfield and Wilson identified the same motivations with the city-manager plan later in the century: "Making local government 'businesslike' meant 'getting rid of politics,' which in turn meant curtailing the representation of low-status minorities. In its early years, the [council-manager] plan appealed to a good many people as a convenient means of putting the Catholics, the Irish, the Italians, the labor unions, and all other 'underdogs' in their places."

Reformers recognized that machine politicians won votes not only by providing patronage employment, but also from the provision of rudimentary social services. The reform movement was divided, however, over the appropriate response. Social reformers and the most prominent women among municipal reformers argued for the professionalization of social services, while many structural reformers argued for shortening government's agenda. Jane Addams, for example, believed machine politics "would disappear once the city itself provided the services currently offered by the boss." Women's municipal activism embraced the tasks of public education, child welfare and juvenile guidance (especially for adolescents), charity, and public health ("municipal housekeeping"). When a committee of the National Municipal League wrote its municipal program, however, women were excluded from the committee and their concerns from the reform agenda. The program diagnosed municipal ills "as a problem of institutional structure and governmental machinery." This meant that the National Municipal League not only endorsed model political and administrative arrangements, but also a very limited sphere for local government.

In the Progressive Era, municipal reformers in the nation's big cities only rarely prevailed against the strong partisan loyalties of machine supporters, not least because so many reformers were hostile to immigrants, who were a large portion of the electorate. By contrast, the municipal reform movement celebrated triumphs across the United States as small cities and towns adopted commission charters. The commission plan gained prominence once it was adopted for Galveston, Texas, after a hurricane destroyed that city. Galveston's successful comeback made the commission plan "the core of urban progressivism." The National League of Municipalities endorsed the commission plan as its model city charter. Armed with the plan, with editorials, speakers, and advice from the National Municipal League, good government organizations in smaller cities across the country campaigned to reorganize local governments. . . .

In my narrative I present politics in southwestern cities in three periods. The first is from the first reform charter (usually a commission charter) to the adoption of city-manager government. The adoption of city-manager charters in most places initiates the period of big-city reform, which is concluded by the adoption of district elections for city council members. These "periods" are not altogether concurrent with major twentieth-century historical markers (say, World War I or the New Deal). Moreover, they are not concurrent across cities. Dallas, for example, may fairly be said to exhibit big-city reform politics from well before World War II until 1976; San Diego, from 1931 to 1988; while in Albuquerque big-city reform is more short-lived, from 1946 to 1974. . . .

REFORM INSTITUTIONS AND POLITICAL CULTURE

Municipal reformers were prolific in the invention of public organizations and administrative arrangements. The National Municipal League and the Short Ballot Organization were just the beginning. Municipal reformers organized municipal research bureaus and nonpartisan slating groups; campaigned for civil service, commission government, and the city manager; and promoted city planning, the authority, autonomous commission, and special districts to further economic development (of which the best known southwestern examples are the Los Angeles Department of Water and Power and the city's Harbor Commission; the Port of New York Authority shares their progressive origin).

Reformers were also assiduous in arranging the rules of government and elections. Reformers' aims of loosening the ties of politicians and their constituents on one hand, and limiting the number of constituents on the other, informed their designs. To those ends reformers endorsed nonpartisanship, citywide and nonconcurrent elections, selection of the mayor by the city council, and a variety of barriers to registration and voting. The twentieth-century reformer Richard S. Childs counseled the importance of "wieldy constituencies" for the success of municipal reform. Leaders of big-city reform governments understood the principle well. Reform governance worked in part by selectively mobilizing "wieldy" constituencies from the unwieldy societies of their metropolitan settings.

Reform designs worked much as reformers intended. Reform regimes governed a political life of low participation and little public dissent. Thus the solution to the consent problem was, in the first instance, the exclusion of most urban residents from the political system. As a result, the characteristic political community of reform government was relatively small, affluent, and Anglo. Reform governments did not reflect, in their personnel or their policies, the divisions and preferences of their diverse big cities. Reformers wrote the rules to win the game of local politics; their great accomplishment was to create political communities that looked like Winnetka in social settings that were much larger and more diverse. . . .

Municipal reformers not only wrote the rules to win the game of local politics, they also enjoyed a rhetorical monopoly, a monopoly of public discourse in southwestern cities. By "public discourse" I mean discourse "heard" by all citizens. Reformers and their supporters owned the mass media and, in the absence of well-organized opposition that could force public debate, the media excluded opposition voices. There were African-American, Spanish, and labor newspapers in the Southwest, often oppositional, but their readership was small and surely confined to a target audience. Thus, although there were alternative voices in local politics, they were not heard beyond their restricted audiences. . . .

The function of . . . public discourse was didactic, explaining government, politics, and the common good. As a consequence, public discourse made moral and cognitive contributions to the strength of reform governments. At the same time, the narrowness of public discourse made it extremely difficult for the most energetic critics of local government—people of color—to make claims that majority constituents recognized as legitimate, and so to find allies, form coalitions, and participate successfully in local politics. Indeed, until well after the Second World War, most Anglo citizens were likely ignorant of their complaints. We may look to New York's ethnically balanced tickets or to Chicago for contrary examples. In Chicago the events surrounding the election of Harold Washington were surely tortuous and filled with conflict. Nevertheless, African Americans in Chicago could—since descriptive representation, majority rule, and ethnic succession were all understood rules of the game—make the claim, "It's our turn." Because in reform regimes there were turns neither in principle nor in fact, reform rhetoric made it difficult to find allies, just as reform rules made descriptive representation impossible.

As this discussion suggests, the values politicians voiced were given meaning in the practice of local government. After each electoral victory, promise is made practice in political institutions, electoral arrangements, policy processes, and political outcomes of all sorts. This is why political ethos does not wither away, either in Chicago a generation after the death of Richard J. Daley or in the Southwest a generation after the organizing rules of reform regimes were dismantled.

What of class? There is overwhelming evidence about the class difference in sources of support for machine and reform government. Everywhere, machine politicians claimed strong support from working-class voters, while municipal reformers could count on middle-class voters. In fights over the adoption of reform charters, labor unions and working-class voters almost always opposed municipal reform, while middle-class and affluent voters usually supported it.

In the Southwest, too, the middle class has been at the center of municipal reform politics. Its role was not to design reform institutions, or organize campaigns to secure them. Rather, the Anglo middle class has been the core constituency of local politics. There were two reasons for this. For one, southwestern cities have been, since the Second World War, somewhat more affluent than the machine descendants of the Northeast and Midwest. No government that alienated affluent Anglo voters (as Daley did their counterparts in Chicago) could survive. Second, the electoral arrangements and political boundaries of reform cities were designed to exclude poor and working-class voters, creating an electorate more middle class than its surrounding community.

From the perspective of the leaders of big-city reform, the middle class was an appealing constituency because its wish list was short. This made it possible to secure their support while pursuing growth and annexation policies that required substantial public subsidy. Reform governments in the suburbs, like Winnetka, were constituted somewhat differently. There high turnout rather than low participation was characteristic. In both suburban and southwestern settings, the preponderantly middle-class electorate was shielded by its homogeneity from demands for redistribution. . . .

CONCLUSION

Early in this century, the strategic location of the Southwest advantaged proponents of municipal reform and provided a disabling environment for reform's antagonists. The result was that almost without exception the small cities and towns of the Southwest adopted reform (that is, commission or city-manager) charters. In the years that followed, reform government proved difficult to bring to life. Nevertheless, reformers could count important accomplishments, of which restriction of the electorate was probably the most important. At midcentury southwestern cities witnessed another wave of charter revision and elite organization; the institutional arrangements of municipal reform were refurbished. As a result, the postwar decades saw the flowering of big-city reform.

Big-city reform was a political system characterized by very low participation and little effective competition. Incumbents could as confidently count on reelection as any machine politician. Popular support was found in affluent Anglo communities, to whom amenities (libraries, better schools, parks) were carefully targeted. The pursuit of growth as conducted by these governments also served their core constituents, as subsidies to developers in effect subsidized middle-class homeowners. The results were a small, contented political community that had good government and knew it was good, and political leaders well insulated from such popular discontent as might exist. The great achievement of big-city reform was the creation of political communities that looked like Winnetka from their sprawling and diverse metropolises.

This accomplishment became, after 1960, a barrier to local government's continuing legitimacy. African-American and Mexican-American communities, long marginalized or excluded, voiced their discontents with increasing insistence, and focused their sights squarely on the institutional arrangements that politically disabled them. Their critique of big-city reform was joined by Anglo, middle-class communities. Wholly committed to growth policies that played the whole against its parts, big-city reform distributed discontents that created pluralities of affluent, Anglo voters who wanted to abandon at-large elections in favor of district representation, and government by civic statesmen in favor of government by politicians. The result was that between 1974 and 1990, the central political institutions of big-city reform were dismantled.

Chapter 7

Modern Urban Leaders: Reformers, Bosses, Crooks, Saints, and Scoundrels

In some cities it wasn't always the party boss who had the power. In New York, for instance, when Tammany Hall fell from power, it wasn't a politician but an appointed official, Robert Moses, who took over the direction of the big public works projects like building the expressways. Of course, Moses frequently had to compromise and make deals with the politicians and the wealthy to get his projects accomplished, but he single-handedly changed the face of New York City and the surrounding areas like Long Island. It was an authority not grounded in winning elections or courting voters, but in heading obscure public authorities. In many ways he was not as accountable as even the political bosses had been. His decisions frequently hurt the poor farmers on Long Island and poor neighborhood residents in New York City who stood in the path of proposed expressways and parks. But his projects also knit the city together, made movement between the different boroughs and the many suburbs possible, and provided recreational facilities for the city's millions of inhabitants. This was a very different face of power than the party bosses of earlier years. There were figures like Moses in other cities and suburbs in the country even though they weren't as well known. People other than mayors and aldermen have power in American metropolitan regions. Some, like Moses, who head public agencies, have even more power than elected officials in arenas like housing, transportation, and economic development.

We are used to thinking of the political leaders of cities as being White men because throughout American history White men like the New York bosses or Richard J. Daley of Chicago have most often been the mayors of American cities. However, after the 1970s, African Americans began to ascend into the most important positions of political power in many of America's largest and most important cities. They included mayors like Richard Hatcher of Gary, Indiana; Harold Washington of Chicago; Marion Barry of Washington, D.C.; Maynard Jackson of Atlanta; and Tom Bradley of Los Angeles. Today, there are about forty African-American mayors of cities over 50,000 population and Black city and county officials have increased from 715 in 1970 to nearly 6,000 today.[1] The story of how Mayor Bradley transformed Los Angeles is included in these readings as one example of African-American mayoral rule. Information on Latino mayors of Miami and Santa Fe are provided to round out the picture of minority mayors in American cities.

It isn't just the biographies and achievements of individual politicians and ad-ministrators that are important, it is the complexity of the political problems facing modern urban politicians and how they have coped in different ways. The story of Ed Rendell, who served as mayor of Philadelphia throughout most of the 1990s, and his struggle to bring his city back from the brink of economic disaster provides a snap shot of modern mayors, the problems they face, and how they try to inspire and lead their cities even in difficult economic times. In his inaugural address, he declared: "Make no mistake, our situation is worse than we thought it could ever be. . . . Change must surely come, but the good news is that if it does come, this city cannot only survive; it can come alive again with a thriving economy, strong neighbor-hoods, and a dynamic downtown that can serve as a magnet to conventioneers, tourists, and suburbanites alike." Philadelphia's current mayor, African American John Street, is now spending $295 million to build new housing on some of the city's 31,000 vacant lots and to replace some 26,000 abandoned housing units.[2]

Most cities in the United States did improve in the 1990s and the beginning of the twenty-first century. They began to come back, to gain new jobs, new housing, and more resources because of the economic boom. But the long-term battle for the future of the cities is not over and not every city has a mayor like Ed Rendell. The trajectory of American cities during the recession and uncertain economic times that began in 2001, especially after the terrorists' destruction of the World Trade Center in New York and part of the Pentagon in Washington D.C., is less cer-tain. Creating a positive urban future will demand strong leadership.

This section contains a portrait of African-American Mayor Tom Bradley and the multi-racial coalition that he put together that could not withstand the city's race riot. The struggle of Mayor Bradley to cope with the special problems and op-portunities of Los Angeles is instructive for all American cities.

There is a darker side to American city politics. If city bosses and powerful fig-ures like Robert Moses have ambiguous legacies, there are others who participate in corruption, crime, and patronage. San Francisco's city bureaucrat Thomas May-field illustrates this side of urban life. Mayfield ran gang prevention programs un-der previous mayors and later directed a group of former gang members who pa-trolled public transportation and public housing projects. According to the *San Francisco Weekly,* he gave out jobs to former "gang members, low-income resi-dents, troubled teens, and former drug dealers." Some argue that such programs saved the lives of youth who would otherwise have ended up permanently in prison. Others argue that it only perpetuated crime and corruption for the sake of minority voter support for various San Francisco mayors.[3]

If any city has convoluted politics and colorful politicians, it is Miami with its contests between African Americans, Whites, Puerto Ricans, and Cubans for power at the city and county levels. The Latinos in charge haven't done much better governing than the White political bosses of Northern and Midwestern cities or African-American mayors like Marion Barry of Washington, D.C., who have succumbed to corruption, drugs, or the misuse of power. In the late 1990s, Miami was so chaotic that voters considered disbanding their city government to be governed by the county instead. That referendum failed because Latinos and Blacks were more supportive of city government than Anglos, who had lost faith in their city government completely. This turmoil was followed with a mayoral election so full of vote fraud that the city commission chairman was sent to jail. City managers, police superintendents, and other key bureaucrats were changed every few months as various mayors were first elected and then thrown out of office by court decisions.

The story of Miami's political turmoil also includes the role that lobbyists played in obtaining city contracts—contracts often counter to the public interest but profitable for the private firms who hired lobbyists and corrupted politicians. Lobbyists in the past were less involved in urban politics, but with multi-million dollar contracts now available in cities, they have become a fixture in most big cities.

Another alternative in modern urban politics has emerged in Chicago. There has been in "the windy city" the creation of a new machine with elements of the old machine welded to a structural and civic reform agenda without fundamental political reform. Once again, a Mayor Daley rules the city and, once again, he rules supreme. Since 1989, Richard M. Daley, the son of the famous boss Richard J. Daley, has dominated Chicago politics and government. Daley's multi-million dollar mayoral campaigns resemble the national presidential campaigns of Presidents Clinton and Bush. His high-tech campaigns are run by professional consultants and public relations officials. They are funded by the business community—especially those wanting construction contracts from city hall and the new global or service economy in the city. Campaign contributions from the global economy sector have also become very important in Los Angeles mayoral and aldermanic elections. The "new" economy contributed 68 percent of the contributions to Los Angeles Mayor James Hahn's campaign and 56 percent to the successful aldermanic candidates in 2001. This appears to be an important new trend in many American cities.[4]

In Chicago, however, coupled to the high-tech, modern campaigns are patronage precinct workers from the old days of traditional machine politics in Chicago. Together they combine to create "The New Daley Machine."

The social movements that opposed the earlier Daley are not strong. Likewise, splits in the African-American community and in the broader reform movement, let Richard M. Daley rule unchallenged. The City Council has become once again a rubber stamp. In the period from January, 2000, to December, 2002, there were only 16 divided roll call votes, all of which the mayor won handily.[5] There is no consistent, well-organized, opposition in the council to propose clear alternative programs.

To Mayor Daley's credit, he has adopted good management techniques, kept many of the positive programs like freedom of information, neighborhood economic development, and affirmative action in jobs and contracts that had been put in place by a previous reform administration. For the moment, in Chicago however, this "Machine Politics-Reform Style" is dominant.[6]

The final vignette is about the woman mayor of Santa Fe. Mayor Debbie Jaramillo is pushing a progressive agenda of limits on campaign spending and overdevelopment of her city for the wealthy to the detriment of the poor; expanding direct democracy; and eliminating racial and sexual discrimination. This Hispanic woman mayor illustrates the diversity in political and governmental styles and how much difference a single leader can make.

U.S. cities and suburbs today have variously conservative, pragmatic, new machine, and progressive mayors, aldermen, and public officials all vying for power. We do not know which will dominate the future of American urban politics.

Notes

1. Dennis Judd and Todd Swanstrom, *City Politics,* New York: Longman, 2002, pp. 402–403.
2. Rob Gurwitt, "Betting on the Bull," *Governing,* July 2002, pp. 28–34.
3. George Cothran and David Pasztor, "Crime and Patronage in San Francisco," *SF Weekly,* Web Archives, 1998. *http://www.sfweekly.com/archives/1998/081998/feature1-1.htm.*
4. Timothy Krebs, "The Los Angeles Regime," Unpublished paper, Midwest Political Science Association Meeting in Chicago, Illinois, April 25–28, 2002 Tables 1 and 2.
5. Dick Simpson, Ole Adeoye, Ruben Felician, and Rick Howard, "Chicago's Uncertain Future Since September 11, 2001," *Urban Affairs Review,* Vol. 38, No. 1, September 2002, pp. 128–134.
6. See William Grimshaw, *Bitter Fruit: Black Politics and the Chicago Machine 1931–1991,* Chicago: University of Chicago Press, 1992, Chapter 9.

24. Robert Moses of New York City

Robert Caro

Not all the powerful people in our cities and suburbs are elected officials. This article on Robert Moses shows how some unelected officials can shape the physical form of cities and suburbs for generations as well as how they can affect the lives of thousands of people who live in the path of grand plans and bulldozers. Was Robert Moses right or wrong to do as he did? Were the citizens and elected officials and the state right to grant him these powers?

Robert Moses is the man who, more than any other individual, shaped modern New York. He had been the most powerful figure in New York City and New York State for more than forty years—more powerful than any mayor or governor, or any mayor and governor combined. . . .

A key element of the image of Robert Moses that had for forty years been created and burnished by him was that he was the very antithesis of the politician, a public servant—uncompromisingly above politics who never allowed political considerations to influence any aspect of his projects. After all the reasoning went, he built most of his projects through public authorities, which were also outside politics. No journalist or historian seemed to see authorities as sources of political power in and of themselves. . . .

Born on December 18, 1888, to a wealthy German Jewish family active in the settlement-house movement, Moses had been educated at Yale and Oxford, and had returned to New York to earn his Ph.D. in political science at Columbia and join a municipal-reform organization as a researcher. In 1914,

SOURCE: From *The Power Broker.* Copyright © 1974 by Robert A. Caro. Used by permission of Alfred A. Knopf, a division of Random House, Inc. Also in Robert A. Caro, "The City-Shaper," *The New Yorker,* January 5, 1998, pp. 38–55.

at the age of 25 he was filled with idealism—he had devised an elaborate plan to cleanse New York of Tammany Hall's influence by eliminating patronage from the city's corruption-ridden civil-service system—and with ideas, many of them about public works. "Everything he saw walking around the city made him think of some way that it could be better," Miss Frances Perkins [a fellow reformer] had told her oral-history interviewer. "He was always burning up with ideas, just burning up with them."

REMAKING NEW YORK CITY

The biggest idea of all concerned the western shoreline of Manhattan Island from about 72 Street up to about 181st Street. That six miles of shoreline, below the high cliff of Riverside Drive, was popularly called Riverside Park; but, unlike the park's landscaped upper level in 1914, the part along the edge of the Hudson was nothing more than a six-mile-long wasteland of mud and rapidly eroding landfill and through its entire length ran four tracks of the New York Central Railroad, lined by high, sharp-edged fences that for seventy years had cut the city off from its waterfront. Since the locomotives that towed the endless trains carrying cattle and pigs south to the slaughterhouses downtown burned coal or oil, the "park" was constantly covered with a thick, gritty, foul-smelling black smog. Huge mounds of raw garbage lay piled there, waiting for scows to collect it and carry it out to sea. There were several large shantytowns in it, inhabited by derelicts so intimidating that their shacks were avoided even by the police; at night the residents of Riverside Drive apartment houses could see the derelicts' open fires glowing in the darkness by the river. But one Sunday in 1914, as a group of young men and women were taking a ferry to a picnic in New Jersey, Robert Moses was standing beside Frances Perkins on the deck, and as the ferry pulled out into the Hudson, and the bleak mudflats shrouded in smog spread out behind them, he suddenly said excitedly, "Isn't this a temptation to you? Couldn't this waterfront be the most beautiful thing in the world?" And, Miss Perkins was to recall, he began to talk faster and faster, and she realized, to her amazement, that "he had it all figured out. How you could build a great highway that went uptown along the water. How you'd have to tear down a few buildings at 72 Street and bring the highway around a curve," how the railroad tracks would be covered by the highway, and cars would be driving serenely along it with their passengers delighting in the river scene, how there would be long green parks filled with people playing tennis and baseball and riding bicycles, and elegant marinas for sailboats.

Looking up from the typescript [of the oral history interview] (bound, I still remember, in a gray loose-leaf notebook), I realized that what Robert Moses had been talking about on that long-ago Sunday was what I knew as Riverside Park and the West Side Highway—the great park and road that, as long as I could remember, had formed the western waterfront of Manhattan Island. Although many other plans had been conceived for the waterfront, this immense public work would be built by him—in 1937, almost a quarter of a century after the ferry ride. And it would be built—this urban improvement on a scale so huge that it would be almost without precedent in early-twentieth-century

America, this improvement that would in addition, solve a problem that had baffled successive city administrations for decades—in very much the same form in which he had envisioned it as a young municipal reformer just out of college.

I had previously been aware only of the Robert Moses of the 1950s and 1960s: the ruthless highway builder who ran his roads straight through hapless neighborhoods, the Robert Moses of the Title I urban renewal scandals—some of the greatest scandals of twentieth-century New York, scandals almost incredible both for the colossal scale of their corruption (personally "money honest" himself, Moses dispensed to the most powerful members of the city's ruling Democratic political machine what one insider called "a king's ransom" in legal fees, public-relations retainers, insurance premiums, advance knowledge of highway routes and urban renewal sites, and insurance-free deposits in favored banks, to insure their cooperation with his aims) and for the heartbreaking callousness with which he evicted the tens of thousands of poor people in his way, whom, in the words of one official, he "hounded out like cattle." Now I saw something very different: the young Robert Moses, the dreamer and idealist. How had the one man become the other? . . .

Moses the Power Broker

In the terms in which I have always thought about New York politics, elected officials—mayors and governors in particular—the principal repositories of the political power that plays so significant a role over our lives: in a democracy, after all, ultimate power theoretically comes from the ballot box. But Robert Moses had never been elected to anything. And yet Robert Moses had held power for 44 years, between 1924 and 1968, through the administrations of five mayors and six governors, and, in the fields in which he chose to exercise it, his power was so enormous that no mayor or governor contested it. He held power, in other words, for almost half the century we observe this week—the century that began when, on January 1, 1898, the five boroughs were united into a single city (which became, with that unification, the greatest city in the New World). And during that century he, more than any mayor or governor, molded the city to his vision, put his mark upon it so deeply that today, thirty years after he left power, we are still, to an astonishing extent, living in the city he shaped.

The legislative act that unified New York created a city of five boroughs, but only one of them—the Bronx—was on the mainland of the United States, so the new city was really a city of islands. It was Robert Moses, more than any legislature or any other individual, who tied those islands together with bridges, soldering together three boroughs at once with the Triborough Bridge (and then tying two of them, the Bronx and Queens, even more firmly together with the Bronx-Whitestone and Throgs Neck Bridges), spanning the Narrows to Staten Island with the mighty Verrazano, tying the distant Rockaways firmly to the rest of the metropolis with the Marine and Cross-Bay spans, uniting the West Bronx and Manhattan with the Henry Hudson. Since 1917, seven great bridges have been built to link the boroughs together. Robert Moses built every one of those bridges.

He built every one of the expressways that cut across the city, carrying its people and its commerce—15 expressways, plus the West Side Highway and the Harlem River Drive. If a person is driving in New York on a road that has the word "expressway" in its title, he is driving on a road built by Robert Moses.

He built every one of the parkways that, within the city's borders, stretch eastward toward the counties of Long Island, and he built every one of the parkways that, beyond those borders, run far out into those counties, thereby shaping them as well as the city. There are eleven of those parkways in all. And he either built or rebuilt—rebuilt so completely that they became largely his creations—five parkways stretching toward, or within, Westchester County, so that he built a total of 16 parkways. In New York City and its suburbs, he built a total of 627 miles of expressways and parkways.

He created—or re-created, shaping to his philosophy of recreation—every park in the city, adding 20,000 acres of parkland (and 658 playgrounds) in a city that had been starved for parks and playgrounds; since he left power, several new parks have been built, and several older parks—most notably Central Park—have been restored to their pre-Moses form, but most of New York's parks are still, today, essentially the parks of Robert Moses. And for the use of the city's residents he created, outside the city's borders, on Long Island, another 40,000 acres of parks, including not only Jones Beach, which may be the world's greatest oceanfront park and bathing beach, but other huge parks and beaches—Sunken Meadow, Hither Hills, Montauk Point, Bethpage, Belmont Lake, Hempstead Lake, and eight others.

And bridges, roads, parks, and beaches are only a part of the mark that Robert Moses left on New York. During the time in which he controlled—controlled absolutely—the New York City Housing Authority, the authority built 1,082 apartment houses, containing 148,000 apartments which housed 555,000 people: more people than, at the time, lived in Minneapolis. Those apartments are mainly for persons of low income. For persons of higher income, he created, under urban renewal programs, tens of thousands of additional apartments. He was the dominant force, moreover, behind such supposedly private housing developments as Stuyvesant Town, Peter Cooper Village, Concord Village, and Co-op City—and such monumental features of the New York landscape as Lincoln Center, the United Nations headquarters, Shea Stadium, the New York Coliseum, and the campuses of Fordham, Pratt, and Long Island Universities. He changed the city's very shape, enlarging it by adding to its shoreline more than 15,000 acres of new land, tying together small islands within its borders with rock and sand and stone, so that, for example, Ward's Island and Randall's Island were united, and Hunters and Twin Islands were joined to Rodman's Neck, so that their combined area would be big enough to hold the mile-long crescent of his Orchard Beach creation. He built public works that, even in 1968 dollars, cost $27 billion (a figure that would have to be multiplied many times to put it in today's dollars). He was the greatest builder in the history of America, perhaps in the history of the world.

He shaped the city physically not only by what he built but by what he destroyed. To build his expressways, he evicted from their homes 250,000 persons, in the process ripping out the centers of a score of neighborhoods many of them friendly, vibrant communities that had made the city a home to its people. To build his non-highway public works, he evicted perhaps 250,000 more; a 1954 City Planning Commission study of just seven years of Robert Moses' eviction policy was to call it "an enforced population displacement completely unlike any previous population movement in the City's history." And, since the people he evicted were overwhelmingly Black, Hispanic, and poor, the most defenseless of the city's people, and since he refused, despite the policy of the city's elected officials, to make adequate provision (to make any substantial provision at all, really) for their relocation, the policies he followed created new slums almost as fast as he was eliminating old ones and, tragically, were to be a major factor in solidifying the already existing ghettoization of New York—the dividing up of its residents by color and income.

Immense as was Robert Moses physical shaping of New York, however, his influence on the city's history cannot be measured merely by the physical. All told, during the decades of his power he used that power to bend the city's social policies to his philosophical beliefs, skewing, often despite the wishes of its mayors and other elected officials, the allocation of the city's resources to the benefit of its middle, upper-middle, and upper classes at the expense of the city's lower middle class and its poor, and particularly at the expense of the new immigrants. These were Blacks and Puerto Ricans, mainly, who had begun arriving in New York in substantial numbers not long after he came to power in the city. His power also has to be measured by zoning policies on Long Island that guaranteed suburban sprawl and by decades of systematic starvation of the subways and commuter railroads that he viewed as rivals for his roads and the revenue they produced, a policy that exacerbated the highway congestion that has made traffic jams an inescapable part of New Yorkers' lives.

The more I thought about Robert Moses's career, the more I realized that his story and the story of New York City were, to a remarkable degree, one story. . . .

He had unveiled a plan of bridges, tunnels, expressways, parkways, and parks for the metropolitan region almost forty years earlier, on February 25, 1930, when, before 500 civic leaders assembled in the Grand Ballroom of the Hotel Commodore for the Park Association's annual dinner; he pulled a drape away from a huge map of New York City hanging behind the dais—a map covered with red lines indicating highways and bridges and tunnels, and green areas representing tens of thousands of acres he wanted to acquire for new parks. For almost forty years, he had been filling in that map, turning lines into concrete, green ink into green spaces. But in 1967 his outline was still far from completed. He had built a network of great urban roads—far more urban roads than any other man in history—but there were gaps in that network: gaps on Manhattan Island, where a Lower Manhattan Expressway, across Broome Street, and a Mid-Manhattan Expressway, across 30 Street (an eight-lane highway a hundred feet in the air, above some of the busiest streets in the world, through a forest of skyscrapers), and an Upper Manhattan Expressway, at 125 Street, would, he was sure, solve the metropolitan region's worsening traffic congestion, and other gaps, like the one on Fire Island. . . .

The Human Cost

One of the implications of Robert Moses' career that I was examining was the human cost of the 15 massive expressways he had built within the city itself. What had been the effect of these giant roads on the neighborhoods in their paths, and on the residents of these neighborhoods? I had decided to try to show this by focusing on one neighborhood, and had selected East Tremont, through which, during the 1950s he had built the Cross-Bronx Expressway on that route which had demolished a solid mile of six- and seven-story apartment houses—54 of them—thereby destroying the homes of several thousand families, although there was available just two blocks away the parallel route that would have required the demolition of only six tenements—but which would have also required the demolition of the "Tremont Depot" of the Third Avenue Transit Company, in which several key Bronx Democratic politicians had hidden interests, and which they didn't want condemned.

Up until the day—December 4, 1952—on which the eviction notices signed by "Robert Moses, City Construction Coordinator" and giving the recipients 90 days to move arrived, East Tremont had been a low-income but stable community of 60,000 persons, predominantly Jewish but with sizable Irish and German populations. Its residents had been poor—pressers, finishers, and cutters in the downtown garment district—and their apartment houses were old, some without elevators and almost all with aging plumbing. But the rooms were big and high-ceilinged—"light, airy, spacious" was how the residents described them to me—and the apartment houses were precious to the people who lived in them, because, rent-controlled as they were, their residents could afford, so long as they kept them, to live in their community. As long as they had those apartments, they had a lot—a sense of community; and continuity; in some of those buildings, two and three generations of the same families were living, young couples who moved away often moved back. "The reason we moved back to that area was that we loved it so much," said one young woman who had moved back shortly before the notices came. "There was no reason for an older person to be lonely in that neighborhood," said one who lived there. If they lost their apartments, they knew, they could not afford to live in the city, and would be scattered to the winds. And then the notices from Moses arrived. "It was like the floor opened up underneath your feet," one woman told me. "There was no warning. We just got it in the mail. Everybody on the street got it the same day. A notice. We had 90 days to get out . . . We all stood outside—'Did you get the letter?' 'Did you get the letter?' Three months to get out!" (There was no need for such haste: construction of the East Tremont section of the expressway would not, as Moses was aware, begin for three years. The 90 day warning was merely "to shake 'em up a little and get 'em moving," a Moses aide explained to me.)

The community tried to fight. It was an era before community protests became newsworthy, and the protests they made received scant notice in a press that in those days did not give much space to such protests, but they fought hard, led by a young housewife; Lillian Edelstein, who had never imagined herself in such a role but felt she had no choice ("What if we were separated? What would Mom do? I was fighting for my home. And my mother. And sister. And daughter. I had a lot to fight for.") and who turned out to possess not merely energy and determination but an indefinable, and inspiring, air of command. And since every one of their elected officials—their assemblyman and their state senator, as well as Bronx Borough President James J. Lyons and Mayor Wagner—was, at first, on their side, they thought they had a chance. In the New York City of the 1950s, however, when it came to the construction of large-scale public works projects, what counted was not what elected officials wanted but what Robert Moses wanted, and in a very short time the residents lost—and Moses immediately began to apply the "relocation" techniques he had perfected on other projects.

As soon as the City Real Estate Bureau took title to the buildings, the heat and the hot water were cut off in many of them, and for much of the ensuing winter the only warmth for the families trying to remain in their apartments came from small inadequate electric heaters they themselves bought or gas ranges turned on all the time. The building superintendents had been fired, so there were no services. Some of the tenants began to move, and as soon as the top floor of an apartment house was empty, the roof and that top floor would be torn off "While people were still living in it, they were tearing it down around their heads!" Mrs. Edelstein told me. When an apartment on a lower floor was vacated, its windows were boarded up—a signal to looters that there were empty premises to be broken into. All requests for watchmen, as for heat and hot water and superintendents, were referred by the city agencies to Moses, who simply ignored them. The looters came: at night, the remaining tenants could hear them tearing the pipes out of the wall to be sold for scrap. A few small frame houses that were on the route were torn down, and their lumber stacked in their back yards—and fires were set. When the first apartment houses were completely emptied, their basements were left as gaping pits filled with broken glass and jagged shafts of steel. Despite parents' pleas, no fences were built around them, and the parents lived in fear that their children would fall into them. Demolition on so immense a scale had other consequences—"The rats were running like cats and dogs in the street," Mrs. Edelstein was to recall. Grime filled the air so thickly that sometimes the neighborhood seemed to have been hit by a dust storm.

In a very short time, the 54 buildings were gone. Then, after construction started, there came month upon month and year after year of earthshaking dynamite blasts, since the expressway was, in that neighborhood, being cut through a trench in solid bedrock. The air was filled with rock dust from the great excavation—a deep gash in the earth 120 feet wide and a mile long, through which rumbled mammoth earthmoving machines and herds of bulldozers and dump trucks—and the gritty dust seeped into rooms even through doors and windows that had been closed and sealed with towels. East Tremont had, of course, been cut in half by the road, and the southern half was isolated from the shopping area along East Tremont Avenue, and it was hard for the remaining residents to get to stores. The residents of the apartment houses that bordered the mile-long excavation on both sides—perhaps one hundred buildings—began to move out, and as more and more moved one of the principal reasons for staying—friends who lived near you—began to vanish, and so did the sense of community. Still more tenants disappeared from East Tremont. Some landlords were happy to see them leave the rent-controlled apartments, and replaced them with welfare families, who demanded fewer services and moved more often, so that rents could be raised more often. The gyre of urban decay spiraled and widened, faster and faster, and more and more residents began to move. East Tremont became a vast slum.

I spent many days and weeks, terrible days and weeks, walking around that slum.

I had never, in my sheltered middle-class life, descended so deeply into the realms of despair. When I entered these buildings, on the floors of their lobbies would be piles of animal or human feces, and raw garbage spilling out of broken bags; the floors were covered so thickly with shards of broken glass that my feet would crunch on it as I walked. The walls would have been broken open and the pipes ripped out, for sale by junkies. An atmosphere of fear hung over East Tremont, of course. I remember one elderly man, with a kindly face, sitting on a stoop; "You're going to be out of here by dark, aren't you?" he asked me. When he feared he hadn't made himself clear enough, he added, "Don't be around this place after dark!" I remember the people who lived in these buildings: almost all were Black or Hispanic. Wanting to interview them to find out what living in East Tremont was like, I would knock on the doors of apartments. Over and over again, in my recollection, the same scene would be repeated. At my knock, there would be a scurry of children's feet behind the door, but no reply. If I persisted in my knocking, I would hear footsteps coming to the door, and then a voice—in my recollection it was always the voice of a little boy—would ask, through the closed door, the same question: "Are you the man from the welfare?" Usually, when I said I wasn't, the door wouldn't be opened. Sometimes, however, it was, and I would be allowed inside—and sometimes that was worse. To this day, I see, in my mind, a Black woman, about thirty years old, sitting with several little children around her, no matter what question I asked, she replied, "I've got to get my kids out of here. I've got to get my kids out of here."

If the days I spent interviewing residents of the great East Tremont slum were terrible, the days I spent interviewing former residents of East Tremont—people who had lived there before it became a slum—weren't much better. These people had lived in East Tremont when it had been a neighborhood, their neighborhood, and they had been driven away by Robert Moses, either by the demolition of their homes or by the neighborhood's consequent deterioration. Their stories, too, were part of the human cost of this highway and I wanted to find as many of them as possible and interview them.

I found them in a great variety of locales. Some—the luckiest or the most affluent ones—had found apartments in sterile high-rise middle-class housing developments in far reaches of the Bronx. Some, less affluent, were living in small—in many cases, too small—apartments in various neighborhoods in the Bronx or in Queens or in Brooklyn. Others were living with their children in the Westchester or Long Island suburbs. And still others, the unluckiest, had come to rest in "the projects," the city's immense, low-income, and quite dangerous public housing.

I asked these couples—or widows or widowers—to compare their present lives with the lives they had had in East Tremont, and the general picture that emerged from their answers was a sense of profound, irremediable loss, a sense that they had lost something—physical closeness to family, to friends, to stores where the owner knew you, to synagogues where the rabbi had said Kaddish for your parents (and perhaps even your grandparents) as he would one day say Kaddish for you, to the crowded benches on Southern Boulevard where your children played baseball while you played chess: a feeling of togetherness, a sense of community that was very precious, and that they knew they would never find again. . . .

The People Without Power

Conversations with the Long Island farmers [who Robert Moses had displaced with later development projects] brought home to me in a new way the fact that a change on a map—Robert Moses's pencil going one way instead of another, not because of engineering considerations but because of calculations in which the key factor was power—had had profound consequences on the lives of men and women like those farmers whose homes were just tiny dots on Moses's big map. I had set out to write about political power by writing about one man, keeping the focus, within the context of his times, on him. I now came to believe that the focus should be widened, to show not just the life of the wielder of power but the lives on whom, and for whom, it was wielded; not to show those lives in the same detail of course, but in sufficient detail to enable the reader to empathize with the consequences of power—the consequences of government, really—on the lives of its citizens, for good and for ill. To really show political power, you had to show the effect of power on the powerless, and show it fully enough so the reader could feel it.

25. How Mayor Tom Bradley Transformed Los Angeles

Harold Meyerson

Before the 1960s, nearly all mayors of major cities were White males. Power had often moved from the hands of White Anglo Saxon Protestants to the Irish or Italians or other White ethnic groups but it remained in White hands. Although African American Tom Bradley failed to win his 1969 campaign for mayor, he prevailed in 1973, leading a biracial coalition when Blacks were only 14 percent of the population.

When police lieutenant Tom Bradley first began to spend his weekends walking precincts for liberal candidates all across the city, Los Angeles was in many ways still a tight little town. Though Blacks and Jews had been pouring into postwar Los Angeles for nearly two decades, the city was still largely run—and its officials handpicked—by a White Protestant financial and merchant elite. By the early '60s, however, the old order was beginning to weaken. There were too many Blacks, too many Jews, too many Democratic activists bent on changing L.A.'s politics. The old guard simply could not maintain its stranglehold on the city. Worse yet, thousands of those activists belonged to Democratic clubs, and they had begun to travel across town to help out in each others' campaigns.

It was during the 1962 campaign of Ed Roybal, who was endeavoring to become L.A.'s first Latino congressman, that Tom Bradley first met Maury Weiner, who later became Bradley's first chief-of-staff. This convergence of a New York Jew with the son of a Black Texas sharecropper to assist a Latino liberal was emblematic of a rising political force that the guardians of WASP L.A. were powerless to stop. Seven years later, when then-Councilman Tom Bradley first ran for mayor, liberal L.A. turned out 15,000 volunteers to walk precincts all over town. It was Stand-at-Armageddon-and-Battle-for-the-Lord time. The 1969 Bradley campaign was a crusade—for civil rights, to rebuild the inner city that had burned in the Watts Riots just four years earlier, and to redeem the reputation of the city where Robert Kennedy had been killed, where the cops were notoriously racist and the incumbent mayor a right-wing demagogue.

The crusaders did not prevail that year. Sam Yorty, the demagogue, outdid himself in the mayoral run-off, accusing retired police lieutenant Bradley of having all kinds of entangling alliances with the Communist Party, the Black Panthers and the antiwar students then taking over college campuses. Undaunted by his defeat, Bradley spent the next four years reassuring White L.A. that he was neither a closet Eldridge Cleaver nor a secret Joseph Stalin. In 1973, he was elected mayor—in a city that at the time was just 14 percent Black.

Give the man, and the moment, their due: Bradley's election was a ground breaking achievement in American race relations—and in democratic politics. No non-White had ever been elected to govern so many Whites. If ever Angelenos had had occasion to feel pride in themselves, that was the time. It was hard not to be enthused about, even moved by, the new mayor. Bradley had no great rhetorical skills; there was no dazzle about him, just sheer, unyielding diligence. He had put himself through UCLA, risen through the ranks of a racist police department, and won election to the City Council with biracial support—the first elected Black council member in the city's history. With a determination as raging as it was quiet, he had built a base in Black L.A.,

SOURCE: Harold Meyerson, "How Tom Bradley Transformed—and Didn't Transform—Los Angeles," *LA Weekly*, Web Archives, 1998. http://www.laweekly.com/ink/archives/98/45news3b-meyerson.shtml. Reprinted by permission of the LA Weekly.

forged ties with non-Black L.A. when many Black activists scorned such connections, and overcome, with his characteristic dignity, the calumnies that Sam Yorty had heaped upon him. That first, bright period of Tom Bradley's administration was one of the few instances in modern urban history where a mayor made his city look—and feel—good.

No one could live up to the kind of advance billing Tom Bradley got, though for his first term as mayor, he made a run at it. City government was opened up to previously excluded groups. Where Sam Yorty had shunned federal funds for social programs, Bradley made sure L.A. received its due, and then some. There were policy and personnel shifts in the city departments—except in the LAPD, where the city charter made it all but impossible to reform what was clearly the city's most retrograde and dangerous institution.

Then a fellow Angeleno—Ronald Reagan—became president, and the federal spigot began to run dry. Like most postwar mayors, Bradley turned to the only other source of economic stimulus: the business community, most particularly developers. Under the aegis of his Community Redevelopment Agency (CRA), developers were encouraged to rebuild downtown in the image of countless other downtowns, one glass-and-steel tower after another, bringing high-income jobs to Figueroa and Flower streets, saving the city's center from middle-class abandonment. But all the new high-rises and malls did little for the inner city.

It was not Tom Bradley's fault that the auto and steel industries pulled up stakes to reconsolidate in the Midwest, or that the end of the Cold War led local aerospace to halve its workforce, or that the devastation of the Mexican economy and civil wars in Central America sent hundreds of thousands of immigrants scurrying to L.A., creating a vast pool of low-wage labor. But the gap between the overdeveloped city of the Westside and the increasingly underdeveloped city of South-Central was steadily widening, and Bradley was slow to respond. It was only in the late '80s, when his Westside supporters were coming to view him as a stooge for developers, that he reversed course, declining to approve new projects in some of the city's more congested pockets of affluence.

The inner city proved tougher to deal with. In his last term in office he was moving toward policies of linkage—requiring developers to set aside funds for affordable housing, redirecting CRA funds to afterschool programs. Then came the recession of the early '90s, and development shuddered to a halt. There were no longer funds to redirect. And in April '92, the two unsolved dilemmas of his mayoralty—the police and inner-city poverty—combusted in an explosion that shook the city, the mayor, and what remained of his citywide alliance, to their core. I remember watching his aides clustered just outside the First AME Church on the night the city ignited, frantically debating how they could safely get Bradley past the irate crowd in the parking lot and back to City Hall. It was a consummation to his 20 years as mayor that no one could ever have wished.

He had groomed no successor—to himself, to his coalition, to his regime. With federal urban funding rejected even by the new Democratic president, with the crosstown liberal coalition of the civil rights days a dim memory at best, with White and Black L.A. both retreating into their separatist shells, Los Angeles in 1993 elected a white Republican businessman to succeed

Bradley—the same year that a white Republican prosecutor, for many of the same reasons, unseated a Black incumbent to become mayor of New York. When Tom Bradley left office, his era of urban politics was already dead.

I last saw Tom Bradley about five months ago, at the annual breakfast of the Jewish Labor Committee, the kind of event at which he'd been a fixture for over three decades. The room was plainly his; pols and rabbis, labor leaders and old-timers all came over to greet him; he imparted a genuine sense of warmth to the morning, as if he'd become a symbol of a warmer time. He'd suffered a stroke in 1996, of course, and he couldn't speak, but he came to the podium to offer a kind of tacit blessing when the JLC presented an award to Assembly Speaker Antonio Villaraigosa.

The speaker may well be facing some of the same challenges Bradley faced as he geared up to run for mayor—and some different ones, too. If Villaraigosa decides to run for mayor in 2001, he won't face the kind of race-baiting Tom Bradley had to endure, but neither can he count upon the kind of citywide cross-racial alliance that Bradley both championed and benefited from. The city today is at once more tolerant and less organized than the city that first elected Tom Bradley.

The growing disorganization is part of a vast national decline in political participation. The growth in tolerance, I'd like to think, is one of Tom Bradley's triumphs.

26. Mayor Ed Rendell of Philadelphia

Buzz Bissinger

Mayors are key to the health and direction of cities because they provide the leadership necessary to cope with their problems. Such was Ed Rendell of Philadelphia. He faced formidable problems and provided leadership. Sometimes, even leadership, vision, and compassion aren't enough.

E d Rendell was a complicated man of many hues. But it also became clear from the very beginning that he represented the very essence of what a politician should be in this country but almost never is, a man unafraid to be human.

This humanity was made all the more remarkable by what he inherited on that first Monday in January, 1992. The literal second he became mayor, he found himself at the helm of a city utterly on the brink, so many hundreds of millions of dollars in debt that it could not pay its own bills. Almost simulta-

SOURCE: Buzz Bissinger, *A Prayer for the City* (New York: Random House, 1997), pp. xii–xiii, xix–xxi, 21, 24–25, 335–337, and 339–340. Copyright © 1997 by H. G. Bissinger. Used by permission of Random House, Inc.

neously, he entered into negotiations with the municipal unions the likes of which had never been seen in the modern history of the American city, and sought givebacks and concessions so enormous it seemed almost lunatic to publicly talk to them.

Intertwined was the crisis of unabated job and population loss, and the crisis of public housing so nightmarish that even the president himself became aware of it, and the crisis of trying to create new jobs. . . .

URBAN ENTERPRISE ZONES

[Early in his term, Mayor Rendell went before the Senate Finance Committee in Washington, D.C. to testify about the urgent need for urban enterprise zones to stimulate investment in America's depleted inner cities through the use of business tax credits.]

After about an hour, Rendell's turn to speak finally came. Forty-eight years old, he was neither intimidated nor nervous. Much of his life had been spent in the public eye, and while he was a devoted Democrat, his political philosophy reflected that of a man who simply said what he thought and what he felt regardless of how it came out. He sat on a red leather chair, his six-foot-tall body hunched over the table as if he had slightly miscalculated the distance between table and chair so he was leaning a bit more than he really needed to and might tip over altogether at any moment. He wore a gray suit, but because of the way clothing instantly rumpled around the large and rounded frame that he constantly fought to keep at 235 pounds, a pair of sweatpants and a sweatshirt would have fit him better. He gestured sharply with his hands as if he were trying to catch a fly. He spoke with a passion that reached just a notch below outrage, the exact passion that he used with nine-year-olds when they trudged into his office and sat there, first glum, then transfixed, as he described the vagaries of what it was he did for a living. His voice had a gravelly edge, phrases coming out of him in rat-a-tat bursts. He never stammered but apparently considered the idea of pausing between sentences a sign of unforgivable weakness.

He told the senators how his city—the city of Philadelphia—had lost $2 billion of its tax base over the past 20 years, after the city had raised various taxes 19 times. He talked about the violence of the inner city, how simple disputes, disputes that in his teens had been settled with a punch thrown here and a punch thrown there, were now being settled with guns and knives and the inevitable end product of someone dying over nothing at all. He talked urgently, as if the words couldn't keep up with the fervor of his belief in them. He worked hard to make the members of the Senate Finance Committee believe that he wasn't looking for a taxpayer handout, a reversion to the wonder days of revenue sharing, when mayors could live out their edifice complexes, but that he was seeking a way, at minimal public expense, of bringing an obliterated portion of the American landscape back to life.

"We in the cities are very confused," said Rendell as he hunched forward. "We see a great deal of support—and we think it's meritorious—of aid to the Soviet people. But we are perplexed why you don't give a similar package to cities that are on the brink. We're also confused at how readily you found money for S and Ls, how readily you found money for Desert Storm." His words were sharp and unflinching, and they had an impact.

"We had no choice [on S and Ls]," countered Senator Bentsen, the chairman of the committee, with simmering indignation that made his fine whiskey twang go suddenly sharp and raspy, as if a piece of metal had gotten stuck in his throat.

"I submit we have no choice here," countered Rendell with equal indignation. . . .

When Rendell spoke about the city, there was a passion in his voice, and not some thin veneer of playacting. He didn't minimize the city's problems, particularly its financial ones, but instead of deflecting and blaming and saying the answer lay in increased help from the federal and state governments, he said that the city had no right to ask anyone for anything until it got its own house in order. Radical change must come from within, he said, and voters admired him for that. . . .

MAYOR RENDELL'S INAUGURAL ADDRESS

"Make no mistake, our situation is worse than we thought it could ever be. Projected deficits in the years ahead number in the hundreds of millions of dollars. And the shame of it is that those deficits do not even begin to tell us the costs of their consequences. These costs—the costs of unsafe streets, of dirty neighborhoods, of struggling schools, of shut-down health clinics and recreation centers—these costs are simply incalculable.

"We have put off difficult choices for far too long. We have been too willing to accept the old way of doing things. In the face of long-term challenges, we have opted for short-term fixes. And we have shown virtually no courage or backbone in standing up to pressure against outside interests.

"Change must surely come, but the good news is that if it does come, this city cannot only survive; it can come alive again with a thriving economy, strong neighborhoods, and a dynamic downtown that can serve as a magnet to conventioneers, tourists, and suburbanites alike.

"To make this change a reality, I want to issue a few challenges:

"To everyone involved in government, to no longer accept the old way of doing things, but to challenge them, change them, and get results.

"To the seventeen city council members on this stage with me today, to put aside politics, partisanship, and personal gain to forge a working relationship with me second to none in this city's long history.

"To our municipal unions and their four fine leaders, to join with us and help this city survive and flourish as other unions have joined together with their employers to keep those businesses afloat.

"To the people of Philadelphia, to be willing to accept short-run sacrifices and pain that will allow us to get through the near future and lead to tremendous long-run gain for all of us.

"And lastly, a challenge to myself, to stand tall, to stay the course, and make the difficult choices unflinchingly, regardless of what the pressure to do otherwise might be and regardless of the political risks involved.

"I cannot and will not falter.

"We cannot and will not fail.

"The stakes are too high.

"The cost of our failing is unthinkable. . . ."

THE JOB CRISIS

[Despite the loss of individual plants and even the famed Philadelphia Naval Yard, Philadelphia did survive and partially recover. In 1996 it gained 100 more jobs than it lost. In 1997, the number of jobs in the city increased by 3,300. Philadelphia began its comeback under the leadership of this pragmatic but optimistic mayor.]

The mayor sat in his customary spot at the table in the Cabinet Room, surrounded by a clump of executives judiciously dressed in innocuous shades of blue and gray and beige. The executives seemed as mousy and nonthreatening as their wardrobes, but the mayor knew exactly what was going on, how this was little more than a setup and how, once you cut through the obsequious slick of legalese and corporate-speak, he was basically being asked to lie.

The more he listened on this August day in 1995, the more his face turned ashen, and it wasn't just the disingenuousness of what he was hearing that was troubling him. It was the realization that his city, and all cities like it that had once been the definition of American industrial might and strength, were on the verge of a certain kind of extinction.

The subject at hand in the Cabinet Room was a plant closure, and the number of jobs at stake was so small as to seem irrelevant: 240. But in the realm of the mayor and the city, where every job counted and was fought over, the loss was significant. Beyond the actual number, there were the deeper reverberations of the psychic loss. The jobs were at the Breyers Ice Cream factory. They were the jobs that had helped lay the foundation of the city, and Breyers, beyond being the maker of the country's top-selling ice cream, was a hallowed name in the industrial arc of Philadelphia. It was here that Breyers was founded in 1866, when William A. Breyer used a hand-operated freezer to produce his ice cream and then sold the delicacy from a wagon. His "pledge of purity" caught on quickly, and in 1924 a then massive plant was built in West Philadelphia, adorned by a huge neon sign in distinctive script that could be seen from miles away on one of the city's expressways, a stable beacon keeping an eye over the quilt of working-class row houses that spread beneath it. But Breyers, like so many other companies in the 1990s, was undergoing corporate restructuring. And although the explanation for such restructuring could be debated by economists from now until the end of the century—how to some degree corporate shedding is the natural reaction of capitalism when new jobs requiring new skills inevitably take the place of old ones—the set of victims seemed forever constant: the city and those who lived and worked within it.

In a six-minute meeting at the end of August, the company that now owned Breyers, Unilever, a multinational conglomerate, had told its workers that the plant was closing. Several days later Rendell met with representatives of

Unilever and Breyers to see if anything could be done to keep the plant open. Given his innate optimism, he refused to believe that any situation was hopeless. But his hands were clasped together instead of conducting their concerto, and this wasn't a gesture of prayer but more a gesture of weary acceptance. He offered to modernize the existing plant or help Unilever, with its more than $2 billion in assets, build a new one. "We think we can compete," he said softly, sounding like a parent begging a school to give his problem child one more chance. "We think we can do a better bottom line. I don't want to waste our time, but we think we can compete." Loans, cheap land, tax benefits— they were all available just as long as Unilever did not close the Breyers plant. "It's got a strong identification with the city of Philadelphia," Rendell said, hoping that might count for something.

And then he sat there quietly as Jerry Phelan, a senior vice president for manufacturing, explained the rationale of Unilever in maintaining its competitive edge in the ice-cream business. "I hate to use the word, but we did computer modeling studies," said Phelan somewhat sheepishly. Those models, which took every need into account except the human ones, made it clear that the only way to keep pace with the competition was through purchase and consolidation and plant closures. First it was at Good Humor, where the studies said that four plants, all of them in industrial cities, needed to be closed. Then it was at Gold Bond Ice Cream, where, as Phelan put it, they "took out" three of six plants, as if they were enemy machine-gun nests. Then it was through an investment at Klondike, where the computer studies said that two of the three existing plants had to go. Then Unilever purchased Breyers from Kraft, and the computer modeling studies said there were nine manufacturing plants, and that was too many, and there was an overcapacity problem, and some of these plants had to be taken out as well.

"We have a great workforce here," said Phelan, trying to be complimentary but not realizing the tragedy of what he was saying. "It has nothing to do with labor. It has nothing to do with gas rates. It's a question of capacity, where do we take it? It is really that simple. . . . We have a capacity issue that we have to address if we want to be competitive, and we want to be competitive."

The computer modeling study gave Unilever a choice of plants to close—the one in Philadelphia or the one in the Boston suburb of Framingham. The Framingham plant was built in 1964, when the suburbanization of industry was exploding. It was all on one level, and its former owners had poured a significant amount of money into it in 1991. The Philadelphia plant was 68 years old and awkwardly laid out in terms of the modern requirements of mass production— too many levels, too much useless square footage. Millions could be spent to modernize it, but other than pleasing the mayor and the workers who earned their livelihood there, what was the point? "If you do that," said Phelan, sitting close to the mayor, on his left, "you still end up with a 70-year-old plant. . . ."

So Rendell went outside to meet with the reporters. Refusing to lie, he characterized the meeting as fruitless because a decision to close the plant had been made before the meeting. And the four corporate representatives, like prison escapees, quietly snuck out a side entrance. They went back to their jobs, while the 240 workers at the Breyers plant learned for certain that they were losing theirs. The mayor gave his impromptu press conference, then trudged the hundred feet back to his office. In the cocoon of privacy, his mood was still somber. He moved to the round table and peered at his schedule to see what was next, because there was always something next. But then he looked up, and the dispassion with which he suddenly spoke seemed far more frightening in its own way than any of his eruptions of the past four years.

"We have clearly stopped and delayed the death of the city of Philadelphia through relatively heroic measures. Will the disease kill this patient? Meetings like this make me feel if I was the most competent public official in the history of the United States and was here for the rest of my life, I don't think I could save it."

27. Lessons in Miami Politics

Robyne S. Turner

It is almost completely impossible to stay up-to-date with Miami politics. Vote fraud and corruption seem to be constant. Cubans seem no better (and probably no less) able to govern than Whites or African Americans who control other cities. No account of modern urban politics would be complete without these examples of continuing old style machine politics even in the twenty-first century.

There has been a considerable amount of political turmoil in Miami, the "Magic City," during the last year. The city changed its charter, avoided dissolution, weathered a bribery scandal and fiscal crisis, elected a new mayor, and currently confronts a vote fraud scandal. The breadth of these problems raises the question, How much can one city, take and survive? While in 1992 Hurricane Andrew challenged the city's ability to deal with physical damage, the 1996–97 scandals are challenging the political foundations of this Sunbelt gateway to Latin America. The city seems to have survived for now, but the ride may not yet be over.

In the summer of 1996 Miami celebrated its 100th birthday. The celebration was interrupted by a federal sting operation, dubbed "operation green palm," Caught in this fraud and bribery caper were the Miami city manager, Cesar Odio, and Miami's only African-American commissioner, Miller Dawkins. Both men entered a plea agreement to avoid trials and began serving their sentences just as another crisis broke. In December, 1996 the city declared a fiscal emergency. The interim city manager had uncovered a

SOURCE: Robyne S. Turner, "Tropical Heat: Lessons in Miami Politics," *Urban News*, Vol. 12, Nos. 1 and 2, Spring and Summer, 1998. Reprinted by permission of the author.

$68 million deficit. Instances of fiscal mismanagement led the city to declare a fiscal emergency requiring state notification. Florida Governor Lawton Chiles appointed a fiscal oversight board to approve a fiscal plan to eliminate the deficit and to oversee city expenditures during the implementation of that plan.

As the crisis emerged, a mayoral candidate, Xavier Suarez, contended that the situation was blown out of proportion. He felt that his opponent, Mayor Joe Carollo, had acted rashly in notifying the state of the supposed crisis and threatened to sue if the state did not quickly release control over the city's finances (whom he would sue was not clear). Mayor Carollo pointed out that it was during the previous Suarez administration (1989–93) that the crisis had its roots. The private audit firm that worked under both administrations denied liability, stating their reports warned of this disaster, while the city commission pled ignorance of any fiscal problem. This vignette provides a fairly clear portrait of the city's style of politics and provides the first glimpse of the tempestuous governing style that would be assumed by Suarez, were he elected again.

A POLITICAL ICEBERG, DEAD AHEAD

The Coalition for a New Miami, funded by local, primarily Anglo, business leaders, proposed a ballot initiative in response to the fiscal and fraud scandals. They wanted voters to decide whether the city of Miami should be disincorporated. The point of the dissolution initiative—the Miami Question—as it came to be known, was that voters would be better off without the city, instead allowing the territory to become unincorporated and governed solely by Dade County. This initiative was characterized as the only way for Miamians to be free of corrupted government.

Such an austere response provoked the powers that be at city hall to proffer their own solution to these crises—change the city charter. The proposal would change city government from a city manager structure to an executive or "strong" mayor form and would switch commission representation from five at-large seats to five district seats. Miami was faced with a legal challenge to change to district elections to create opportunities for minorities to be elected to office. The convicted commissioner Dawkins occupied the designated "black seat" in the at-large system and was replaced in 1997 by an Hispanic commissioner, Humberto Hernandez, in a special election. This left Miami without an African-American commissioner for the first time in 30 years. The mayoral/manager changes would give the mayor the power to hire and fire the manager, appoint the chair of the city commission, veto council action, and appoint commission committees. The success of Alex Pinellas, the strong mayor of Dade County, was not lost on the Hispanic politicians of Miami who wanted to harness similar political power in Miami.

The scene was set for an epic showdown on September 4, 1997, when the dissolution initiative and the charter change referendum would be on the same ballot. Surprisingly, there was little anguish in the months preceding the election. There was a subtext on Spanish language radio that the Miami Question was an attempt to eliminate Cuban political control of the city. Public opinion polls, though, showed that voters did not think the Miami Question was a reasonable option; both Hispanic voters and black voters had strong ties to the city and supported its retention. Minorities also supported the charter changes for district representation. Not surprisingly, then, the Miami Question was defeated (though the city commission had reversed the wording to help voters, and a "yes" vote indicated keeping the city intact). The charter changes were approved.

The results of this election indicate that people were concerned about several different issues. One issue was whether or not their taxes would increase if they were governed solely by the county. Most who supported retention of the city claimed that taxes would perhaps double if the county had to provide all services to the city. The second, and perhaps more important issue, was that minorities not only had personal ties to Miami, but especially for Cubans, Miami represented political power. The dissolution question was raised by Anglos and found its greatest level of support (though not a majority) in the Anglo-dominated Coconut Grove and Brickell Avenue neighborhoods. Results of a poll conducted by the *Miami Herald* before the election, indicated that symbolic politics was as much a factor as pocketbook issues [*Miami Herald,* 1/26/97: What would the losing the city mean to you?]. When asked if they thought their taxes would be lower if the city government were abolished, more non-Cuban Hispanics and Anglos thought "yes" than did Cubans and Blacks. When asked if the city's cultural and historical importance would be lost if the city were dissolved, nearly 70 percent of Cubans and more than 50 percent of Blacks said "yes," but less than 40 percent of Anglos and non-Cuban Hispanics said "yes." Perhaps even more revealing was the question about whether Miami would lose its importance to the Hispanic communities in Florida and Latin America if the city ceased to exist; 60 percent of Cubans said it would be a loss, and less than 20 percent of Anglos agreed.

The election results confirm that minority neighborhoods were most opposed to dissolution and most supportive of the charter changes. Minimal pockets of resistance were most prevalent in the Anglo neighborhoods. The Miami Question failed; 86.8 percent voted to retain the city. Similarly, the charter changes were approved as a single item on the ballot with 79.5 percent of the vote. The vote by various neighborhood areas (for which the Dade county election office provides estimates of demographic characteristics of registered voters by precinct) is shown in Table 7.1.

Miami did not go gently into the tropical moonlight after this vote. A new mayor had to be chosen to fill the newly created executive mayor position. The firestorm that erupted during this campaign still smolders and offers a lesson in multi-minority urban politics.

SHOWDOWN IN MIAMI: CAROLLO V. SUAREZ

Two familiar faces in Miami politics quickly ascended to headline the race for mayor of the city. The incumbent mayor, Joe Carollo, was ready to move into the new and improved mayoral chair. His chief competition was former Miami mayor, Xavier Suarez (1985–93) who was ready to make a political comeback after losing an earlier bid for the same office in Dade County. Both are

TABLE 7.1   Neighborhoods, Racial/Ethnic Character, and September 4, 1997, Referenda Results

Neighborhood	Size and Nature of Predominant Ethnic/Racial Group	Percent Voting "Yes" on "Yes" on Miami Question	Percent Voting "Yes" on Charter Changes
Edison/Wynwood	80% Black	85%	78%
Miami/Biscayne	52% Anglo	61	66
Brickell/Grove	57% Anglo	70	66
South Little Havana	75% Hispanic	89	81
Central Little Havana	82% Hispanic	92	84

Cuban, 40-something, assumed to be Republicans in the nonpartisan race, and ready to lead Miami into the next millennium.

The campaigns kicked into high gear but with a characteristic Cuban accent—literally on Spanish language radio and television. The candidates were not to be found in the English-speaking media in the two months between the charter change and the election. The *Miami Herald* and its Spanish language partner, *El Nuevo Herald* carried few stories and fewer accounts of appearances by the candidates. Instead, as politicians are wont to do in Cuban Miami, they began a verbal blitzkrieg, assaulting each other's credibility, loyalties, and past performances as mayor, primarily on the Spanish airwaves and at appearances within the Cuban community, *mano a mano*.

At one campaign appearance the candidates' supporters literally resorted to fisticuffs after verbal taunting escalated to snipes and character assassinations. While these anecdotes may seem to trivialize the political process, they actually serve to reveal how isolated Miami city politics has become. There is not even the pretense that Anglo or Black votes are necessary to win an election. Politics has retreated into an insulated arena that, instead of encouraging a race- and ethnicity-neutral strategy, exercises an exclusionary ethnic-based strategy.

On election day, November 4, 1997, three new commissioners were elected, including Arthur Teele as the lone African-American commissioner. He was well known in the community and had strong name recognition after he too had lost his bid to be Dade County mayor. The other two new commissioners are Hispanic. The council carried over one long-time Anglo commissioner, J. L. Plummer and one Hispanic commissioner, Tomas Regalado. The commission thus has three Hispanics (Cubans), one Anglo, and one African American.

The mayoral election unexpectedly ended in a runoff between Carollo and Suarez. Carollo had been expected to win outright, but ended up with only 49.9 percent of the vote because Suarez took 61 percent of the absentee ballots, forcing Carollo into a runoff. The unexpectedly strong showing by Suarez in absentee ballots produced extensive controversy that is currently in the courts. Carollo was so incensed that he filed a lawsuit alleging voter fraud in the absentee ballots. The runoff went on as scheduled. Xavier Suarez won the runoff election, setting in motion more political eruptions.

TABLE 7.2   **Total and Absentee Vote Percentages by Candidate for Primary and Runoff Elections**

	Carollo	Suarez
Total Votes		
Primary	49.9%	47%
Runoff	47	53
Absentee Ballots		
Primary	35	61
Runoff	35	65

ELECTION AFTERMATH

The first response to the Suarez victory came from the state attorney's office as it responded to the Carollo lawsuit. The state's attorney arrested several vote brokers (employed by both candidates' organizations to collect absentee ballots), and suspicious absentee ballots, evidence of ballot tampering, and "dead man" votes were found. Corruption was not limited to Suarez's campaign, for Carollo's people found themselves under investigation, as well. Carollo vowed to continue his fight, hoping to have the election results voided. His lawsuit went to trial on February 9, 1998. The state legislature also launched an inquiry into fraudulent registration and voting, prompted by the Miami situation. They concluded that the abuses were so extensive that loopholes in the state's implementation of the "motor voter" law must be closed.

The second and still reverberating response to the election was Suarez's breakneck approach to changing city government in Miami during his first month in office. Self-named "Typhoon Suarez" and "Hurricane Suarez," the mayor went on a binge to fire and hire the police chief, the city manager, and other high-level city staffers. He appointed re-elected commissioner, Humberto Hernandez commission chairperson. The Hernandez appointment was within the powers of the mayor but raised concerns because the commissioner is currently under federal indictment for bank-fraud in a real estate deal. It also raised concerns because it was widely rumored that Hernandez was instrumental in delivering the "Little Havana" vote to Suarez in runoff election.

THE POWER AND THE GLORY

The newly elected Mayor Suarez was intent on shaping his administration in the first days by firing the city manager and attempting to fire the police chief. The city manager, Eduardo Marquez (who was the second manager to replace the convicted former manager, Cesar Odio) had considerable financial skills and had been instrumental in working with the state oversight board to develop a financial recovery plan for Miami. But his close ties to the former Carollo administration seemed to taint him politically in the eyes of Suarez, and therefore he could not be trusted or perhaps respected within the new administration. Suarez had campaigned on the notion that the fiscal crisis was a

TABLE 7.3   Suarez's Share of the "Little Havana" Vote

Neighborhood	Suarez's Percentage of the	
	Primary Vote	Run off Vote
Central Little Havana	46%	54%
South Little Havana	48	53

political fabrication or at least an overstatement that had brought unnecessary supervision from the state. Marquez had a diametrically opposite view of the situation.

Suarez deflected attention from the fiscal crisis by appointing the first of several interim city managers, Alberto Ruder, a long-time city employee who oversaw the Parks Department. This interim manager was not as qualified as former manager Marquez, but was loyal to Suarez. It was assumed he would carry out the hatchet job on the police chief, Donald Warshaw, who refused to resign.

With the new interim manager in place, the mayor fought two flanks at once—the popular police chief who refused to go quietly and the state fiscal oversight board and Wall Street, who were not convinced that Miami's fiscal crisis was overstated. The Governor rebuffed Suarez's claims that the fiscal crisis was over and observed that "weird" things were going on in Miami. Indeed, after the mayor (in his bathrobe) made a late night and unannounced visit to a constituent to query the citizen about a complaint letter, others, including acclaimed columnist Carl Hiaasen of the *Miami Herald,* suggested the mayor had a mental disorder (prompting threat of a lawsuit from Suarez). Furthermore, the mayor was thwarted by the city attorney, who pointed out to the mayor that his powers to fire staff did not extend to the police chief. Only the manager could hire and fire staff and then only for cause. Ruder, not wanting to get embroiled in a controversy, resigned as the interim manager. His replacement, another long-time city employee, similarly resigned after three weeks, when it became clear he would not be allowed by Suarez to exercise independent decision-making authority. He had teamed with the city attorney to reverse staff resignations ordered by Suarez, incensing the mayor. Thus, after only six weeks on the job, the mayor had been through three managers.

While looking for a fourth manager, the mayor took a day to fly to New York City to meet financial investors and to convey to them personally the view that the fiscal crisis was over, if indeed it had ever existed. Suarez desperately felt that the crisis was ruining the image of Miami and severely hampered his political power. Unfortunately for the mayor, the Wall Street community was not convinced and sent the mayor home to find a new tack. The mayor resumed budget talks with the city commission, trying to decide whether to institute a new fire service fee and a hefty increase to the garbage fee, which were the politically charged issues. The mayor also needed to identify funds to finance a new basketball arena downtown to which the city had committed to pay for with Dade County. The last thing Suarez wanted now was to have to back out of the deal, leaving Dade County Mayor Pinellas to save the team.

Suarez was advised to find an experienced city manager in order to restore some credibility to the city's operations. The manager of Miami Beach, Jose Garcia-Pedrosa, was appointed and quickly confirmed by the city commission at the end of December, bringing the first moments of stability to the city since Suarez took office. The new manager agreed to defer any review of the police chief and agreed to work with the state oversight board on fiscal matters.

With a city manager in place, Mayor Suarez was determined to continue playing the part of the recalcitrant rebel who would not be subordinate to the city attorney or the governor. He expected this strategy to play well to his core constituency, older Cubans, who viewed Suarez as a source of political power and respect. When the oversight board convened in Miami for a regularly scheduled meeting, the mayor did not attend. Instead, he dispatched his close friend, a state representative, to address the board and convey the message that they were an unnecessary body and that their review was unwelcome. On the morning of the meeting, however, the mayor was heard on Spanish language radio denouncing the board and reminding listeners that he would not bow to the board's control. The board was not amused and reiterated its purpose and its resolve to monitor Miami until the board was satisfied that the crisis was over.

In the meantime, Mayor Suarez quickly learned that violating the city charter would not be seen merely as spirited politics. The state's attorney concluded that when the mayor fired staff and reorganized the administration, he had overstepped his powers and violated the city charter, usurping power assigned to the city manager. In addition, the mayor had violated the "sunshine law" by convening a public meeting of the city's sports authority without the required public notice, thus invalidating any business conducted at that time. The mayor entered into an agreement to receive six months of supervision by the state's attorney office in lieu of a charge and possible conviction of exceeding his legal authority. Currently, the mayor is under review for several actions that may have violated that agreement. His most egregious act was leaving a voice-mail phone message for an editor at the *Miami Herald* telling him to give the city and his administration more flattering coverage. The mayor threatened to pull all city advertising if the paper did not show the mayor and the city more respect. This action got national as well as local media attention for its First Amendment implications.

POSTSCRIPT

On February 9, 1998, the court began hearings on allegations of vote fraud and absentee ballot abuses brought by Carollo. Judge Thomas S. Wilson ruled on March 4 that the November election was void and that a new election must be held within two months because of a "pattern of fraudulent, intentional and criminal conduct." Suarez was personally exhonerated of connection to the absentee ballot fraud, however.

This left open the question of who the legal mayor of Miami was. The city attorney issued an opinion that the city commission could name an interim mayor, but in a March 6 meeting the commission declined to do so, in part because Carollo had filed a new suit which sought to continue his service as mayor, since the November results had been discarded, until the new election produced a new mayor. However, charter changes passed the previous September had been implemented, and there was no "old" mayoral seat to which Carollo could return.

Carollo thus asked that the state appellate court determine which charter was in effect and that it reinstate him. The court agreed and, moreover, set aside the lower court order for a new election, ruling that the machine vote totals alone from November be considered, since the contested and voided ballots were those cast by absentee voters. On that basis, the court in essence declared Carollo the winner.

Suarez appealed these findings, but on March 24 the appellate court denied his appeal and denied his request that the case be certified to the state supreme court. That decision appears to end Suarez's legal remedies in the state system, but he may file a voting rights case in federal court. He has also mentioned the prospect of circulating a petition which would put a question on the November, 1998 ballot that would grant the mayor more powers if passed. Such a charter change would require another mayoral election if voters approve it.

Carollo, meanwhile, has returned to office, removed Humberto Hernandez as commission chair, and appointed himself interim chair until he ascertains which commissioner is sufficiently loyal to him to be given the job. He has also forced out some of Suarez's staff, but kept the police chief. The city manager's job seems to depend upon his ability to develop a city budget that will pass scrutiny of the state oversight board. The commission has passed one such budget, but the board rejected it. On March 31 the commission developed a new mix of taxes and fees, which still must be reviewed by the board.

Although Carollo has publicly asserted that the rule of law now prevails in Miami and that the city is not a "banana republic," political banter filled the air when he was sworn back into office, and Hernandez has declared political war on Carollo. As the skirmishes continue, however, there is some evidence that the Cuban community has now turned its attention away from city hall and toward questions of U.S. policy concerning Cuba.

The 1997 election in Miami was important. Both principal candidates were Cuban, in contrast to the recent past of Puerto Rican, Cuban, and Anglo mayors. The campaign did not unify the electorate, nor did it incorporate Anglo or Black voters; it was instead confined and insulated within the Cuban community. Charter changes and the mayoral turmoil may have dulled voter interest in city affairs and reduced feelings of political efficacy even more. Certainly the increase in mayoral powers raises the stakes for those who enter the political arena, but recruiting a serious non-Cuban candidate for the office may be even more difficult now than it was in 1997.

CONTINUING TURMOIL

In March, 1998 Joe Carollo was reinstated as Mayor by an appeals court ruling, ending the tumultuous three month reign of Xavier Suarez. Miamians assumed a period of tranquility would begin, but alas, political corruption, power-grabbing, and arrests seem to be the continuing saga of this troubled and politically beleaguered city.

On May 28, 1998 City Commissioner Humberto Hernandez was arrested on state vote fraud charges stemming from an investigation of the 1997 Miami mayoral race. Hernandez won election despite having been removed by the Florida Governor because of federal bank fraud charges. It was assumed he delivered the vote from his Little Havana district for Suarez. Governor Chiles removed Hernandez from office again, leaving his seat vacant as well as the seat of the City Commission Chairman.

The presence of only four commissioners gave Mayor Carollo an opportunity to get rid of the City Manager, Jose Garcia-Pedrosa, who was fired on June 2. Carollo knew he had a chance to force the commission's support for his decision because of a city charter rule stipulating the necessary majority to call for a reconsideration of the mayor's decision. Smelling a rat, the Commission voted 4–0 to reconsider and reinstated Manager Pedrosa. Exactly one and one-half hours later, Mayor Carollo fired Pedrosa again, citing irreconcilable differences with the manager; much of which had boiled over during Commission meetings; the two also resorted to hurling insults about disrespect on Spanish language radio. The interim manager is Police Chief Don Warshaw. He was the first interim manager on the Suarez team when that mayor hoped to get him out of the Police Chief's office.

The Commission (now back at a five-person roster) considered its next move with Carolla adamant that a Suarez appointee not be left as manager; to reinforce his message he threatened release of new details of a political relationship between Hernandez and Pedrosa. Pedrosa resigned, leaving Warshaw as mayor and police chief. The financial oversight board met in late July [1998] to receive Miami's final five year budget plan, found it lacking, and sent the city a letter threatening to assume responsibility for city operations if a reasonable plan is not submitted within one month.

Hernandez is currently in jail awaiting his federal trial in September. The federal prosecutors convinced a U.S District judge that if Hernandez tampered with evidence and witnesses to throw off state prosecutors in his vote fraud case, he might do the same in his federal case. Portions of the damning evidence in the state case were released in the media. A political associate of Hernandez wore a wire and the tape transcripts reveal what seems to be a very brash and cynical politician who had little fear of arrest and no remorse for corrupting the vote process.

One potential new player is the Mesa Redonda (Round Table), a business elite of 25 Cuban-American leaders, which met in June to discuss combating corruption and minimizing its impact on business. They are acting out of civic responsibility, since Cubans have gained wealth and political influence, and have called in an expert from a Chicago business group who claims to have been successful in tackling such problems. Nothing has come of that meeting thus far.

28. Lobbyists in Miami

Manny Garcia and Tom Dubocq

Lobbyists weren't a major force in urban politics for most of the nineteenth and twentieth centuries. Formerly the major utilities such as the gas and electric companies employed city lobbyists because the city granted the franchises under which they operated. Now, however, major cities have multi-billion dollar budgets. Hiring lobbyists—often former city officials—to gain multi-million dollar contracts is worthwhile. Miami may lead the way in both lobbyists and corruption—but many other cities have similar arrangements. In San Diego in 2003, for example, a lobbyist for strip joints gave bribes to city council members as campaign contributions.

Five years ago, when Humberto Herandez was a Miami city attorney, he helped negotiate a $371 million garbage recycling contract. It was billed as a cost-saving measure.

But the contract could cost taxpayers at least $1 million a year more than they pay today, experts say.

"I did my damnedest to kill it," said Dennis Carter, a retired county executive.

Yet thanks largely to the influence of a string of politically connected lobbyists—including some who flocked to court to support Hernandez after his latest arrest on vote fraud charges—the contract won't die.

"This is not the best contract, I've got to say," acknowledged Joe Pinon, who as an assistant city manager recently reviewed the 30-year contract with Bedminster Seacor Services Miami Corp. for the first time. "I said, how the hell did we get into this?"

The answer to that question speaks volumes about the workings of government in Miami-Dade County. Lobbyists often play key roles in shaping public policy to fit their clients' needs, capitalizing on their relationships with the politicians they helped elect. Taxpayer needs come second.

Ordinarily, lobbyists do their work in relative obscurity for compensation seldom disclosed. But this deal was different because Bedminster sold the contract to Compost America, a publicly traded company that is required by law to file documents with the Securities and Exchange Commission.

SEC documents and other records provide a rare glimpse into how the public's business is really done. Altogether the lobbyists and unidentified "certain individuals" stand to make more than $2 million in cash and stock—for work in a deal whose public benefit is questionable at best.

The contract calls for Miami to turn over its garbage to Bedminster after the company builds a $58 million recycling plant in Northwest Dade.

SOURCE: Manny Garcia and Tom Dubocq, "Political Ties: How Miami's Garbage Contract Could Cost Millions Extra," *The Miami Herald*, December 9, 1997, Web edition. Copyright © 1997 by Miami Herald. Reproduced by permission of Miami Herald via Copyright Clearance Center.

Miami now pays the county for its garbage disposal. Using controversial technology, the plant would convert Miami's trash into compost, which would be sold to farmers.

Those pushing the deal read like a Who's Who of influence peddlers and the politically connected:

- Orlando Garcia Jr., by his own description "like a brother" to Hernandez, got a piece of the deal as it was being negotiated by Hernandez, then an obscure city attorney. Garcia had no experience in garbage; his main source of income was from liquor sales. Years later, while a Miami city commissioner, Hernandez helped keep the contract alive.
- A team that includes Julio Gonzalez Rebull Sr., Pedro Roig, Erelio Pena and other unnamed "individuals" will share more than $640,000 plus stock when the recycling plant finally opens. Rebull, Roig and Pena are consultants and lawyers with close relationships to the Miami city commissioners who voted on the project.
- Jose Ferre, the eldest son of Maurice Ferre, will receive more than $400,000 for consulting services regarding tax-free bond financing for the project. Jose Ferre inherited the deal while his father was a county commissioner. He replaced his younger brother Francisco, who died in a plane crash. Both sons got into the deal through their father.
- Michael Benages, a lobbyist who declared publicly that he was "friends for a long time" with Miami Mayor Joe Carollo, was brought into the deal when Carollo began questioning it in late 1996. Benages met privately with Carollo and appeared at two public meetings. His pay: options to buy 50,000 shares of the company's stock at $2 apiece. Carollo opposes the deal.
- Tomas Andres Mestre, a wealthy South Dade trucking company owner who stands to make more than $1 million in the deal, hosted a fundraiser and gave $1,500 in campaign contributions to Miami-Dade Mayor Alex Penelas in 1996. That year he got a no-bid county contract that is vital to the project's future.
- State Rep. Luis Morse used his public position to get an attorney general's opinion for Bedminster, even though he was also a private lobbyist for the company. He said in an interview that he did not remember the incident.
- Jose Garcia-Pedrosa, Miami's on-again, off-again city manager, represented Bedminster as a private lawyer. But when the company came before the City Commission in February for a contract extension, Garcia-Pedrosa did not publicly disclose his prior relationship with the firm.

Perry Senn, whose Texas firm unsuccessfully bid for the contract, believes that something is terribly wrong with the political system here. "It was so corrupt," he said.

"Bedminster had purchased the right team to help them get the job. I knew politics was great in Miami, but nothing like this. There is no way I would do business in the city of Miami again. Never."

Lobbyist Rebull, whose firm was hired to publicize the deal, insisted the project is a good one. Rebull said he did not recall details of his financial agreement with Bedminster, but was surprised at the six-figure amounts reported to the SEC.

"I have never in my life done anything incorrectly," he said. "To imply any wrongdoing, it's totally wrong."

WHY LOBBYISTS?

. . . The Bedminster deal was especially complex. It needed action from both city and county government.

So the New Jersey company turned to platoons of lobbyists, politically savvy operatives who help politicians get elected, raise money and make decisions.

"When you're dealing in the political arena, there are people trained and skilled in certain areas," said Nelson Widell, Bedminster's executive vice president. "The folks that we used down there were people who knew their way around."

The firm used lobbyists to help secure the contract with the city. Then it needed help hashing out an agreement between Miami and the county. And then it needed help securing financing, zoning approval and environmental permits.

Lawyer Antonio Zamora, hired on a monthly retainer "to advise the company concerning governmental relations, lobbying and public relations," bristled at the suggestion that he was a lobbyist. "I'm a lawyer," he said. "I find that offensive."

Zamora could not explain why he registered as a lobbyist in the county when Bedminster was seeking financing. "I have no idea," he said.

The Miami Herald research shows that most of the governmental work was done by two main lobbyists, Francisco Ferre and zoning expert Tom Carlos. The others did little more than appear at public meetings and meet with politicians whose votes were critical.

"They came as a package," Carlos said of the other lobbyists. "This minority group is politically active. I'm sure that was one of the reasons they were hired."

Widell said no one pressured the company to hire specific lobbyists. "Politics is tough everywhere," he said.

It's easier when a company knows the political ropes. And Bedminster certainly learned them.

After Senn failed to get the contract, he sued the city and Bedminster. Bedminster hired a team of influential lawyers to defend itself. The lead lawyer: Garcia-Pedrosa. Others on the legal team: Roig, Zamora and Armando Lacasa. Hernandez represented the city. Senn lost the lawsuit.

Five years later, Hernandez, then a city commissioner, brought up a "pocket item" at the end of a long City Commission meeting in February. He wanted the city to allow Garcia-Pedrosa, then city manager, to give Bedminster another two-year extension to build the compost plant.

In exchange, Bedminster would underwrite the costs of recycling in the city for the next two years. The discussion lasted barely three minutes. Garcia-

Pedrosa told *The Miami Herald* he saw no reason to mention his prior relationship with Bedminster during the City Commission meeting. "I don't think there was anything for me to say," Garcia-Pedrosa said.

The manager later passed the contract on to the city attorney, even as his own staff questioned whether it still made financial sense for the city.

"That contract looked good at one time. Compared to what the county is charging today, it doesn't look good, in my opinion," said Clarance Patterson, Miami's sanitation director until March. "I had a fiduciary responsibility to point out the shortcomings."

If the original deal looked bad, the two-year extension doesn't bode well for taxpayers, either. Bedminster agreed to pay $788,306 to cover the city's recycling costs. But city staff estimates that it won't be enough. The staff estimates that recycling costs are really $1.9 million.

Hernandez, who did not return phone calls before he was jailed last week, could not be reached for comment.

DEAL ONCE MADE SENSE

. . . The Bedminster deal once was a smart move for the financially strapped city of Miami. Garbage disposal costs were soaring. Miami had no way to pay for them.

So the city decided to seek proposals for a composting plant. That way, it would avoid the ever-increasing costs of dumping its garbage in landfills.

Composting was controversial in its own right. A company called Agripost spent 13 years trying to build a composting plant in North Dade, right across from an elementary school. It closed in 1991, barely two years after it finally opened. Odors were making the schoolchildren sick.

It was around that time that Miami began seeking bidders.

Senn thought his firm, Ecology Concepts, had a lock on it. He said he helped city officials write the specifications. "I wrote the [request for qualifications] for the city of Miami. I gave it to the Solid Waste Department. I gave it to the Legal Department," Senn said.

He contributed money to city commissioners.

He said they wanted more. "They all wanted a piece of it," he said.

Senn felt sure his firm would be rated on top. He had experience running a similar plant in Florida.

But in July 1992, Miami's commissioners threw out the responses from the companies that answered their proposal. They wanted to rebid the contract.

ENTER A FORMER MAYOR

First, Ferre steps into picture, then his sons replace him.

A new game began to unfold.

It began with a man named Martin Firestone, a former Washington, D.C., communications lawyer who once put together an unrelated deal involving Maurice Ferre, Miami's former mayor. The deal fizzled, but the friendship remained.

Firestone had met Bedminster's principals through a New Jersey law firm when he was living in the Keys.

When Miami decided to explore composting, Bedminster turned to Firestone. He said he helped the company prepare its presentation to the city. He also did something more significant. He introduced Ferre into the deal.

A skilled negotiator with a public profile, Ferre could use his old contacts at Miami City Hall to get Bedminster what it wanted.

For his work, Firestone will be paid $100,000—if the plant is built and operating. He said in a recent interview that he did not know the contract was still alive. "Any manna that might fall from heaven would be gratefully accepted," he said.

After several meetings with the Bedminster folks, Ferre decided that Bedminster had a viable proposal. "I said, you know, it does make sense," Ferre said.

So he, too, joined the team.

Ferre said he brought in lobbyist Julio Gonzalez Rebull Sr. as a partner. It was a smart move. Rebull was close to many of the Miami commissioners who would vote on the plan, especially J. L. Plummer. Rebull once called Plummer his "best friend" in a campaign advertisement.

Ferre was out of public office at the time. "I would get a fee and a portion of the deal and the right to purchase stock," he said.

But in March 1993, Ferre decided to throw his hat into the political ring again, this time for a seat on the County Commission.

"Fortunately, I never signed any papers," Ferre said. "I turned everything over to my sons."

BEDMINSTER GETS NOD

By the time Ferre left the deal, it was clear that Bedminster had the votes to get the contract. A selection committee, made up of city workers and outsiders, ranked it first. City commissioners rarely overturned selection committee recommendations.

The contract came before the Miami City Commission on April 15, 1993. Xavier Suarez was mayor, though the position did not yet carry executive power. Plummer, Victor De Yurre, Miller Dawkins and Miriam Alonso sat as commissioners.

One by one, competing firms complained about the selection process.

Jose Villalobos, representing Senn's firm, said the process was "not kosher." He pointed out that Ecology Concepts received 18 points for technical expertise from one member of the selection committee when the member voted the first time. But a year later, the same member, a man who worked for the U.S. Conference of Mayors, gave the firm zero points in the same category.

One firm complained that its representative waited in a line at the clerk's office to turn in its bid, but it was then rejected for being 11 minutes late.

Several firms questioned whether Bedminster even met the specifications. They pointed out that Bedminster's "low bid" had hidden charges that made it more expensive than those of the other companies.

Bedminster guaranteed that its price would always be $10 a ton lower than the county's, a provision that somehow got dropped from the current contract.

Bedminster's president, Charles Carter, called all the criticism "smoke and mirrors."

"I think the staff has cut through all the B.S. and the emotion and focused on establishing a recommendation based upon the track record of the proposer: someone who does what they say they do, and can stand behind it," Carter said.

Suarez suggested there might be a better way to select firms "in an ideal world." "We would have a lot less lobbying, certainly of this commission, on behalf of all these groups," he said.

The final vote in favor of negotiating with Bedminster was 4-1. Only Alonso objected.

The lobbyists sat in the audience, the first part of their job complete.

"My brother represented Bedminster. He put together a group of consultants, as is often done, to answer that RFP [request for proposals] successfully," Jose Ferre said. "The work was really done when [the contract] was issued."

The contract negotiated that year was a very good deal for Bedminster. Under its original terms, the city would pay Bedminster to dispose of 204,000 tons of waste—even if the city did not produce that much garbage.

The small print virtually guaranteed that the city would come up short. Bedminster would not have to accept any "tree stumps or limbs over two inches in diameter"—the size of a big twig. But the city said it had more than 56,000 tons of yard waste every year. A good deal of it is larger than two inches. . . .

29. The New Machine: Mayor Richard M. Daley of Chicago

Dick Simpson

The old Chicago Democratic Machine might have died, or at least atrophied, with the death of Richard J. Daley in 1976. Some historians argue that he was the last of the "big city bosses." But a new machine has arisen in Chicago as well as in other cities and suburbs. The unanswered question is whether Chicago's "New Machine" is the precursor of the future of urban politics in America or an anomaly that will soon disappear.

The split within the African-American community and splits within the reform coalition that had elected Harold Washington led to the election of Richard M. Daley as mayor in 1989. But Daley also won because he ran a high-tech modern campaign that differed from the campaigns of his father and earlier machine candidates. His victories completed the unraveling of Mayor Harold Washington's progressive coalition and brought about the creation of a new regime.

The regime that now governs Chicago, which I call the New Chicago Machine, retains some aspects of the past but has new elements. The previous Richard J. Daley progrowth machine had been composed of real estate developers, major downtown businesses, labor unions, major institutions like universities, and the Democratic Party. Although the Democratic Party, labor unions, and major institutions continue to support the new Mayor Daley, most of the older downtown commercial, real estate, and financial businesses that had supported his father are no longer central to the new regime. Of the 21 companies that had composed the powerful Chicago Central Area Committee in the 1950s and 1960s, only a couple contributed a total of a few thousand dollars to Richard M. Daley's multimillion-dollar 1999 campaign. Daley's support, at least in terms of financial contributions, now comes more from wealthy lawyers, lobbyists, bankers, stock traders, and the construction firms and unions that depend on contracts from City Hall. In 1999, bankers, lawyers, and stock and options traders gave Richard M. Daley more than $463,000 to run a modern Clintonesque campaign with political consultants, public opinion polls, press secretaries, direct mail, and television ads to supplement the work of the old-time precinct captains. As Daley would later say, "People aren't what they used to be. People don't vote for parties. They vote for the person. It's all television money and polling now. It's not parades. It's not torchlights and songs."

Don Rose and James Andrews, who served as political consultants for one of his opponents, describe the new urban political machine under Richard M. Daley:

> In the late 1980s it cost upwards of $4 million to run a rigorous campaign for mayor of Chicago. . . . The massive infusions of cash necessary for such campaigns simply cannot come from golf outings and putting the squeeze on patronage workers. . . . Such money now must come from institutions where the benefits of government run, not in the hundreds of thousands of dollars, but in the millions: law firms, financial organizations, and developers. Thus, the $50,000 or $100,000 contribution to candidates becomes the ticket to municipal . . . access for such institutions. . . . The term that emerged for this process . . . was "pinstripe patronage."

SOURCE: *Rogues, Rebels, and Rubber Stamps: The Politics of the Chicago City Council from 1863 to the Present.* Boulder, CO: Westview, 2001, pp. 247–249 and 287–290. Copyright © 2001 by Perseus Book Group. Reproduce with permission of Perseus Book Group via Copyright Clearance Center.

> This, then, is the next and higher stage of the new urban political machine, which must spend millions upon millions to feed the media monster (rather than the families of precinct captains) and utilize contemporary technologies such as computerized mailing and phone banking.
>
> The important cogs in the machine are not the ward bosses and the sewer chiefs of old, but development-businessmen . . . and lawyer-lobbyists.

The regular Democratic Party has also changed. The Shakman Decree has made trading government jobs for precinct work unconstitutional. Although the old machine still exists, it is weaker than it was in Richard J. Daley's heyday. Some Democratic Party precinct captains who still work city precincts got their jobs at the city, county, park district, or other local governments before the Shakman Decree took effect and remain loyal to the party. Other "volunteer" precinct captains with government jobs believe that party precinct work will bring them raises or promotions. These old-time precinct captains, however, are now linked with what has been called a new politics of candidate-oriented, media-based, synthetic, high-tech campaigns. For the funding of this new media-based campaign, Daley in 1999 received only $47,000 from political figures and party organizations. The party no longer provides the finances needed for the media-based campaigns; the candidates must raise this money on their own.

The 1999 campaign finance disclosures also reveal Daley's spending habits as a candidate. Daley spent $3.41 million during the 1999 primary, whereas his campaign contributed less than $3,000 to other political campaigns. Instead, Daley's largest expenditure was for promotional material, campaign consultants, consulting fees, polling, mailing, paid advertising, printing, and other associated political services. In all, this category accounted for nearly $2.4 million of his $3.4 million in campaign expenses, or 68 percent of his total expenditures. The second largest category of Daley's expenditures, 21 percent of his campaign spending, included salaries for his campaign staff, reimbursements for staff expenses, and insurance and hospitalization for injured personnel. Another 3.55 percent was spent for office space, telephones, office equipment, and travel for campaign staff. Thus modern, high-tech, media-based mayoral campaigns require huge sums of money for consultants, media, and professional staff. The days of precinct captains delivering simple brochures and campaign promises door-to-door are gone. . . .

THE NEW DALEY MACHINE

Richard M. Daley also governs in an era that is different from his father's. Although boosterism and bossism may have served his father well, these qualities are not enough for his son to govern. Although Richard M. Daley is more enlightened and modern than his father in his attitudes and policies, he has not completely abandoned the machine politics that brought his father and him to power.

Richard M. Daley was elected mayor after "Council Wars," a time of pronounced racial and political polarization in the city and the city council. He had to defuse those tensions if he was to be effective. He could not resurrect the patronage army and tyrannical control of the old Daley machine, neither could he roll back the clock on affirmative action and minority empowerment. Daley avoided most political reforms but has cast himself as a civic or good government reformer streamlining city government, improving the city bureaucracy, keeping taxes low, and limiting waste if not corruption at City Hall.

Daley quickly tamed the city council, which had been chaotic under Mayor Eugene Sawyer. His power over the council was strengthened by the fact that between 1989 and 1998, he appointed seventeen of the fifty aldermen to the seats they held. When an alderman resigned or died, the mayor appointed a successor until the next election, and the appointee most often won reelection. Needless to say, these appointed aldermen were grateful for the mayor's help, felt a debt of gratitude, and usually sided with the administration on major votes. Daley also gained more power because the Independent or opposition bloc in the council was divided. Only racial issues, property tax increases, and some environmental legislation motivated significant levels of opposition in the council. The rest of the time the vast majority of the aldermen were willing to support the mayor. Further undercutting the opposition, the mayor implemented a number of managerial and budget reforms, including the unusual step for a Democratic mayor of privatizing some city positions.

Citizens' job performance ratings for Mayor Daley have been high. They were highest just after he won primary elections (60 percent of the voters said that he was doing a good or an excellent job after the 1989 primary and 62 percent after the 1991 primary). They dropped to below 50 percent in 1990 and 1992, but in comparison to Mayor Sawyer, who had only 38–41 percent approval, Daley's positive ratings remained solid. However, there is a major racial bias in the ratings. Only 18–35 percent of African Americans in the early 1990s said the mayor was doing a good or an outstanding job. Daley has not yet become the mayor of all the city and all its diverse racial groups, but he is gaining more of the Black vote in each election.

Chicago in the 1990s clearly was different from the Chicago of earlier years. Perhaps most emblematic of the change was the 1996 Democratic National Convention. For the 1996 convention, Chicago was spruced up with newly paved streets, flower boxes, banners, and signs along the routes to the new United Center, where the convention would be held. In 1968, the clash between protestors and police in the streets and pro- and anti-Vietnam delegates in the convention hall defined the event. Although in 1996 there were incidents in which the police were sued for harassing dissidents, the convention was marked by only a few orderly, regulated, peaceful protests. In contrast, Democrats made a gigantic show of unity as they joined together to renominate Bill Clinton and Al Gore as their presidential and vice presidential candidates. By every standard the convention was successful, including the all-important test of a unified Democratic Party triumphing in the November elections two and a half months later. Chicago handled the 1996 Democratic National Convention effectively and got positive publicity from this well-reported event. Many of the media news programs made explicit contrasts with the 1968 convention and praised the new Chicago under the new Mayor Daley.

The new Daley regime and the public policies that it produces are an amalgam that William Grimshaw has called "Machine politics, reform style." While keeping the support of the old machine organization, Richard M. Daley has run slick, modern campaigns. Unlike his father, he has not become a party "boss." He holds no official position in the Democratic party, but he does maintain his own loyal army of precinct workers and political operatives. On the other side of the ledger, he has kept, to a certain degree, the affirmative action and good government reforms such as freedom of information, instituted under Mayor Washington. He has extended the ethics ordinance and has undertaken antimachine and antiunion government actions such as the privatization of janitorial services, only to indulge in "pinstriped patronage" in letting those contracts. He has been a "builder mayor" supporting big government projects, office building in the downtown, and upscale housing projects in the neighborhoods adjacent to the Loop. At the same time, following Mayor Washington's job retention strategy of preserving manufacturing jobs, he has supported zoning policies to protect manufacturing plants and to create new high-tech industries in other neighborhoods. In response to the desires of the new service and global economy business elite, he has provided for better amenities and beautified the city, especially the downtown, with more parks, flowers in street medians, and wrought iron ornamental fences around parks and schools. The greatest image of the new Chicago is no longer State Street but Millennium Park, being constructed across from Michigan Avenue, and Navy Pier on the lakefront as a playground and tourist attraction.

The old "city of the big shoulders" is being remade into the global city capital of the Midwest. Although the new regime that surrounds Daley includes some party hacks and wheeler-dealers from the past, more prominent are wealthy lawyers, bankers, and investors who make up the new business elite of the city. Meanwhile, down on the second floor of city hall, Mayor Richard M. Daley rules over a rubber stamp city council, as his father did fifty years ago.

However, this new machine is very unstable. In March 2000, Daley had a health scare that appeared at first to be a heart attack or stroke (which killed his father and Mayor Washington). We are told by the media that he only has high blood pressure, which is treatable with standard medication. But, as this scare reminds us, Richard M. Daley will not rule forever; and, like his father and Mayor Washington, he has groomed no successor.

Second, the economy that supports Mayor Daley is fragile—some call it a bubble economy based on high-tech stocks that cannot maintain their inflated values. In an economic recession, the legal and financial sectors that underpin the new global service economy will be hard hit. A government of retrenchment like the government under Mayor Ed Kelly in the 1930s will require very different allies and policies.

Most of all, there is a steady racial change in Chicago, and Whites are already a minority. The 2000 census showed a 37 percent Black population, a 31 percent White population, a 26 percent Latino population and 6 percent other social categories. As the fastest growing population, Latinos will inevitably play a more important role in Chicago politics. They may not be willing to continue as a junior partner, as they have in the reigns of Mayors Harold Washington and Richard M. Daley.

30. Success in Santa Fe: Mayor Debbie Jaramillo

John Nichols

In the 1980s and 1990s in the United States many cities experimented with "progressive" governments which favored neighborhoods over downtown development and traditional business-based power elites. Cities like San Francisco, Chicago, and Santa Fe experimented with these types of social reformist governments. This is the story of the progressive takeover of Santa Fe local government. It also highlights one of the many women mayors like Chicago's Jane Byrne and San Francisco's Diane Feinstein who came to power in the last decades of the twentieth century and will more frequently in the twenty-first.

In the struggle between rich and poor, folks like Valentin Valdez usually end up holding the short end of the stick. But not in Santa Fe.

Valdez is a retired janitor who, since childhood, has climbed in the mountains that surround New Mexico's historic, picturesque, and increasingly trendy capital city. Several years ago, as he hiked on Atalaya Mountain, Valdez came across a parcel of land that had traditionally been known as a place of great spiritual significance to members of Santa Fe's large Hispanic community.

Now, however, what Valdez had always thought of as public space was being divided into lots where developers planned to build $500,000-and-up homes for wealthy emigres from California.

"I realized that greed was destroying our community," says Valdez, a soft-spoken man of 71. "I realized that if we did not fight back, the rich people would just roll over the poor people—like they have for a thousand years."

The fight back that Valdez describes has evolved into a remarkable story of municipal transformation that, in less than two years, has seen Santa Fe's City Hall wrenched from the hands of a conservative, pro-development establishment and handed over to one of the most progressive local governments in America.

Where Santa Fe's mayor and city council once could be expected to rubber-stamp extravagant development proposals and then march off to drink cocktails with their rich contributors, local officials are now voting for development moratoriums and then heading out for union rallies or Green Party meetings.

In Santa Fe, where class issues were once ignored, local pols now speak candidly about economic disparity. "People know class differences exist, but politicians in most places never talk about it," Mayor Debbie Jaramillo declares. "Well, here in Santa Fe we do talk about it. How can we avoid the subject? It's so blatantly obvious what's going on—you have rich people forcing

SOURCE: John Nichols, "Success in Santa Fe," *Progressive*, August 1995, pp. 32–36. Reprinted by permission of *The Progressive*, 409 E. Main Street, Madison, WI 53709, www.progressive.org.

poor people out of their homes, their communities. This isn't something I'm making up. This is something we see every day. And this is what people elected us to do something about."

The new mayor and council have also appointed openly gay and lesbian officials for the first time, placed Greens on planning bodies, and so shaken up the status quo that discussions of local government are now spiced with phrases like "populist coup" and "revolution."

"Compared to the history of politics at this City Hall, our taking over could be viewed as a revolution," admits Jaramillo, who began her political journey as a militant neighborhood activist in 1986 and seven years later was sworn in as mayor. "I think that those who saw the election as a revolution did so because the shift that was made was from a good-old-boys club, real pro-development-type government to one that was led by a woman—and a Hispanic woman at that—who was talking about putting the interests of working people and poor people first."

So marked has the shift been that national observers are beginning to point to Santa Fe as a model for progressives nationally. It illustrates the possibility of building coalitions involving Greens, unions, the elderly, minorities, and the white working class, and it highlights the issues that can help sustain such coalitions.

"I think the left has to start thinking about putting development and affordable-housing issues to use as tools for coalition-building and for getting important things done. And Santa Fe shows how that can happen," says Steve Cobble, a former official in the Presidential campaigns of the Reverend Jesse Jackson. "If the left is serious about environmental issues and issues of wealth and poverty, this shows a way to build coalitions and to succeed."

Former New Mexico Governor Toney Anaya, a Santa Fe resident who was one of the most progressive governors in the nation during his tenure in the 1980s, shares Cobble's view. "The model from Santa Fe could go to other places. In fact, it should go to other places," says Anaya. "The model of building coalitions around issues such as development is something that progressives need to understand if we're going to really start winning at the local level and, eventually, at the national level."

While left coalitions have won control of a number of cities around the country over the years—from Burlington, Vermont, to Berkeley, California—the Santa Fe example is unique, not only in the makeup of the coalition, but in the distinct emphasis on class issues. Then again, everything about Santa Fe is unique.

With roots that stretch back more than seven centuries, to the time when the Pueblo Indians established a village on the site of the current city, Santa Fe is one of the oldest and most distinct communities in North America. So appealing was the site that the Spanish conquistadors fought the Indians for the turf—eventually establishing a thriving commercial center that boomed as the terminus of the Santa Fe Trail in the Nineteenth Century. Shortly after the beginning of the Twentieth, it was named as New Mexico's capital. . . .

Santa Fe remained a relatively quiet, culturally diverse state-government town until the 1970s, when improved transportation links and a growing reputation as a "new-age" center began to draw increasing numbers of newcomers—particularly wealthy Californians—to what locals refer to as "the city different." . . . [M]any were so drawn to the scenery and the relaxed lifestyle that they decided to stay. Santa Fe's population has boomed from around 40,000 in the 1970s to more than 60,000 today with another 45,000 living in the surrounding county. And for the first time in three centuries, the 1990 census showed there were more Anglos than Hispanics living in the community.

"Suddenly, you started to see mansions in the hills," explains Valentin Valdez, whose family has lived in Santa Fe for generations. "And in the neighborhoods, over the last few years, you started to see the houses being bought up not by the children of people from Santa Fe but by people from Hollywood with big checkbooks."

Indeed, housing values skyrocketed in Santa Fe during the 1980s. The median price for a home rose 28 percent between 1990 and 1993. And simple adobe homes in once humble neighborhoods near the city center now sell for $300,000, just as one-room apartments can go for as much as $1,500 a month.

"The whole city has experienced the most incredible process of gentrification in the last 20 years," says City Councilor Cris Moore, a Green Party activist who was elected along with Jaramillo in March 1994. "A lot of wealthy people came as tourists and then decided to retire here. The problem is that, while they have driven up housing prices and taxes, there has been no parallel increase in wages. So the natives—the people who have always lived here—are under intense pressure to sell their homes to millionaires from California."

Longtime residents such as Valdez, who built his adobe home on the city's east side more than forty years ago, now find themselves property rich but cash poor. As home values rise, property-tax bills have jumped so quickly that people like Valdez—who lives on Social Security and a small pension—must take out loans simply to afford to stay in their homes.

In a matter of a few years, Valdez saw his Apodaca Hill community turn from a homey, low- to middle-income enclave into what the local newspaper, The New Mexican, now refers to as "a million-dollar neighborhood." . . .

The problem as the 1990s dawned was that Valdez did not want to sell out and move—as many of his neighbors have—to affordable areas thirty and forty miles from town. An even bigger problem was that the prospects for the children and grandchildren of working-class people like him buying their own homes were rapidly disappearing.

"I was afraid that one of these days it would just get to be too much, and I would lose my home, my land—where my roots have been all my life," explains Valdez. "I felt so sad; the native people were being forced out of their own home town. We had to respond or this wasn't going to be our town anymore."

The fight back was slow to develop. Santa Feans had always been taught to appreciate tourism, and the live-and-let-live atmosphere of the community—reflected in shop signs that read, "Shoplifting is Bad Karma"—was traditionally quite welcoming to newcomers.

"In the 1980s, particularly, Santa Fe became very tourist-oriented, very tourist-hungry—to a fault," says Anaya. "Santa Fe was very pro-development—the city council never met a development it didn't like."

What older residents began to realize, however, was that the tourism boom and the development frenzy were turning their city into a place they could no longer afford. It was Debbie Jaramillo who, as a young housewife and mother, took the lead in 1986 in one of the first high-profile anti-development campaigns. She led a petition drive to prevent a road project that would have torn up an existing neighborhood in order to promote development of surrounding areas. Jaramillo was so vocal, and so effective, that in 1988 she was elected to the city council as a lonely—but seldom silent—foe of the direction in which Santa Fe was then headed.

Though she lost on a lot of issues by a 7–1 margin, the councilor succeeded in putting development issues on the public agenda, and in making a name for herself. To call Jaramillo's council tenure controversial would be an understatement. Speaking to *The New York Times* about wealthy newcomers, she said, "These are conquerors who did not need arms to take over our town. They have come instead with their big money and their higher education."

In 1993, she told a reporter for *The San Diego Union-Tribune* newspaper—which was doing a feature on wealthy Californians moving to the Santa Fe area—that Hispanics in northern New Mexico were considering burning down million-dollar houses in order to fight what they saw as a white invasion of their region. Jaramillo's in-your-face approach shocked the traditional power establishment in Santa Fe—a mixture of wealthy Hispanics and Anglos that in the late 1980s and early 1990s was led by Mayor Sam Pick. An ardently pro-development official, Pick was backed by a like-minded majority on the city council.

Jaramillo challenged Pick for mayor in 1990, winning almost 30 percent of the vote. But when she ran again in 1994, she was written off by many local pundits who portrayed her as too strident. She was even accused of being a racist—since she was so impassioned in her criticism of newcomers, the vast majority of whom happened to be Anglos.

In fact, Jaramillo worked hard to combat racism, building broad-based coalitions around shared economic concerns. But her opponents ignored this work.

"I think a lot of times they figured that if they could turn it around, turn the discussion onto another topic, then they wouldn't have to deal with the real issues," says the 43 year-old mayor. "They figured they had an easy one—call her a racist and pretty soon people will be talking about racism, not economics. It was a way to get away from the real issue that was at hand. I saw it as kind of a tactic to skirt what needed to be addressed."

In the 1994 campaign, however, Jaramillo would not be deterred. Though the pro-development front runner, Councilor Peso Chavez, outspent her three-to-one, and though she was undercut by a third candidate who ran on a somewhat more moderate anti-development platform, Jaramillo forged a coalition that is all too rare these days.

"I think her victory was not so much due to practical organization as to the impression that she was the anti-establishment candidate, and people knew that the establishment had let them down," says Moore, who supported Jaramillo. "She got a good deal of Hispanic support—particularly from senior citizens—and she also attracted a lot of Anglo support from liberals, anti-development folks, union members, Greens, and whatever exists of the left."

Running on the defiant slogan, "Es Tiempo" ("It's Time"), Jaramillo purchased newspaper ads that declared, "What is popular is not always right, what is right is not always popular," and said, "It's time City Hall turns its attention to the needs of its citizens, instead of focusing attention on the needs of developers, politicians, and special interests."

Jaramillo made issues of economic disparity a vital part of her campaign, saying, "It's time to reverse the trend that's adding to the economic and ethnic split of our city. We must quit neglecting less affluent neighborhoods and uplift pockets of deterioration."

While other candidates harped on crime and gang issues, Jaramillo noted that she had been in a gang as a youth, and said, "Social conditions such as poverty, poor housing, and lack of economic opportunity are major contributors to crime. We must address crime by addressing the root causes."

Former Governor Anaya thinks that Jaramillo's progressive positions on economics were a powerful tool in the under-financed candidate's political war chest. "The awareness of class is very real here," said Anaya. "There is more of an open discussion of class in Santa Fe than you'll find elsewhere. Why? Part of the reason is that everything is so very apparent. You have your $800,000 houses on the ridge tops—rich people, many of them newcomers, looking down on the rest of us. It's not hidden—it's obvious. On the other side you have your local families, families that have been here for generations, having to sell out because they can't afford property taxes that were driven up by the arrival of the out-of-staters. Debbie simply let people know that she saw what they saw—and they responded."

The last polls before the election showed Jaramillo trailing by twelve points, but when the votes were counted she had won easily with 39 percent of the vote in a 12-candidate field. In addition, the election swept in an anti-development, progressive majority on the eight-member council, which meant the new mayor could turn her bold words to action. That prospect chilled local developers—who had poured money into her leading opponent's campaign in the final days before the election.

Newspaper editorials warned the mayor that she would have to be careful lest her election might "scare" business. But Jaramillo doesn't really think "scare" is the proper word.

"Scare is just a term they like to use—I think the reality is that the election angered a lot of powerful people," she says. "There was a combination of things that I saw happen whenever I spoke to the truth, when I said what needed to be said. The reactions were varied. I saw some people get real defensive and try to turn on me—call me 'racist' and all that—but I knew that was because I talked about the real issues. There is a genuine understanding of what's really going on in this country—who's better off, who's not, who's getting the short end of the stick. But to hear it in a political context is rare in itself. So when I say it, period, I think people are taken aback by it—they just don't expect politicians to talk seriously about wealth and poverty."

So far, Jaramillo has shown little willingness to trim her sails. She filled the council seat she had to give up to become mayor with an openly lesbian community activist, and—though Jaramillo is "a Jesse Jackson Democrat"—she showed few qualms about appointing members of Santa Fe's well-organized Green party to local commissions.

The new council has funded an innovative tenant hot line, passed resolutions calling for environmental-impact studies of projects at the nearby Los Alamos nuclear facility, and endorsed union organizing in the local private sector.

The mayor and council are currently considering a bold city charter proposal, which would impose limits on campaign spending and expand direct democracy with initiatives, recalls, and referendums. It also would bar the passage of any city ordinance, resolution, referendum, or policy that "discriminates on the basis of race, age, religion, color, national origin, ancestry, gender, sexual orientation, physical or mental handicap, or medical condition."

On the key development front, Jaramillo and the council have moved quickly—although not always as quickly as some local activists would like. The city has launched a number of projects aimed at providing affordable housing. A 46-unit resort-condominium development that failed was acquired from the Resolution Trust Company, with the goal of making units available for low- and moderate-income families. The city is also purchasing plots of land where affordable housing can be built.

Jaramillo has proposed a plan that would require all developers to set aside a certain proportion of future developments to include affordable-housing units—which by law would have to be mixed in with more expensive units. In fact, the debate now is not about whether this is a good idea, but on where to set the standard of affordability—Santa Fe planners identify a $120,000 home as affordable, but Moore thinks the figure should be closer to $80,000.

In order to more effectively direct growth—which often follows patterns of available water—the city also is purchasing the private Sangre de Cristo Water Co.

In the boldest act so far, city and county officials voted in June to impose strict limits on development in the mountains east of Santa Fe, the very area where Valentin Valdez saw treasured open spaces being claimed by developers just a few years ago. Calling it the most important piece of local legislation in decades, Councilor Frank Montano declared that the growth-control ordinance would "protect the mountains not just for those that live today, but for those that live after us, and after them."

Following the vote, Valdez approached Moore, the Green councilor who had taken the lead on the growth-control initiative, and as the two men hugged, Valdez whispered, "You've done well, my friend." Moore, who has emphasized the need to build community coalitions to support the new council's bold initiatives, replied, "No, we've done well."

The question of whether the Santa Fe progressives can really alter patterns of development—and of economic disparity—remains unanswered. Some local activists say Jaramillo and the new council have not been as hard as they should be on land speculators. Others say there is simply no way to do enough.

"I think we're moving in the right direction. We're getting some balance. But it may be the old theory of locking the barn door after the horses got away," says Anaya. "There's still too much development, still too much pressure for development. We've lost a lot of the Santa Fe I'd like to have seen retained. And I'm not sure we can reverse the influx of outsider hordes pushing the brown people out of town."

Still, a genuine confidence radiates among many activists after passage of the growth-control legislation.

"You can make a difference here," observes David Arbin, a local architect and neighborhood activist who has been involved in several land-use fights. "At this level you can make a swing. Maybe it's not everything that everyone would want, but what we're doing here matters."

And Arbin thinks it will ultimately matter to progressives in communities across America. "Remember," he says, "the Populists started in little towns in Oklahoma and Kansas back in the 1890s, and they ended up writing the agendas that Bob LaFollette and Franklin Roosevelt and others eventually instituted. Why shouldn't a little city in New Mexico be the place where the next set of progressive agendas gets written?"

Exercise
Studying Power in Your City

The purpose of these exercises is to allow you to map the distribution of power in your community much as you mapped the distribution of race and wealth in earlier exercises. Based upon the information you gather here, you should be able to determine whether your community is a reform or machine-run city. You can further discover the balance of power in your city council or county board and between local political parties or political factions. You will learn whether there are any occupational or business-interest group biases among governmental officials.

These exercises will also allow you to trace the influence of money on local politics and which sectors of society are most likely to make up the informal public private partnerships which constitute the governing regime. Lastly, you will compile a list of the 10 to 15 most powerful people in your community and learn what makes them so powerful.

(continued)

(continued)

REFORM OR MACHINE REGIMES

A reform city administration is one that does not depend upon the particular resources of a political machine. Instead, it depends upon civil service rather than patronage jobs. In such a reform administration, the city and metropolitan region isn't governed by a single political party. Finally, a reform administration distributes its city contracts by a public bidding process rather than to campaign contributors with clout.

Checking newspaper stories on city government for the last year and official city documents either in hard copies or on the Internet will allow you to determine roughly how many city jobs are civil service jobs requiring skills and passing objective tests as opposed to the number that can be appointed by the city administration without special qualifications or tests. You can also determine whether there have been any lawsuits alleging patronage hiring or bid rigging by your local governments. Further checking newspaper articles through the index of your local newspapers, Lexis-Nexis, or other Internet search engines will also locate charges of corruption in local government.

Next, determine how many seats in the city council are held by which political party or different political factions such as pro-mayor and anti-mayor factions in cities or suburbs with nonpartisan elections. Determine key divided roll call votes in your city council and how many aldermen voted with and against the mayor and his or her administration during the last year. The city council divided roll call votes are sometimes listed on the city's Website and at other times will be recorded in an official government document such as the City Council Journal of Proceedings. (See, for example, the Chicago City Clerk's Website at **http://www. chicityclerk.com.** You may simply select all divided roll call votes or the ones mentioned prominently in newspaper stories for the last year.) This research will tell you the division between political parties or political factions in your local government.

Next determine the professions and occupations of the mayor and city council members from official city biographies or newspaper stories about them. How active is the industry or group each represents on major issues before the city council as determined by the divided roll call votes of the last year. If the information is easily obtained, also determine if occupations of elected officials a decade ago were the same as the present officials.

To determine the public/private partnership which governs the city determine the largest contributors to the successful mayoral candidate in the last election. (Campaign contribution data are usually available from your state or city Board of Elections or County Clerk's Websites. If they are not available electronically, every state requires that they be made available in some form at the appropriate Board of Elections or County Clerk offices.) Did city contractors and developers, the institutions of the global or service economy (such as banks, insurance companies, and law firms), labor unions, interest groups, or downtown merchants give the mayor the greatest amount of campaign contributions? What does this tell you about the alliance or regime that probably governs your city in addition to elected officials such as the mayor and the aldermen?

YOUR CITY'S LEADERS

To determine the key leaders in your city go to the newspapers and locally published magazines (either in hard copies in your library or on the Internet). See who these publications identify as leaders in your city. City leaders will appear most often in publications as sponsors, supporters, or opponents of major public and private projects. If someone is listed in news stories about such projects more than once a year, they are probably a community leader. Supplement this list with an interview with one city council member or city government official and one major business leader. (If this exercise is being done by a class, select different public officials and business leaders to interview so that the same people are not interviewed over and over.) Ask the persons you interview to name the ten most influential or powerful individuals in your community. From the published lists and the lists from interviews, select the 10 to 15 individuals listed most often. What are the characteristics of these leaders: (1) Are they administrative officials who are not elected like Robert Moses of New York City? (2) Are they elected public officials like the Mayor? (3) Are they business leaders? Determine their institutional basis of power and see if you can find at least one news story that provides a biography of the most powerful leaders. What makes them so powerful?

What is the race and sex of the key leaders in your community? Does their race and sex reflect the racial and sexual distribution of the general city and metropolitan population as shown in the last census?

Chapter 8

Structures of Local Government

Local government policies and decisions depend upon more than colorful personalities like George Washington Plunkitt and Robert Moses. They are determined by factors other than the existence of machine or interest group politics. Government structures and processes provide the framework within which the laws, economic development, and social policies are made.

We begin this part with court decisions, charter debates, reform proposals, and newspaper accounts of attempts to change urban governance rules and structures. Some of the proposed changes concern the laws governing elections and others involve city council proceedings. Whether public officials are elected by wards or at-large, by plurality or systems of proportional representation are factors that affect the racial characteristics, outlook, background, perspectives, and accountability of local officials. Similarly, city council rules determine to some extent whether the council will be effective and representative of the voters who elected them or simply a rubber stamp for the mayor's programs and policies.

Of all the government processes, the level of citizen participation and their level of satisfaction with their local governments are the most important. Citizen participation has waxed and waned since the 1960s. Minorities have been incorporated to differing degrees into local power structures. And beyond government itself, more than 10,000 neighborhood and community organizations have involved citizens in directly delivering services and pressuring governments to better meet their communities' needs. Yet citizens, and especially minority groups, evaluated the success of local government differently. They evaluate some officials and local government policies and projects positively and some negatively. But it is often difficult to get local governments to conform to citizen expectations.

Most Americans now live in metropolitan regions. While there is a case to be made that urban sprawl is not as bad as most social scientists and media commentators have maintained, our metropolitan regions are not well governed. Some large cities like Houston have taken over some regional functions beyond their city boundaries. Other metropolitan regions like Minneapolis-St. Paul have created regional councils to facilitate regional planning and to redistribute tax resources to communities in the greatest need but with the least financial means to cope with those needs.

Full regional government has not been adopted in most places, because as Jones and Hays reveal in their citizen surveys, most of us don't see ourselves as regional or metropolitan citizens. However rational regional government might seem, most of us don't want to be governed by it. Until that changes, only incremental cooperation between multiple sovereign local governments will be possible.

There is an additional outside constraint on our local governments. There has been a major change since the terrorist attacks of September 11, 2001. Cities are now prime terrorist targets but mostly helpless to prevent such attacks. The economic development of the urban renaissance of the 1990s and the first of the twenty-first century is jeopardized. Greater expenditures on public safety are required at the same time that an economic recession has forced major state and local government budget cuts. Cities and suburbs are having to do more with less. Insurance for major urban projects in the private sector is more costly or impossible to obtain. Grand plans for costly public developments and improvements in urban life are being postponed or canceled. City, suburban, and metropolitan futures are becoming more uncertain than they seemed in the era of affluence.

We begin with a discussion of local government structures. The fights over the structures of local government include reformers' attempts to reign in the evils of machine politics by proposing structural changes like at-large and nonpartisan elections of aldermen and granting more powers to mayors. They include ethics laws governing city contracts and expenditures of city funds. These structural remedies for political ills of cities have not always worked as expected. The fight over structures continues in U.S. cities today in the adoption of new city charters by cities like New York and Los Angeles; the provision of home rule taxing powers in state constitutions; and efforts since the 1960s by the courts to achieve better racial representation through ward rather than at-large elections of city councils, which reversed the earlier effort by reformers to elect the "best people" concerned for the entire city through nonpartisan, at-large elections.

Structural changes matter and create controversy. One unusual change adopted by city government in the last few decades was ordered in a federal court case in Peoria in 1991. The problem the court addressed was quite common in most U.S. cities. Despite large minority populations, especially of African Americans, the most common system of at-large elections deprived Blacks of representation on city councils equal to their numbers in the city as a whole. The usual solution imposed by the courts, has been to require ward elections of at least some city council members.

In Peoria, Illinois, until a federal lawsuit was filed in 1987, only one Black had been elected to the city council in their entire history. The suit maintains, "Black residents and voters . . . have had less opportunity than White residents to participate in the political process and to elect representatives of their choice." Because of this, Peoria changed to a system of five ward and five at-large elections for their city council. But to guarantee full Black participation and representation, the at-large elections were to be held under a system of cumulative voting. Under this system in Peoria, a voter may vote for any number from one to five at-large candidates. If they cast a "bullet vote" for a single candidate, the candidate will be awarded five votes; whereas, if they vote for five candidates, each of the candidates will receive one vote. The effect of this method (which is used extensively in Europe and other parts of the world as a system of proportional representation) is to allow political, racial, or ethnic minorities to indicate the intensity of their support for candidates so as to get at least some members of their group elected. Cities, even smaller cities like Peoria, make a good testing ground for such political systems before they are adopted more broadly.

A common experience over the last few decades in the United States is adoption of new city charters or amendments to existing city charters. Not all cities have charters. For example, Chicago does not, it is governed by the State of Illinois' Cities and Villages Act. However, most cities have a single document, which at the state and national level we would call a constitution. At the city and suburban level of government these documents are called charters. Charters and charter amendments usually have to be approved by the voters in a referendum. In talks in front of the Los Angeles Charter Reform Conference before the new city charter was adopted in 2000, various speakers stressed that charters pass when a consensus is formed in favor of the changes before they are sent to the voters. Because of this consensus, for instance, the 1925 Los Angeles Charter received approval by 87 percent of the voters. On the other hand, Chicago's proposed 1907 city charter was soundly defeated because the business leaders of the charter convention failed to create a broad consensus and a number of reformers as well as ethnic groups opposed it.[1]

One reason that many cities are changing their city charters and their political structures is that the old system of rule by a regime of business people and the mayor—called in Los Angeles, the "Committee of 25"—no longer runs the cities. The multinational corporations that are now so important to the economic life of global cities don't have the same concerns and knowledge of the individual cities in which they do business as did the local firms for most of the twentieth century. Beyond changes in the regime, older political structures don't allow as much political participation and older methods of running city government are not up-to-date. So cities change as they try to cope with current problems like the decline of the middle class and the growing division between the poor and the rich. In addition, civil service systems become more inflexible, independent units of government have multiplied, commissions and boards of city agencies and separate units of government don't encourage accountability and citizen participation. Finally, many local problems go beyond city or small suburban boundaries and require regional solutions which may not be possible with current local government structures. All of these frustrations drive political structural changes to "modernize" and improve city, suburban, and metropolitan regional government.

At the center of many complaints about our cities are frequently the most representative institutions, the city councils. Efforts are constantly made to reform the city councils and to force councils to adhere to the reforms that have been adopted. An entire book could easily be compiled of writings—particularly from local newspapers that cover the sessions and antics of city councils. In 1988 the City Club of Chicago made ten recommendations for reforming the Chicago City Council.[2] The recommended reforms were along four dimensions: (1) public disclosure of the debate, voting, and expenditures of aldermen; (2) reforms of the council committee system; (3) procedural reforms of the council; and (4) reforms to guarantee greater citizen participation. The City Club has issued a report card on their ten specific reforms since 1989 when Richard M. Daley first became mayor. In the first report card, the city council received passing grades on only four of the ten proposed reforms. In the most recent report card, Chicago managed to get a passing grade in six reforms, but an excellent grade in only two. You may wish to grade your city council on these same dimensions to see how it would fare.

Reference

See Judd and Swanstrom, Chapter 9: "The Fractured Metropolis," Chapter 11: "Urban Sprawl and Regional Governance," and Chapter 14: "The Challenge of Governance." In Ross and Levin see Chapter 4: "Formal Structure and Leadership Style" and Chapter 7 "Citizen Participation and Decentralization."

Notes

1. Maureen Flanagan, *Charter Reform in Chicago,* Carbondale: Southern Illinois University Press, 1987.
2. Dick Simpson, Jennifer Arneson, Lisa Dushkin, and Ann Gentile, *Chicago City Council Reform,* Chicago: University of Illinois at Chicago and City Club of Chicago, 1988 and 1991. Also in Dick Simpson (ed.), *Chicago's Future in a Time of Change,* Champaign, IL: Stipes, 1993, pp. 276–286.

31.   Restructuring City Government: Joyce Banks, et al. *v.* City of Peoria, Illinois

City government in many American communities has been restructured in the last decades of the twentieth century and will, undoubtedly, be changed again in the twenty-first century. Some cities, like New York and Los Angeles, have adopted new charters and some cities like Chicago have gained "home rule" powers under new state constitutions or laws. Some like Indianapolis and Minneapolis-St. Paul have experimented with various forms of metropolitan government. More cities and suburbs like Peoria, Illinois have had to change the structure of their city council because of court decisions to guarantee "one man, one vote" under civil rights legislation passed in the 1960s.

On March 7, 1987, members from the African-American community filed a lawsuit in federal court to stop the City of Peoria, the Park District, and the Public School District from holding its April elections and to force them to create new electoral districts to give minorities a greater opportunity to be elected to public office. The lawsuit charged that the "at-large" election system prevented minorities from electing candidates of their choice.

The suit was settled with a consent decree and since 1991 Peoria has operated under a council/manager form of government in which the mayor is elected as one of the at-large members of the City Council. The Council is now comprised of five ward representatives and five at-large members. One of the most interesting aspects, which differs from nearly every other American city is that the at-large members are elected by a system of cumulative voting that allows minorities greater voice in the electoral process.

DEFENDANTS' ILLEGAL PRACTICES

. . .

8. The City of Peoria under the present electoral system excludes Black representation and participation and minimizes, dilutes, or cancels out Black voting strength and access to the political process.
9. The City of Peoria is governed by a manager-aldermanic system with three at-large elections and five single member district elections under which the City Council, the city governing board, is composed of eight members.
10. Under this electoral structure only one black citizen in the history of the City of Peoria has been elected to any seat on the City Council. In 1983, a Black was elected from District 1, one of the single-member districts.
11. Black residents and voters of the City of Peoria, Illinois, have had less opportunity than White residents to participate in the political process and to elect representatives of their choice or to influence the election of representatives of their choice.
12. The Plaintiffs are not challenging any action taken by the Peoria City Council or its members heretofore elected or appointed, except as specifically related to the adoption of this form of government.

DEFENDANTS' STATUTORY VIOLATIONS

13. The present electoral system of voting for members of the City of Peoria City Council under the present form of government has the *result* and *effect* of diluting, minimizing, and cancelling out Black voting strength in the City of Peoria, and thus denies to Black citizens and registered voters of the City of Peoria the meaningful right to participate in the city election process and to influence the election or to elect candidates of their choice to the City of Peoria City Council, in violation of the rights of Plaintiffs and their class secured by Section 2 of the Voting Rights Act of 1965, as amended, Pub. Law. No. 97-205, 96 Stat. 134 (1982), 42 U.S.C. Sec. 1973 *et seq*.
14. Elections in Peoria and Peoria County are marked by a high degree of racially polarized voting.
15. The Black population in Peoria is a geographically compact, politically cohesive, distinct population, and is capable of constituting a majority in a single-member district.
16. Plaintiffs have no plain, speedy, or adequate remedy at law to secure redress. Unless restrained and enjoined by this Court, Defendants, their agents, employees and appointees, will continue to deny Plaintiffs their rights under the Voting Rights Act. By virtue of the foregoing, Plaintiffs have suffered and will continue to suffer immediate and irreparable injury.
17. The right to vote and the right to equal participation in the electoral and political processes is the most fundamental right in a democracy. The

SOURCE: *Banks et al. v. City of Peoria et al.*, Case No. 87-1018, U.S. District Court, Central District of Illinois, March 9, 1987.

harm to plaintiffs in allowing further elections under a system that dilutes that most fundamental right far outweighs the harm to the City of Peoria and the people of Peoria that a slight delay in the scheduled electoral process would cause.

18. The public interest is best served by full and equal participation in the electoral processes of all eligible citizens. The public interest is not served by a continuation of an electoral structure that dilutes the strength of over 15% of the citizens of the City of Peoria. . . .

AMENDED ELECTORAL STRUCTURE FOR THE CITY COUNCIL

The City Council of the City of Peoria shall hereafter be elected as follows:

1. The Mayor of the City of Peoria will continue to serve a four-year term and will continue to be elected at-large.
2. There will continue to be five members of the City council elected from single-member districts. The five districts as currently in place in the City of Peoria will remain undistrubed at this time and would continue to be reapportioned after every decennial census. The terms of the current members of this City Council elected from these districts will not be disturbed.
3. In the 1991 election there will be five at-large City Council seats up for election and the at-large general and primary election for those seats will be by means of cumulative voting. That is, each voter may vote for one, two, three, four, or five candidates at such election. If a voter votes for just one candidate, that candidate shall receive five votes. If a voter votes for just two candidates each of those candidates shall receive two and one-half votes. If a voter votes for just three candidates each of those candidates shall receive one and two-thirds votes. If a voter votes for just four candidates each of those candidates shall receive one and one-quarter votes. If a voter votes for five candidates each of those candidates shall receive one vote. The maximum number of votes each voter may cast in the at-large elections will be five. The five candidates who receive the highest number of votes in the general election will be declared the winners of the at-large seats.
4. There will continue to be primary elections for the at-large Council seats to reduce the candidate field down to ten and, for the district elections, down to two.
5. The elections in all other respects will be governed by the law of the State of Illinois. . . .

THE COURT FINDS

1. This Court has jurisdiction over the subject matter of this action and the parties thereto.
2. The provisions of this Consent Decree are fair, adequate and reasonable and are not contrary to the laws of the State of Illinois or Federal Law.
3. This Consent Decree is in the best interest of the parties and the public.

32. Charter Reform in Los Angeles

James Ingram and Xandra Kayden

One of the ways of remaking cities is to change their governmental structures by amending their city charter. Citizens may agree to change their city's charter because they are frustrated living there, the society has changed in major ways, and their current city government is unable to respond effectively because of financial or legal restrictions imposed by the current charter. But proposed new charters or charter amendments are only successfully adopted if a broad consensus of interest groups and citizens agrees on the nature of the existing problems and the proposed solutions. Two talks given at a conference on charter reform sponsored by UCLA and USC explain why this is the case. Professors James Ingram and Xandra Kayden in their talks made the need for consensus in charter revision clear. Sufficient consensus was achieved that Los Angeles successfully implemented its newest city charter on July 1, 2000.

THE HISTORY OF CHARTER REFORM BY JAMES INGRAM

I have a feeling of deja vu because meetings like this concerned with the future of Los Angeles and charter reform have been going on, at least as revealed in my research, since 1887. So you and I are here engaged in a process of perfecting Los Angeles, of making the City of Angels live up to its name—if that's possible at all.

I can only address one simple theme here, what I see from having studied the city's charters and the many charter amendments. There is a need to form a consensus in order to allow real charter reform to occur. . . .

The Need for Consensus

The city began the process of charter reform in 1887 and elected its first board of freeholders. Most historical accounts neglect this because the charter that the freeholders wrote was not passed by the voters. Stung by their failure at the polls, they immediately formed a new board of freeholders, and wrote the 1889 charter that governed the city up until 1925. What marked the 1889 charter and allowed it to succeed where the previous charter failed, was that the board of freeholders worked on forming a consensus, making sure that the various groups in the city would agree upon the charter they would be voting on. Again in 1925, a board of freeholders met to assemble a charter to govern the City of Los Angeles, and here again the crucial need for consensus was

SOURCE: James W. Ingram, "The History of Charter Reform" and Xandra Kayden, "Societal Change and Charter Reform," talks given at the Los Angeles Charter Reform Conference, 1998. http://www.sppsr.ucla.edu/dean's/forum/chref.htm. Reprinted by permission of the authors.

met. But on every other occasion, in 1898, 1900, 1912, 1916, 1934, 1970, and 1971, Los Angeles failed to find a consensus for charter reform. We've had lots of efforts like this that are concerned with building a new charter, but most of them have failed because the framers haven't been able to agree on what the charter is to be about. So this ongoing process of perfecting Los Angeles has taken its toll on charter reform.

The board of freeholders for the 1925 charter was a very forward-looking group of people. They made sure that the city could pursue growth through its power, its water and harbor facilities. They made sure the city would deal with social concerns as well. They actually provided that employers had to give their workers two hours off in order to go and vote during the many city elections. And so social reform and developmental reform marked the 1925 charter that was produced. . . .

[A]mendments have been many. Since 1925 when this charter was formed, the voters of Los Angeles have looked at 518 different charter amendments and they've actually passed 394 of them. With all of these amendments, the charter of Los Angeles today is so big that I didn't bother to try to bring it in here. It became so patched up and changed around that it bears little resemblance to the forward-looking document that the charter framers of 1925 produced. Therefore, I'm hesitant to completely attribute the flaws of the present charter to those forward-looking looking freeholders of 1925. Before this charter went to the voters on May 6, 1924, they made sure that they formed a consensus among themselves and among the various groups in the city that they represented. A number of the freeholders really didn't care about the issue of district representation, but because they knew that many people in the city were very concerned with that issue, they put it on the ballot so that the people would be able to choose whether or not they would go with district representation. Another aspect of governance that is particularly relevant for a 464-square-mile city, is the issue of boroughs. Article 30 of the original 1925 charter actually contained an entire article on borough government, and would have allowed the city to deal with some of the issues that are not being dealt with today. . . .

The economic and population growth that occurred after the 1925 charter was passed is exactly what the framers wanted to create. So the fact that the city is home to people from different cultures, religions, languages, and ethnicities is a measure of the success of the 1925 charter. Therefore, I see some of my experience as a citizen of Los Angeles today as validation of that 1925 charter. However, that doesn't mean that a charter that was written for one million people can adequately address the needs of several million people.

Consensus Achieved

What I'd like to convey to you in this short time I have is that the reason the 1925 charter actually passed is that a consensus was formed before the charter was ever sent before the voters, and the voters ratified it in great numbers because they approved this consensus. 87 percent of the voters in that election said "yes" to the 1925 charter. All but two of the 978 election precincts that comprised the city in that May 6, 1924 election, approved the charter with a majority. In fact, a vast majority of the city's precincts gave well over two-thirds of their votes to approve this document that was put into effect in 1925. This was a document ratified by admittedly one of the most Anglo cities in the entire country, but also by groups in the city of all different backgrounds. It's not simply from one elite group of patricians who wanted to impose their will upon everyone else. They addressed the needs of people across the city. The 1925 charter even contained a provision for a municipal housing commission. Two decades before the federal government entered into public housing through the Wagner Housing Act the city charter of Los Angeles provided that the city could build housing to meet the needs of the people who were underserved by the city's current housing market. The 1925 charter also created a social services department to both provide public charitable assistance, and to coordinate the efforts of private charitable groups. So, if we stereotype these people as dead White male patricians who only cared about doing what was best for their small group, then we do them a real disservice much as people 70 years from now could do us a real disservice by lumping together all of our different goals and interests into one conceptual box. Just as many motives, interests and ideals as are represented in this room today were represented among those people who framed the charter in 1923 that the voters approved in 1924 and became the governing law in 1925. So the theme here is that consensus and a future orientation are essential if we want to make a charter that has the kind of venerability and lasting power that the 1925 charter has. I will now allow Professor Kayden to make this more relevant by putting it in the context of current events. . . .

SOCIETAL CHANGE AND CHARTER REFORM BY XANDRA KAYDEN

I'm going to talk about what's driving reform now and what the issues are. I'm not going to say the most obvious things because I think we've heard a lot of them. It seems to me that there are three issues: the frustration with living in the city, the changes in the society of Los Angeles, and the inability of the city government to respond to demands because of financial constraints, a complex decision structure within city government and the inability of the city to bring about consensus; that's a theme you may hear frequently.

Societal Changes in Los Angeles

Now in terms of the changes in society. Despite Jim's very strong argument for the social equity and liberal nature of the people who wrote the 1925 charter, it nevertheless remains true that in 1925 Los Angeles was the most White, Anglo-Saxon, Protestant, middle-class city in the nation. It's now the most ethnically diverse city in the world. If there is a relationship between culture and political structure, it would behoove us to rethink how our city government functions.

One of the differences in terms of who the new people are is that they are immigrants who come from non-Western societies which are more communitarian. So culturally they bring a different approach to thinking about authority, to thinking about government. And, also of course, the most important factor about them is that they are immigrants. The last time we had major immigration in America, people came into a party system. There is that old proverbial notion that you're met at the boat by your local precinct captain who provides you with a house, a job, and in return for that you will vote early and often. That system incorporated those immigrant groups into the political structure, and the sense of loyalty that followed the very definite economic war lasted for generations. We were a very partisan nation up until the 1950s and 1960s. Today when immigrants come to Los Angeles, there's no incorporating mechanism. There's no outreach to them from the city or from the political structure, because we don't have a political structure on the ground in Los Angeles. So everybody is kind of left to their own devices.

The other thing that characterizes immigrants is that they tend to look homeward, so we have many foreign language newspapers in the city. This is not unusual. Our parents and grandparents did the same thing, except that many of the immigrants who came at the turn of the century didn't plan to go home again. Some did, in fact Italians returned at a very high rate—almost the same rate at which Mexicans return. But today we live in a very different society because people can go back and forth. You can call home, you can reach home on the Internet, you can travel back and forth very easily. That wasn't the case in the past. Also many of the immigrants who came in the 1970s and '80s were middle-class people because the immigrant law of 1965 provided entrance to the United States if you had something to offer. So they think in terms of middle-class priorities, but they are not tied here to Los Angeles and that's an important thing for us to think about. How do we get their focus to change when the most important issue for any immigrant community is survival? How do we incorporate these different communities into the city?

The consequence of the progressive reforms that occurred about the same time as the charter came about, was that in their effort to eliminate undue corruption and undue political influence, they also advocated nonpartisan elections in the city. Nonpartisanship had a major impact of the decline of local parties. Obviously, that wasn't the only reason they declined, but it was an important one. Another thing to bear in mind about the local parties is that once they went, Los Angeles particularly but many American cities in general, were ruled not by the parties, but by the civic associations.

Civic Culture in Los Angeles

California is known for having had a high civic culture. Civic culture can be defined by the scenario of coming to a stop sign, being the only one on the street, and stopping. That kind of incorporation of value and behavior is what made California the clear representation of American goals and values—that, plus active participation in organizations. We don't have that kind of active participation in organizations today. There's a very famous article, famous mostly because it's brilliant, called, "Bowling Alone" by Robert Putnam. This thesis is that there are more bowlers in America today but there are fewer bowling leagues. In a bowling league you go to the bowling alley once a week, one person gets up makes a fool of himself and everyone else sits around and chats. What they're chatting about is the person making a fool of himself, everyone's friends and relations, and what's going on in their world, namely, the political world. We don't have that kind of communication today. It's not that we are necessarily unhappier as individuals, but we don't share our views with each other except in a private way over the Internet or the newspapers or in the radio or television we listen to, by only paying attention to those with whom we agree. It's harder to get consensus if you only talk with people with whom you agree. It's also hard to believe that you're going to make a difference in the world if you're all alone. When you're part of a group, you tend to feel you can have an impact. This lack of communication is a phenomenon going on worldwide in the developed nations, and political scientists use that to explain why there is a decline in confidence in our institutions. That is part of what is driving the effort for charter reform in the city.

Business and Civic Culture

Another part of the old civic culture that doesn't exist anymore is from the 1960s and '70s when Los Angeles was run by the "Committee of 25" made up of the top businessmen in the city. As I interviewed the secretary of the group, Steven Gavin, one day, he said that they didn't call the mayor in all that time. They only called the mayor in before he wrote the budget. Well, that committee doesn't exist anymore for several reasons. The nonpartisanship in Los Angeles enabled the group to stay together, but it broke apart when Tom Bradley ran for governor. People started choosing sides in their support for governor, and once Deukmejian was elected he sent a message to the business community that he was not pleased with their nonpartisanship.

The other reason the group doesn't exist today, is that the top corporations in the city, who have reformed in a group called the L.A. Business Advisors, are multinational corporations and don't do business in the city of Los Angeles. ARCO doesn't even own its own building—the ARCO Tower is rented. It's not that they don't feel the responsibility to be good civic citizens, but they don't really have a grasp that the changed economy in the city is principally small business, people who employ under a hundred employees. On the whole, small business isn't going to come up with the kind of money that large corporations come up with, nor do they have the clout individually or collectively.

The Media and Civic Culture

There have been other declines in our civic culture, one of them is one of my favorite institutions, The *Los Angeles Times*. The *L.A. Times* thinks of itself as a national institution. It doesn't cover a great deal of what goes on at the local level. The *Daily News* has much better local coverage. The other important issue is that newspapers used to define the agenda for the local television news, but that is no longer the case. Local television news is driven by technology and the major issue is "if it bleeds, it leads," and we have the technological capacity to cover, as we all know, instant crime. Evidence last week that now we've advanced from police chases to the actual committing of the crime. And if we don't have enough violence, we borrow it. We will get four or five stories on the local news, perhaps only two of them occurred in Los Angeles, but it's hard to tell. That has an impact on public attitudes about the city, about the community. And it has a profound impact.

The other thing about Los Angeles in terms of its civic culture is that it was private city. We don't have many public institutions, we don't have many public places. People came here because they wanted their own backyard, their own home, their own access to the ocean and to the mountains. I used to say that when you talk about people who contribute so much money in politics, particularly in Hollywood, what they're concerned about are rain forests. They're not concerned about what's going on in South Central, unless of course we happen to have a major crisis.

The Decline of the Engines of Middle Class Incorporation

Another characteristic about Los Angeles that contributes to the frustration driving reform today is the decline of engines of middle class incorporation. By decline of middle class incorporation, I mean we don't have the large employers. The aerospace industry, the defense industry—that's what brought many people into the middle-class, and brought many people to Los Angeles. They're not there anymore. We risk becoming a city that is more divided between the rich and the poor than any city in America, and the strength of America always was that we were a middle-class society. Most of us are not going to be as rich as the rich in L.A., and that has an impact on who we think we are and who we think we can be. Now we're moving to a different kind of economy which may turn out to be very successful in the long run, but in the short run this adds to the sense of frustration and the decline of the feeling of a civic culture.

The Inflexibility of City Government

This leads me to the civil service. We have one of the most inflexible civil service systems in the country. It's not that the employees are mean, incompetent, or don't care. It's that the structure doesn't lend itself to flexibility. The frustration a lot of people in the city feel comes from the fact that they haven't been able to get the kinds of things they want out of the civil service, and there are structural reasons for that. Also, as you know, Los Angeles has very powerful city unions. In order for charter reform to be effective, those unions must be engaged in the process of how they're going to change themselves. It's probably its going to be downsizing. I don't want to go on at length, but there are other issues that charter commissions will have to deal with. One of these issues is not just the relationship between the mayor and the council, but the roll of commissions. Commissions were a way for everyone to feel that they were incorporated into the decision-making process. However, one consequence of incorporating public decision is a decline in the efficiency they were working toward. How do you get coordination of departments if each department must answer to a separate board? We tend to have, as Eric Shockman would put it, a vertical structure, not a capacity for the mayor to coordinate what the agencies do. We need to rethink that. Eric, who also has an article in this book on the charter, makes the point that the commissions only really represent a small segment of the city. We want to increase participation on a broad range of the population. Commissions don't do that. Commissions generally all tend to be drawn from one sector of the population. There is the issue about the relation of the mayor to the council. It's always been difficult and some, particularly I, have argued that this mayor could have been more responsive to the city council, but there are reasons why it's structurally frustrating. Charter commissions ought to think about what would make it possible to sustain coalitions. You can't legislate or structure leadership, but you can take some of the road blocks away, and in the end it comes down to the sense of frustration that pervades a lot of the experience of the city. It is interesting as I've listened to discussion in charter reform. The people who are closest to the city, the people who work in it, who work in city hall will tend to ask why we need charter reform. And the people who are furthest from it are the most eager for it. That in itself is instructive—I want to reiterate the message that Jim gave.

There are two reasons we need charter reform. One is the charter and one is the reform process. The reform itself ought to happen in the way that we build consensus, and that is important for Los Angeles. I also think that now is the opportune moment for charter reform because of the term limits, which means that everybody now in office will either be out of office or in their last term by the time a new charter is voted into effect if it is voted into effect.

Chapter 9

Citizen Participation
in Local Government

Although local government structures are important, the political processes by which officials are elected and appointed, policies and laws are made, and citizens evaluate and participate in their local government are more important. The federal government during the 1960s, especially with the civil rights movement and the national war on poverty, began to promote citizen participation. It required "maximum feasible participation" in developing community action programs, urban renewal, and model cities programs. At this same time, neighborhood organizations began to deliver a wide variety of services such as affordable housing and economic development, some of which were paid for by federal grant funds such as Community Development Block Grant funds distributed by the local governments. Larger cities experimented with various forms of neighborhood government.

The effort to promote citizen participation in local government was substantially curtailed by the federal budget cuts and the abandonment of a National Urban Policy by the administration of President Ronald Reagan in the 1980s and has never fully recovered. Nonetheless, the ideology of citizen participation and the call for more power to people in the neighborhoods in the form of neighborhood government and community organizations continues even if it doesn't triumph.

The Civil Rights movement and the national urban policies adopted since the 1960s have also brought a growth in the number of minority elected officials—especially African Americans and Latinos. While in 1960 there were no Black or Latino mayors in major cities, by 1991 there were 33 Black mayors in cities over 50,000 in population and a number of Latino mayors. The number of minority city council members, county board presidents, county board members, school board presidents, and school board members is much greater. There has been some "political incorporation" of various minorities in different cities, defined as "an equal or leading role in a dominant coalition that is strongly committed to minority interests."[1] Howard, Lipsky, and Marshall claim: "Incorporation brought tangible shifts in public policy. Cities where it occurred not only experienced a sharper increase in city minority employment and in the percentage of city contracts awarded to minority businesses, but appointed more minorities to city boards and commissions, established many minority programs, created police-review boards, and were in general more responsive in delivering services than cities in which minority representation was either negligible or was coopted." There is no doubt that all minority groups have been empowered since the 1960s. However, numerous obstacles to reform still limit cities' ability to help minority communities enter the mainstream of social, economic, and political success.

One of the most successful forms of political participation and neighborhood improvements has been community organizations. One example, as discussed in Chapter 4, is Dudley Street in Boston. This Roxbury neighborhood is 40 percent African American, 30 percent Latino, 24 percent Cape Verdeans (from islands off the coast of West Africa), and 6 percent mostly elderly Irish and Italians. Despite its racial and ethnic diversity along with widespread poverty, the neighborhood has improved itself through the Dudley Street Neighborhood Initiative with the assistance from a local community foundation. Like the Dudley Street Neighborhood Initiative, there are more than 10,000 neighborhood organizations utilizing different strategies to preserve and improve their communities. Advocates claim that this is the best and most successful form of citizen participation in cities today.

Citizens not only participate through elections and community organizing, they also evaluate the effectiveness of their local governments. Dissatisfaction with city government and the services it may fail to deliver can fuel massive citizen participation as it did in the elections of Harold Washington in Chicago in the 1980s. Chicago citizen surveys now show that even when there is more citizen satisfaction with local government, citizens evaluate different branches of city government differently, the same governmental officials differently over time, and general city government differently from individual officials. Since different racial groups are affected differently both symbolically and materially, Blacks, Whites, and Hispanics have very different perceptions about how well their local governments are doing.

In the early 1990s, about 60 percent of Chicagoans generally rated Mayor Richard M. Daley as doing a good or excellent job as mayor although between elections this rating could drop by as much as 15 percent. However, this generally high rating masks the fact that only 23 percent of the African Americans surveyed agreed that the mayor was doing a good job. In contrast to their relatively positive ranking of the mayor, only 15 to 28 percent of Chicagoans thought their city council was doing a good job (again with significant racial differences in the evaluation). Just as citizens evaluate Congress poorly but their own Congressman highly, 30 to 50 percent of Chicagoans thought their own individual alderman was doing a good job while they thought the city council as a whole was performing poorly.[2]

It is argued that elections do a better job of holding local officials accountable than public opinion does. But the low turnout in most local elections, the existence of local political machines or powerful local business elites, combined with the lack of information about local government that most citizens have, make elections a less reliable method of accountability than they should be. The fact that public opinion surveys generally show greater dissatisfaction of Black and Latino voters suggests that local governments can do better in satisfying all their citizens with their services, their policies, and their accountability.

Citizens not only have a general response to their local governments but they have specific responses to important public policies as well. One of the greatest concerns of citizens at the end of the twentieth and the beginning of the twenty-first century has been economic revitalization. There was in the 1990s and until the economic crisis triggered by the terrorist attacks of September 11, 2001, an urban "renaissance" in the country. One place where this has occurred was Providence, Rhode Island.

A detailed study of public opinion by citizens of Providence found that more that 70 percent reported that they believed that things in Providence were headed in the "right direction" and only 10 percent thought it was "off on the wrong track." Similar numbers felt that downtown Providence was "better off " in 1999 than five years previously. Generally, citizens thought fire services, garbage collection, and police protection were the best services (63 percent – 81 percent rated them as good or excellent) while they thought schools and street repair were bad. As with the Chicago study, there were major differences among the racial groups, which perceived services like police protection very differently. Even in a city like Providence where there were generally positive feelings about downtown revitalization, problems like race relations still remain unresolved.

It is reasonable to suppose that if citizens had greater participation in local government decision-making, especially a voice in making those decisions that most affect their lives, they would be more supportive of their government. Local governments vary enormously in the degree to which they involve citizens directly in the governing process. Small towns, some small suburbs, and towns and villages in New England, with their centuries-long tradition of town hall meetings, are accessible and accountable. Citizens may not avail themselves of the opportunity to attend town hall meetings in order to participate in making government decisions directly, but they can. While citywide town hall meetings may not be a workable strategy in major metropolitan regions, paying attention to citizen views and allowing for greater effective citizen participation is desirable.

In short, the issue of citizen participation in local government involves: (1) neighborhood government, community organizations, and methods of obtaining "maximum feasible participation" which can be encouraged by federal and state governments; (2) continuing the efforts to increase minority incorporation in the local government and in the private/public regime that directs and implements public policy; (3) encouraging the multifaceted work of community organizations even in poor communities; and (4) taking seriously citizen evaluations of their local government, local government officials, and policies.

Notes

1. Rufus P. Browning, Dale Rogers Marshall, and David H. Tabb, "Minority Mobilization in Ten Cities: Failures and Successes," in Rufus P. Browning, Dale Rogers Marshall, and David H. Tabb, eds., *Racial Politics in American Cities*. New York: Longman, 1995, p. 9.
2. Barry Rundquist and Gerald Strom, "Citizen Evaluations of Chicago City Government," in Dick Simpson, ed., *Chicago's Future in a Time of Change*. Champaign, Illinois: Stipes, 1993, pp. 263–268.

33. Neighborhood Empowerment

Ann Gentile and Dick Simpson

In American cities, two of the principal ways of encouraging meaningful citizen participation in local government have been to fund and empower existing community organizations and to create new institutions of neighborhood government. The policies of the federal government over the last half-century have differed to the degree that they have made community organizations, citizen participation, and

neighborhood governments priorities. National government policies have had profound impacts at the local level.

_____

Since the 1960s, citizen participation at the neighborhood level has been both encouraged and inhibited by government. The national government has required citizen participation in determining the use of federal funds and in moni-
toring programs. City governments have encouraged citizen participation by establishing advisory councils, by holding public hearings on city programs,
budgets, and legislation, and by asking for neighborhood input in physical planning. In the 1960s, citizen participation was a major goal at the federal level and
a major demand of city governments. Twenty years later, however, the tide
turned against neighborhood government, and advisory neighborhood boards
and councils have too often become perfunctory. Yet, the earliest hope of constituting neighborhoods as the loci of a revitalized democracy remains, and we now
have 20 years of experience to instruct us on what has worked and what has not.
    To some extent the wave of government-connected citizen participation
might be said to have begun in its current form in 1964 with the establishment
of the Community Action Program that began the nation's War on Poverty. Urban Renewal had begun earlier in 1954 with required citizen participation in
developing plans for community development, and Model Cities programs followed with even more stringent participation requirements in 1966. But the
War on Poverty demanded not only that local boards direct the Community
Action Agencies but that there should be "maximum feasible participation" in
developing community action programs. This translated into requirements that
at least one-third of the agency board members be representatives of the poor
themselves. In some cases this led to local boards whose members could politically challenge the established city officials. By 1966 the Congress became disturbed at the political implications of this citizen participation. Its remedy was:

> to earmark as much of the Community Action budget as possible for special pro-
> grams such as Head Start, Legal Services, New Careers, service to narcotic addicts,
> and emergency loans to low-income families, thus leaving less money for locally
> initiated activities including citizen organization.

Even so, the net effect was to create "a new decision-making center . . . outside the existing institutional structure with influence over some limited social
service resources."
    The general Community Action Programs ultimately were eclipsed by the
Model Cities Programs, which began with 75 planning grants in 1967. As the
newer program with greater funding, Model Cities soon began to surpass
Community Action Programs as the vehicle for citizen participation. However,
citizen participation was more circumscribed in the Model Cities Programs as

SOURCE: Ann Gentile and Dick Simpson, "Neighborhood Empowerment," *Social Policy*, Vol. 16,
No. 4 (Spring 1986), pp. 25–30. Reprinted by permission of the author and M. E. Sharpe, Inc.

local political forces began to reassert control. A positive major difference between Community Action Program boards and Model Cities boards was that the representatives of the poor were chosen by actual elections in Model Cities. Unfortunately, many of the elections were eventually controlled by the more traditional political forces. Despite the problems, an analysis of Model Cities Programs in 1974 concluded:

> Citizen participation has sought and found new resident leadership, forced some important changes in government, brought democracy and decision-making closer to the people, and involved at least some of the poor in the actual workings of government. Most importantly, it has created a feeling in large segments of our population that government really cares.

Programs like Urban Renewal, Community Action, and Model Cities gave way in 1974 to more manageable and restrained community action under the Community Services Administration. Restrictions were tightened on the use of federal funds, and Community Development Block Grants eliminated Model Cities programs. Neighborhood boards were no longer required to determine the expenditure of funds; instead, two nonbinding public hearings would determine the flow of expenditures in neighborhoods scattered throughout a city. This led to a broadened citizen participation but to less power since citizens could no longer exercise a veto on public expenditures. As a result governance at the neighborhood level was undercut.

The trend continued during President Jimmy Carter's administration, when there were many more "citizen participation" requirements written into the laws governing all kinds of federal programs, but citizen participation was removed to national or regional advisory boards, reduced to testimony at agency public hearings, or limited to the opportunity to intervene in the complicated federal rule-making process. By 1978 there were over 226 federal public-participation programs, including 155 grant-in-aid programs, which required some form of citizen participation. Yet nearly all of these participation requirements provide either only public notice of hearings or advisory commissions without budget or veto powers. By 1975 more than 45 federal agencies employed 1,267 Advisory Committees with 22,125 positions. Although the number of citizens directly advising federal agencies had increased, the president's National Commission on Neighborhoods in 1979 concluded:

> Mandated citizen participation is both a permanent and a proliferating fact of public life. Unfortunately, most of it has not brought citizens into positions of real power.

By the 1980s there were attempts to eliminate guaranteed rights of citizen participation. While these general threats have been turned back, the Community Development Block Grant program has allowed only limited participation in decision-making, although many community groups have received vital federal funding for key neighborhood projects from these grants:

> All too often over the last decade federal block grant funds have been spent by the local government without real involvement by the neighborhoods. Token public hearings have not provided a real opportunity for effective participation. If

neighborhoods are to provide the locus for citizen participation in government then neighborhood organizations will have to be granted real powers that affect actual expenditures.

Or as the *Chicago Tribune* put the fundamental issue graphically in a criticism that could apply to many cities:

Traditionally Chicago mayors have used the money to enhance their popularity with voters. Former Mayor Jane Byrne viewed community development funds as a somewhat private reserve that could be tapped for political purposes.

President Ronald Reagan's administration cut funds that traditionally allowed community organizations to provide government services directly, and many of the government programs that provided support to low-income neighborhoods were cut back. In the President's proposed budget of 1981 the Legal Services Corporation, VISTA, Community Services Administration, Neighborhood Self-Help Development Program, and CETA were to have been eliminated. Programs scheduled for deep cuts were Title XX Social Service Programs, CDBG, Section 502 Loan Development Program of the Small Business Administration, the Subsidized Housing Program including Section 8 HUD housing, and Community Health Centers. Many of these proposed cuts were only partially adopted by the Congress, but they demonstrated the efforts of the Reagan administration to cut federal funding for domestic programs, including those that promoted citizen participation at the neighborhood level.

GRASSROOT DEVELOPMENTS

Many cities began to experiment with various forms of neighborhood government including advisory councils, decentralized delivery of government services, and formal governmental bodies at the neighborhood levels. The War on Poverty caused some community corporations such as ECCO in Columbus, Ohio, to be spun off with semi-governmental powers and Community Action Program funding. However, various spin-off agencies dwindled as the general Community Action Program declined, or they became strictly neighborhood development or service corporations without any explicit political or governmental agenda.

Three other forms of neighborhood government have emerged at one time or another in more than 100 cities around the nation. They are formal neighborhood advisory councils officially established by the city government, independent neighborhood groups that claimed some governmental or political powers, and, finally, neighborhood groups that have been either organized by or incorporated into a city government's Department of Neighborhoods or official neighborhood program. With federal government budgetary cuts and local political changes, these programs continue to exist in a number of cities but without the power envisioned for neighborhood governments when they emerged in the 1970s.

Neighborhood government and the neighborhood empowerment movement seem to have lost much of their momentum, at the same time as the number of neighborhood organizations is growing and there has been the need to create more neighborhood sites to house the homeless, feed the hungry, support the jobless, and tutor, nurture, and educate the children. There are more than 10,000 neighborhood organizations from block clubs to large civic groups in the United States, but there are still only a few with the formal powers of a neighborhood government.

The best way to understand all of the efforts at neighborhood government and the changes in the 1980s is not through statistics but through case studies. While each neighborhood government began for different reasons, operated at different budget levels, and utilized very different techniques, they were all founded to maximize citizen participation, and all had direct connections to their local city governments.

Washington Advisory Neighborhood Commissions

In 1974 Washington, D.C., enacted a city charter that gave advisory powers to commissions in 36 neighborhoods, two of which were the DuPont Circle and the Adams-Morgan commissions. They served neighborhoods where racial minorities composed the majority of the population. The DuPont Circle Commission sought originally to strengthen participation in government by allowing citizens to vote on which way the commission should proceed on all neighborhood issues. The movement for complete inclusion of citizens through the mechanism of voting would have ensured that the Washington City Council members knew that the decision of the commission was, in fact, the will of their constituency. However, the DuPont Advisory Commission finally settled for a minimum winning coalition style, where only the nine member commission would vote. The citizens participated by attending the bimonthly meetings, where they were entitled to voice their opinions on problems facing their neighborhood.

The aim of the commission's advisory recommendations were centered in the areas of zoning classification and reclassification. Developers saw the deteriorating neighborhood as fair game for commercial development and condominium conversion. However, the DuPont Circle Commission saw the needs of the neighborhood differently and, as a result, fought to defeat each zoning proposal targeted at destruction of their residential environment. They even went so far as to declare their area of Washington, D.C., a historic district, a bold tactic unwelcomed by the Washington City Council. Sensing that their power was being usurped, the city council created roadblocks to deter the DuPont Circle Commission. They began by limiting the amount of information on zoning proposals the commission received, making it difficult for the commission to act effectively on particular proposals. The commission never conceded to the pressure because they knew that if the city council continued to run interference for developers they were legally entitled to sue under rights guaranteed in the city charter.

A second neighborhood advisory commission in Washington, D.C., the Adams-Morgan Commission, went a step further in connecting itself to government. They pressured the mayor into allowing their commission a voice in decisions concerning licensing and permits in their neighborhood. The commission also worked with the Adams-Morgan Organization to fight the practice of bank redlining. Since the neighborhood was predominantly composed of minorities, savings and loan institutions frequently refused financial credit to its residents. Despite the odds, the Adams-Morgan Organization and the commission through legal action were successful in halting this discriminatory procedure.

The Washington neighborhood advisory commissions provided a vehicle through which citizens were able to participate directly in government. Frank Smith a one-time member of a Washington advisory commission sums it up:

> The commissions . . . help the neighborhood movement solve two of its problems. They provide legitimate elected neighborhood representatives and official neighborhood boundaries. They are helping many of the older civic groups by providing some funds, by giving awards, and by giving support on critical issues. The more levels of government the better. It keeps decision-making closer to the people.

THE 44TH WARD ASSEMBLY

Chicago is a city where citizen participation is a rarity. In the winter of 1971 one of the authors ran for alderman of the 44th Ward of Chicago on a platform of citizen participation. If elected, he promised that a 44th Ward Assembly would be established to allow citizens direct participation in government. The first 44th Ward Assembly was duly created and began meeting on January 9, 1972.

The purpose of the 44th Ward Assembly was to serve as a governing council for the entire ward. Specifically, the ward assembly had four functions:

1. To direct and to advise the alderman as to how he shall cast his vote in the city council.
2. To direct and to advise the alderman as to what new legislation he shall sponsor in the city council.
3. To establish priorities for programs to be undertaken by the alderman for the benefit of the ward.
4. To make possible free and responsible debate on all issues that affect the welfare of residents of the ward.

To reflect the diversity of the ward and to make the decisions binding and effective, it needed to have some attributes of a representative assembly. In order to achieve this, two sets of voting members were elected by the citizens of the ward. One set of voting members consisted of two elected representatives from each of the 61 precincts within the ward. The second set of voting members consisted of one representative chosen from each organization with more than 25 members residing in the ward. Any citizen of the 44th Ward was also automatically a nonvoting member, guaranteed the right to speak or debate at the monthly assembly meetings. The alderman served as chair of the assembly.

In 1974 the assembly expanded with the addition of a Community Zoning Board, Traffic Review Commission, and a Spanish-speaking assembly, *Asamblea Abierta*. The accomplishments of the ward assembly are numerous. Perhaps most important was the existence of the assembly itself as a model of neighborhood government. It provided the necessary volunteers to deliver a 44th Ward almanac with reports on the state of the neighborhood and a guide to city services to 30,000 families. It conducted a fair every year with displays of community art, photographs, ethnic foods, community organization exhibits, and children's games for the 3,000 people who attended. The assembly also undertook special drives such as fund drives for local private food pantries to feed the hungry of the community.

In the area of services, the 44th Ward Assembly identified sites for four playlots and parks that have been built. It planned truck load limits to restrict trucks over five tons of weight on side-streets in the neighborhood. It coordinated special service efforts on trash baskets, garbage pickup, and street sweeping. Moreover, Chicago's anti-redlining law, which has since become the model for cities throughout the nation, was developed by the assembly. It offered amendments to a variety of city legislation on issues such as unit pricing and condominium conversions that became law.

The three other branches of the 44th Ward neighborhood government also had notable achievements. The Community Zoning Board heard over 40 zoning cases, including the controversial legislation to down-zone the lakefront of the community to prevent further high-rise construction. The board was upheld in all of its decisions by other government agencies except one zoning decision in which the community itself was divided. The Traffic Review Commission modified one-way streets and approved stop signs and traffic lights. The Spanish-speaking assembly undertook a number of ambitious projects, including suing the city of Chicago for discriminating in the hiring of Latinos. The number of Latinos hired by various agencies of local government increased greatly as a result.

These instruments of neighborhood government worked, producing good and innovative laws, providing governmental services as rights not favors, promoting community projects and events, and allowing citizens in the community to have a sense of control over their own destiny. The 44th Ward proved that neighborhood government can be a practical reality even in a city like Chicago. It lasted ten years under two different aldermen. However, when the Democratic machine recaptured the aldermanic seat in 1981, the units of neighborhood government were dismantled. Only the election of another alderman committed to neighborhood government in all Chicago wards can reestablish the 44th Ward's neighborhood institutions.

Northwest District Association

The Northwest District Association of Portland, Oregon, was founded in 1969 as a direct result of expansion on the part of big corporations. Developers wanted to utilize a deteriorating residential area in the northwest section of the city to meet their need for land. The residents saw the oncoming changes planned for their neighborhood, and quickly rallied together to halt the corporations. They won the battle and from this fight the Northwest District Association was created. The association hired Mary Pederson as a staff organizer, who later influenced the city government in 1974 to create an Office of Neighborhood Associations, which she eventually headed.

> Pederson's first-year budget was $104,000 from hard tax funds. Portland's non-partisan city government, led by Mayor Goldschmidt, never viewed the burgeoning network of neighborhood groups as a political threat as did partisan governments in some of the cities of the East and Midwest.

The connection of the Northwest District Association to the Office of Neighborhood Associations enabled a direct citizen linkage to city hall.

The Northwest District Association had the responsibility of providing the community with services such as food, clothing, and jobs for the needy, within the limits of a low-budget organization. With the support of the Office of Neighborhood Associations these services were affordable, since the city government supplied the association with free office space and staffing, allowing the Northwest District Association to stay afloat during the Reagan administration cutbacks in the early 1980s. The Northwest District Association turned to additional outside help from the academic arena; they hired professional researchers to conduct surveys and opinions polls in their neighborhood. Such techniques guided the association decision-making process concerning housing and other needs of the community and enabled them to predict upcoming problems and to develop long-range solutions.

One major experience of the association shows how citizens participating in government at the neighborhood level can make a positive impact on their community. A developer received a building permit to construct an apartment building, which was agreeable with the Northwest District Association. However, as construction was underway they realized a motel was destined to stand on the land.

> The association mobilized 500 angry residents at a mass meeting, where city officials promised the new housing would be limited to rental apartments. When the building was completed, the association found it being used as a motel. Follow-up resulted in a lawsuit being filed against the city.

It should be noted that this occurred prior to the creation of the Office of Neighborhood Associations. Afterwards the coordination between the city and the association was much improved, and lawsuits were no longer required to protect the neighborhood.

The Northwest District Association started out as a means to save a residential neighborhood from "developers destruction." It brought about government-connected citizen participation with Portland's City Hall, by displaying the unity of the people in the community.

> Coordinator Geri Ethen of Northwest feels that the association would survive even if all city supports were withdrawn: "It would be at a smaller scale, it would drop some programs and focus on land-use issues, maybe even raise enough funds locally for a half-time staff member. Too many neighborhood people realize the need for the association to let it die. They just care too much about their neighborhood."

KEY ISSUES

Whether in the form of an advisory commission, neighborhood assembly, or a more traditional community organization, the key ingredient for effective neighborhood government was guaranteeing citizens' rights to services and a voice in the decision-making process within their community. Since the 1960s, the goals and objectives of successful neighborhood groups seem to have remained the same, with each neighborhood organization fighting for its survival in the political arena. The three case studies provide some understanding of what needs to be accomplished today in neighborhoods across the United States, to create effective government-connected citizen participation.

All three organizations were especially concerned with physical developments and land use in their community, as well as neighborhood services and city jobs. Why is community development and land use such a major issue? Since the late 1960s, cities have faced growing pains as middle and high income families first migrated to the suburbs and then began to resettle into selected city neighborhoods. The cities were originally left with a population composed mainly of low- and middle-income residents as a result of this demographic flow. In the 1970s, urban renewal programs began to revitalize deteriorating neighborhoods with little compassion for its previous residents. Developers recognized that money-making schemes lay ahead, and they become involved in the renovation of inner cities. In their plans condominiums would replace low-income apartment buildings, strips of taverns and nightspots would shut down the corner grocery store. The tide would shift, bringing with it young professionals in higher income brackets.

Residents in low and middle income areas organized to halt the overhaul of their neighborhoods by developers. Any deteriorating neighborhood is fair prey for wrecking balls and developers. Control of the zoning, or at least a voice in the planning process, is a key issue for any neighborhood. Since city government officials often side with the developers on plans for inner-city revitalization, these three neighborhood organizations connected themselves with their city governments to guarantee themselves a voice in the decision-making process on land use and government services.

These neighborhoods recognized the need to provide more than just a voice in planning decisions, however. They offered concrete services themselves and provided a mechanism for supervising the services provided by government and by private institutions like banks. Thus, the neighborhood commissions controlled licensing, they and the 44th Ward Assembly curbed bank redlining, and all three neighborhood governments supervised services like one-way streets and the provision of government jobs. . . .

34. Citizen Participation in Urban Politics

Christopher Howard, Michael Lipsky, and Dale Rogers Marshall

This article explores two important issues: the rise of African-American and Latino elected officials and the rise of urban populism or neighborhoods and grassroots organizations in political power. Both are important to the future of U.S. cities.

ELECTORAL POLITICS

The rise of minority mayors has often been cited as the best evidence that disadvantaged groups have made gains in urban politics over the last 30 years. The change has indeed been dramatic. Whereas there were no Black or Latino mayors of cities with populations greater than 50,000 in 1960, there were 27 Black and three Latino mayors of cities this size by 1985. By 1991, there were 33 Black mayors in cities this size. They became the elected leaders of some of America's largest cities—New York, Chicago, Los Angeles, Detroit, Atlanta, San Antonio, Newark, and Denver, among others. Some, like Newark's Kenneth Gibson and Atlanta's Andrew Young, were veterans of the civil rights movement and the War on Poverty.

The total number of Black elected officials, who far outnumber Latino officials nationally, grew 138 percent between 1970 and 1975, 40 percent from 1975 to 1980, and 23 percent between 1980 and 1985. Part of the explanation for the declining rate of growth lies in demographics. The 1970–75 surge came primarily in cities with large Black populations. Comparable data for Latino officials are unavailable. What is clear is that between the early 1970s and 1990, the total number of elected officials grew at a faster rate than the rate of growth of Latino populations in Arizona, California, Florida, New Mexico, New York, and Texas.

By the 1980s, there were few cities left with large minority populations that had not elected a Black or Latino official. As rapid as these changes have been, continued growth in the number of minority elected officials is likely to be less rapid. Minorities are currently declining as a percentage of population in many urban areas as White professionals return to the central cities. Faster growth can be expected for Latino officials than Black officials, principally because of faster growth in the (naturalized) Latino population. Of course, minority population size does not fix a ceiling on the potential number of minority elected officials, but the clear (not perfect) split of recent urban elections along racial or ethnic lines indicates that this factor is important.

As one might expect with such a large increase, no one model of political organization predominated. Based on an investigation of 10 northern California cities over 20 years, Browning, Marshall, and Tabb produced a study that identified four general patterns of minority mobilization and incorporation in urban electoral politics. In descending order of minority influence, these patterns are biracial electoral alliance, cooptation, protest and exclusion, and weak mobilization. The key to higher levels of responsiveness—the degree to which minority demands are translated into public policy—is not simply representation but incorporation into the governing coalition. Election to city council, for instance, is less meaningful if the council member represents the minority party or is excluded from the dominant faction of the

SOURCE: Christopher Howard, Michael Lipsky, and Dale Rogers Marshall, "Citizen Participation in Urban Politics: Rise and Routination," in George E. Peterson, ed., *Big City Politics, Governance, and Fiscal Constraints* (Washington, D. C: Urban Institute Press, 1994), pp. 203–214. Reprinted by permission of The Urban Institute Press.

majority party. A tradition of protest and activism helped to accelerate the process of incorporation, but was not in itself sufficient to produce tangible benefits to the minority community. Blacks and Latinos achieved the highest levels of incorporation in those cities in which they formed alliances with liberal Whites.

Incorporation brought tangible shifts in public policy. Cities where it occurred not only experienced a sharper increase in city minority employment and in the percentage of city contracts awarded to minority businesses but appointed more minorities to city boards and commissions, established many more minority programs, created police review boards, and were in general more responsive in delivering services than cities in which minority representation was either negligible or was coopted.

A number of scholars have questioned the significance of these findings because the sample communities came from a relatively prosperous region of the country with a reputation for liberal views and included only two major cities, San Francisco and Oakland. Subsequent testing of the thesis that "protest is not enough" has borne out the primary finding, with several important qualifications. First, inclusion in a dominant coalition does assure a much stronger minority position than does just representation, but the value of political incorporation will be tempered by the larger context of the urban political economy. In a context of fiscal crisis, the need for economic development constrains the kinds of redistributive policies that Blacks and Latinos might have been expected to favor. Second, entrenched party machines have created barriers to incorporation in cities such as New York and Chicago. Third, as New York City and Miami demonstrate, Blacks and Latinos cannot be assumed to be natural political allies; they have at times worked at cross-purposes. Mollenkopf warns of a possible rollback of minority gains in New York City. Thus, even incorporation may not be enough to provide minorities with meaningful control over urban public policy.

These qualifications bring into question the impact that minority electoral participation has had on the Black and Latino communities. Students of urban politics have divided sharply in their assessments of how effectively minority officials have worked within these constraints. Most would agree that incorporation seems to have increased levels of political participation and trust in government among minorities. Their disagreements relate to the size and distribution of material benefits. Among the optimists, Bette Woody has argued that

> Black mayors. . . . blended a sophisticated mix of managerial reform principles, good government and grass roots participation, designed to compete in regional and national arenas for a larger slice of the social and economic pie. . . . The Black mayors thus proved some of the more successful practitioners of an amalgamation of populist and socially responsive goals on the one hand and on the other, leaders of the fight for management reform and sound government operation.

Less-sanguine observers have emphasized the degree to which benefits have accrued disproportionately to more-upwardly mobile Blacks and Latinos, leaving behind a significant underclass. In their view, the election of minority officials and federal initiatives like the War on Poverty have helped to create a Black middle class of government employees but failed to alleviate poverty. William Nelson, Jr., offered a typical judgment of this group:

> The upsurge in the election of "new breed" Black politicians to public office has been most effective in the promotion of the social and economic interest of upwardly mobile, elite sectors of the Black community.
>
> Elected on reform platforms that promised profound changes in the policy-making process, Black mayors have almost uniformly embraced corporate-centered strategies that have virtually precluded the redistribution of major benefits to broad segments of the black community.

A third perspective—and in our view the most persuasive—has emphasized the numerous obstacles to reform common to Black, Latino, and White officials. Decentralized and overlapping authority, the product of "good government" reforms, has lowered the potential for any one city official, including the mayor, to affect public policy. Weak political organizations and candidate-centered elections have depressed voter turnout and produced officials who owe sustained allegiance to no group. Where urban machines have dominated, competing views have been ignored and new actors discouraged from participating. Perhaps most important, city officials, regardless of race or ethnic background, have come under increasing pressure to make economic development their overriding policy objective. The combination of slower rates of economic growth, the exodus of more-affluent residents to the suburbs (and, hence, declining tax bases of many cities), public resistance to tax increases, and the increasing mobility of capital has limited cities' ability to engage in redistribution. Meanwhile, the national government, a prime sponsor of programs for disadvantaged groups in the 1960s and 1970s, has reduced aid to the cities—a policy some have termed "fend-for-yourself federalism."

As a result, many mayors who campaigned on a progressive or populist platform have actively pursued corporate investment once in office. Coleman Young of Detroit and Tom Bradley of Los Angeles are the most commonly cited recent examples; Andrew Young of Atlanta, Federico Peña of Denver, and Lionel Wilson of Oakland also fit this pattern. These same pressures have changed the types of candidates likely to run for office, the tenor of their campaigns, and the substance of their message. Referring to the second generation of minority mayors (e.g., Wilson Goode of Philadelphia, Kurt Schmoke of Baltimore), one observer has written: "More pragmatists than pioneers, professionals than preachers, coalition builders than confrontationists, they came to power during a period of drastic cutbacks in federal money for cities, and they are hawking economic progress and managerial expertise."

Moreover, minority officials have faced an additional set of constraints. Their core constituency has become a smaller portion of the electorate as affluent Whites and other racial and ethnic immigrants have moved to the cities. As the Black middle class has grown, its participation in civic matters has declined or dispersed over a larger metropolitan area. Traditional Black organizations like the NAACP have lost membership and support. In this third view, then, Black and Latino officials on the whole have been as constrained, or as ineffective, in addressing the poverty-related problems of their constituents as their White counterparts. Ironically, the process of generating real benefits for the Black middle class may have undercut political support for minority officials and reoriented urban politics more along income and class divisions than along racial lines.

Looking back over the last quarter century of minority participation in electoral politics, we foresee three issues becoming more important in the near future. The first is that of growing income disparities and class divisions within the minority community. Although these disparities are most obvious within the Black electorate, Miami and Los Angeles provide comparable evidence for Latinos. These schisms are most evident in Atlanta, Chicago (since Harold Washington's death in 1987), Cleveland, and Philadelphia. According to Carolyn Adams, "it is increasingly difficult for a single Black candidate to appeal to the disparate socioeconomic groups within the Black community."

A second and related issue is that of generational succession. The mature generation of minority officials, which grew up with the civil rights movement and various federal antipoverty programs in the 1960s, succeeded in replacing more conservative businessmen, politicians, and civil rights leaders because they better represented the views of a population coming of age. There is some evidence, still mostly anecdotal, that this process is repeating. In New York City, for instance, Black leaders divided sharply over their responses to racial incidents such as the Howard Beach murders and Washington Heights riots. A younger generation of ministers and lawyers has gained visibility in characterizing these incidents as the most obvious signs of a profoundly racist society and has challenged city leaders, regardless of color, to be more open and aggressive in confronting racism. These leaders regularly question the wisdom of working through the Democratic party to achieve their goals, and sometimes advance independent candidates and policy platforms. Alternatively, pragmatic mayors like Goode and Schmoke may represent the future generation. James Jennings suggests that neither set of leaders will alone speak for the Black community. They will instead share power, and ideally will discover ways to combine their respective resources to effect meaningful policy change.

The extent to which the next generation adopts the politics of confrontation will have a profound effect on the third issue in minority electoral politics, the growing importance of multiethnic electoral coalitions. Demographic changes will continue to force minority officials, even in cities where minorities now outnumber Whites, to develop closer alliances with White constituencies. The increasing racial and ethnic diversity of cities will create the potential for many different types of coalitions. Obviously it will be difficult to forge such alliances if the parties view each other more as the problem than as the solution. At such a moment of political flux, the side that expands its constituency by mobilizing disadvantaged citizens who currently refrain from participation may well tip the balance of power in its favor.

URBAN POPULISM

Most scholars use the term "neighborhood movement" or "citizen movement" to capture the diversity of grass-roots organizing and protest that emerged during the 1970s and 1980s. One 1978 survey identified over 1,000 community and neighborhood groups organized around 40 different issues. Gary Delgado estimated the number of these groups at over 8,000 by the mid-1980s. Neither of the terms for these activities, however, is adequate. Although neighborhoods did reemerge as important actors in urban politics, considerable activity took place elsewhere. Statewide organizations like Massachusetts Fair Share and national organizations such as the Associated Communities Organized for Reform Now (ACORN) were central actors. Nor is it clear whether "neighborhood" refers to a geographic entity, type of organization, or a particular set of values. "Citizen movement" is a catchall phrase whose vagueness seems designed to capture as many developments as possible under one heading. Those who use this term tend to highlight the more progressive organizations and ignore the more conservative and even reactionary elements. Further, the inclusion of "movement" in both terms overstates the unity of these organizations.

A different conceptual framework is needed. The richness and ambiguity of these efforts may be better understood through the concept of "urban populism": urban because the majority of these organizations operate in cities; populism because, like the agrarian populists of the late nineteenth century, they are openly suspicious of concentrated power, whether in the form of big business or big government. Urban populists stress local solutions to local problems and build upon the strength of community churches, ethnic associations, and similar organizations. They work through and around existing institutions, much as their nineteenth century counterparts did. Their membership also cuts across traditional political divisions of left and right, liberal and conservative. This term also captures a central tension. Whereas many urban populists affirm the highest democratic ideals, others demand local control to preserve their communities racially and culturally—a reminder of the racism that tainted populism a century ago.

The analogy to agrarian populism should not be taken too far, however: urban populism of the 1980s and 1990s has been geographically fragmented and oriented toward short-term goals; urban populists have devoted little attention to fundamental critiques of capitalist democracy and have created nothing like the Farmers Alliance or the People's party. Still, the similarities appear close enough to make the analogy useful.

The roots of urban populism are as numerous as its branches. All of the protest movements of the 1960s appear to have influenced it. The combination of Nixon's reelection, the end of the Vietnam War, and the winding down of civil rights/Black power compelled many activists to rethink their approaches to social change. Some began to focus on tangible issues in their local communities. A 1976 poll of leaders in 32 grass-roots organizations found that 12 traced their roots to the civil rights movement, 6 to the National Welfare Rights Organization (NWRO), 6 to Saul Alinsky's Industrial Areas Foundation (IAF), and 6 to the Students for a Democratic Society (SDS) or to the antiwar movement.

Because the predecessor movements had different goals and used different strategies, the community organizations that emerged were remarkably diverse. Some of the activists who came through the civil rights movement and SDS favored the creation of alternative institutions such as food co-ops and credit unions. Welfare rights advocates argued for mass protests leading to systemic breakdown. Organizations like ACORN, a descendant of NWRO, emphasized grass-roots organizing around local issues. Some SDS veterans preferred to use the media to mobilize the population around long-term goals. And many organizations have employed any number of combinations of these strategies.

Admittedly, some elements of urban populism did not spring from the protest movements. Many White, working-class neighborhood groups originated as a response to major development projects (e.g., highways and stadiums). These projects either displaced working-class whites directly or displaced Blacks who moved into white working-class neighborhoods. These groups were essentially conservative; they wanted to shield their neighborhoods from outsiders. They were less interested in organizing for more political power or a better distribution of goods and services than in being left alone to determine the character and composition of their neighborhoods. Some of the best-known groups, such as Restore Our Alienated Rights (ROAR) in South Boston and BUSTOP in Los Angeles, developed in opposition to court-ordered school busing. Although these organizations used the same rhetoric of community control as other urban populists, their motive was racism and their politics were the politics of exclusion. Whereas some of these organizations are truly inclusive and progressive, a "parochial and reactive 'Not in My Backyard' stance" appears to have become more prevalent over time.

Perhaps the least well-understood element of urban populism has been the growth of alternative organizations providing goods and services. Examples of typical organizations that spread rapidly in the 1970s and 1980s include community development corporations (CDCs), which promoted economic development, affordable housing, and job training in particular neighborhoods; rape crisis centers; battered women's shelters; food co-ops; and housing co-ops. Despite their diversity, all of these groups originated out of a desire to meet basic human needs in a decentralized, democratic, face-to-face setting. Their brand of urban populism may have been less confrontational than the practice of ACORN and ROAR, but distrust of big government and big business runs through all of them. Such an attitude would seem to create conflicts between many of the new non-profit social service agencies and the government whose funds support them. The relationship persists because of mutual need: alternative organizations need to survive and governments need to develop flexible mechanisms to deliver public services in the wake of new service demands, fiscal constraints, and widespread public dissatisfaction with the results of established agencies and approaches.

Pressure to create these kinds of alternative organizations has increased in recent years. Spurred by the decrease in national funding for cities and the increasing mobility of capital, many neighborhood groups have created local development organizations to fill in the gaps left by state and market.

"It's been a remarkable transformation," says Norman Krumholz, professor of urban planning at Cleveland State University and former city planning director under three

Cleveland mayors. "What began in the early '70s as a group of grass-roots activist organizations, very strident in style and confrontational in expression, has been transformed into a set of enormously competent community development corporations
that are now doing economic development, housing, and commercial development."

Many of these goods and services are desperately needed, and the involvement
by community organizations signals an expansion of their influence in urban
politics. On the other hand, participation has forced these same organizations
to stress collaboration over confrontation. Their housing and development
projects often require a coalition of public and quasi-public agencies,
churches, foundations, and private banks, none of which is legally required to
cooperate. Put simply, "the era of 'baiting the establishment' is ending."

"While LDCs [local development corporations] offer a route to community
preservation and autonomy, their search for funding restricts their usefulness
as independent neighborhood advocates and produces inherently co-optative
tendencies." Thus, urban populism provides further evidence of the rise and
routinization of citizen participation.

Not surprisingly, the strengths of urban populism are also its basic weaknesses. First, alternative organizations that develop and remain outside existing structures of economic and political power can provide citizens with new
avenues of political participation; such organizations are also by definition incapable of affecting the larger questions of public policy. To date, many of
these organizations have eschewed electoral politics. Those representing less-
affluent citizens fear cooptation by local governments and middle-income
groups. They also believe that no matter how populist the rhetoric, elected officials will ultimately emphasize economic development without sufficient attention to redistribution. Many of those concerned with consumer and environmental issues claim that nonpartisanship is a key to their credibility. Other
organizations steer clear of partisan politics to preserve their tax-exempt status. Unless these organizations find some means of influencing traditional arenas of politics, they will be forced to continue reacting to decisions made elsewhere. And to the extent that they are financially dependent on government,
they may be reluctant to advocate significant change.

Second, although the range of strategies and tactics has given urban populism tremendous flexibility in achieving local objectives, this same diversity
has hindered its ability to transcend local issues and become a unified, national movement. Urban populists have succeeded to the extent they have
previously because of their emphasis on short-term goals. There is no inherent reason why tenant groups in New York City cannot forge alliances with
environmental activists in Seattle. But so long as the democratic ideal of urban populism gives priority to values of community over values of justice
and equality, the conservative and clannish tendencies of urban populism
will persist.

Finally, urban populism has yet to succeed in incorporating the urban
poor. With few exceptions, the majority of populist organizations operate in
working-class and middle-class neighborhoods. So far, the principal unifying
force of urban populism has been the Reverend Jesse Jackson, whose broad
democratic vision recognizes the value of community and places it within a

larger framework of justice and equality. Whether Reverend Jackson (or any-one) can accommodate urban populism's conservative tendencies, and mobi-lize those who consider electoral politics pointless, remains to be seen.

35. Citizen's Views on Urban Revitalization in Providence

Marion Orr and Darrell M. West

This article explores citizen attitudes about city success, quality of life, and downtown improvement as well as satisfaction with specific services and politi-cal leadership in Providence, Rhode Island. It ends with suggestions about what cities that wish to be seen as having "turned the corner" must do to bring citi-zens around to their viewpoint.

Once Providence was dismissed as a factory town with empty mills and exiting population; but in the year 2000 we are justly called a "renaissance city," with evi-dence everywhere of renewal and rebirth.
—Mayor Vincent "Buddy" Cianci, Budget Address, January 2000

All residents of Providence should share in the pride of being part of the renais-sance that is capturing the imagination of our nation.
—Mayor Vincent "Buddy" Cianci

The media have hailed the development of downtown corporate offices, ho-tels, convention centers, sports stadiums, concert halls, waterfront festival markets, and downtown malls as sure signs that a central city is experiencing an "urban renaissance." Newspapers and magazines have carried articles on so-called "renaissance cities." Atlanta, Baltimore, Boston, Chicago, Cleve-land, and Philadelphia have all been featured as "comeback cities" and "hot cities." In such stories, journalists typically interview politicians and business leaders whose accounts are often positive and upbeat. Few of these articles, however, report the views of ordinary citizens.

Providence, Rhode Island's state capital, has recently received consider-able attention in the national press as a "comeback city," drawing raves for its artful waterfront, quality restaurants, shiny downtown showpieces, and attracting visitors lured by the television show set in (and named for) the

SOURCE: Marion Orr and Darrell M. West, "Citizen's Views on Urban Revitalization: The Case of Providence Rhode Island," *Urban Affairs Review*, Vol. 37, No. 3, January 2002, pp. 397–419. Copy-right © 2002 by Sage Publications. Reprinted by permission of the publisher, Sage Publications.

city. The *New York Times* observed that "after years of decline, Providence is again becoming an economic and cultural force in New England." *National Geographic Traveler* featured the city in a cover story titled "What's Hot in Providence." A recent front-page story in *USA today* proclaimed Providence as the symbol of urban renaissance in America's medium-sized cities. According to *New York Times* journalist Carey Goldberg, Providence is "a national model for how to make a run-down old city hot again." In 2000, touting its "remarkable rebirth," "quality of life," and low housing prices, *Money Magazine* named Providence "the best place to live in the northeast." As Providence Mayor Vincent Cianci unabashedly asserts, "The headlines say it all."

The question of whether the kind of revitalization taking place in Providence and other "renaissance" cities has actually benefited city residents has been widely discussed and debated in the literature. However, no study has systematically researched citizens' views of downtown revitalization. In this article, we present a detailed case study of Providence to determine what factors influence citizens' feelings about "hot cities" or "renaissance cities." In particular, we are interested in what dimensions of city life contribute to citizens' sense that their city has experienced a "renaissance." What role does political leadership play in influencing how residents feel about whether their city is headed in the right direction? How important are citizen views about traditional public services such as schools, police and fire protection, and garbage collection? What about less tangible factors, such as public opinion about race relations and job opportunities? Do demographic qualities affect how residents feel about whether a city has experienced an urban renaissance?

To study citizen opinions about the factors affecting views of urban revitalization, we undertook a random survey of Providence residents. In the cross-sectional survey of city residents, we examine how residents feel about Providence and what impressions guide people's views on urban revitalization. Later, we undertake a multiple-regression analysis to ascertain what parts of city life bear the strongest relationship to overall views about Providence. When citizens conclude that a city has "turned around" and experienced a "renaissance," what factors spark those impressions? Is it the quality of the city's political leadership? Is it satisfaction with specific city services?

In the next section, we provide a historical and political overview of Providence's downtown revitalization. For many readers, this section will serve as an introduction to the "new" Providence, as the city has yet to receive attention from urban scholars. Located less than an hour south of Boston and a stone's throw away from Hartford, Connecticut, Providence's emergence as a popular destination seems almost incomprehensible. It is a medium-sized city with few great historic moments. For decades, Providence was considered an old, gritty, fading industrial city, reputed to be New England's organized crime capital. Next we turn to the survey, examining citizens' overall impressions of Providence's revitalization, public services, and political leadership. This is followed by an analysis of the factors that shape citizens' views on three dimensions of urban revitalization—city direction, quality of life, and downtown improvement. We conclude with some observations about the multidimensional nature of urban revitalization. . . .

DOWNTOWN REDEVELOPMENT IN THE CAPITAL CITY

The early 1970s marked a sense of urgency, energizing civic and public leaders to work toward revitalizing the city's central core. The Nixon administration's decision to close the Navy shipyard in nearby Newport, rising gasoline prices, and record unemployment were major events that jump-started Providence's downtown redevelopment efforts. The first major effort was the construction of a downtown civic center, completed in 1973. With strong support from Mayor Joseph Doorley, Rhode Island's governor, and civic and business leaders, voters approved two bond referenda totaling $11 million to help finance the civic center. Civic leaders claimed that the civic center would become the keystone of a New Providence.

Other significant downtown projects followed. A few months after the official opening of the civic center, the Trinity Repertory Company, an award-winning regional theater company, opened the doors of the newly renovated downtown Majestic Theater. Originally opened in 1917 as a vaudeville house, the Majestic fell on hard times after suburbanization left many downtown buildings empty. Today, the theater has an annual budget of $5.2 million, employs 130 artistic and administrative staff, generates more than $20 million in economic activity each year, and serves as one of the central points for the city's large arts community. The construction and opening in 1974 of the Rhode Island Hospital Ambulatory Patient Center and the Rhode Island Hospital Trust Tower (the state's largest office building) signaled that Providence's embryonic renaissance was gaining steam.

Two key events in 1974 would accelerate the tempo of Providence's downtown revitalization. First, to provide focused corporate involvement and resources to the short-term and long-term challenges facing the city's downtown area, the Providence Foundation, a nonprofit organization comprising the chief executive officers and top managers of some of the region's leading businesses—Fleet Bank of Rhode Island, Narragansett Electric, Gilbane Properties, The Providence Journal, CVS Pharmacy, Textron, Providence Washington Insurance, Bell Atlantic, and others—was formed. Providence Foundation leaders proposed downtown projects and worked to make them happen. As a significant business group, the Providence Foundation has provided credit, technical expertise, in-depth analyses of problems, prestigious endorsements, donations, and organizational support for an array of downtown projects and programs. As Clarence Stone and others have shown elsewhere, the downtown business elite in Providence has played a leading role in the city's "comeback."

The other crucial event in 1974 was the election of the energetic Vincent Cianci as mayor. In his first inaugural address, Cianci called for a "new beginning" and a new "spirit of adventure and excitement" for the city's downtown, its neighborhood, and waterfront. Using the formal authority of Providence's strong-mayor system, the young Cianci (he was only 33 years old) forged a powerful mayoral-centered regime and, working closely with city's business leaders, worked to transform downtown Providence.

With unchallenged control over most aspects of the city's political system, Cianci negotiated tax breaks for prospective investors, condemned properties for redevelopment, and generally made deals with corporate entrepreneurs. During his first 10 years in office, Mayor Cianci concentrated on expanding and leveraging Providence's share of federal urban development action grants (UDAG) and community development block grants (CDBG), using the federal dollars for projects ranging from parks to community development. From 1975 until 1982, more than $600 million of CDBG funds, plus federal, state, and private-sector dollars, had been pumped into downtown and the city's neighborhoods. For example, in 1975, the Biltmore Hotel, which had served for decades as the city's grand downtown hotel, closed its doors. The hotel was operating at 20 percent occupancy and was in serious need of renovations. Resisting suggestions to transform the hotel into housing for the elderly, Mayor Cianci secured a $3 million low-interest loan from the federal government and convinced the city council to provide a 10-year tax break for the hotel's new investors. The 245-room hotel reopened in February 1979, restored to its original grandeur, and remains a center of the city's downtown activity.

Union Station and the old Loew's Theater were restored. Davol Square, an old industrial complex, was transformed into a modern marketplace and office center. South Main Street, a commercial strip of restaurants and boutiques in the center of the Rhode Island School of Design, was substantially refurbished. By the early 1980s, the future of Providence appeared to be taking shape. Service industries were increasing. Banks, insurance companies, and hospitals and health care corporations were beginning to dominate the local economy. Providence was finally positioning itself to survive in the postindustrial economy.

Filling the Void: The Corporate Community and the Exit of Mayor Cianci

In 1984, just as Providence's redevelopment regime was gaining traction, Cianci resigned—forced out of office after physically attacking a man he accused of having an affair with his wife. He pleaded "no contest" to assault charges and was given probation. For many city residents, especially Providence's large Italian community, Mayor Cianci was simply defending his honor. Across the city, many believed that the optimism sparked by Providence's downtown renaissance outweighed the popular mayor's crime. Meanwhile, Providence's municipal government was hit by a big corruption scandal. "Cianci was never charged, but thirty members of his former administration were indicted on charges of extortion, larceny, and conspiracy." . . .

Buddy Cianci "reentered politics and took over once again as mayor." After a judge ruled that his "no contest" plea was not a conviction and under Rhode Island laws he could serve as mayor, Cianci ran as an independent in 1990 and won a closely contested three-way contest for mayor. He was reelected in 1994 and 1998, the latter time without opposition.

Providence Renaissance: Act II

During his second stint as mayor, Cianci did not lose his appetite for downtown projects, large or small. He concentrated on attracting residents and businesses to move into the downtown area by offering incentives to develop abandoned buildings. He successfully lobbied the legislature to provide income tax and sales tax breaks for artists who live and work in the refurbished upper-floor loft and studio spaces in downtown Providence. New Englanders come from surrounding cities to dine at one of Providence's many appealing restaurants. City government has played a part in the city's restaurant scene through a model restaurant loan program. In 1998, a downtown ice skating rink opened, with a surface twice the size of the one at New York's Rockefeller Center and fully funded by the private sector. Investors have committed to constructing four new hotels in downtown Providence, including a 370-room Marriott.

More large-scale projects are under way. A state bond issue won voter approval in November 2000 to help fund the rerouting of an interstate highway that currently cuts through the downtown area. The relocation of Interstate 195 will open access to more than 60 acres of land for riverfront development. Work is already under way on the second leg of the Providence riverwalk, and the city is preparing a new wave of waterfront projects, including Heritage Harbor, the $50-million Rhode Island history museum due to open in 2002. Ground breaking is expected at the 140,000 square foot festival marketplace, including a market and a multiscreen cinema complex near the downtown mall. In the arts and entertainment district, city officials are negotiating with an off-shoot of Robert Redford's Sundance Institute to build a multiscreen arts and cinema complex near the Providence Performing Arts Center. Finally, in Downcity, Providence's "old downtown" area (just south of the current redevelopment activity), there are plans to continue the renovation and conversion of empty office buildings into artists' lofts. A coalition of nonprofits and business leaders is exploring ways to finance Downcity business renovation, including establishing a multimillion-dollar revolving fund that would help cover the costs.

Providence leaders' efforts to revitalize the city's downtown area have not only translated into rave headlines; an expanded tourist trade has also resulted. Since 1996, the number of conventions, a central component of downtown revitalization in all cities, has risen. Bookings, room nights, and convention proposals all have increased. The number of bookings at the Rhode Island Convention Center has risen steadily—from 19 to 46. Also telling is the number of room nights, which has more than doubled over the past five years. Similarly, the number of convention proposals increased from 96 in 1997, peaking to 157 in 1999. In March 2000, Amnesty International–USA held its national convention in Providence. The National Trust for Historic Preservation and the National Fraternal Order of Police will hold conventions in 2002 and 2003, respectively.

In the remainder of this article, we report the views of city residents. Although there is little doubt that Providence has come a long way from its depths of recession in the mid-1970s, it is not clear what residents think about the city's revitalization and what factors help shape their opinions. In March 1999, we conducted a random telephone survey of 324 Providence residents.

The survey was broadly representative of the city's demographic diversity. The sample slightly overrepresented nonwhites and those with a college education but generally was within the margin of error in terms of the city's demographic composition. The survey had a margin of error of plus or minus 5.5 percent. Finally, we compiled data on the demographic background of residents to have controls for factors such as gender, sex, age, race, education, and income. Because it is known that people of various backgrounds have different life experiences, we wanted to see whether views of a city's "hotness" were affected by demographic factors.

CITIZENS' OVERALL VIEWS ON URBAN REVITALIZATION

We wanted to get a sense of the citizens' overall impressions of Providence, their opinion of the city's revitalization. We relied on three measures of revitalization. First, given that the city's downtown revitalization is relatively recent and ongoing, we asked the respondents whether they believed the city was headed in the right direction. Specifically, we asked, "Generally speaking, would you say things in Providence are going in the right direction, or have they gotten off on the wrong track?" Our second measurement of Providence's revitalization is based on the respondent's subjective perception of his or her "quality of life" as a resident of the city. We asked, "How satisfied are you with the overall quality of life in Providence? Very satisfied, somewhat satisfied, or not very satisfied?" Third, we wanted to gauge Providence residents' opinion of the downtown improvement efforts. We asked, "Compared to five years ago, would you say downtown Providence looks better off, about the same, or worse off?"

Table 9.1 shows the results of the Providence citizens' overall impression of the city's revitalization. We found broad support for the notion that Providence has done an admirable job of revitalizing itself. More than 70 percent of those interviewed reported that they believed things in Providence were headed in the "right direction," but only 10 percent thought it was "off on the wrong track." A similar percentage of respondents felt that downtown Providence was "better off" in 1999 than five years previously. Only 3 percent reported that downtown Providence was "worse off."

Political scientist Mark Schneider has shown that subjective life quality is related to such "aspects of personal life as aspirations, expectations, happiness, and satisfaction." When asked about their satisfaction with the overall quality of life in Providence, 30 percent said they were "very satisfied," 54 percent felt "somewhat satisfied," 13 percent were "not very satisfied," and 3 percent expressed no opinion.

In short, it is not just positive press or the pronouncement of local boosters that marks the sense of urban revitalization in Providence. Citizens themselves report that the city has turned around and is headed in the right direction. Providence residents, however, appear to be less enthusiastic about their quality of life. This is an interesting finding. City residents appear to be exposed to an objectively revitalized downtown but subjectively feel that the quality of their personal life experiences is modest at best. This finding raises the issue of

TABLE 9.1   Three Dimensions of Urban Revitalization (in percentages)

City direction	
Right direction	72
Wrong track	10
Don't know/no answer	11
Satisfaction with life quality	
Very satisfied	30
Somewhat satisfied	54
Not very satisfied	13
Don't know/no answer	3
Downtown improvement	
Looks better off	72
Looks about the same	9
Looks worse off	3
Don't know/no answer	16

SOURCE: Brown University Survey, March 6–8, 1999.

the relationship between downtown revitalization and residents' perception of their quality of life.

Downtown Revitalization and Citizen Assessment of Public Services

There is a longstanding literature showing that city residents consider traditional public services—schools, police and fire protection, garbage collection—foremost when rating a city's quality of life. Providing services always has been a major function of local government. Robert Lineberry observed that "public services are the grist of urban politics. . . . Virtually all the rawest nerves of urban political life are touched by the distribution of urban service burdens and benefits." Bryan Jones and his associates maintain that "delivering services is the primary function of municipal government." Decisions about city service agencies, they add, "comprise the bulk of the benefits provided to citizens provided by their governments." Richard C. Rich has observed that "public services provided by U.S. cities *do* shape the quality of life."

In one of largest surveys assessing the quality of life in local communities (more than 7,000 local residents were surveyed), the public's evaluation of how well local government provided basic services was a key part of the respondents' evaluation. "The public's evaluation of how well these services are being provided, if at all, in their neighborhood is an indication both of the quality of life in that particular place as well as a measure of citizen satisfaction with local government."

In our survey, Providence residents were asked to assess the quality of municipal services. We asked, "How would you rate the following Providence

**TABLE 9.2   Providence Citizens' Assessment
of City Services (in percentages)**

City Services	Excellent	Good	Only Fair	Poor
Police	15	48	23	12
Fire	32	49	7	1
Garbage	19	52	20	6
Street repairs	6	21	31	40
Public transportation	11	44	17	7
Public schools	6	23	28	21

city services (police protection, fire services, garbage collection, street repairs, public transportation, and public schools): excellent, good, only fair, or poor?" In other words, we examine the tie between services such as police, fire, and garbage collection and overall satisfaction with the city.

Table 9.2 displays the results of Providence residents' assessment of municipal services. The activity receiving the highest percentage of excellent or good ratings was fire services (81 percent), garbage collection (71 percent), police protection (63 percent), public transportation (55 percent), public schools (29 percent), and street repairs (27 percent). The wide range of views reported here demonstrates that citizens are capable of drawing sharp distinctions across different aspects of city life. The nearly 60 percentage point variation in positive ratings shows that some services are viewed quite positively, but others garnered poor ratings.

Although the results are not reported in Table 9.2 the survey found wide variation among various demographic groups in the city. For example, police protection was rated more highly by Whites (70 percent excellent or good) than nonwhites (49 percent excellent or good). Nonwhites (36 percent) rated public schools more positively than Whites (24 percent). There also were differences in ratings by neighborhood. The area giving the police the highest ratings was the working-class area of Mt. Pleasant/Elmhurst (79 percent), followed by Downtown/Federal Hill/Smith Hill (75 percent) and the West End/Silver Lake/Hartford/Olneyville/Manton (69 percent). On the more affluent and largely White East Side, 66 percent rated the police positively, but in the city's poorest section and largely minority neighborhoods of South Providence and Elmwood, only 46 percent gave the police excellent or good ratings. The area giving public schools the lowest ratings was the East Side (16 percent excellent or good), followed by South Providence/Elmwood (23 percent). On street repairs, the area giving city services the highest ratings was Mt. Pleasant/Elmhurst (34 percent), followed by Downtown/Federal Hill/Smith Hill (33 percent), the West End/Silver Lake/Hartford/Olneyville/Manton (26 percent), the East Side (25 percent), and South Providence/Elmwood (19 percent).

Restaurants, Taxes, and Jobs in a "Renaissance" City

It is often argued that factors such as employment opportunities, taxes, and the state of local race relations influence how people feel about the quality of

TABLE 9.3   Providence Citizens' Assessment of City Life (in percentages)

City Services	Excellent	Good	Only Fair	Poor
Restaurants	31	43	13	4
Employment	10	32	31	15
Taxes	4	18	32	32
Race relations	2	32	38	15

life in urban America. In the 1978 HUD survey, a large majority of the respondents reported that "cities" had the "best restaurants" when they were growing up. When asked whether large cities still provided the best restaurants, "smaller numbers, but majorities nevertheless, say that large cities still have the best" restaurants. Good restaurants are a major draw to cities.

Mayor Cianci and other local promoters take pride in Providence's dining-out experience and point to it as an indicator of the city's "renaissance." As noted, city hall has encouraged the development of new restaurants through a low-interest loan program. Providence's restaurant scene also benefits from its ties to Johnson & Wales University, a nationally renowned culinary arts school headquartered in downtown Providence. The city's reputation for fine cuisine was recently featured in the *New York Times*. When we asked Providence citizens to rate the city's restaurants as an aspect of the quality of life in the city, 74 percent responded that they were either excellent or good (see Table 9.3).

Part of the logic of urban growth politics is that the creation of jobs in the central city will have a broad impact on the quality of life. The existence of employment opportunities is a major draw to a city and affects how residents feel about a city. When we asked city residents to rate employment opportunities in Providence, only 10 percent characterized them as "excellent," 32 percent as "good," and 46 percent as "only fair" or "poor." Providence residents are not as sanguine about employment prospects as the promoters of economic growth are.

We hypothesized that the nature of race relations affects how citizens feel about a city. Experiences across the nation suggest that high levels of racial tensions can hamper revitalization efforts. Cities where race relations are more harmonious are likely to do a better job at becoming "hot." As indicated, Providence is increasingly becoming a multiethnic, multiracial city, We wished to ascertain Providence residents' views on race relations. As Table 9.3 shows, only 2 percent of the respondents rated race relations in Providence as "excellent." A majority of citizens (53 percent) characterized the city's race relations as "only fair" or "poor." Our data suggest that Rich's speculation that the city's growing racial diversity poses "political problems for the city" in the future has some bases of support.

Paul Peterson, in his influential work *City Limits,* reminds us of the impact high taxes can have on a central city. Higher taxes reduce a city's competitiveness as an attractive site for commerce, industry, and residents. When asked to rate taxes as an aspect of life in Providence, a large majority of Providence citizens—64 percent—gave a negative response (see Table 9.3).

POLITICAL LEADERSHIP AND URBAN REVITALIZATION

"Leadership is not a process of presiding over what is inevitable. It is about making something happen that, given the ordinary course of events, would not occur." It generally is believed that the quality of political leadership influences how residents feel about the overall direction and quality of urban existence. Local observers in Providence have noted that Mayor Cianci has used his formal and informal leadership to transform a decaying, old textile city into a city of national prominence.

Strong leaders and innovative vision should make city dwellers feel better about a locality and lead them to give the city high marks in terms of urban revitalization. Because Providence has a strong-mayor system and Mayor Cianci claims credit for being the primary architect of the city's turnaround, we asked citizens, "How would you rate the job Buddy Cianci is doing as mayor—excellent, good, fair, or poor?" In line with the generally positive press Mayor Cianci has received throughout the 1990s, his political leadership earned very favorable ratings. Seventy-seven percent thought he was doing an excellent or good job, 14 percent believed his job performance was only fair, 3 percent felt it was poor, and 6 percent had no opinion. Whites (83 percent) were more likely to view him positively than nonwhites (65 percent). Women (78 percent) were slightly more likely than men (74 percent) were to be positive about Cianci's performance. In terms of age, Cianci was rated most favorably by those age 65 or older and 45 to 64 (82 percent each), compared to 75 percent for those ages 25 to 44 and 69 percent for those ages 18 to 24. New arrivals (those living in Providence five years or less) rated Cianci almost as positively (75 percent) compared to those who have been in the city 20 years or more (78 percent excellent or good).

EXPLAINING CITIZEN VIEWS OF PROVIDENCE'S REVITALIZATION

We have established that citizens hold favorable opinions about city revitalization but have quite divided views regarding a range of city services and aspects of city life. In general, they feel more positively about the city's political leadership and services such as fire and police than qualities such as the public schools, taxes, and street repairs. The unanswered question is, What parts of city life bear the strongest relationship to overall views about Providence? When citizens conclude that a city has turned around and become revitalized, what sparks those impressions? Is it the quality of the political leadership? Is it satisfaction with specific services? Is it less tangible qualities, such as race relations, city schools, or taxes? To examine those questions, we undertook regression analyses of our three dimensions of urban revitalization: city direction, quality of life, and downtown improvement.

In the model for citizen views about the city being on the "right" or "wrong track," the factors that bore the strongest relationship to city direction were ratings of police protection, sex, age, and race. Residents who felt police protection was good were more likely to feel the city was headed in the right direction. The same was true for men, young people, and Whites. Conversely, factors such as political leadership, taxes, and nightlife bore no significant relationship to city direction.

Providence's resuscitation from a gritty industrial city into a revitalized tourist attraction of national prominence is an ongoing enterprise. A large majority of respondents in our survey believed the city was moving in the right direction. In general, it is clear that police protection was most crucial in helping to shape these views. Like many major cities, Providence has witnessed a significant drop in its crime rate during the 1990s, for which the police have been given much credit. In 1998, serious crime in Providence was at its lowest point in 30 years. Other than demographic background, this satisfaction with police service was the only aspect of city service and living that bore a strong relationship with citizens' overall views about the city direction.

One of the downsides of a rejuvenated downtown is that as more people flock to the city center, the opportunities for criminal mischief multiply. Public officials in cities experiencing the kind of "renaissance" Providence has enjoyed should be mindful that public safety plays a significant role in shaping residents' views about whether the city is on the "right or wrong track."

On our second dimension of urban revitalization—satisfaction with the overall quality of life—two factors stood out as major predictors: those who felt street repairs are good and those who gave favorable ratings to race relationships within the city. In addition, young people were more likely to report high satisfaction with Providence's life quality.

In a classic study of Oakland, California, conducted in the early 1970s, Levy, Meltsner, and Wildavsky argued that "in no small part, streets contribute to the quality of urban life." Our findings provide some confirmation of this assertion. Residents believing that the city had done a good job on streets and street repairs were much more likely to report that they were satisfied with the quality of life within the city. Most of us take streets for granted. However, streets and street repairs are crucial life quality measures because they tap everyday dimensions that residents care about. This is suggested by the frequency in which citizens contact local government officials concerning streets. In his survey of the literature of who contacts government agencies and why, Philip B. Coulter found that the second most popular subject of contact concerns streets. In Providence, a city with limited mass transit options, the quality of the streets was a major contributing factor to how citizens defined their overall quality of life.

Mayors and other public officials have had to develop a delicate balancing act between promoting downtown revitalization and tending to the concerns of their voter base. Indeed, some of the nation's "best" big-city mayors were able to promote economic development and address the public service needs of city residents. According to urban historian Melvin Holli, Mayor Richard J. Daley, who successfully revitalized Chicago's downtown Loop, won public support "because he paid close attention to the delivery of public services," giving substance to the slogan "The City That Works." Baltimore's William Donald Schaefer, who oversaw Baltimore's downtown restructuring and was often criticized as a "bricks-and-mortar" mayor, never lost sight of the significance of providing good public services. Dissatisfaction with schools, police protection, street repairs, and other routine services heighten residents' discontent and hasten their exodus out of the city. Mayors, although occupied with issues of economic development, risk ignoring important public services at their own peril.

As W. C. Rich has written in his study of Providence, "Mayor Cianci has been very careful to make sure some of the Urban Development Action Grant funds are spent in the neighborhoods. Every neighborhood gets new sidewalk." In his 1999 inaugural address, Cianci proudly stressed that since 1990, 73 miles of city streets were resurfaced, 42 parks refurbished, thousands of sidewalks replaced, brighter streetlights installed in 80 percent of the city, and state-of-the-art equipment provided to the police department. In other words, Mayor Cianci has tried to balance downtown revitalization with provision of basic services.

In a city that is 30 percent nonwhite, relations between Whites and minorities significantly affected how citizens felt about the overall quality of life within the city. Those residents who believed race relations were good were more likely to approve of the city's quality of life. We know from Detroit's and other cities' experiences how heightened racial tensions can hamper efforts to rejuvenate a city's central business district, weakening the capacity to create a "renaissance." Providence's political leadership has been successful in navigating the tensions that often exist in a multiethnic/multiracial city. However, as the city's Hispanic and Asian communities continue to grow, how the city's leaders incorporate them into the local governing regime and address their concerns will become a critical factor in the city's future.

The contrast between the factors affecting life quality and city direction demonstrates that urban revitalization is multidimensional in nature. There is not a single consistent factor that explains citizen belief in a city's turnaround. Rather, city residents draw distinctions between a belief that a city is headed in the right direction and that an area has a high quality of life. Our results suggest that cities cannot focus on service delivery to the exclusion of more general issues of community climate. Sometimes, civic leaders spend all their time on bricks, mortar, and service delivery, not recognizing that community factors also count for a lot with residents. Based on our findings, narrow, technical approaches to governing that do not also work to improve the "spirit" of a city will not be as successful as those that function at both levels.

Our final dimension of urban revitalization—downtown improvement—taps into the city's political leadership. It has been surprising that the quality of political leadership within a city does not explain much of citizen views about a city being revitalized. In part, that is because it is difficult for mayors to claim credit for abstract successes such as a city being headed in the right direction or citizens being satisfied with the overall quality of life within the city. The one aspect of revitalization where political leadership can be shown to matter is on the physical restructuring of downtown.

Providence has undergone a renaissance in part because the downtown area looks much better compared to five years ago. Mayor Cianci is widely credited with having the vision and political abilities to attract the resources for new office buildings, an upscale downtown mall, and relocating rivers that opened up new walkways and parks. Cianci frequently claims credit for the downtown turnaround as well, peppering his speeches with concrete evidence of progress in the downtown area. In looking at the factors that explain why people feel the downtown has improved, one of the strongest predictors was the quality of political leadership. People who felt that Cianci had done a good job as mayor were much more likely to say that downtown Providence looks better. These individuals recognized that Cianci's charismatic personality and strong leadership abilities were important determinants in the downtown's turnabout. Between working with private developers and tapping into valuable state and federal revenue sources, the mayor is seen as instrumental to the Providence renaissance.

Chapter 10

Metropolitan Politics

There has long been a discussion in the United States about creating a unified metropolitan regional government that would subsume both cities and their suburbs. There are examples like Indianapolis where this has been done and places like Miami where the voters have voted down the dissolution of city government in order to create a single general county government. For the most part, suburbanites since the mid-twentieth century have not wanted to be annexed by the major city from which so many of them fled in the first place. In fact, between 1921 and 1979, reformers have placed referendums on the ballot 83 times to attempt city-county consolidations. They succeeded only 17 times and only 3 of those came in major metropolitan areas of more than 250,000 people.[1]

The current effort in metropolitan politics is to create at least unified metropolitan wide planning and the sharing of tax resources for the benefit of the entire region. In the first article in this chapter, Myron Orfield recounts the mostly successful effort in Minneapolis-St. Paul to accomplish this through state legislation. While business leaders in various cities, such as the members of the Commercial Club of Chicago, have tried to emulate the Minnesota model, most have not achieved political success.[2]

Many cities face the problems of regional governance. For instance, Houston has not adopted regional forms of government, but the city government there, like other cities elsewhere, has met some of the regional needs for water and airports. Business and political leaders in Houston are beginning to recognize the need for some form of regional governance, but the forces preventing it seem likely to prevail in the immediate future.

The reason that there is not a strong move towards regional government is that citizens don't want it. They have not, for the most part, become what Jones and Hays call "Metropolitan Citizens." In their study of the St. Louis metropolitan region, Jones and Hays found that only 7 percent of the people living outside the city believed that there was a very close connection "between the quality of life in the City of St. Louis and the quality of life in [their] local community." There is some support for centralized decision-making around some policy areas and limited redistribution of tax revenue to help the poorer areas of the metropolitan region. But urban politics is not yet producing the metropolitan citizens necessary for any major moves towards metropolitan governance.

Finally, Gregg Easterbrook, among other journalists and urban scholars, argues that sprawl may not be the great evil that most urban planners and scholars suggest. Sprawl, when you are tied up in a traffic jam on the streets or the expressways, may be irritating, but it is not "statistically significant." People fled the city because they wanted to. Easterbrook contends that they have a right to more yard space, better schools, lower crime, and better amenities. He states that road construction is not necessarily inferior to public transit construction; both have their place. Smart growth is in everybody's interest, but sprawl, according to some urban observers, is not necessarily bad.[3]

Notes

1. Dennis Judd and Todd Swanstrom, *City Politics*. New York: Longman, 2002, pp. 332–333.
2. Commercial Club of Chicago, *2020 Plan*. Chicago: University of Chicago Press, 2002.
3. Gregg Easterbrook, "Suburban Myth," *New Republic,* March 15, 1999, pp.18–22. This article was originally included in this anthology, but it was dropped because of anti-Semitic remarks in another unrelated on-line article for the *New Republic* in October 2003.

36. Metropolitics in Minneapolis-St. Paul
Myron Orfield

Urban politics in general and metropolitan regional politics in specific is affected not just by policies of the federal government and local political decisions; the states play a key role as well. Myron Orfield is a law professor and state legislator in Minnesota. This is his account of how he built the necessary coalitions and passed the state legislation to transform the Minneapolis-St. Paul metropolitan region. Both his specific tactics and his general approach can be used more widely to restructure metropolitan regions throughout the country.

While Myron Orfield did not succeed in passing his legislation in the early 1990s, by the end of that decade he had created a new metropolitan coalition that was successful in partially reorganizing the structure of metropolitan planning agencies and in increasing the tax sharing system that had already begun in Minneapolis-St. Paul.

"**M**etropolitics" began with studies, sewers, and maps and moved on through mayoral associations, the Minnesota State Legislature, and the governor's office. Issue by issue, bill by bill, the coalition was forged. Today it spans the central cities, inner suburbs, and low–tax base developing suburbs, hundreds of metropolitan churches, environmentalists, civic groups such as the League of Women Voters and the Citizens League, and the Twin Cities metro area's communities of color. It is strong and continues to gain influence and credibility. . . .

SOURCE: Myron Orfield, *Metropolitics: A Regional Agenda for Community and Stability.* Washington, D.C.: Brookings Institution, 1997, pp. 104–128. Copyright © 1997 The Brookings Institution Press. Reprinted by permission.

THE 1991–92 LEGISLATIVE SESSION: FROM MAPS TO BILLS

My first step in the ensuing legislative history was to draft a bill requiring the Met Council to do a comprehensive study of the economic health of the city and the first ring of "fully developed," older suburbs. In what the committee chairman said was a first, I testified in the Senate myself on behalf of the companion bill, because its Senate author was too busy. The Fully Developed Area Study, initially opposed by the council, produced two reports that began to shed light on regional polarization. These reports largely confirmed the social and economic decline of the inner suburbs but offered few solutions.

The Metropolitan Infrastructure Stability Act

In January 1992, I introduced the Metropolitan Infrastructure Stability Act, a bill that required subregional pricing of sewer infrastructure. Before 1987, the Met Council had "priced" sewer infrastructure so that developing areas paid a higher share of the cost of new sewers to support their growth. In 1987, the legislature imposed a uniform pricing system through which the whole region shared the cost of new sewer capacity. This move seemed to have originated outside the council, because its staff had opposed these changes. Staffers argued that it was unfair for the older areas of the Twin Cities region to pay for this capacity and that spreading the costs of sewers made the possibility of more urban sprawl too easy. My bill was drafted by Minnesota House Research in consultation with a Met Council attorney and with the help of several of the council's planning staff members. In short, the Metropolitan Infrastructure Stability Act would have overturned the uniform regional debt-service fee and made the growing areas pay a larger part of the cost of new sewer capacity. This looked like a perfect issue to begin building a coalition between the central cities and older suburban communities. It seemed manageable in scope and did not involve race or class issues, and the status quo was hard to defend in terms of policy. . . .

In a sequence of events that became predictable, this bill was immediately and strongly opposed by the Builders Association of the Twin Cities, several powerful developers, real estate agents, and growing cities. House leaders soon let me know that builders and real estate agents were among the largest contributors to the political process and warned me to step back. The Met Council moved quickly from a neutral position on the bill to outright opposition. After the session ended, one developer of expensive homes invited me to lunch and told me that he and several other developers had written large personal checks to hire additional lobbyists to kill the bill and that they would continue to do so. . . .

In this seemingly hopeless battle, Irv Anderson, chair of the Local Government Committee and soon to be Speaker of the House, took an interest in the bill at my urging. He understood its equities. As added motivation, in 1980 when Anderson first ran for Speaker, Gordy Voss, then a state representative, was instrumental in a controversial internal Democratic coup that resulted in another House member's becoming Speaker. The bill received a hearing in Anderson's committee and, on a rapidly gaveled voice vote, was sent straight to the floor of the House, avoiding damaging potential referrals to other committees.

Had the bill passed, it could have significantly increased sewer fees for residents of developing suburbs. As it moved to the floor of the House, the bill gathered opponents—six or more lobbyists from the building industry, lobbyists from the real estate industry, growing cities, and labor unions—in addition to Voss, McCarron, and the South Minneapolis state senator and the council member. Although the bill was dead in the Senate, its opponents were still afraid it would be amended to one of the large omnibus bills on the floor in a long, late-night session.

As the forces opposed to the bill grew more powerful, in exchange for withdrawing the bill the Met Council and the Waste Control Commission agreed to finance a $400,000 infrastructure study of freeway and sewer financing to be done independently at the University of Minnesota. This compromise resulted in two significant studies that provided detailed evidence of both the historical pattern of infrastructure subsidies and the virtues of pricing infrastructure regionally. These studies showed conclusively that, after the central cities, the northern suburbs were the largest subsidizers of the southwestern suburban infrastructure expansion.

This debate taught me several lessons. Builders and real estate agents, partly because of the amount of money they gave to both political parties, were some of the fiercest opponents in the legislative process. Without Irv Anderson's help, the bill probably would have died in committee. The political world of the northern suburbs was also more complicated than I had thought. Though seemingly sympathetic on many issues, these suburbs had their own alliances, which had to be considered. Clearly, the pattern of regional polarization was not well understood and was difficult to explain. Without significant preparation and communication, not even my colleagues in Minneapolis could be relied on to support regional reform policies.

THE REGIONAL FAIR HOUSING COALITION

After the 1991–92 session, I began to concentrate on building an alliance with the northern suburbs for regional reform. . . .

Color maps, which powerfully and simply conveyed complex patterns and trends, were critical to these discussions. In late 1992, with $750 of my own money. I bought a Datanet Mapping package, a rather primitive type of geographic information system (GIS) software. Speaker Dee Long assigned me a staff member one day a week who helped collect and interpret census and agency data over the summer of 1992. By early 1993, I had developed a series of GIS maps that illustrated the region's changing demographics. My maps and presentations of the pattern of regional polarization soon found a receptive audience throughout the region: I made more than 70 speeches in 1993 and more than 100 in 1994. Local officials especially liked the maps showing placement of new regional infrastructure, locations of new jobs, fiscal disparity between communities, and patterns of tax base polarization. Soon I could not keep up with requests for my maps and gave them to the State Planning Agency to be reproduced and distributed. By late 1993, the State of Minnesota had sold 5,000 copies of the first set of regional demographic maps.

Because of the political unpopularity of city issues and the socioeconomic and racial divisiveness of metropolitan policies, getting maximum visible support in the suburbs was critical. For regionalism to succeed, it had to become a suburban issue. At first, the suburbs (no matter how badly off) saw no reason to join in a political alliance with the central cities. Foreign to their worldview, the very idea smacked of a sort of political degradation. In addition, some suburban city officials did not want to publicly acknowledge any problems. An extensive series of meetings began—first with individual officials, then in larger groups—using maps and presenting arguments for regional reforms that demonstrated the self-interest these suburbs had in regionalism. . . .

North Metro Mayors Association: Inner Suburbs, Low Tax Base

Most inner-suburban city officials understood the inevitable deepening of their cities' problems. None of the cities that were members of the North Metro Mayors Association had enough property tax base to adequately support community services. After the fiscal disparities distribution, they still had one-third less tax capacity per household than the southwest and east developing suburbs. Believing in the axiom that economic development followed major public infrastructure expenditures, the association had become disgruntled about the disproportionate metropolitan freeway designation and sewer spending in the southwestern quadrant.

The North Metro Mayors Association exists as an organization to win approval for northern highway projects and sewer projects, to preserve the present fiscal disparities system or increase local government aid payments to its member suburbs, and to acquire new programs and resources in response to the explosive growth of social needs in the northern inner-suburban area. However, troubling cross-currents disturbed this seeming consensus. . . .

In January 1993, the North Metro Mayors Association called a large public meeting of all the north suburban city, school district, and county-elected officials and other community leaders. The meeting focused on demographics and the outline of regional reform in terms of housing, transportation reform, fiscal equity, and structural reform. Afterward, the North Metro Mayors Association and its member cities endorsed the outline of regional reform and would later endorse all of the specific bills of the Metropolitan Community Stability Act. . . . Even Mayor [and future governor, Jesse] Ventura was in favor of the agenda. This support gave enormous momentum to metropolitan reform and helped persuade other suburban communities to join us. . . .

Support from Low-Income, Minority, and Good-Government Groups

Once the North Metro Mayors Association had signaled its strong support for regional housing reform, building a strong base for regional fair housing in the central cities became the next imperative. Because fair housing initiatives were so divisive in older regions, we had approached local community development groups early on. We hoped to head off any anxiety about loss of city-dedicated housing resources or the massed political power of disenfranchised groups. By engaging these groups early on regarding the issues surrounding fair housing and in the design of a local bill, we avoided much mistrust.

This venture had two strong suits. Solution and design of the proposal came from the bottom up, not the top down. It was a legislative solution with broad community input, not a litigation-based court decision lacking grassroots input. In addition, metropolitan reforms were not presented as alternatives competing for resources and power but as complementary methods that would *gradually* reduce the overwhelming nature of central-city problems and provide resources for community development through metropolitan tax base sharing.

More meetings were held in fall 1992 and winter 1993 at the offices of the Urban Coalition, which represented the interests of low-income and minority communities. Its research arm independently came to the conclusion that the regional dynamics of concentrated poverty had to be more widely understood. We simultaneously contacted the Legal Aid Society, which was just beginning a lawsuit against the Minneapolis Public Housing Authority and associated entities. Good-government groups were also important in building a coalition for fair housing and other regional reforms.

At the Urban Coalition meetings, a great deal of time was spent on demographics and the implications of growing regional polarization for low-income communities in the central cities. Confirming the suspicions of many activists, members presented real evidence of the huge societal expenditures going to build exclusive communities on the metropolitan fringes, in a development pattern that had severe detrimental effects on central-city neighborhoods. This group dealt methodically with the implications of the housing and other metropolitan reform bills for low-income communities and community development groups. Community development groups then moved to support the multifaceted regional reform agenda (and specifically the fair housing bill) to complement continued community development efforts within the central cities. . . .

The fair housing bill caught the Met Council between a rock and a hard place. During the 1970s the council had established a housing and redevelopment authority, and through its housing policy, it had for a time tied the allocation of regional resources to the progress a requesting community made regarding affordable housing. On the one hand, the Comprehensive Choice Housing Act (the housing bill) expanded the council's power in an area where it had always sought to widen its authority; on the other hand, its members were Republican appointees connected with a legislative Republican caucus strongly opposed to fair-housing issues. Initially, we sought the Met Council's input on the housing bill and made dozens of individual changes for council staff in 1992–1993. By the time the bill was introduced, it was as much the council's as our own, and the council supported it.

After the bill's introduction, as Republican opposition mounted, the council changed its position and opposed the housing bill. Severely criticized for this about-face by the editorial board of the *Minneapolis Star Tribune,* the council again reversed its position and supported the bill. The Minnesota Housing Finance Agency (MHFA) reviewed the bill carefully, offered several suggestions that were incorporated, and never took a formal position on the bill.

Amid increasing controversy, the pro-housing forces attempted to establish direct communications with the governor's office concerning the housing bill. Early on, the governor's office had informed us that it would follow the Met Council's lead. We made particular efforts to contact the governor's deputy chief of staff, Curt Johnson. Johnson had been a community college official in Inver Grove Heights, where he saw firsthand the needs of low–tax base suburbia. At some point, he made the leap from this job to the Citizens League, a historically powerful proponent of regional planning. Johnson would later become a coauthor, with Neal Peirce, of the book *Citistates*, a strong call for a more powerful commitment to regionalism. On the road in national speaking engagements with Peirce, Johnson's views sounded compatible with the "metropolitics" I have proposed in this book. In local politics, however, that compatibility seemed to disappear.

Throughout the debate, Johnson kept the pro-housing and metropolitan reform forces at arm's length and did not return telephone calls. At the same time, he condemned this coalition as bad politicians and poor policymakers in numerous conversations with reporters and editorial boards. At this point, he began referring to the bill's "quotas" and sometimes called the housing bill a "quota bill." This was particularly hurtful coming from the former head of the Citizens League. The bill's supporters had hoped that if political circumstances made it difficult for Johnson to join them, he could provide counsel, or at least maintain neutrality. Instead, his actions made our approach to moderate Republicans (who looked to Johnson for guidance) quite difficult. It was not until 1995 that we finally convinced several of these moderates to support the fiscal parts of the regional agenda.

Early in the 1993 session, the Republican members from southwestern suburban areas made clear to the governor that if he did not veto the housing bill, they would no longer sustain his veto power in the legislature. Without the threat of a veto in an overwhelmingly Democratic legislature, the governor's power would be severely curtailed.

Of immediate concern to the governor was a campaign finance reform bill that contained provisions to limit gubernatorial campaign contributions substantially. Despite the popularity of these provisions, Arne Carlson, a governor with great fund-raising capabilities, strongly opposed them. In a tumultuous closed meeting the Republican legislative leadership told Carlson that if he signed the housing bill, they would not sustain a veto of the campaign finance bill. After this meeting, the governor's opposition to the housing bill crystallized, and his office refused to negotiate. On April 23, 1993, shortly after the governor's meeting with the Republican caucus, he outlined his objections to the housing bill in a letter urging me to withdraw it. He stated he would then appoint a blue-ribbon committee to seek a compromise over the interim for the next session.

Governor Carlson substantively objected to the bill because the term "barriers" was ill defined. In fact, the housing bill defined barriers as including "zoning requirements, development agreements, and development practices" that unreasonably impede the development of moderate-and low-income housing. This definition was agreed on after lengthy negotiations with the North Metro Mayors Association and the Association of Metropolitan Municipalities. The city and suburban representatives who drafted this language (in concert with the governor's appointees at the Met Council) believed that it provided sufficient legislative guidance in terms of barrier removal. They wanted more specific delineation of the term by a neutral administrative law judge in the rulemaking process. It was unlikely that any process could produce a better definition supported by so broad a coalition of city governments. I informed the governor that we would be willing to negotiate further.

The governor also asserted that the bill ignored the "single most obstructive barrier to low-income housing—land cost." But the bill directly addressed these issues by seeking to curtail unduly restrictive, large-lot zoning provisions and encourage higher-density multifamily development. The governor's office had been repeatedly told that any suggestions that the governor supported would be incorporated, and I reiterated this offer.

In addition, the governor objected to the bill as an affront to local prerogatives. The North Metro Mayors Association and the Association of Metropolitan Municipalities (organizations whose function is to protect these prerogatives) disagreed. Further, the governor had recently directed the council to study the consolidation of local governments. It was therefore difficult to reconcile his interest in consolidation with his respect for local prerogatives. Again, I offered to negotiate on this point.

Governor Carlson stated that the Local Government Aid (LGA) and Homestead Agricultural Credit Aid (HACA) penalties were outside the Met Council's charter, that the council was unequipped to use such power, and that such an exercise could result in gross injustice to cities. In response, his concern for local prerogatives again exceeded the concern expressed by the North Metro Mayors Association and the Association of Metropolitan Municipalities. Moreover, the agencies in his administration charged with policy in this area—the Met Council and the Minnesota Housing Finance Agency—had not raised any concerns about these powers. The governor could offer no specific precedent or authority that would prevent the council from exercising such powers. However, we offered to delete the penalties.

The governor countered that the bill had too many penalties and not enough incentives. I informed him that pro-housing forces had offered a package of incentives in the negotiating process but that his office rejected these incentives. The council, negotiating on his behalf, was quite emphatic that the Carlson administration would support no new spending in this area. I told the governor that virtually any incentive he approved would be included. After this exchange, the governor's office cut off all contact with me and the pro-housing forces. Dozens of calls to Tom Weaver (Representative Charlie Weaver's brother, and one of the governor's chief lobbyists) and Curt Johnson were not returned. The debate on the House and Senate floors became nasty and acrimonious. Representative H. Todd Van Dellen (Republican-Plymouth) argued strenuously in opposition: "The suburbs exist for a reason.

They give people something to shoot for." The bill passed 79 to 51, 11 votes short of an override.

All House Democratic members voted for the bill, except for four representing the southwest and east developing suburbs. The only Republican member voting in favor represented Saint Louis Park, an inner-ring community. The rural Democratic members followed the lead of their metro counterparts, as did the rural Republican members.

In the Minnesota Senate, because of the governor's veto threat, the housing bill was amended in its entirety into the omnibus tax bill. The Democratic leaders in the Senate did not think the governor would veto the entire tax bill that financed all of state government simply because he opposed the housing bill. They were wrong. On the Senate floor, Edward Oliver of Deephaven, in the southwest developing suburban area, repeatedly stated that the bill was "social engineering" that usurped local powers. A sarcastic senator asked him whether the 22,000-square-foot lot size requirements practiced by one of Oliver's communities were "social engineering." Thereafter, a motion to delete the housing provisions from the tax bill failed by a single vote.

When the tax bill came up in the conference committee late one night in May 1993, Commissioner Morrie Anderson of the Department of Finance represented the Carlson administration. Doug Johnson, Senate tax chair, and Ann Rest, House tax chair, were the lead conferees. Anderson announced that the housing provision was a "veto item." Both Johnson and Rest repeatedly tried to find some compromise to prevent the governor from vetoing the entire tax bill. As they offered each option (including the removal of all penalties), the only reply, repeated over and over, was an ominous, mechanical "That is a veto item." The housing provisions were finally extracted at 2:30 a.m. when it became clear that no compromise was possible.

The housing bill was again brought up and was amended on the floor of both bodies to meet all of Governor Carlson's objections stated in his letter of April 23, 1993. Specifically, all penalties were removed, and mechanisms were created both to define barriers to affordable housing more fully and to identify incentives for producing such housing. Further, based on an oral request from Tom Weaver, the requirement of Administrative Procedure Act rulemaking was eliminated from the bill. The toothless housing bill was now essentially a "request" (without penalties) to communities to remove their housing barriers. The bill passed by slightly larger margins and was promptly vetoed on May 23. In his veto message, perhaps because the pro-housing forces had responded to each of his original objections, the governor raised a series of entirely new ones.

Although this bill was vetoed, tremendous energy and awareness had been raised in a very short time. The endurance of a coalition on this difficult issue was itself an important step forward, and the forces behind the bill were dedicated to the pursuit of housing reform. We realized that the going would be tough, but we believed that we could only achieve ultimate success by continuing to put the issue before the public.

37. The Challenge of Regional Governance in Houston

The Houston Chronicle

The following article traces the regional history and new opportunities of the Houston Metropolitan Region. It suggests some of the optimistic factors that might make some form of regional governance possible in areas like Houston. Houston is now the tenth largest city in the U.S. and the fourth largest metropolitan region. Many American cities face Houston's problems of regional governance, but its approach is unique.

W hile Houston shares many characteristics with other fast growing urban centers in twentieth-century America, it has dealt with regional governance issues differently than most. A combination of different structural rules, demography, and political culture shaped this uniqueness and leaves Houston with an atypical pattern of challenges and opportunities as we approach the end of the century. To understand this exceptional situation, a brief review of regional governance is in order.

TRADITIONAL PATTERNS

In 1900, the Houston urban area included about 50,000 people: 44,633 in the incorporated city and a few thousand living around the edges. Liberally defined, the urban area included 70–80 square miles, or less than five percent of Harris County. By 1990, the Houston urban area included about 3.2 million people and extended over 2,000 square miles. Most of Harris County had been integrated in the regional metropolis, along with much of Fort Bend County, northern Brazoria and Galveston counties, and southern Montgomery County. About half the urban population lived in the City of Houston, which had spread over nearly 600 square miles, and had extraterritorial jurisdiction over most of the remainder.

Throughout most of the twentieth century, regional governance needs were dealt with rather effectively in Houston. Several structural and political factors contributed to this result. Among the most important were:

- **A dominant incorporated central city.** Houston aggressively used its expansive authority under its home-rule charter and liberal annexation powers to annex new suburban growth and thwart the emergence of municipal rivals in the region. Houston was thus the reverse of St.

SOURCE: "Greater Houston: The Regional Dilemma" *The Houston Chronicle* online. Available at http://www.chron.com/content/interactive/special/GHP/section2.html. Copyright © 1996 Greater Houston Partnership. Reprinted by permission.

Louis. Houston became a highly elastic city able to reshape its boundaries as the metropolitan area changed and grew. Armed with extraterritorial jurisdiction, Houston could monitor and partially control growth outside its city limits as well as block any new incorporation in adjacent areas.

As a home-rule city, Houston had broad powers to take the lead in addressing regional problems. In the 1950s the City developed and implemented a regional water plan assuring adequate supplies of surface water until well in the next century. In the 1960s the City began building a new international airport that has become a key hub for regional fliers. The City has also been able to expand its reach by securing dominant representation on important functional boards such as the Port of Houston Authority and the Metropolitan Transit Authority. This ad hoc structure made it possible to provide leadership on most regional issues.

- **Harris County accounted for virtually all of the population.** Regional governance was also made easier by the fact that Harris County (the largest county in the eastern half of Texas) included virtually all the metropolitan population until the 1970s. As a result, in cases where the City's reach seemed insufficient to address a regional need (as with building a baseball stadium in the 1960s), the county could step up to the plate. And since the great majority of Harris County voters were also residents of the City of Houston, city-county conflicts were muted.

- **Impact of independent school districts.** Somewhat ironically, the ability of the City of Houston and Harris County to address regional policy issues was enhanced by fact that neither had responsibility for public educational services in the Houston area. This immunized, to a great extent, city and county officials from the bitter educational battles when local schools were desegregated in the 1960s and 1970s. The fragmentation of educational policy-making into nearly 30 independent schools districts made it impossible to address public educational issues on a regional basis. Annexation by the City does not change school district boundaries. This also spared key governmental decision makers from messy entanglements in the racial/ethnic, financial, and instructional quarrels that raged in this sector. In addition, local citizens, assured that their schools would continue to be run by local elected officials, gave more leeway to regional authorities than would likely have been the case otherwise.

- **Impact of at-large districts.** Finally, for most of its history, Houston area elected officials ran from large districts which encouraged "big picture" perspectives. State House and Senate members ran at-large in Harris County until 1965, and the eight Houston city council members were elected at-large until 1979. All legislators now represent single member districts, but five of the fourteen council seats (plus the Mayor and Controller) run at-large in the City.

- **Influence of business on regional issues.** In addition to these structural factors, a number of political considerations contributed to a regional bias in making most public policy decisions in the Houston area. One significant factor, for example, is the great influence historically exercised in Houston by pro-growth business leaders. Typically, these were White males who had come to Houston as young men to make their fortunes, succeeded, and then worked to ensure the engines of growth that enriched them continue for future generations. While unabashed supporters of free enterprise conservatism in general, they looked to government to provide the needed infrastructure for sustained economic development. So while Houston was characterized as a low-tax, low-service city, most business leaders were supportive of building the docks, airports, water systems, and flood control structures required for the region to prosper.

Like Atlanta leaders, Houston business leaders worked to minimize racial conflicts for both moral and practical reasons. Rarely holding public office themselves, leaders like Jesse Jones, George R. Brown, and Leon Jaworski sought regional solutions to regional problems. Generous supporters of federal, state, and local candidates, they usually found ways to get things done for Houston. There were, of course, notable disagreements among business leaders (Jesse Jones and Hugh Roy Cullen fought over zoning for 30 years), but they were able to reach a consensus on most issues that they deemed important to Houston's future.

- **Minimum amount of political opposition.** Selling that pro-growth consensus was usually possible in the Houston area. Most voters, like the elites, were Whites who had moved to Houston for economic reasons. They were not rich, but most were considerably better off than their relations in rural areas and small towns across Texas and the South. Blacks were largely excluded from the political process until the 1960s, and when they became significant players, their priorities did not often clash with business leaders.

    Alternative power bases to challenge local private and public elites were few and ineffective. Political parties were almost entirely focused on federal elections until the 1970s, and then only gradually began to contest state and finally local offices. City politics were officially and unofficially non-partisan. Labor unions were weak, ethnic and community organizations largely ineffective, and participation in elections was low.

    City-suburban conflicts were muted by the relative lack of difference between people inside and outside incorporated areas. Outside the incorporated areas there was an absence of political community in many new suburban areas as well as a widespread expectation—and acceptance—that the City would eventually annex the area, as it had previous growth zones.

In sum, while Houston did not join Miami, Jacksonville, Nashville, and Indianapolis in a formal city/county consolidation, area leaders found the ways and means over the years to address the regional needs of one of the fastest growing metropolises in the country. But over the last 20 years or so that ability has clearly declined, for reasons we next turn to.

FRAGMENTATION THREATENING REGIONALISM

Houston's unique combination of structural and political elements that encouraged or at least permitted a regional focus have been undermined in important regards. The most important structural changes include:

- **Erosion of the City of Houston's preeminent position.** The political costs of annexation increased sharply in the 1970s as evidenced by Clear Lake's long, but ultimately losing fight to avoid incorporation. Political leaders have been less willing to pay those costs since that struggle, so annexation slowed dramatically in the 1980s, leaving the City with a shrinking share of the region's population.

    The Federal Voting Rights Act and tighter state rules now give the City less leeway than was the case before the Clear Lake annexation. The City remains the single most powerful entity in the metropolitan area, but it has been fighting to keep its regional prerogatives even as it uses them less and less.

- **Changes in Harris County's role and influence.** Harris County has assumed more of a regional burden but remains hobbled by restrictive state rules that require legislative authorization for most new county initiatives and a governmental structure that is highly fragmented. In addition, a significant share of the metropolitan population (close to 15 percent and rising) now resides outside the Harris County lines in surrounding counties. In the 1960s the County was the appropriate bonding authority for the Astrodome, but in the 1990s a larger regional tax base may be required for supporting regional projects such as sports stadia.

- **Changes in political districts.** Today most elected officials aside from judges represent single member districts in the Houston area, few of which bear much resemblance to the overall regional population. Members are understandably more focused on narrower constituent interests than was the case in the 1960s or 1970s. About half the area legislators have non-City of Houston electorates. This proportion will grow after the 2000 census.

- **Demographic changes.** Political diversity has tracked demographic change. White males dominated elective politics through the 1970s, but today Houston's public officials are far more reflective of the metropolitan population. Ethnic and gender differences are joined by sharper partisan splits. The regional legislative delegation is closely split between Democrats and Republicans, with most City members in the former group and suburban members in the latter.

- **Changes in Houston's business community.** The region's business community is larger, and less unified than 20 years ago. Building a consensus within groups like the Greater Houston Partnership is much more difficult than was the case in the old Chamber of Commerce, not to mention the [elite business group] of the 1940s and 1950s.

- **More cynical political climate.** The general political climate has become more cynical, making leadership more difficult at all levels of government. City officials are now constrained by harsh term limits. In addition, the initiative process means that even when City officials agree on a major policy change, it may very well be taken to a public vote with uncertain results.

- **Suburban residents have gotten more feisty.** Many suburban residents have now lived in unincorporated communities for 20–25 years. Most either intentionally left the City of Houston or moved here from incorporated suburbs in other parts of the country. The idea of forcible annexation without a local vote is anathema to most. And, especially in upscale planned communities like The Woodlands, Kingwood, and much of the area, residents have significant political resources to resist annexation. They will not go quietly as did many annexed residents in the 1950s, 1960s, and 1970s.

Taken together, these factors make it far more difficult for local leaders to seek regional solutions to area problems. The region continues to change, and new problems arise, but the governmental sector is basically static, frozen in place since the 1970s. Regional cooperation as currently exists is largely ad hoc, as in response to the threatened loss of Houston's sports teams. Can Houston do better? In our view, yes.

A Window of Opportunity

While recognizing the evident difficulties, there are good reasons for optimism in addressing the problems that confront the Houston metropolitan area.

Houston city leaders worry that Houston could go the way of St. Louis or Detroit in the twenty-first century—declining into a poorer, under populated, mostly minority urban core abandoned by all who are able to leave.

Suburban communities are in limbo. Most are unable to incorporate, but resist being forcibly annexed at some uncertain date. Opinion surveys show modest public interest in local governmental structures in general, but strong feelings that some things need to be dealt with locally (public schools, public safety, neighborhood upkeep), while there is a general acceptance that other problems (economic development, the environment, transportation) require regional solutions. This ambivalence gives local leaders some opportunities to try new approaches that combine a significant degree of local autonomy in some areas with area-wide means in others.

Reason for Optimism

Houston's unique demographics also provide reason for optimism. The city-suburban split is not nearly as pronounced as in many large metropolitan areas. White flight occurred from the City in the 1960s and 1970s as public schools desegregated, concerns about public safety rose, and developers used special utility districts in unincorporated areas to create affordable housing. But the oil busts of the 1980s, with a net loss of nearly 200,000 jobs, caused property values to plummet in many suburban areas and eased the ability of minority residents to follow Whites into the suburbs.

As a result, between 1984 and 1996 Houston has become one of the most desegregated metropolitan areas in the United States. . . .

In 1970 [downtown] areas were densely populated (138,493 residents) and overwhelmingly African American (86.3 percent). But over the next 20 years there was a massive out-migration as areas like the Fifth Ward and Third

Ward lost over half their populations. By 1990, the total African-American population in these inner city neighborhoods had fallen from 119,518 to just 46,319, a decline of 61.2 percent. At the same time, the Hispanic and other non-Black population was growing. As a result, African Americans made up just 55.8 percent of the population counted in 1990.

When African Americans moved out of older inner city neighborhoods, they did not migrate into adjacent Anglo or Hispanic neighborhoods. Instead, they followed the white migratory patterns of the 1960s and 1970s and relocated to growing suburban areas where housing had become much more affordable, schools had better reputations, and crime rates were lower.

For the same reasons, much of the new Hispanic growth of the 1980s also occurred in suburban areas. [L]arge demographic shift[s] occurred in five largely Anglo school districts from 1975 to 1995. In 1975 these districts on the western side of Houston's metropolitan area had fewer than 8,000 African-American and Hispanic students, or just 10 percent of the total enrolled student population. By 1995 there were 67,317 African-American and Hispanic children enrolled in these districts, or 37.3 percent of the total enrollment.

At the same time that minority growth has been shifting to the suburban and unincorporated areas, there has been a modest but growing increase in the Anglo population inside the Loop. Inner city Houston, like Washington, D.C., is getting "Whiter" in the 1990s as the outer suburban areas become less Anglo in population makeup. Consequently, the concerns about racial and economic "tipping" that David Rusk expresses in his book *Cities Without Suburbs,* seem less relevant in the Houston metropolitan area. Consequently, the economic and racial/ethnic disparities between the central city and suburbs are narrowing, not increasing. Houston is not Detroit, nor it is likely to become such in the foreseeable future. Seattle may be a more appropriate and comparative case, where inner-city revitalization has accelerated around the downtown area.

The economic vitality of the City of Houston (which includes the great proportion of highly compensated jobs in the area and most suburban commercial centers) and the extreme fragmentation of the unincorporated areas where 400 municipal utility districts deliver basic services, create opportunities for positive sum solutions where both areas gain. This win/win opportunity is essential given the relative balance of political power between the City of Houston and unincorporated areas because it is unlikely that one party can force a regional governance solution at this point in time. The devolution of federal authority back to states and localities is increasing pressure for communities to find local solutions to urban problems. With less federal money and controls, Houston, like other cities, will be under increasing pressure to improve the delivery of public services.

A final reason for optimism is a growing recognition among civic leaders that the old governance structures are increasingly inadequate as the urban area steadily expands, and changes internally. Houston's leaders have a well-deserved reputation as "can-do" people who have historically risen to meet new challenges to the community's growth and prosperity. That spirit is essential again in addressing the growing problems of one of the most dynamic metropolitan areas in the country.

38. Metropolitan Citizens in St. Louis

E. Terrence Jones and Elaine Hays

The efforts to create regional governments and metropolitan decision-making processes have most often failed because people don't feel like metropolitan citizens. Sample surveys in St. Louis and its suburbs reveal the attitudes of citizens about different aspects of metropolitan governance. Presumably, these are very similar to the attitudes held by citizens in different cities and suburbs in the country. Changing those attitudes will be central to any successful efforts at improving coordination and governance at a metropolitan level.

WHY METROPOLITAN CITIZENSHIP MATTERS

As urbanization has spilled first past central city boundaries and then beyond suburban units during the twentieth century, the metropolitan areas created by this diffusion have struggled with how to make collective decisions about entire regions which now encompass thousands of square miles and include hundreds of governments. Individual municipalities and counties remain fully capable of dealing with issues confined within their boundaries—building codes or traffic enforcement, for example—but an increasing number of problems—air quality and transportation networks, to name two—are arguably best handled at the metropolitan level.

The past five decades have seen numerous attempts to develop and implement regional decision making structures and procedures. Some are formal like Minneapolis-St. Paul's Metropolitan Council, an overarching body responsible for selected functions, or Jacksonville-Duval County, a merged central city and urban county. Others are more fluid and ad hoc, like Chattanooga's visioning initiative or Chicago's Metropolis 2020.

These efforts to develop "regionalism on purpose" have usually been top-down projects. Some members of the region's elites, most often drawn from the corporate community, have determined that greater centralization is needed. The typical rationales given to justify these reforms are to achieve lower costs through economies of scale or to enhance economic competitiveness with other regions. The efficiency argument dominated the earlier years of regionalism, the 1950s and the 1960s, while the intrametropolitan contest for jobs and tourism has emerged more recently.

Everyday citizens have occasionally acquiesced in shifting some decisions from smaller to larger governmental units or public-private partnerships but they have not been the driving force. For them, localism has been and continues to be the prevailing focus. As Gerald Benjamin and Richard P. Nathan

SOURCE: From a paper prepared for a poster session at the American Political Science Association meeting, September 1, 2001. Reprinted by permission of the authors.

note, "although local government boundaries may seem irrational to people interested in changing political structures to advance regional purposes, many citizens carefully pick the places in which they live and work and come to identify strongly with them."

Within the United States, there have long been three citizenships: national, state, and local. But as regions increasingly become more important for each person's quality of life, as their individual well-being becomes more associated with how their region is faring in the intraregional competition, they must also become metropolitan citizens. As Clyde Mitchell-Weaver and David Miller comment, "if metropolitan regionalism is to take root in more than a few favored locations, . . . a critical factor is the political elaboration of a new popular feeling of regional citizenship." Put more bluntly by John Baricevic, St. Clair County (Illinois) Board Chairman, "it's not easy being a regional leader if there are no regional followers."

STUDY DESIGN

To probe what kind of collective purpose exists among the citizenry within today's more complex metropolitan areas and what, if anything, explains which residents have how much of it, we surveyed a probability sample of 800 persons in the St. Louis metropolitan area in March 1999. The respondents represent all persons 18 or older living in a household with a residential telephone in the eight largest counties in the St. Louis (Missouri-Illinois) region. The Missouri units of government are the City of St. Louis, St. Louis County, Franklin County, Jefferson County, and St. Charles County, while the Illinois units are Madison County, Monroe County, and St. Clair County. These counties constituted the St. Louis Metropolitan Statistical Area prior to 1990 and presently have over 95 percent of the population in the expanded 12-county MSA.

The completed interviews were weighted by age, gender, and county to match the age/gender distribution within the 1990 U.S. Census and the 1999 populations as estimated by the St. Louis Chapter of the American Statistical Association. The study was sponsored by the East-West Gateway Coordinating Council, the metropolitan planning organization for the St. Louis region.

We explored four aspects of regionalism:

1. *Connectedness:* To what extent do citizens see that the quality of life in their local community is linked with what happens in other portions of the metropolitan area?
2. *Decision Level:* Which level of government (municipality, county, regional body) is best able to make decisions for land use planning, air and water environmental regulation, transportation planning, economic development, and parks and open space?
3. *Equity:* Should the more affluent areas within the region assist the less well off segments?
4. *Representation:* Should local government elected officials be more concerned about what is best for their own local community or for what is best for the entire region?

MEASURING REGIONALISM: CONNECTEDNESS

St. Louis is one of many metropolitan areas where the central city has been experiencing hard times. Population and jobs have dropped dramatically over the past 50 years, poverty levels have risen, and housing abandonment increased. At the same time, most of the remaining parts of the region have fared well. To what extent do the approximately 85 percent living outside the City of St. Louis see its problems affecting their communities?

Not much. Only 7 percent say there is a very close "connection between the quality of life in the City of St. Louis and the quality of life in [their] local community," 34 percent reply somewhat close, 56 percent not very close, and 3 percent express no opinion.

Looking inward out rather than outward in, residents in the more settled parts of the Missouri side of the region—the City of St. Louis and St. Louis County—were asked about the links between their areas and the three suburban/exurban counties bordering them. This trio—Franklin, Jefferson, and St. Charles—have collectively grown from about one hundred thousand persons in 1950 to approximately six hundred thousand today. Again, the bonds are tenuous; 11 percent characterize the connection as very close, 46 percent as somewhat close, 31 percent not very close, and 12 percent have no opinion.

Like many other metropolitan areas such as Chicago, Kansas City, Philadelphia, and Washington, the St. Louis region crosses state lines with the Mississippi River dividing it between Illinois (about 20 percent of the population) and Missouri (approximately 80 percent). Neither state's residents see much connection between their local community and the other state although, as the more dependent entity, the links are slightly stronger for the Illinoisans; 6 percent of them characterize the connection as very close, 58 percent somewhat close, 29 percent not very close, and 7 percent have no opinion. For Missourians, the response distribution is 5 percent very close, 34 percent somewhat close, 40 percent not very close, and 21 percent no opinion.

Measuring Regionalism: Decision Level

As many metropolitan areas have shifted responsibility for policy making from a smaller government like a municipality or a county to a larger unit such as a special district or a metropolitan planning organization, policies which have obvious regional implications have been the ones first to be transferred. Common among these are land use planning (e.g., a broad master plan), air and water environmental regulations (e.g., regional air control standards), transportation planning (e.g., an integrated plan for public transit and highways), economic development (e.g., a targeted region-wide strategy), and providing parks and open space (e.g., a trail system for the entire metropolitan area).

Among three options for making these decisions—the local municipality, the county government, or some regional organization—the regional approach fails to receive majority backing for any of the five policy areas although a plurality prefers it for air and water environmental regulation (46 percent, followed by the county at 20 percent and the local municipality at

19 percent) and transportation planning (40 percent, trailed by 27 percent for the municipality and 19 percent for the county).

Municipalities—the most local alternative—remain the top selection for land use planning (41 percent with the county and a regional body each receiving 22 percent), providing parks and open space (41 percent with 23 percent for the county and 21 percent for the municipality), and economic development (33 percent with 29 percent for the regional body and 21 percent for the county).

Measuring Regionalism: Equity

With the exception of Minneapolis-St. Paul property tax sharing scheme, no metropolitan area has a policy in place that systematically shifts some revenues to less prosperous portions of the region. What redistribution that exists within the U.S. political system occurs largely through the federal taxation system, primarily individual and corporate income taxes. Nevertheless, residents are open to the concept; 62 percent say they favor and just 23 percent oppose "a proposal which would have the better off parts of the St. Louis metropolitan area share some of their tax revenues to help meet the needs of the worse off parts of the area." Another 8 percent would want more specifics before committing one way or the other and 7 percent have no opinion.

Moving from a generic expression to a more concrete suggestion, given two options for dealing with inner-city issues, 58 percent select "problems in places like the City of St. Louis and East St. Louis affect all communities within the St. Louis metropolitan area and so everyone should help solve them" while 32 percent choose "people in places like the City of St. Louis and East St. Louis should solve their own problems and not expect the people in the suburbs and rural area to help." These results roughly parallel those from a January 1998 survey of 1,725 Cleveland metropolitan area citizens: 58 percent disagreed but 41 percent agreed that "people in bigger cities like Cleveland, Akron, and Lorain should solve their own problems (and) people in the suburbs and rural areas should not be expected to help."

Measuring Regionalism: Representation

One of the challenges faced by elected officials is where their primary loyalties lie. Should members of Congress, for example, place a higher priority on the needs of their districts or should they emphasize the overall interests of the country? Applying this dilemma to the metropolitan level, 67 percent reply that "when local government elected officials are making decisions," they should be more concerned about "what is best for the entire St. Louis metropolitan area" and just 21 percent think that they should stress "what is best for their own local community." Again, the results are quite similar to those found in the Cleveland region where 66 percent said "what is best for the entire Northeast Ohio area" should be more important while 21 percent indicate that they should do "what is best for their own community."

Measuring Regionalism: Interrelationships

Is regional citizenship a unifying perspective, one which combines connectedness, decision level, equity, and representation? Or are each of these separate and distinct dimensions where some citizens score highly regional on one but not on the others? To help address this question, cumulative scores were constructed for each of the four aspects of regionalism and then correlated with one another.

The results show that three of the four facets—decision level, equity, and representation—are all interrelated. Individuals who prefer having regional bodies making decisions of policies like land use and economic development also disproportionately support redistributing taxes from the more to less affluent portions within a region and back having their local elected officials place primary emphasis on regional concerns when making judgments. Conversely, those who opt for having municipalities or counties handle the selected policies are more likely to oppose shifting revenues and having their mayors or county councilpersons give too much weight to metropolitan-wide interests.

Connectedness, on the other hand, is only significantly related to equity with a greater sense of togetherness leading to higher support for redistribution. There are no links, positive or negative, between connectedness and either decision level or representation. This means that a sense of mutual interdependency contributes to burden sharing but does not spill over into greater support for regional bodies or for local elected officials to emphasize regional factors.

WHO ARE THE REGIONALISTS: PERSONAL VARIABLES

Demographically, which types of citizens are most likely to be region-minded citizens? Earlier studies of voting on urban reform issues, conducted during the 1950s and 1960s when many proposals for local government consolidation were on the ballot, pointed to social class as key factor. Those with more years of formal education are apt to be more regional, supposedly because they appreciate the need for a more comprehensive approach. So, too, those with greater incomes should understand the interdependence within metropolitan areas.

Education matters significantly for three of the four dimensions, all except connectedness. For decision level, equity, and representation, the more formal learning people have, the more regional their perspective. Income, on the other hand, is only a factor for decision level where those with higher earnings are more supportive of having regional bodies make the determination. Wealthier individuals are no more likely, however, to support burden sharing or having their local representatives assign greater weight to regional factors.

Younger citizens, especially those under thirty, are more regional on equity and representation It could very well be that younger adults are less rooted in their immediate local communities and more open to a broader view. African Americans and parents of children 17 or under are more likely to support burden sharing, perhaps because most would be net beneficiaries of such policies. On the other hand, there is no relationship between gender and metropolitanism.

WHO ARE THE REGIONALISTS: CONTEXTUAL VARIABLES

Where one resides matters when it comes to regionalism. Dividing the St. Louis metropolitan areas into three segments according to how dense its development—urban (high density), suburban (moderate density), and exurban (low density), the urban segment is distinctly more metropolitan-minded on all four dimensions and the suburban component is more regional than the exurban on decision level and representation. It is easier to appreciate the interdepedency looking from the inside out than from the outside in.

Living in a racially diverse neighborhood, on the other hand, does not lead to greater support for regionalism nor does it matter whether one is in an incorporated or unincorporated area. Although one might anticipate that variety in the immediate environment might lead to greater acceptance of regional interdependence, such is not the case. Being a municipal citizen might conceivably lead to being less metropolitan (more loyalty to the local government) or more so (added support for governmental services) but neither seems to be the case.

CONCLUDING COMMENTS

Despite many scholarly assertions that, at least economically and ecologically, metropolitan area residents are indeed all in it together, a great many St. Louis metropolitan residents do not yet accept the message. At best, one in ten think the connections across counties and state boundaries are very close and substantial minorities see almost no interdependency. Until more citizens accept and embrace this key tenet, metropolitan-wide initiatives will never be seen as essential as opposed to possibly desirable.

The mixed support for centralizing decisions for selected policies is more encouraging. Eighteen months after this survey was conducted, for example, strong majorities in the St. Louis region's five largest counties voted to establish parallel park districts and to fund them with a one-tenth of a cent sales tax, providing half the proceeds remain in the home county. The dollars headed toward regional purposes will largely be used for a metropolitan-wide trail network.

Having majorities backing redistributive policies and encouraging their elected officials to weigh regional factors higher than local concerns must be interpreted with more skepticism. Assisting those in need and embracing the greater metropolitan interest are, of course, the socially respectable responses. When the issue is stated abstractly, many are predisposed to say the "right" thing. Here, as in most public policy debates, the devil lies in the details. In April 2000, for example, St. Louis Countians, the largest jurisdiction within the region, rejected a use tax which would have modestly shifted levy proceeds on out-of-state purchases from the more to the less affluent communities. In the survey, they backed redistribution as a principle. At the polls, they rejected a specific proposal.

A recent commentary on regionalism states that "if a substantial percentage of regional residents declare, and practice, their regional citizenship, they can successfully tackle almost any regional challenge (but) if only a small percentage are committed to regional cooperation, they can tackle few challenges successfully." If St. Louisans are any measure, metropolitan citizenship has considerable room to grow.

Chapter 11

Changes in Urban Politics Since September 11, 2001

U rban politics has changed since September 11 and we don't fully understand all the implications yet. In the month immediately following the terrorist attacks, some newspaper columnists wondered if the terrorists could undo American cities in ways that previous crises haven't. Could we be thrown back into the days of high crime, fear, and middle-class flight to the suburbs after the successful 1990s in which many cities made a major comeback from earlier problems?[1] Thus far, we seem to have escaped these reversals.

However, our cities have become terrorist targets. Savitch and Ardashev explore why terrorism so often occurs in cities and why global cities, in particular, are frequent targets. Their data demonstrates that cities indeed are most often the sites of terrorist attacks. We cannot expect that we will be free of such attacks no matter how good our defenses against them may become. So occasional acts of terrorism are a new urban reality for Americans in the twenty-first century.

The September 11 attacks on cities have also affected urban scholarship.[2] The costs to New York City are fairly clear in terms of lost revenue and the cost of rebuilding the section of the city that was destroyed. But what about cities that did not suffer these attacks directly—what is the collateral damage from these events? On the one hand, smaller and weaker units of local government were badly harmed as were state governments, which depended upon sales and income taxes as a major source of income. By 2002, for instance, the state of Illinois was cutting its budget by 6 percent and its workforce by 4,500 state employees as well as closing prisons and making Medicaid cutbacks, which closed private hospitals. Illinois faced further major cuts in social services and local government funding because of an overall debt in 2003 of $5 billion if major budget changes were not made. Many state governments faced even worse cutbacks. *Governing* magazine estimates that states' total debt by 2002 alone was more than $40 billion and that the situation would only worsen in 2003.[3]

School district deficits soared even before the current recession with Texas owing $1.89 billion; Michigan, $926 million; Illinois $917 million; and Pennsylvania, $818 million during the 1998–1999 school year. Illinois Governor George Ryan's proposed 2002–2003 state budget would cut $100 million from state subsidies for education, $40 million of which was proposed to be cut from the Chicago Public Schools. In many states, half of the school districts showed expenses exceeding revenues and these are not one-time deficits but repeated deficits, which only grew in the period of recession following the September 11 attacks. In Illinois under a new Democratic Governor, Rod Blagojevich, school financial cutbacks continued to mount.

The editors of the *Urban Affairs Review* report that in the quarter ending September 2001, general state tax collections were down 3.4 percent and city revenue collections declined about 4 percent. Certainly, state budgets had major cuts in 2002, but cities seem to have fared better than expected. For instance, the $4.6 billion budget for the city of Chicago in 2002 rose by only $101 million from 2001, and it did not require the cutbacks that were feared. Mild winters in 2002 and 2003 saved the city $10 million in snow-removal costs and cuts in nonpersonnel expenses along with 625 employee layoffs kept the Chicago city budget in balance. In 2003 Chicago had another $116 million cut and now has the smallest city workforce since the reign of Richard J. Daley in 1976. Cities have less reliance on sales and income taxes than state governments and were able to weather the recession better, but cutbacks in both state and federal funding are now having negative impacts, including political fallout like the recall of Governor Gray Davis of California.

Cities that had been relying much more on tourism dollars (and various tourism taxes such as the hotel tax, sales tax, and entertainment taxes) were hurt in the immediate aftermath of September 11 when tourism to all U.S. cities plummeted. It is uncertain when tourism will flourish in American cities once more. At the same time cities were losing revenues, costs for public safety and public health were greater without new funds from the federal government to cover these additional costs.

It may be too soon to render a final verdict. We don't know the final effects of the September 11 attacks. We know that as Americans were changed individually by these events, so will our cities be changed in the decade ahead. The recession that has continued after the Iraq War reversed many of the gains that cities had made in the affluent 1990s.

Paul Kantor has argued that "New York City's experience suggest that the hand of terrorism is profoundly changing urban politics. The events of 9/11 struck a city that was already serious off balance due to long-building sources of political fragmentation and exclusion that obstruct political leadership, making it difficult to overcome festering social divisions or steer the city in new directions." Political and governmental problems that existed before 9/11 were exacerbated by the terrorist attacks and the recession that followed.

In a journal article on the effects of 9/11, I argued that "Despite the impacts of September 11, Chicago politics and government have remained mostly unchanged, although the Chicago City Council has become more of a rubber stamp council. Chicago's future depends on success in preventing future terrorist attacks in the United States, on Chicago's not being attacked, and on decisions by private firms to continue to locate and build in central cities."[4] On the other hand, Richard Murray, Bob Stein, and Stephanie Post in their study of Houston since September 11, maintained that Houston weathered the attacks rather well despite a continuing economic recession depressing the local economy. No change in Houston's politics are expected as a result and the mayor was successfully reelected in the spring of 2002.[5] Houston was even one of the few American cities to gain jobs in 2002. So the effect was different in different cities.

But there is at least one common result. Neal Pierce argues that the combination of the terrorist attacks of September 11, the cost of the Iraq War, and the tax and budget policies of President Bush have resulted in "a fiscal Code Orange." States and cities are under major fiscal constraints, which are making the task of governing them more difficult.

It is not yet known whether the New York, Chicago, or Houston experiences are typical of most U.S. cities. What is the situation in your city or suburb? Will the economic recession following September 11 accelerate deterioration in local politics or government? Does it depend on whether or not there are further attacks? Or has politics and government in your community simply gone back to politics as usual?

Notes

1. See Clarence Page, "Terrorists Have Also Threatened Urban Recovery," *Chicago Tribune,* October 21, 2001, Section 1, p. 19.
2. See Susan Clarke, et al., "Urban Scholarship After September 11, 2001," *Urban Affairs Review,* Vol. 37, No. 3, January 2002, pp. 460–467.
3. Penelope Lemov, "Deficit Deluge," *Governing,* May 2002, p.20.
4. Dick Simpson with Ola Adeoye, Ruben Feliciano, and Rick Howard, "Chicago's Uncertain Future Since September 11, 2001," *Urban Affairs Review,* Vol. 38, No. 1, September 2002, p. 128.
5. Richard Murray, Robert Stein, and Stephanie Post, "Houston's Future After 9/11," http://www.uh.edu/cpp/lanierconference_papers.htm.

39. Terrorism in Cities

H. V. Savitch with Grigoriy Ardashev

This article was written before the September 11 terrorist attack and updated with minor revisions. The authors conclude that terror is more common in cities. It originates in places with high social breakdown but is transmitted to globally oriented, target-prone cities. It is a new urban reality.

An unmistakable transition has occurred in which cities have become the central venues of terror. Not only has terrorism taken on a global cast with international linkages, it is also apparent that cities have become the stage on which this tragic drama is played. There are many reasons why this has occurred. For one, the assets of cities make them rich targets. Densely packed and heterogeneous with a great mix of industrial and commercial infrastructure, cities are the wellsprings of prosperity and economic growth.

SOURCE: H. V. Savitch with Grigoriy Ardashev, "Does terror have an urban future?" *Urban Studies,* Vol. 38, No. 13, (September, 2001), pp. 2515–2533. Available online at http://www.tandf.co.uk/journals/carfax/00420980.html. Reprinted by permission of Taylor and Francis, Ltd., and the authors.

This is not just true of the post-industrial world, but also of less developed nations. Research shows that, amongst the poorest nations, cities remain their major source of hope. The migration from the countryside to the urban *favelas* of Latin America and shanty-towns of Africa provides ample evidence of a search for economic survival in cities.

Secondly, cities have become "nodes" for a vast international network of communications. Economic complexity and global interdependence have converted cities into powerful command centres, directing billions of dollars in investment, managing millions of people and controlling thousands of work sites around the globe. This may be an enormous sign of power, but it is also a very visible sign of vulnerability. A well-placed explosion can produce enormous reverberations and paralyse a city. This, in fact, was the motive behind the bombing of New York's World Trade Center in 1993 and 2001. The simple idea of collapsing two buildings in a highly populated, densely built, "global city" not only damages people and property, but also creates a contagion of fear and economic rupture.

Thirdly, urban heterogeneity puts different social groups in close proximity to one another. While social pluralism provides rich synergies, under certain conditions it can be a nesting-ground for terrorist organisations. A sense of relative deprivation sharpens as different groups come into closer proximity. Word gets around more quickly and socialisation proceeds more rapidly in densely packed environments. This kind of environment provides an abundant source of recruitment for potential terrorists. Beirut provides a ready example of how different groups living under conditions of hopelessness and in proximity to one another can engage in mutual attack. Similar ecologies of terror also pervade Belfast, Sarajevo and Hyderabad. Rather than directed from lower classes upwards towards élites, terror and conflict occur between groups operating at the same level—Hindus fighting Muslims in Bombay or rival criminal gangs in Bogota. Religious groups or underworld gangs simply battle it out.

Lastly, cities have considerable symbolic value. They are not only dense agglomerations of people and buildings, but guardians of national prestige and assets. They hold the tangible symbols of military, political and financial power for great national powers. A blast in a mountain town or in the countryside may arouse local concern, but is generally of little or no consequence for the rest of the world. But an attack on Wall Street, a massacre in Piccadilly Circus, the bombing of the Eiffel Tower, or poison gas in a Tokyo metro arouses international alarm. Any such event will be instantly telegraphed to a larger world and will provoke a much larger audience. If terrorists thrive on anything, it is media attention and widespread recognition. Graphic images of terror can be used both to intimidate the public and to enlist its sympathy. Publicity acquired through less violent means also serves the terrorists' cause—not just because it introduces them to the world, but also because it induces a sense of vulnerability into the population at large. There are two sides to this tactic. On the one side, vulnerability entails the dread of attack and mass fear. On the other side, it softens up the opposition, predisposing it to try to "understand" the terrorist cause. Liberal societies, accustomed to tolerance, are apt to wonder why individuals would resort to such brutal, impersonal acts and even blame themselves for provoking terrorism. Broadcasting the other side's position makes the public sensitive to the grievances that motivate terrorists, enabling potential sympathisers to come to the fore. Media attention and constant publicity also impart terrorist causes with quasi legitimacy. The more one hears about a set of grievances, the greater the chance it will gain a place on the public agenda and become part of a wider discourse.

Finally, media attention strengthens the bargaining hand of those who resort to violence, by allowing quasi terrorist organisations and their allies to identify alternative paths to reconciliation. During the 1970s and 1980s, Palestinian terrorists hijacked planes demanding that authorities negotiate directly with them. By the 1990s, a substantial part of that movement had managed to portray themselves as a nonviolent alternative to more radical "rejectionists." In effect, the cessation of terror became a bargaining chip, based on the idea that people would prefer to deal with more moderate and predictable elements than face "uncontrollable consequences."

This paper explores the extent to which cities have become the targets of terror and the tactics involved. More theoretically, we address the issue of whether there is something intrinsic to cities in a newly globalised world and something unique in their role as nerve-centres of an international economy that puts them at higher risk. We also examine the question of what kinds of cities are most vulnerable to terror. Put simply, we ask whether terror has shown a disproportionate and rising presence in cities, where has this occurred and what best explains this occurrence.

CITIES AS TARGETS FOR TERROR

Researchers well know that rising urbanisation is also accompanied by an increasing gross national product. The logic behind this suggests that cities convert surplus products into other uses and operate more efficiently to make wealth possible. But what might be the association between urbanisation and terror? Does terror or do more collective forms of violence occur in conjunction with rising urbanisation? A number of scholars have suggested that there is no causal relationship between cities and terror (defined more broadly to include all types of security such as crime and public safety). They claim that there are few clear linkages between urbanisation and most dimensions of security.

There is a point to this position. Using a narrow definition of insecurity as acts of terror, we find no correlation between levels of urbanisation and incidents of terror. . . .

[T]rying to determine whether rising levels of urbanisation are related to terror is not the same as examining whether cities are more or less vulnerable to terror. The proposition that urbanisation is not strongly related to terror or collective violence may be true. But its converse, that terror or collective violence is related to concentrated urban environments may also be true. Not all cities are ripe for terror, but some cities may be especially susceptible to terror.

TERROR AND THE URBAN-RURAL DICHOTOMY

As defined here, terrorism consists of international, violent attacks upon people and property, often with little discrimination, in order to intimidate them and instil widespread fear. In order to expand the sphere of intimidation, terrorists show that anyone can be vulnerable to attack. Richardson puts an

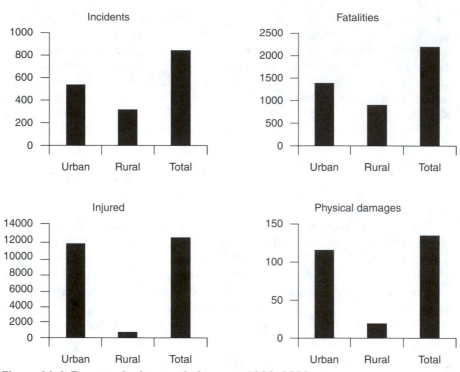

Figure 11.1 Terror and urban-rural cleavage, 1993–2000
SOURCE: US Department of State (1993–2000).

TABLE 11.1   Terrorist Incidents, 1993–2000

	Total Incidents	Fatalities	Injured	Physical Damage
Urban	534	1,326	11,762	117
Rural	306	829	769	19
Total	840	2,155	12,531	136

SOURCE: U.S. Department of State.

accent on the symbolic character of terrorist targets and describes terrorist acts as a method "to communicate a message to a broader audience." For all these reasons, terror is associated with acts of random violence, aimed at almost any segment in a given society. Most people can be struck by it, regardless of whether they are noncombatants, children, teenagers or the elderly. This randomness puts everyone in a target area at risk and heightens the capacity for intimidation. The governmental literature on terrorism provides complementary definitions. The U.S. Department of State defines terrorism as

premeditated, politically motivated violence, perpetrated against noncombatant targets by sub-national groups or clandestine agents, usually intended to influence a wider audience.

Here the emphasis is also put on "subnational groups" or "clandestine agents," and this has become an increasingly prominent characteristic of terror. During the past 30 years, terror has often been carried out by secret groups lacking an address, rather than by states that can be held accountable. To be sure, some states like Libya, Syria, Iran and North Korea conduct state-sponsored terrorism. However, international condemnation exerts substantial pressure and most of these states are anxious to erase that mark of disrepute.

We proceed with the simplest dichotomy between "urban" and "rural" areas. Figure 11.1 displays incidents of terror within each of these distinct areas. Incidents are broken down according to outcome (people killed, injured, or incidents of property damage).

Within a span of just eight years, cities incurred over 500 such incidents and over 13,000 casualties. More than 250 cities across the globe experienced at least one terrorist act. Note, too, a higher incidence of terror in cities than occurred in rural areas. The total number of urban incidents is more than a third higher than elsewhere. The number of persons killed in cities constitutes 61 percent of total fatalities, while the proportion of people injured zooms to 94 percent of total injuries. Not surprisingly, urban terrorism takes more than six times the toll in physical damage.

With just a few exceptions, these data hold up—regardless of country or region. Even relatively rural nations or regions have a propensity to attract terror into urban cores. . . .

A PROFILE OF CITIES SUBJECT TO TERROR

We find an enormous range of cities subject to terror and neither industrial, demographic or geographical patterns readily emerge. The pattern varies from cities in less developed nations to advanced countries, from densely populated, close-knit cities to those resembling townships and from cities in western Europe to others in Africa and Asia. Putting this in more specific terms, Srinagar (India), Athens, Sanaa (Yemen), Paris, Istanbul and Lima led the list, followed closely by Jerusalem, Algiers and Dushanbe (Tajikistan). The largest number of fatalities occurred in Nairobi (291 killed in one incident). Following Nairobi are Colombo (108 killed in three incidents) and Jerusalem (77 killed in nine incidents). Injuries are another story and Nairobi (with 5,019) accounts for nearly half the total. Next are Colombo (1,510 injuries), New York (1,004 injuries in eight incidents) and Jerusalem (584 injuries). [Not included in the New York total are the 2823 killed on September 11, 2001.]

In just eight years, the number of incidents and physical damage more than doubled. Casualties also rose, although the trajectory is more irregular and with the high point occurring in 1998. We estimate that 64 percent of the brunt of terrorism is absorbed by cities. Whether or not there is a causal pattern to this kind of violence is not as significant as the consistent disproportion of urban incidents over the years.

What can we make of both the salience of terror in certain cities and its overall growth? Clearly, the symbolic value and strategic composition of cities have put them at the forefront of confrontation. While our analysis does not allow for prediction, we believe this is likely to continue. Harking back to our initial observations, there are other reasons why cities are so vulnerable. Cities are the media centres for the world. They contain international newspapers, news organisations, television and radio broadcasting studios. A terrorist attack in a strategic urban core is a shot heard instantly around the world. As one terrorist in Algeria expressed it

> Is it preferable for our cause to kill ten enemies in an *oued* (dry river bed) of Telergma when no one will talk of it . . . or [is it better to kill] a single man in Algiers, which will be noted the next day in the American press?

This logic explains why Paris, London and New York would be on the list. These cities are of a global class and central components in the world's media networks. It might also explain the role of "secondary world cities" like Athens, Istanbul, Jerusalem, Rome, Berlin and the like. For various reasons (geographical junctures between continents, religious centres, national capitals), these cities are vital links in the chain of international urban centres. Thus they too would yield big pay-offs for ambitious terrorists. But what explains terror in so many other cities? Why would cities like Srinagar, Sanaa, Lima and Dushanbe find themselves high on the list? By the standards of the International Monetary Fund, 22.5 percent of the cities where terror occurred are classified as advanced economies (Paris, Athens, New York, Jerusalem, Tel-Aviv, London, New York, Rome, Vienna). Many other terrorised cities are in developing or transitional economies (Sanaa, Addis Ababa, Nairobi, Lagos). Reconciling and explaining these differences require a broader framework and we now turn to that task.

SOCIAL BREAKDOWN, RESOURCE MOBILISATION AND TARGET-PRONENESS

As we see it, three factors contribute to the rise of urban terror. These factors are: social breakdown, resource mobilisation and target-proneness. Two of these factors—social breakdown and resource mobilisation—are directly drawn from the literature on collective violence and modified for our purposes. The third factor—target-proneness—is drawn from our own analysis of terror. These factors operate, both singularly and cumulatively, to lubricate, feed and steer urban terror. Essentially, we argue that cities with high cumulative standing on these factors also incur high levels of terror. These levels of terror are encapsulated in the terror score for each city. Taken in conjunction with our earlier discussion on the vulnerability and susceptibility of urban environments to terror, these factors help to explain its predominance in particular kinds of city. While the cumulative nature of these factors may not account for all cities experiencing terror, they do account for much of it. Finally, we speculate that past patterns of terror are likely to continue. . . .

We label our third factor "target-proneness" and define it as the incentives or values within a city that make it attractive to attack. Targeted cities have a high value for terrorists; either because they are global centres, and terrorists want to transmit an international message, or because they are proximate to conflict (availability) and terrorists are more concerned about conveying a localised (i.e., national) message. Although their means are brutal, terrorists are often "rational actors" willing to take risks in order to achieve highly valued ends. While different cities may be target-prone in different ways, all major cities offer the common advantage of high visibility and substantial resonance.

Global centres like Paris, London or New York possess enormous resources (stock exchanges, banks, embassies, news media, political capital, etc.). These are ideal cities that can be used to export the terrorist message, thereby gaining larger sympathy. Religious fundamentalists were anxious to use Paris as the object of attack because it was the visible seat of the French government and because of its international standing. Similarly, Irish Republican extremists used London because it embodied what was left of imperial Britain. In much the same way, Islamic fundamentalists first chose in 1993, and subsequently in 2001, New York's World Trade Center. More than anything else, the World Trade Center personified the might of U.S. capitalism, its global reach and the sheer material prosperity of the West. The very severe attacks in Nairobi and Aden were ways of violently assailing U.S. territory (respectively by bombing the embassy and exploding a warship).

At another extreme of target-proneness, we find cities like Srinagar, Lima, and Dushanbe. Terrorists choose these cities because they are most available and because their audience is localised—that is, for reasons of their own, terrorists have little motive to export their message to an international audience. These cities can be viewed as the nearest urban target and they can be seen as valuable hostages. Srinagar is at the seat of conflict between Islamic separatists and the Indian army over the fate of Kashmir. Terror cells are rooted in that city and operate against the Indian army on a constant basis. Control over Srinagar also symbolises dominance over the larger area of Kashmir. Lima is a prize sought by revolutionaries. The Peruvian struggle is largely confined to an insurrection carried out by the "Shining Path"—an organisation that is as much involved in criminal activities as in political revolution. In Dushanbe, religious extremists are also connected to international drug-trafficking. These organisations finance efforts to destabilise the region, stop democratic reforms and overturn secular regimes. Terrorist attacks aimed at establishing Islamic religious rule in Tajikistan are initiated from the northern parts of the republic that are beyond governmental control, yet they are most often carried out in Dushanbe.

A remaining group of target-prone cities combines elements of both high value and availability. In a sense, they are hybrids whose value may not be as high as world-class cities, but whose availability and importance to more localised conflicts are immense. Athens, Istanbul, and Jerusalem fall into this category. There are geopolitical reasons for this. These cities are located at the junctures of two worlds—West and East. They are major cities with high target value and all three are not just national capitals but have enormous significance as historic-symbolic sites. Athens is the seat of Western civilisation; it has a substantial economic base; and it is a transport crossroads for western Europe, the Balkans and the Middle East. Few cities better combine international visibility with being proximate to localised conflicts. Istanbul literally occupies two continents. It too has a substantial economic base and it occupies a similar position in the midst of localised ethnic and religious conflict. The last member of this urban triumvirate, Jerusalem, speaks for itself. It is amongst the world's best-known religious symbols; it is the seat of a vibrant economy and has an Anglophone media. Jerusalem also exemplifies the very essence of the Arab-Israeli conflict.

At least half of our international message cities lie at the global nerve-centre of the new economy. These include New York, London and Paris. A strike at any one of these has ramifications throughout the world. Any such attack could upset the flow of international finance, the value of capital equities and the management of multinational corporations. Two of the other cities in this category, Jerusalem and Athens, are flashpoints of international tension—respectively holding sacred religious sites and/or a unique geopolitical proximity to the source of conflict. Further down the line, Istanbul, Cairo, Vienna, and Rome also magnify the pay-off for terrorists. While not as deadly for international traffic, a strike in any one of these cities could be contagious, setting off waves of panic and military action.

All this highlights the fact that terror is exportable from socially deprived areas to socially privileged cities. Egyptians and Lebanese gravitate to New York. Algerian terrorists make their case in Paris. Irish Republican terrorists pronounce their wishes in London. Chechens are alleged to do the same in Moscow. The existence of transnational communities in these cities is an important component for successful attack because terrorists require some base of local support. Also, the contrast between the great, burgeoning wealth in these cities and the dire, unrelenting poverty of their fellow-nationals gives terrorists a rationale for retribution. While justifying terrorist brutality may not be easy, furnishing a reason for it is feasible. And a cogent rationale can bolster terrorist claims over issues of national rights (Albanians), economic inequity (radical Muslims) and social polarisation (Irish Catholics).

Finally, international message cities play a paramount role in the new "borderless world." These cities have begun to act as mini sovereignties, moving about to compete for the Olympic Games, court multinational corporations or sell their products abroad. Here we find ironies in how great cities have begun to refract the twin pressures of global economics and global warfare. While cities are increasingly free-floating and delinked from their national economies, so too has terrorist warfare become "borderless," similarly transcending national locations. Further, as globalisation evolves and cities attain a strategic niche in a fluid, market-driven world economy, terror too has been able to find its place in a new type of inchoate, formless warfare.

40. Terrorism and Governability in New York City

Paul Kantor

New York City's experience suggests that terrorism is profoundly changing urban politics. The events of September 11, 2001 struck a city that was already seriously off balance due to long-building sources of political fragmentation and exclusion. Despite Mayor Giuliani's image of control during the weeks of emergency, deeply rooted forces conspire against sustained governability. Since these problems are found in other cities, terrorism will pose similar problems for them.

There is little doubt that the tragedy of 9/11 has thrown New York City off course. The question is how much and in what ways. Despite recent boom years when New York appeared to be rebounding from days of urban crisis, the terrorist act has brought into sharp relief deeply rooted imbalances in the city's governance capacity. This problem assumes greater importance in the wake of the attack and is likely to confound the city's successful recovery. Furthermore, this dilemma will pose dangers elsewhere.

New York City's traditional political strength is its open, competitive, and pluralistic system of governance. Its traditional weakness is the excessively fragmented character of this political order. All too often, political conflicts are resolved by expanding budgets, launching new programs for special interests, and avoiding necessary fiscal retrenchment at times of declining revenues. Although political changes during the 1990s helped to check some of these tendencies, they never significantly altered the deeply rooted forces underpinning this system. Consequently, the city is politically unprepared to effectively plan or mobilize support for an effective recovery program.

During the 1970s, the state fiscal monitors that were established to restore the city's credit and contain its appetite for spending more or less displaced elected officeholders from strategic policy making. Their role gradually lifted after New York City reentered the bond market on its own after 1981. What emerged in subsequent years were disturbing signs of increasing fragmentation of decision-making power even as new mayoral electoral coalitions were emerging that seemed to promise greater order. This was due to three countervailing forces: the continued decay of traditional party politics, the flawed character of new mayoral electoral coalitions, and the proliferation of new independent governmental entities.

SOURCE: Paul Kantor, "Terrorism and Governability in New York City: Old Problem, New Dilemma," *Urban Affairs Review,* Vol. 38, No. 1, September 2002, pp. 120–127. Copyright © 2002 by Sage Publications. Reprinted by permission of the publisher, Sage Publications.

First, the decline of the Democratic Party as a balance wheel in imposing control over nominations, campaign fund-raising, and elections for local offices has hit an all-time low. Contenders for the major offices increasingly ignore party chieftains in electoral contests that have become increasingly candidate centered. Media campaigns, private fund-raising, and civil service union electioneering have now largely replaced the once-fabled power of the party machines. Just how far disorganized politics has come is suggested by the widespread corruption scandal that engulfed Democratic Party bosses and some key mayoral aides during the late 1980s. This led to indictments of many officials, including a member of Congress, and to the suicide of the Queens party boss. Investigations convincingly revealed that the mayor was unconnected to this alternative political system, part of which was being operated from the basement of city hall, but they also showed that greed for personal enrichment alone lay behind most of the kickback schemes (because so little of the take was recycled back into the party machine).

The decay of the Democratic Party has enabled recent mayoral contests to become essentially nonpartisan campaigns. On the Democratic side, the mayoral primary has become a catch-as-catch-can match among contenders, some of whom, like Al Sharpton, have had virtually no ties to the Democratic Party yet are able to win large percentages of the primary vote (more than one-third of the vote in Al Sharpton's case). Outside of the Democratic Party, Republican mayoral candidates have been able to mount winning campaigns by assembling their own media-driven electoral machines that owe little to party but much to personal fund-raising. In Giuliani's case, this meant assembling support from big special interest fund-raisers in the uniformed service unions, people who do business with the city, developers, and real estate interests. Michael Bloomberg avoided those financial ties to special interests only by using his vast personal wealth to bankroll his mayoral campaign. In doing so, he conducted the most expensive mayoral campaign in history and gravely weakened or even destroyed New York's model campaign finance system. By spending $75.5 million, mostly his own money, Bloomberg paid the almost unbelievable amount of $100 per vote to win.

The decline of party has had the effect of producing new sources of faction and stalemate. As mayoral elections become increasingly nonpartisan and candidate centered, candidates are more dependent on raising their own money to build their own political networks, increasing the role of money and special interests in politics. Simultaneously, however, the decaying Democratic organization has maintained its hold on city council elections and on other political offices at the state and federal levels. The result: growing stalemate between the mayor and city council on many major legislative issues such as budget, education, and finance in a pattern of divided government. This also has produced a lack of unity among officeholders in lobbying for more aid from state and federal sources, undermining the political influence of New York City in intergovernmental politics. The arrival of term limits for members of the city council in 2001 has also helped throw mayoral-council politics out of balance. Last year, 35 incumbents out of the 51 council members were forced to retire and were replaced by new council freshmen. Their ability to work together and pose a counterweight to the mayor remains uncertain.

Second, the Center-Right mayoral coalition that elected three out of the past four mayors is a deeply flawed means of bringing about governability. Since the days of the fiscal crisis, mayors have been unable to build very inclusive electoral coalitions. The city's first African American mayor, David Dinkins, was able to mobilize the poor, minorities, White liberals, and other groups including business in an effort to defuse the racial tensions of the Koch years. Yet his coalition proved unstable, and conflicts over race plagued his administration. After a single term, he lost to Rudolph Giuliani in 1993. In contrast, by winning the support of homeowners, Whites, Catholics, and working-class ethnics in the outer boroughs while excluding people of color, White liberals, and the poor, Koch and Giuliani were able to maintain an alliance with leading business interests while containing the demands of service-demanding groups. This kind of governing coalition is like a keg of gunpowder, however. The longer mayors rely on this electoral strategy, the more they risk bottling up racial resentments and precipitating explosive political confrontations with the very groups whose electoral presence is growing most rapidly (and who already have achieved a majority of the resident, though not the voter, population). During the 1990s, New York became a majority-minority city as White non-Hispanic persons fell from 43.2 percent in 1990 to 35 percent in 2000. Due to a large increase in Hispanic births and migration, the number of Latinos surged from 24 percent to 27 percent while the African-American population dropped slightly to just below one-fourth of the population.

Race relations during the Koch and Giuliani years were almost always poor. Confrontations with Mayor Giuliani were minimized during the later 1990s only by the growth in budget revenues that enabled the mayor to avoid cutting programs and by the rise in private-sector employment opportunities. As time passes and the exclusionary impact of this electoral strategy increases resentment and isolation among marginalized groups, this power base becomes more difficult to sustain. It becomes most unstable at precisely this time, however—after the good economic times are over and the city must pull in its belt. When that happens, mayors who inherit this power structure have two choices. One is to try to maintain this coalition by relying on appeals to White racial and neighborhood resentments, as Mayor Koch did during the fiscal crisis years. The other is to somehow broaden this coalition by uniting groups around issues that have wide appeal.

Mayor Bloomberg has chosen the latter strategy. During the election, Bloomberg won 47 percent of the Hispanic vote in large part because Democratic candidate Mark Green had been abandoned by minority politicians after a bruising and racially charged campaign. Since 9/11, Bloomberg's challenge has been to broaden his coalition to include Latino and African-American voters, but he must do so while contending with a budget gap that approaches $5 billion. Coping with the latter requires across-the-board cuts in virtually all services but especially in the costly social services and in the municipal payroll—areas that are likely to have a disproportionate impact on the very voter groups he needs most to include. Yet those groups feel that their priorities have been postponed long enough after years of exclusionary politics. In effect, Bloomberg's attempt to alter the voter coalition inherited from the past is happening at a time when changes in population and fiscal resources make this most difficult. Mayor Bloomberg has yet to establish a stable political base. The events of 9/11 will make it harder to do so.

The third source of political fragmentation stems from growing reliance on private benefit corporations (PBCs) to buffer the city's economic decision making from mainstream electoral politics. PBCs such as the Port Authority, the Metropolitan Transportation Authority, the Empire State Development Corporation, and others are independent of political and fiscal control of the elected general-purpose government of the city, but they more or less control the city's infrastructure and key economic development projects. They are the city's so-called "money-generating" governments and are highly responsive to bond holders who expect to be paid back from the revenues and user fees that PBC projects are expected to generate from airport fees, rents, transit fares, tolls, and the like.

While reliance on PBCs makes sense for a cash-pressed city at the limits of its borrowing ability, PBCs proliferated dramatically in recent decades, displacing local elected officials from large areas of public policy. In 1960, there were only 6 PBCs in all of New York City, but by the end of the century, there were 36. Through them, the city's capability for financing large undertakings has increased, but its ability to govern and remain very accountable to the city electorate has diminished.

Not surprisingly, the task of rebuilding the World Trade Center site and planning a recovery has been handed over to yet another PBC, the Lower Manhattan Development Corporation (LMDC), a subsidiary of the powerful Empire State Development Corporation. The LMDC has a board that is evenly divided between gubernatorial and mayoral appointees and has access to part of the $20 billion emergency recovery aid promised by federal officials. Studded with blue-ribbon appointees, mostly from the worlds of business and finance, the LMDC rightly sees its role as more than simply cleaning up the trade center site. It has embarked on programs to attract new businesses into Lower Manhattan and assist existing businesses and residents to recover from the losses sustained in the attack. Furthermore, it has organized a number of taskforce committees to consult with interested groups including area businesses, residents of nearby neighborhoods, families of victims, and others in planning a recovery program.

Yet by casting its lot with another independent government corporation that is dedicated to regenerating the downtown business area, state and city officials have bypassed the opportunity to seriously rethink the economic future of the city in a postterrorist world. One effect of 9/11 has been to call into question the competitive advantage of a dense and centralized central business district in which the giant skyscraper is the dominant office site. Several months prior to 9/11, the Group of 35—top leaders from the private and public sector—issued a report on the future of New York City's office sector due to a growing shortage of commercial office space. It predicted that the city would probably need to add 60 million square feet of office space during the next 20 years. Recognizing the limited space for future office construction in Lower Manhattan, the taskforce concluded that priority should be given to dispersing new office construction to other locations in Mid-Town, Queens, Brooklyn, and elsewhere. The destruction of the World Trade towers has dramatically given impetus to such a plan. In an age of terrorism, global cities like New York, London, and Tokyo provide high-profile "international message" targets for suicide bombers and violent radical groups seeking to dramatize their political demands. The 9/11 attacks have virtually compelled fundamental reassessment of how far and in what shape the new metropolis will go in the direction of dispersal—not whether the continued building of giant skyscrapers in dense locations will continue to be the norm. Eighteen thousand jobs at stock brokerage firms, banks, and insurance companies have already permanently moved since 9/11, according to a senior economist at the Federal Reserve Bank of New York. The problem, however, is that a nonelected special-purpose government committed to regenerating the old downtown is hardly the kind of planner that is capable of rethinking the future of the city. It stands as yet another instance of planning by special interest and the city's lack of governability.

The events of 9/11 also call into question the adequacy of New York's government for building public confidence in its recovery programs. The death of so many people and the destruction of so much property in a single blow means that decisions over the physical reconstruction of the city cannot be left to only nonelected experts and executives who are used to keeping the public at arm's length in their deliberations. The inevitability of a sustained war on international terrorism requires redesigning cities in ways that can reclaim public confidence in homes, neighborhoods, modes of travel, and places of work. This necessitates greater public participation and oversight in the planning of New York City, not less. Yet the city has already drifted in the latter direction and is not well prepared to cope with the political aftermath of 9/11. Its tradition of fragmenting political power and concentrating management of physical infrastructure in special-purpose authorities is ill-suited to rebuilding public confidence in city building in a postterrorist world.

URBAN GOVERNANCE IN A POSTTERRORISM WORLD

The impact of the terrorist attack and its aftermath goes beyond the immediate damage done to people, business, and security in New York City. The terrible events of September 2001 struck a city that was already seriously off balance politically. Long-building sources of political fragmentation and exclusion now obstruct the need to assert greater political leadership, overcome festering social divisions, and steer the city in new directions in the wake of 9/11. Although Mayor Giuliani briefly seemed to fulfill this role during the weeks of emergency, the deeply rooted forces of political decay and exclusion conspire against sustained governability. Decaying partisanship, disorganized politics, reliance on exclusionary electoral coalitions, and the proliferation of entrenched special interests powerfully check mayoral leadership and innovative planning for the city as a whole. New York City faces a difficult task of modernizing its political system if it is to successfully cope with twenty-first-century international terrorism.

Since the forms of division and stalemate are not unique to New York City, it is likely that the hand of urban terrorism will pose similar challenges well beyond the borders of the nation's largest city. Urban politics has changed as a result of 9/11. Yet it is because a new dilemma has surfaced in the midst of an older problem.

41. Fiscal Code Orange for States and Cities
Neal Peirce

A prominent urban journalist, Neal Peirce, has declared that the financial status of cities and states has entered a dangerous phase—a "Code Orange." It has been brought about not only by the terrorist attacks and the recession that followed, but is worsened by the policies being proposed and adopted by the federal government.

Is it time to declare a fiscal Code Orange—a condition of serious financial peril—for America's states and cities?

A seasoned intergovernmental professional, requesting he not be identified, suggests to me the situation is just that serious—and likely to reach Code Red if we don't watch out. Foreign terrorists alone, he adds, can't be blamed for this danger alert. It's a direct result of what he'd categorize as "blind and insensitive" policy directions that our government—especially the Bush White House—are now pursuing.

Personally, I'd put the immediate peril of a U.S. attack on Iraq at the top of the list. Its cost, according to such experts as Delaware's Joseph Biden, the Senate's leading Democrat on foreign affairs, may be as much as $80 to $100 billion. The 1991 Gulf War cost $61 billion—almost $80 billion in today's dollars—and in that case foreign allies picked up 90 percent of the cost, and we had no plans for regime change and long-term occupation.

Assuming a $100 billion total, the National Priorities Project has broken down the cost in taxpayer dollars, by state and city. The figures are disturbing: California $10.1 billion, Texas $5.7 billion, Illinois $4.3 billion, Michigan $2.9 billion, for example. Or by city: Chicago $775 million, Detroit $179 million, St. Louis $75 million, Houston $447 million, Seattle $228 million.

SOURCE: Neal R. Peirce, "Bush, States, and Cities: Fiscal Code Orange?" February 23, 2003, © 2003 Washington Post Writers Group. Reprinted with permission.

The fiscal stakes are immense, even ignoring the moral or military-strategic stakes in an Iraq war that we wage against the will and advice of much of the world. Oregon taxpayers, for example, would pay $368 million toward a $100 billion Iraq war. The same dollars would pay 7,090 elementary school teachers, buy 1,636 fire trucks or place 58,963 children in Head Start.

Small wonder, both on moral and fiscal grounds, that some 80 American cities, from New Haven to San Francisco, Atlanta to Portland, have passed resolutions opposing the war.

But others, including my Code Orange intergovernmental source, see an alarmingly insensitive White House, even without the Iraq issue.

A prime example: slow and paltry federal assistance for local "first responders"—police, firefighters, emergency medical personnel—who will represent our first line of personal defense in any terrorist attack.

The terror peril is linked inextricably to foreign policy and intelligence failures—clear federal roles. Cities, counties and states, gripped by their worst fiscal crisis of modern times by the recession, have been spending billions to provide extra protection since 9/11.

But the Bush administration failed to press hard on a promised $3.5 billion first-responder aid package. And Congress dawdled. The federal fiscal year 2003 budget, belatedly passed this month, earmarks only $1.2 billion for first responders and in hard fact actually *reduces* overall federal aid for local law enforcement and disaster recovery from $11.7 billion in 2002 to $6.4 billion for 2003.

Just as alarming, the Bush budget proposed for 2004 barely corrects that, asking only for $8.4 billion for all law, disaster aid and first responder assistance—even while it asks a staggering, *pre-war,* $379.9 billion for the armed forces.

One would have thought an administration headed by an ex-governor, with former state chief executives in several Cabinet slots, would have more sensitivity. But trace the dollars where you will, this administration's fiscal plans spell deep trouble for mayors and governors.

Take Bush's idea to lift federal taxes on dividend income (channeling most benefits to the 1 percent of taxpayers who earn over $300,000, with no comparable favor for wage earners). That could cost the states $50 billion in the next decade, because so many state income tax forms "piggy-back" on the federal. Governors and legislatures would have a nasty choice: take the political flack for raising taxes in the midst of a recession, or cut funds for critical services. Either way, they'd deepen the recession.

A companion Bush proposal would let people with spare cash (up to $45,000 a year) set up absolutely tax-free investment accounts—part of what would be cumulative $1.8 *trillion* losses to the federal treasury in the next decade. Meanwhile, Mr. Bush would cut child-care and after-school programs, chip away at vocational training, end the Hope VI program that's remade so many ravaged public housing projects into exemplary communities, and make earned-income tax credits (many poor people's best fiscal safety ring) harder to get.

Maybe it's intentional: A red-ink drowned federal government will likely be unable to partner with states and localities in any meaningful way—for years and years to come.

But if Mr. Bush intends that, why didn't he run on such a platform? Virtually nothing in his 2000 campaign suggested he'd advocate rigid ideological positions, foreign and domestic, leading to this kind of result. Having trailed in the popular vote by a half million votes, a consensus-based government of national unity would have been more appropriate.

Is there a solution? Maybe, in 2004—regime change.

Exercise
Studying Your City Government

The purpose of these exercises is to increase your understanding of how your local government actually works and the degree to which the terrorist attacks of September 11, 2001 and the economic recession that followed them have affected your city or suburban government.

To do these exercises you will need to use your city's or county's annual budget, program budget, comptroller's report or audit, and any annual reports published by the agency or unit of government you are studying. Some of these materials may be in the government documents section of your university or public libraries. Some, but not most, documents and information you need may be on the local government's Website, if it has one. However, many of these documents will have to be obtained from City Hall, the County Building, or the agency you are studying.

In larger cities each agency will have a public affairs or public relations official who can get the answers to your questions. In smaller cities, suburbs, and counties, the city or county clerk will assist you if you ask politely *after* you have gotten as much information as possible from library and Internet sources.

In many states, you have a legal right to file a "Freedom of Information" request. This is not normally a useful procedure for students unless you are asked formally to file such a request for the record before the agency representative gives you the material that you have verbally requested. The problem with Freedom of Information requests is that they may take months to process before you get the necessary materials if the agency and the government go through formal channels. Freedom of Information requests are more useful for newspapers, interest groups, or lawsuits in obtaining information that the local government would rather not release. You don't have the time they do to wait for the official response to your questions in a Freedom of Information request.

A SINGLE GOVERNMENT AGENCY

1. Select a local unit of government to study—a department or agency of the city or county governments or a suburban unit of government.
2. Begin by finding out the answers to the questions in this exercise and then write an essay about the agency. The answers to these questions should give you a complete analysis of a single government agency. If you can understand one government agency in this way, you can understand any city agency. The exercise also teaches you how easy or hard it is to get information on government agencies in your city or suburb. You may learn more in trying to find out how government agencies (which are funded by your tax money) work, than in the substantive answers to the questions themselves.

Purpose and Function of Agency

1. What is the legal basis of your agency and its required functions in either city ordinances or state law printed in the State Statutes (i.e., law books)?
2. What are the current programs of the agency? (These are usually listed in agency annual reports, the program budget of the city or county, or the comptroller's report of the city or county. They may be amplified in news reports and direct interviews with the agency personnel.)

Organization and Administration

1. Develop an organization chart and a list of the key executive personnel of the department. For the current personnel, the names and titles of the individuals are needed. (These can be found in department reports and directories of employees.)
2. List the number of budgeted positions in the department or agency for the last three years including the current budget year? (These can be found in the city budget or similar document.)

   2002 _____ 2003 _____ 2004 _____

Agency Budget

1. What was the amount appropriated for the agency's budget over the last three years? (This can be obtained from the city budget.)

   2002 _____ 2003 _____ 2004 _____
2. What was the amount actually spent by the agency over the last three years? (This can usually be obtained from the city budget for past years along with the comptroller's report.)

   2002 _____ 2003 _____ 2004 _____

(*continued*)

SERVICES AND PROGRAM DELIVERY

1. What was the cost per unit of the service delivered by the agency such as cost per ton of garbage picked up or cost per mile of street repaired? (This is obtained by taking the total cost of a program—obtained from the program budget—and dividing it by the number of tasks performed. Not all services can be measured this way.)
2. Have there been local newspaper stories of failures of the agency in its delivery of services?

Public Participation

1. What mechanisms, if any, are there for public participation in guiding the activities or decisions of the agency—public hearings, neighborhood government, and so on? (This is usually provided from interviews with agency personnel, the public affairs officer, or the city or county clerk.)

Overview

1. What is your final evaluation of the agency—how well does it operates and what could be done to improve it?

CHANGES IN YOUR CITY SINCE SEPTEMBER 11, 2001

Compare your city's or suburban town's budget in 2001 to the most recent year's budget. What are the total amounts of spending in each year's budget? Next, consider the money raised from tourism—the hotel tax, sales taxes, and entertainment taxes—for the years since 2001. Are the funds from these sources greater or less this year than in 2001?

If you can find in your city or town budget or in the comptroller's report the total federal and state government funds given to your city or town in 2001 and the most recent year, have these funds gone up or gone down?

Finally, locate the total funds spent on public safety (police department and fire department) and on public health (health department). Have these funds gone up or gone down since September 11, 2001?

Have any major public or private projects or developments in your city or town been started or stopped since September 11, 2001?

What have been the cuts in your state budget since 2001? Have school districts or other smaller local governments had to raise taxes or developed greater debts since 2001?

Have private charitable groups gone out of business or lost funds—have shelters for the homeless or other private endeavors closed?

Have there been any major positive developments in your city or suburban community since September 11, 2001—public displays of patriotism, efforts to create more religious tolerance, more support for the national government, or better voter turnout in elections for example?

Our Urban Future

Urban politics is constantly changing. In some ways local politics and government are at the mercy of much larger forces such as national and global economic trends, changing social conditions like immigration and race relations generally, and changes in federal government urban policies. In other ways, urban politics is changed by local actions such as electing different public officials, creating new community organizations, or organizing a protest demonstration around some public policy.

Many people whose voices are heard in this book, from social workers like Jane Addams to mayors like Rudy Guiliani and Debbie Jaramillo, have changed urban politics at least in their own communities. Others such as social scientists and media commentators are advocates of change.

Particularly now, the future of cities, suburbs, and metropolitan regions is uncertain. The readings and exercises in this anthology have provided you with the information and perspective to help to shape your own community's future. Will racial discrimination and disregard of the poor continue? Will race and poverty continue to be linked? Will racial discrimination be eliminated and race relations continue to improve? Will the better-off members of society barricade themselves in gated communities or join in the effort to make the entire urban region more livable?

Will the growing global economy mean that the gap between the rich and the poor will continue to widen? Will future leaders of cities be conservative or progressive, pragmatic or the bosses of a new machine politics?

Will cities and metropolitan regions be unreformed and ungovernable? Will citizens be active participants or merely subjects of their local governments?

Will the economic recession following September 11, 2001 cause cities to decline or will the renaissance of the 1990s return? Will representatives of all races and genders become leaders as well as citizens of our new cities and suburbs?

The answers to all these questions about the future of urban politics depend not just on national or international trends and events. The thousands of public officials currently in power will not determine the answers by themselves. The future of our communities will be determined by what each of us decides to do—what actions we take in the governments and organizations closest to us. By what we say and do, we will write the future of our cities and suburbs.

Credits

Bissinger, H. G. From *A Prayer for the City*. Copyright © 1997 by H. G. Bissinger. Used by permission of Random House, Inc.

Boles, Jane K. "Local Elected Women and Policymaking: Movement Delegates or Feminist Trustees," from *The Impact of Women in Public Office,* ed. Susan J. Carroll. Copyright © 2001 Indiana University Press. Reprinted by permission of the publisher, Indian University Press.

Bridges, Amy. From *Morning Glories: Municipal Reform in the Southwest*. Copyright © 1997 by Princeton University Press. Reprinted by permission of Princeton University Press.

Cano, Gustavo. "The Chicago-Houston Report: Political Mobilization of Mexican Immigrants in American Cities," a paper delivered at The American Political Science Association Meeting, September 2002. Reprinted by permission of the author.

Caro, Robert A. From *The Power Broker*. Copyright © 1974 by Robert A. Caro. Used by permission of Alfred A. Knopf, a division of Random House, Inc.

Cianci, Vincent A., Jr. From the mayor's "Inaugural Address," January 4, 1999. Available online at www.providenceri.com/inauguraladdress1999.html.

Cleeland, Nancy. "Lives Get a Little Better on a Living Wage," *Los Angeles Times,* February 7, 1999. Copyright © 1999 Tribune Media Services International; Los Angeles Times. All rights reserved. Reprinted by permission.

Doty, Gary. From the mayor's "2001 State of the City Address," January 8, 2001. Duluth Website. Reprinted by permission of the mayor's office.

Garcia, Manny, and Tom Dubocq. "Political Ties: How Miami's Garbage Contract Could Cost Millions Extra," *Miami Herald Online*. Copyright © 1997 by Miami Herald. Reproduced with permission of Miami Herald via Copyright Clearance Center.

Gentile, Ann, and Dick Simpson. "Neighborhood Empowerment," *Social Policy,* Vol. 16, No. 4, Spring 1986. Reprinted by permission of the author and M. E. Sharpe, Inc.

Giuliani, Rudy. "Renaissance Budgeting," from the New York City mayor's weekly column on nyc.gov website, June 11, 2001 and "Mayor Giuliani Unveils $39.5 Billion Executive Budget," press release, April 25, 2001. Available online at www.nyc.gov/html/om/html/2001a/weekly/wkly0611.html and www.nyc.gov/html/om/html/2001a/pr125-01.html. Reprinted by permission.

Goozner, Merrill. "What Ails Post-Industrial Chicago," *Crain's Chicago Business,* October 27, 1986. Copyright © 1986 by Crain Communications Inc. All rights reserved. Reprint permission conveyed through Reprint Management Services.

Gurwitt, Rob. "Black, White, and Blurred: The Subtle Urban Politics of the 21st Century," *Governing,* September 2001. Copyright © 2001 by Rob Gurwitt. Reprinted by permission of the author.

Holli, Melvin G. "Samuel M. 'Golden Rule' Jones, 1897–1904," in *The American Mayor: The Best and the Worst of Big City Leaders* by Melvin G. Holli. Copyright © 1999 by The Pennsylvania State University Press. Reproduced by permission of the publisher.

Houston Chronicle Online. "Greater Houston: The Regional Dilemma." Available at www.chron.com/content/interactive/special/GHP/section2.html. Copyright © 1996 Greater Houston Partnership. Reprinted by permission.

Howard, Christopher, Michael Lipsky, and Dale Rogers Marshall. "Citizen Participation in Urban Politics: Rise and Routination," from *Big City Politics, Governance, and Fiscal Constraints,* ed. Georges E. Peterson. Reprinted by permission of The Urban Institute Press.

Ingram, James W., III. From "The History of Charter Reform," a talk given at the Los Angeles Charter Reform Conference, 1998. Available online at www.sppsr.ucla.edu/dean's/forum/chref.htm. Reprinted by permission of the author.

Johnson, Valerie C. "The Political Consequences of Black Suburbanization in Prince Georges County, 1971–1994," adapted from Ph.D. dissertation, University of Maryland, 1995. Reprinted by permission of the author.

Jones, E. Terrence and Elaine Hays. "Metropolitan Citizens in St. Louis," from a paper prepared for a poster session at the American Political Science Association meeting, September 1, 2001. Reprinted by permission of the authors.

Kayden, Xandra. From "Societal Change and Charter Reform," a talk given at the Los Angeles Charter Reform Conference, 1998. Available online at www.sppsr.ucla.edu/dean's/forum/chref.htm. Reprinted by permission of the author.

Lebow, Edward. "Primary Colors," *Phoenix New Times,* August 30, 2001. Online at www.phoenixnewtimes.com/issues/2001-08-30/feature.html/page1.html. Reprinted with permission of New Times.

McKenzie, Evan. From "Walls Do Not Make Good Neighbors," *Chicago Journal,* June 21, 2001. Reprinted with permission of Chicago Journal.

Mendell, David. "Race Still Midwest's Dividing Line," *Chicago Tribune,* June 21, 2001. Copyright © 2001 by Chicago Tribune Company. All rights reserved. Used with permission.

Meyerson, Harold. "How Tom Bradley Transformed and Didn't Transform Los Angeles," originally published in the *LA Weekly,* 1998. Available online at www.laweekly.com/ink/archives/98/45news3b-meyerson.shtml. Reprinted by permission of the LA Weekly.

Nichols, John. "Success in Santa Fe: Score One for the Revolution from Below," *The Progressive,* August 1995. Reprinted by permission from *The Progressive,* 409 E. Main St., Madison, WI 53709. www.progressive.org.

Orfield, Myron. From *Metropolitics: A Regional Agenda for Community and Stability.* Copyright © 1997 The Brookings Institution Press. Reprinted by permission.

Orr, Marion, and Darrell M. West. "Citizen's Views on Urban Revitalization: The Case of Providence Rhode Island," *Urban Affairs Review,* Vol. 37, No. 3, January 2002. Copyright © 2002 by Sage Publications. Reprinted by permission of the publisher, Sage Publications.

PBS Online News Hour. "Cincinnati One Year Later," available at www.pbs.org/newshour/bb/race_relations/jan-june02/cincinnati_4-12.html. Reprinted with permission from MacNeil-Lehrer Productions.